Studies in Social History
edited by Dr J. F. C. Harrison and C. S. Yeo

The First Shop Stewards' Movement

In the same series

Trade Unions and Society: the Struggle for Acceptance, 1850–1872
by W. H. Fraser

The First
Shop Stewards'
Movement

James Hinton
Lecturer in History at the University of Warwick

London · George Allen & Unwin Ltd
Ruskin House   Museum Street

ISBN 0 04 331059 1

Printed in Great Britain
in 10 point Times Roman type
by Unwin Brothers Limited
The Gresham Press
Old Woking, Surrey

For Jo

Preface

I am indebted to Eric Hobsbawm who first suggested this topic to me and supervised my work on it as a doctoral student. Many others have helped me at various stages of this work, among whom I must mention particularly Terry Brotherstone, Richard Hyman, Richard Kuper, Edward Thompson and the editors of this volume. I am grateful to the staff of the Public Record Office and several other libraries for their help and co-operation, and to the General Secretary and staff of the Amalgamated Engineering Union (as it then was) for permission to consult their records and help in doing so. I am also grateful to Mr Bill Moore of Leeds, the Sheffield Trades Council, the Communist Party and the Department of Economics at the University of Glasgow for making available to me records in their possession. Finally my thanks are due to the staff and students of the Centre for the Study of Social History at the University of Warwick for the unfailing stimulation they supply. That shortcomings remain is not to be blamed on any of those who have helped me.

JAMES HINTON
University of Warwick
April 1972

Contents

Introduction

The history of the British labour movement between 1910 and the early 1920s has a special claim to our attention. However it is measured – by the sheer growth of numbers in the unions; by the working days lost through strikes; by the upsurge of socialist organization, campaigning, ideas; by the intensity and range of debate over the tactics and strategy of the struggle for socialism; even by the victory (albeit the hollow victory) of socialism within the Labour Party in 1918 – these years mark a climax of class-conscious self-activity among the workers which, in Britain, has not yet been surpassed. There was, of course, no revolution. A combination of ruling class flexibility, reformist initiative within the labour movement, and an economic recession which weakened the power and undermined the ambition of the ordinary workers, made possible a new and lasting accommodation of organized labour within the capitalist system. This accommodation was already substantially achieved by 1924 when the first Labour Government took office, and is symbolized by the tacit alliance between Stanley Baldwin and Ramsay MacDonald which was to dominate British politics throughout the inter-war years. Simultaneously the revolutionary movement, consolidated in the Communist Party in 1920–1, found itself relatively isolated from the bulk of the organized working class. In the absence of any renewed spontaneous upsurge on a scale comparable to that out of which it had been born, the Communist Party gradually came to adopt some of the colour of its environment, and to lose sight of the revolutionary tasks for which it was founded. Today, when there is much to suggest that the era of accommodation may be coming to an end, and when revolutionary politics again show signs of becoming a significant force in the working-class movement, there is good reason to re-examine the last great revolutionary period in British history. This book is intended as one contribution towards that end.

At the 1918 annual conference of the British Socialist Party a delegate declared that the shop stewards' movement in the engineering industry was 'the only active revolutionary movement in the country . . . at the present time'. Two months before, in January 1918, the shop stewards had come within a hair breadth of initiating a strike movement against the continuance of the war. The militancy of the engineers was one of the major domestic problems confronting Governments throughout the war years. The movement originated during the war and its power was largely dependent on the exceptional labour shortage created by the demand for munitions. As a mass organization it hardly survived the coming of peace. Nevertheless the shop stewards' movement was to supply the early Communist Party with several of its most important leaders. In many localities the Party's most successful political effort of the inter-war years, the National Unemployed Workers' Movement, drew predominantly on the personnel and the surviving local organization of the wartime shop stewards. Most important of all, it was the wartime practice of the shop stewards' movement which, more than anything else, made possible the development of British revolutionary theory from its various pre-war syndicalist manifestations to the 'sovietist' ideology that underlay the formation of the Communist Party. Clearly the history of this movement is an important part of the history of the British revolutionary movement as a whole during these years.

The militancy of the engineers was itself primarily a product of the breakdown, under war conditions, of their traditional security as a privileged section of the working class. The influx of women and semi-skilled men into the munitions factories and into jobs previously performed only by craftsmen ('dilution') appeared to undermine and render worthless the means by which skilled engineers had habitually sought to defend themselves. Craft unionism had been directed as much against the encroachments of less skilled workers into those jobs preserved for the aristocrats of labour, as against the employers themselves. Immediately we are confronted with a problem: how is it that a movement based upon a privileged stratum of the working class became the central growth point of the British revolutionary movement? Part One of this book seeks to explain this paradox partly by an analysis of the character of the craftsmen's traditional outlook, and partly by reference to the circumstances in which their privileges were challenged. The shop stewards' movement recognized that any struggle to restore undiluted craft privilege would be both undesirable (politically) and hopeless. The movement attempted, with some success, to break down traditional divisions between craftsmen and the less skilled workers, to develop an industrial policy which united the interests of the two groups, and to construct all-grades organization in the workshops. Moreover, there was more than exclusiveness to be found in craft consciousness. Craft work induced a pride and an independence which manifested itself in a tenacious resistance both to managerial encroachments in the workplace, and to the logic of bureaucratization both in industry and in the trade unions. For fifteen years before 1914 the engineers, in the name of the local autonomy in trade policy which had always characterized engineering trade unionism, had fought off attempts of employers and trade union leaders to impose the restraints of national collective bargaining. To the extent that the shop stewards' movement succeeded in taking the craftsmen beyond exclusiveness, it was able to release these traditions of craft control and of local autonomy from the narrow embrace of a defensive craft consciousness, to transform them into weapons of an ambitious class offensive.

In conditions of war collectivism, when the collaboration of employers, state and trade union officialdom pressaged the growth of a bureaucratic regulation of every aspect of economic life, and the withering away of social and political freedoms previously enjoyed, the specifically anti-bureaucratic character of the craft tradition could take on a revolutionary significance. In their struggle against industrial and military compulsion the craftsmen's ideas of craft control could be transmuted into ideas of workers' control; and ideas of local autonomy might develop into the pursuit of dual power not only between the local Workers' Committees and trade union officialdom, but also between the Workers' Committees and the bourgeois state itself. The argument of this book is not that this revolutionary potential of the shop stewards' movement was ever realized, nor indeed came very near to being realized, but that such a development existed as a possibility and was perceived as existing by the revolutionaries. The development of ideas indicated above may have been possible for large numbers of engineers: what is certain is that it happened among a small number of their leaders, thus making possible the ideological transition from syndicalism to 'sovietism' that characterized most sections of the revolutionary movement in the years before the Communist Party was formed.

Even the preliminary stages of this process did not occur among many engineering craftsmen. Part Two deals with the wartime practice of the shop stewards' movement. Shop stewards' organization within the workshops spread rapidly during the war, but the shop stewards' *movement*, local Workers' Committees based directly in the workshops and capable of leading the mass of the workers independently of the existing trade union authorities, became established in only a handful of the largest munitions centres. A series of local comparative studies reveals two main conditions for the emergence of a successful local Workers' Committee during the war. Firstly, the status and privileges of the craftsmen in the area concerned should be intact when war broke out – the advanced technology of the Midlands motor car industry, for example, had substantially undermined craft status before 1914, and Workers' Committees were not successful in the Midlands. Secondly, the threat to this status should be experienced as both sudden and acute. It was in the Northern centres of more or less archaic engineering technology that these conditions were most fully met, and that the national shop stewards' movement was most firmly based.

The explosive force of militancy released by the challenge to the craftsmen's status and economic security remained, for the revolutionary leaders of the shop stewards' movement, a double-edged weapon. While this militancy contained germs of a revolutionary spirit on which they could build, it also contained germs of a merely sectional struggle for the restoration of lost status. The development of the movement hung between these two possibilities, the leadership pulling towards revolutionary politics, the craftsmen at one moment following, at the next retreating into a military exclusiveness. In the end craft conquered class goals among the rank and file of the movement, and the anticipated strike against the war in January 1918 collapsed into a sectional struggle in defence of the (novel) craft privilege of exemption from military conscription.

Nevertheless the significance of the revolutionary possibilities of the shop stewards' movement was not lost upon its leaders; and these possibilities had very considerable impact on the way in which members of the various Marxist groups in Britain viewed the problems of revolution. Part Three examines the contribution to revolutionary theory made by the shop stewards' movement, firstly in its practical fusion of the two trends in pre-war syndicalism (dual unionist *versus* amalgamationist), and, arising from this, in making it possible for British revolutionaries to conceive of an agency of transition to socialism that was neither the Industrial Union of syndicalist theory, nor the parliamentary party of social democratic theory, but the Workers' Committee (or soviet).

It is not intended to deny the obvious influence of the Russian Revolution and, particularly, the work of the Communist International during 1919–20, in persuading British revolutionaries to base their perspectives on a struggle for soviet power. 'Sovietism', however, was not simply an alien import, nor is it to be explained merely by the understandable fascination of British revolutionaries with the experience of their successful Russian comrades. The First World War precipitated an international revolutionary crisis. That the climax had already occurred in the Bolshevik Revolution of October 1917 was far from apparent during the immediate post-war years. October was widely seen, both on the right and the left, as a beginning, not as an end. Reasonable men could anticipate the Hungarian, Austrian, German, Italian, French and even the British revolutions. In particular it was the phenomenon of the soviet, of Workers' Councils, that characterized the international crisis. 'We say that the present period is revolutionary precisely because we can see that the working class, in all countries, is tending to generate from within itself, with the utmost vital energy . . . proletarian institutions of a new type: representative in basis and industrial in arena. We say the present period is revolutionary because the working class tends with all its energy and all its will-power to found its own State.' The shop stewards' movement constitutes the evidence for the truth of Gramsci's claim in one of the least revolutionary nations of Europe. Whatever distortions were later to be imposed on the British revolutionary movement by its subordination to the heirs of a degenerated Russian Revolution, the post-war victory of the theory of soviet power over both syndicalism and parliamentarianism rested upon the authentic, if ambiguous, experience of a section of the British working class movement during the war years. It is an experience that deserves to be rescued from oblivion.

Abbreviations

USC United Socialist Council
WIIU Workers' International Industrial Union
WMV War Munitions Volunteers
WSF Workers' Socialist Federation
WU Workers' Union

Part One

The Context

Chapter 1

The Servile State

The shop stewards' movement was a child of war. Its power was the power of munitions workers in a war whose fate was decided as much in the workshops of Britain and Germany as in the trenches of France. The context of blood and iron is at the same time necessarily the context of intensified social discipline, of domestic repression. And the one informs the response to the other. A munitions worker, through most of the war, could expect to escape the particular horror of the trenches, but there was no exemption from the generalized violence of war. War brutalized and simplified social relations, at home as well as on the front. It lent some of its own violence and its own urgency to the workers' perennial struggles for economic security and for class power. There is no lack of subtle ambiguity in the character and ideology of the shop stewards' movement, but there is a stark simplicity in its perception of the enemy. There were three forces whose collaboration appeared to 'throw the whole constitution into the melting pot',[1] to make imminent defeat at the hands of a home-bred Prussianism – the servile state. This chapter will investigate the nature of that dominating block as it affected the engineers, and of the relations between its constituent parts – employers, Government, trade union officialdom.

EMPLOYERS

The metal industries grew very rapidly during the war (Table 1).[2]

[1] *The Worker*, 8 January 1916.
[2] *Committee on Industry and Trade*, Board of Trade, 1928, pt. IV, p. 132. See also *History of the Ministry of Munitions* (1920–4), vol. VI, pt. 3 (hereafter *MM* VI, 3), pp. 6, 22–9.

Table 1   *Metal workers in Great Britain, 1881–1921*

	1881	927,000
	1891	1,095,000
	1901	1,447,000
	1911	1,765,000
July	1914	1,804,000
July	1915	1,776,000
July	1916	2,077,000
July	1917	2,292,000
July	1918	2,418,000
July	1921	2,491,000

For thirty years before 1911 the labour force grew at an average rate of 3% per annum. From 1915 to 1918 it grew by 12·3% per annum. After the war it only grew 3% in three years.

The engineering industry was, of course, something less than the metal industries as a whole. For the purposes of this study the definition adopted by the Balfour Committee in 1928 is an appropriate starting point: 'an amalgamation of a considerable number of separate industries differentiated by product but united by the fact that the basic metal working operations underlying them are all substantially the same'.[1] We are concerned with the workers who made things of metal, with the foundry and forge workers, and, most important for this study, the turners, the fitters and the more specialized tradesmen employed to cut and to assemble the metal.

Defined in this way the industry has no rigidly distinct place in British industrial organization at the time of the First World War. Many large engineering firms were engaged in primary metal manufacture; others, like those in the vehicle and shipbuilding industry, were engaged in woodworking operations. Large sections of the engineering industry were carried on by firms primarily interested in other activities. 16% of all engineering workers were employed by railway companies; 10% of all skilled engineers worked in iron and steel firms, and 2·8% for local authorities; and others worked on ships, in mines, in the repair shops of every kind of factory.[2]

[1] *Committee on Industry and Trade*, pt. IV, p. 130.

[2] 'Census of Mechanics', October 1915, in *Beveridge Collection on Munitions*, vol. III (hereafter *Bev.* iii), p. 142. This census, unreliable as to the absolute numbers of workers employed in different sections of the industry, is probably reliable as to the proportions. See also G. D. H. Cole, *Trade Unionism and Munitions* (Oxford, 1923), pp. 15, 22.

The internal structure of the engineering industry can be viewed in a number of ways. There were numerous specialist sections, the largest of which were probably shipbuilding and marine engineering, munitions, railway engineering, the cycle and motor car industry, the textile engineering industry, electrical engineering, and machine tools. Of these shipbuilding was the most important, employing about 10% of all metal workers and sufficiently specialized to be regarded as a separate industry. With the important exceptions of the major armaments firms, which were normally involved in shipbuilding, the ownership of the shipbuilding firms did not overlap to any great extent with that of other sections of the industry.[1] Moreover the skills predominantly employed were of a specialized nature. The central engineering skills of fitting, turning, etc., which accounted for over half the skilled workers in the industry as a whole, made up only 28·5% of shipbuilding workers. A further 49% were boilermakers, shipwrights, etc., trades very largely confined to shipbuilding.[2]

But shipbuilding was exceptional. In general the market for engineering skills was not cut up into specialized sections. Skilled workers could move freely from one section to another. At the same time economic differentiation in engineering had not tended to produce new separate industries, so much as specialized sections of one industry bound together by their mutual dependence for components on the great fundamental mass of general engineering firms. The specialized component firm was a rarity: 'In this country we have, except in the cycle trade, practically no one to compare with the component specialist who exists throughout the US.'[3] In general, specialist firms subcontracted work to general engineering firms, and these showed little desire to specialize in a single type of component. Indeed 'some of them seemed to take a special pride in the number of things they turn out; whilst few of them seemed willing to contemplate buying at a cheaper price a component part from a rival manufacturer, even if they were permitted to do so by that rival'[4].

[1] *MM* IV, 4, p. 139; *Committee on Industry and Trade*, pt. IV, p. 370; *Departmental Committee on Shipping and Shipbuilding*, Second report, 1918, XIII, p. 21.

[2] 'Census of Mechanics', *loc. cit.* These figures appear to include marine engineering, which apart from its boilermaking aspect was technically very much like any other kind of engineering.

[3] *Departmental Committee on the Engineering Trades*, 1918, XIII, p. 10.

[4] *Ibid.*, p. 11.

When, in the first year of the war, the Board of Trade attempted to mobilize the engineering industry for arms production, they found great difficulty in discovering the productive potential of the industry because of the vast network of sub-contracting. The specialist firms did not know what their suppliers produced, beyond their own orders; some of the general engineering firms did not know the ultimate destination of what they themselves were producing, sub-contracted as they often were through one or more intermediary.[1]

The Committee on the Engineering Trades of 1918 was impressed not only by the lack of specialization within the industry, but also by 'the smallness of the individual firms and of the capital they employ'. Looked at in comparison with Britain's potential post-war rivals, Germany and the United States, this was certainly the case. But in terms of the British industry's own history, the most remarkable feature was the polarization between large and small firms during the thirty years preceding the First War, in particular the growth of the great arms combines. The armament firms had grown up chiefly around the increasingly complex activity of warship construction, which 'between 1870 and 1914 [grew] from a minor specialist activity to the corner-stone of prosperity in the shipbuilding industry'.[2] But the arms firms – Armstrong-Whitworth, Vickers, John Brown, Cammell-Laird – did not limit themselves to work directly associated with the production of battleships, though this included armour plate and gun manufacture as well as shipbuilding. All of them, in 1914, were contracted for armaments with the War Office as well as with the Admiralty. Armstrong-Whitworth was engaged in civil engineering, merchant ship-building, machine tools and motor cars, as well as in warships and arms; Vickers had interests in railway materials and motor cars.[3] The extent to which these giant companies had penetrated the industry by the outbreak of war is illustrated by the experience of the Board of Trade in its attempts to discover new sources of skilled engineering labour for munitions production early in 1915. A survey of engineering workers in London revealed that 'most

[1] 'Census of Mechanics', *loc. cit.*, introduction; *MM* XII, 1, p. 60; Beveridge to Gibb, 18 January 1915, in *Bev.* i, p. 115.

[2] S. Pollard, 'Laissez-faire and Shipbuilding', *EcHR*, Second series, vol. V, no. 1, 1952, p. 108; Sir John Clapham, *Economic History of Modern Britain*, vol. III (1938), pp. 259ff.

[3] *MM* I, 2, p. 112; *Committee on Industry and Trade*, pt. IV, pp. 273ff.

firms of any standing or capacity' were either directly contracted with the Government to produce arms, or sub-contracted to one of the arms firms, or the Arsenal. In addition: 'Many of the smaller firms are busily engaged in repair and upkeep work on the machinery and plant of firms executing large contracts.'[1] At the same time, the Board discovered, Armstrong-Whitworth had at least 1,500 sub-contractors, mostly in the north-east and Scotland.[2]

During the war the traditional arms firms were remarkably successful in maintaining their predominance in munitions production, despite the massive growth of demand and the anxiety of smaller firms outside the ring to participate in the profits of patriotism. The contracts for machine guns, rifles, and, to a lesser extent, heavy guns went substantially to the traditional suppliers – Armstrong-Whitworth, Vickers, Coventry Ordnance Works (part of the John Brown Group), and the Birmingham Small Arms Company. Where it was necessary to bring in new engineering firms this was effected 'under the tutelage' of the traditional firms. In gun manufacture, for example, 'the unit of manufacture tended to be a group of firms in a certain area supervised by one of the armament firms'.[3] In those fields where less skill and experience were required, primarily shell manufacture, the arms firms found it more difficult to maintain their monopoly. Nevertheless, in the main munitions centres, Clydeside and Sheffield, the new plants that were set up for shell production were under the control of the arms firms (and a few other large engineering firms.)[4]

There was one important sector of the munitions industry where the traditional arms firms entirely failed to establish their predominance. In 1914 the aircraft industry hardly existed. There were eight firms making aircraft, and three – Beardmore, Glasgow, the Government factory at Farnborough and one other private firm – producing experimental aircraft engines. All the aero-engines in service were imported from France. Aircraft construction does not concern us since it was at that time still largely a woodworking industry. But by 1918 'aero-engine production was a huge industry involving innumerable firms of large and

---

[1] 'Armament Workers' Survey', 15 January 1915, in *Bev.* i, p. 86; *MM*, I, 2, pp. 25–6.
[2] Report by Patterson, 16 January 1915, in *Bev* i, p. 109.
[3] *MM* x, 1, p. 61; *MM* I, 3, pp. 54, 61–2.
[4] *MM* VIII, 2, p. 131.

small capacity'. Most of these firms were well established as the work required considerable capital outlay. But they were not the traditional arms firms. It was predominantly the motor car and component firms of Manchester, Coventry and west London which went into aero-engine production, the development of the wartime industry playing a large part in laying the technological basis for the post-war motor car boom.[1]

The works of the arms firms were the largest factories in the country, barring only the Royal Arsenal at Woolwich, which employed 68,000 workers in November 1916.[2] Some impression of their overall dominance is given by the employment figures for the two largest – Armstrong and Vickers (Table 2).[3] 140,000

Table 2   *Employment in the arms firms, November 1916*

Armstrong-Whitworth	
Elswick (Eng.)	47,938
(Shipb.)	9,692
Alexandria	4,873
Openshaw	7,174
	69,677
Vickers	
Barrow (Eng.)	26,872
(Shipb.)	6,235
Ward End	12,114
Crayford	5,083
Erith	9,543
Sheffield	10,807
	70,654

workers were employed in the main works of Armstrong's and Vickers – i.e. 6·5% of the total metal working labour force, or 1 in 15 metal workers. The proportion would of course be far larger if workers in firms substantially controlled by the giants through sub-contracting, or any of the forms of wartime 'tutelage' were taken into account. In particular localities, like Barrow,

[1] Cf. the history of wartime aircraft production, in *MM* XII, 1.
[2] *MM* VIII, 2, p. 15.
[3] *Bev.* V, p. 76, 'Report on Labour in Controlled Establishments'.

Tyneside, or Sheffield, one or more of the arms firms might completely dominate the market for engineering skills.

THE STATE

Behind the arms firms, visibly confronting the engineering workers, stood the enormously expanded wartime power of the state. By the end of the war the Government controlled 90% of total imports and the home production of food, coal and most other raw materials. It controlled shipping and rail transport. It controlled the distribution of food (through rationing) and of raw materials (through allocations). The capital market was under Government control, as were wages and rents. The labour market was controlled by anti-strike legislation, restrictions on the mobility of labour, military conscription. Nearly 3·5 million workers in the metal industries, chemicals and other sectors concerned with munitions production, were employed directly or indirectly by the Ministry of Munitions.

The establishment of the Ministry of Munitions in June 1915 was one of the first acts of the Coalition Government set up under Asquith in May. It represented the new Government's answer to the agitation over the failure of the War Office to organize an adequate supply of shells for the army, which had been partly responsible for the downfall of the former Liberal Government. The agitation was directed against 'bureaucratic administration as applied to business affairs', held by the business community in general to have been primarily responsible for the failures of the War Office. The cry was for 'a man of push and go'; and since 'the conduct of a modern war is simply a form of business', who could conduct it better than a businessman?[1] The Ministry of Munitions, as created from June 1915 by Lloyd George, was 'from first to last a businessman's organization', intended 'to liberate the munitions industries from military direction, and the restrictions of established official routine, and to hand over the task of guiding and co-ordinating these developments to prominent businessmen familiar with industrial problems'.[2] The larger firms loaned over ninety directors and managers to the Ministry for the duration of the war, often keeping them on their own payrolls at the same time. In such an organization it was difficult to tell where business control ended and state control

[1] *Glasgow Herald*, 21 May 1915.
[2] W. Beveridge, *Power and Influence* (1953), p. 126.

began: a few examples will illustrate how closely private capital and state power were interlocked within the Ministry. Until the end of 1917 Alfred Herbert was in charge of machine tool production; he was also head of one of the major machine tool companies. From September 1917 Colonel W. C. Wright, of the Port Talbot Steel Co. Ltd. was Controller of Iron and Steel Production. Most impressive was the representation achieved by the arms firms in the control of gun manufacture. Between 1915 and July 1917 Lieutenant-Colonel W. C. Symon (an employee of Vickers) was in direct control of gun production: he was succeeded by a Captain V. B. Stewart of Beardmores. Beardmores was a subsidiary of Vickers. Following the removal of Sir Percy Girouard (Armstrong-Whitworth) in July 1915, Symon's immediate superior in the Ministry hierarchy was Charles Ellis (John Brown). In May 1917 Ellis was succeeded by Glynn West (Armstrong-Whitworth again).[1]

The problem of labour supply, manpower, was in many ways the most crucial facing the Ministry. Here it was not the integration with business that was most striking, but the continuity with the institutions of labour control erected by pre-war Liberal Governments. The Labour Exchange system was the basis without which wartime labour controls would have been impossible.

'The Act of 1909 had anticipated the War . . . [Together with the Insurance Act it ensured that] the numbers, classes, and even the distribution of the workers [in engineering and shipbuilding] were known with accuracy. Moreover the Exchanges had acquired a special and intimate acquaintance with the labour engaged in these trades and had formed, in many cases, close association with the employers. When, therefore, it became a matter of great national importance to make the fullest and most economical use of the labour in these trades, the experience acquired during the years between the setting up of the Exchanges and the outbreak of war was invaluable.'[2]

It was that same 'storm corps' of 'eager young bureaucrats'[3] who had been mobilized by Lloyd George and Churchill on

---

[1] *MM* II, 1, pp. 17, 151, apps. ii–viii; 86 of the 208 senior officials listed by the official historians were businessmen.

[2] H. Wolfe, *Labour Supply and Regulation* (Oxford, 1923), pp. 68–9; see also Beveridge, *Power and Influence*, pp. 118, 126.

[3] A. Marwick, *The Deluge* (Harmondsworth, 1967), p. 168.

social insurance before the war, who built the wartime labour controls, transferred or on temporary loan from the Board of Trade. Sir Hubert Llewelyn Smith, permanent secretary of the Board of Trade since 1907, was general secretary of the Ministry from its foundation.[1] William Beveridge, leading theorist of New Liberalism and, since 1909, Director of Labour Exchanges, was Assistant General Secretary in charge of the Labour Department and Secretariat.[2] Charles Rey, general manager of Unemployment Insurance since 1912, was responsible for launching the War Munitions Volunteers, and from the autumn of 1915 was Assistant General Secretary in charge of Labour Supply.[3] All three men retained their Board of Trade connections and, in October 1916 when the formative phase was complete, returned to the Board. Humbert Wolfe, from 1912 'among the band of able civil servants who . . . organized the labour exchange and unemployment insurance schemes', served in the Labour Department throughout the war, and was Director of Labour Regulation during 1917–18.[4]

Nowhere was the subordination of workers' to employers' interests in the wartime intervention of the state more decisively illustrated than in the steps taken towards industrial compulsion. The influence of large employers in the Ministry was, from the start, directed towards using the state machine to strengthen employers against unions. In May 1915 William Weir,[5] a leading

[1] Sir Hubert Llewellyn Smith (1864–1945). Oxford and Toynbee Hall. Wrote *The Story of the Dockers Strike* with Tillett in 1890. Joined the staff of the Board of Trade in 1893. After the war he became Chief Economic Adviser to the Government. Retired in 1927, and subsequently directed the New Survey of London Life and Labour (1928–35).

[2] William, later Lord, Beveridge (b. 1879). Director of London School of Economics 1919–37, and Master of University College, Oxford, 1937–45. Author of the Beveridge Report, 1942.

[3] Charles Rey (b. 1877) had joined the Board of Trade staff in 1900. One of the officials sent to study the German labour exchanges, he was appointed General Manager of Labour Exchanges in 1909. In 1918 he became Assistant Secretary to the new Ministry of Labour. Subsequently his interests took him to Africa, where he became Resident Commissioner in Bechuanaland, 1930–7.

[4] Humbert Wolfe (1886–1940). Romantic poet and civil servant. Changed name from Umberto Wolff in 1918. Bradford Grammar School and Oxford. After war returned to labour exhanges, and in 1938 became deputy secretary to the Ministry of Labour, wrote or edited 40 books, 39 of them literary. Other ex-Board of Trade officials included Stephen Tallents and J. B. Adams.

[5] Descended from illegitimate daughter of Burns. William Weir, created 1st Baron in 1918 (1877–1959). Not to be confused with Andrew Weir (Lord Invernorth), who became Minister of Munitions in 1919. William Weir was Director-General of Aircraft Production at the Ministry from December

Glasgow employer who was well connected among the top management of the great arms firms, and who was later to become Director of Munitions for Scotland, called for 'an arbitrary stabilization of working conditions on a war basis'. By this he meant an absolute wage freeze, the abrogation of all trade union restrictive practices and bargaining rights, the direction of labour. His argument was that since 'as a general proposition . . . the existing skilled men, organized as trade unionists, are uncontrollable by the employer', the state should take the employers' disciplinary functions on itself.[1]

This statement immediately became a focus in the national campaign for industrial conscription. Milner and the radical right wanted complete national service, military and industrial conscription. The Clydeside employers lobbied the Ministry demanding 'all sorts of powers over workmen – a sort of martial law – which they themselves might administer, obviously an impossible demand'.[2] On June 3rd, convinced by pressure from employers and army, the new Minister of Munitions, Lloyd George, made a speech in Manchester fully embracing the demand for industrial compulsion:

'It is a war of munitions. We are fighting against the best organized community in the world – the best organized, whether for war or peace – and we have been employing too much of the haphazard, leisurely, go-as-you-please methods which, believe me, would not have enabled us to maintain our place as a nation, even in peace, very much longer . . . We must increase the mobility of labour, and . . . we must have greater subordination in labour to the direction and control of the state.'[3]

The Munitions Act was drafted on the basis of this speech. 'Such was the instruction given to us officials in June 1915. We were told to draft a measure of industrial compulsion and

1917. During the inter-war years he was chairman of the Advisory Committee on Civil Aviation. In 1939 he became Director-General of Explosives at the Ministry of Supply, and in 1952, chairman of the Tank Board. He was also, for a time, president of the British Employers' Confederation.

[1] *Glasgow Herald*, 21 May 1915.

[2] C. Addison, *Four and a Half Years* (1934); W. J. Reader, *Architect of Air Power* (1968), p. 39; *Bev.* i, p. 293, Deputation from Emergency Committee of Shipbuilding Employers' Federation, 9 June 1915; *MM* i, 4, p. 29; *The Times*, 27 May 1915; *The Herald*, 28 May, 19 June 1915.

[3] *The Times*, 4 June 1915.

discipline: it seemed to us fair to do so.'[1] On June 9th Sir Hubert Llewelyn Smith, who, with Beveridge, was the main draftsman of the Act,[2] outlined his primary consideration:

'The shortage of labour directly delays production. It is however, at the present time having indirect effects perhaps even more serious. Practically any workman of any pretensions to skill at all in the engineering and ship building trades has so little difficulty in finding work the moment he wants it that he has little economic motive left for remaining with his employer, if he is in any way dissatisfied, whether with good reason or without.

'On the other hand, the employers, constantly urged by the Government to increase their output, do not feel themselves really in a position to bargain with the men, and have indeed, in many cases owing to the terms of their contract, little incentive to do so. The ordinary economic control of the individual workman has practically broken down. The result is that to a very considerable extent men are out of the control both of the employers and of their own leaders. The question is whether some exceptional form of control or motive not of a purely economical character can be effectively substituted.'[3]

The Asquith coalition represented a balance of political forces that made military conscription, for the time being, unattainable. In the absence of military conscription, the degree of compulsion that could be brought to bear on civilian labour was necessarily limited. Munitions workers could not, for example, be placed under military discipline. The Munitions Act is to be understood as the nearest approximation that could be devised in the absence of military conscription to the ideal of compulsory national service.[4]

---

[1] Beveridge, *Power and Influence*, p. 126. See also *Mun*. 5. 328, memorandum by Beveridge, 17 February 1919.

[2] Wolfe, *Labour Supply and Regulation*, p. xi.

[3] *Bev*. i, p. 292, memorandum on Labour for Armaments, 10 June 1915. For authorship see *MM* I, 11, pp. 98–9.

[4] According to the official history the critical limitation on the degree of compulsion in the Munitions Act was the need to agree the measure with 'the Trade Unions and their members' before submitting it to Parliament: *MM* I, 4, p. 25. These negotiations may have had some effect in reducing the compulsionism in the Bill (though it is not true that the trade unions' members were consulted – the unions did not ballot on whether or not to accept the Bill). But the absence of military conscription seems a more decisive consideration.

B

The Munitions Act became law on 3 July 1915. It tackled the problem of creating a disciplined and mobile labour force on four major fronts. First, strikes on war work were made illegal and arbitration compulsory. In a rising labour market the reciprocal outlawing of the lockout represents a very minimal concession to labour. Second, a War Munitions Volunteers scheme, which had originated on the Tyne and Clyde, was given statutory recognition. By September 1915, 100,000 engineers had volunteered to work (for a six-month period initially) wherever the Government chose to send them, in return for travelling allowances and guarantee of no loss of wages. Unfortunately the vast majority of these men turned out already to be working on essential war contracts. Although Lloyd George had threatened to make the scheme compulsory if it failed to place sufficient men at the disposal of the Government, no attempt was made to do so at this stage. In a modest way, from 1916 onwards, the War Munitions Volunteers scheme was not ineffective as a means of meeting the more acute shortages of skilled labour.[2]

Third, section IV of the Act enabled the Ministry to declare any workshop on munitions work a 'controlled establishment'. This was the one place in the Act where any serious attempt was made to compensate the unions for their sacrifices. In controlled establishments all restrictive practices were suspended by law, and wages and workshop discipline were under the control of the Ministry. In return the amount of profit that could be earned in a controlled establishment was controlled by the Government, and statutory recognition was given to those guarantees against the adverse effects of wartime dilution of labour that had been negotiated by the trade unions in the Treasury Agreement of March 1915. As the chief example of 'that infallible sense of evenness' which, according to the wartime Director of Labour Regulation, characterized the Act, section IV left much to be desired.[2]

The munitions levy was easily evaded by claims for capital expenditure and depreciation allowances and its yield was negligible. The levy was subsequently merged into an excess profits duty which applied much more widely and was more effective, if less ambitious in its attack on war-inflated profits. None of this activity, however, prevented the munitions firms

[1] Wolfe, *Labour Supply and Regulation*, pp. 194–206; *MM* IV, 1, pp. 5–10; *MM* IV, 10, pp. 27–33.

[2] Wolfe, *Labour Supply and Regulations*, p. 105.

from making huge profits out of dilution and the needs of the warfare state.[1] The guarantees against the use of dilution to introduce cheap labour were totally inadequate, and those of the restoration of pre-war practices after the war were of highly questionable value.[2] In any case the supposed legislative reciprocity was inappropriate. No amount of legislative activity of this kind could have protected the engineering craftsmen against the fundamental threat to their economic security implicit in the adaptation of the industry to the needs of war production. The maximization of their independent strength could alone provide such protection: and the whole purpose of the Act was to reduce that strength. Under section IV Munitions Tribunals, composed of an official chairman and an assessor appointed by the Government from each of two panels representing employers and workmen respectively, had the power to fine workers offending against workshop rules laid down by the Minister. Such rules required regular attendance and diligent work (including 'a reasonable amount of overtime, if required'), sobriety and good order, and, in pursuance of section IV (3), that

'No person employed shall insist or attempt to insist on the observance either by himself or by any other person employed of any rule, practice, or custom tending to restrict the rate of production on any class of work, or to limit the employment of any class of person, or otherwise tending to restrict production or employment.'[3]

In this way the state had been brought in to reinforce the disciplinary functions of the employer, though the employer remained responsible for initiating prosecutions under this section of the Act.

Fourth, and most unpopular of all, section VII of the Act laid down that

'A person shall not give employment to a workman who has within the last previous six weeks . . . been employed on or in connection with munitions work . . . unless he holds a certificate from the employer by whom he was last so employed that he left work with the consent of his employer . . .'

[1] S. Pollard, *The Development of the British Economy, 1914–1950* (London, 1962), p. 64; *MM* III, 3, pp. 51–2.
[2] See below, pp. 66–68.
[3] Wolfe, *Labour Supply and Regulation*, p. 366.

Some of the more grossly repressive aspects of the administration of the leaving certificate were removed by the Amendment Act of January 1916. This made it an offence for employers to dismiss a workman without issuing a certificate; prevented employers using the certificates as a device for blacklisting militants; and abolished imprisonment as a penalty for any offence under the Act. But the basic objection to the leaving certificate remained: '. . . this virtually extinguishes the free market for Labour. It means that there is to be no competition between masters for the labour of the workman.'[1]

That, of course, was the intention. The central purpose of the Act, despite all talk of reciprocity, was to redress the balance of power in the workshops away from the workers and in favour of the employers. Even Wolfe had to admit that section VII 'placed no reciprocal restriction on the right (of the employer) to dismiss'. He continues:

'It gave the employer and (what from the workman's point of view was worse) the foreman an extraordinary hold over the individual. However little the workman liked his place of work, he could no longer take his money and go . . . The workman was or might be exposed to harsh or unfair treatment, and only be able to escape from it at the expense of six weeks unemployment. Nor was it merely unemployment that he had to fear. With the appearance of the Military Service Acts, and even before, it was difficult for a skilled man out of work to avoid the recruiting officer.'[2]

The major change in the Munitions Act during the war was the abolition of the leaving certificate following its identification as the major grievance of the skilled men by the Commissioners on Industrial Unrest, in the autumn of 1917. It is debateable how far this represented a victory of organized labour over industrial compulsion. The main function of the leaving certificate was to prevent indiscipline and wage inflation by making it impossible for munitions workers to take advantage of their scarcity in the market. Undoubtedly it had considerable effect as one weapon in the employer's armoury; and when it was removed it certainly became more difficult for employers to risk antagonizing their skilled workers by pressing forward with

[1] *House of Commons Debates*, Fifth series, vol. 72, col. 1600 – William Pringle, Liberal MP for NW Lanarkshire.
[2] Wolfe, *Labour Supply and Regulation*, pp. 110, 221.

dilution, using the tribunals to enforce discipline, or holding down wages. But this point can be exaggerated. The same economic circumstances which made skilled labour scarce also put a premium on its co-operation in the workshops. There were plenty of profits to be earned, and ca'canny or strike action were likely to be at least as powerful weapons as the ability to get another job. The clearest failure of the Munitions Act – as the great mound of information contained in the Daily Reports on actual or threatened strikes considered by the Munitions Council during 1917–18 reveals with some force – was its failure to prevent the everyday use of, or threat of, the strike weapon to enforce wage and other demands.[1] The real victory over industrial compulsion is to be found not in the abolition of the leaving certificate, but in the *de facto* maintenance of the right to strike.[2]

[1] Metal, engineering and shipbuilding

	No. of disputes beginning in the year	No. of working days lost through strikes
1910	96	3,147,000
1911	253	1,265,000
1912	231	1,357,000
1913	391	2,985,000
1914	232	1,308,000
1915	189	357,000
1916	105	305,000
1917	225	3,063,000
1918	420	1,499,000
1919	335	12,248,000
1920	340	3,414,000
1921	151	4,420,000
1922	115	17,484,000

B. R. Mitchell and P. Dean, *Abstract of British Historical Statistics* (Cambridge, 1962), pp. 71–2.

[2] This is not to say that the anti-strike legislation was entirely ineffective. No doubt there would have been even more strikes had they not been illegal. Apart from this generalized deterrent function, the law could only be used productively in quite special circumstances. Early in 1916, a Ministry of Munitions memorandum outlined the main considerations that lay behind the authorities' decision to activate the Munitions Act against strikers:

'(4) Prosecutions of the strikers themselves under the Munitions of War Act would not be undertaken as a matter of course but regard will be had to the circumstances of the case, and, in particular, to the size of the strike. If the strike is a general one, it may have to be left to take its own course. Without recourse to the Union funds it can hardly continue for any length of time, and if, as may be hoped, the

The Munitions Act was not the only piece of wartime legislation to threaten industrial compulsion. From January 1916 the threat intensified from a new angle with the introduction of military conscription. The fear that military conscription would lead to industrial conscription was widespread throughout the labour movement, as Arthur Henderson explained to his colleagues in the Government:

'No one who has studied the recent history of Labour will doubt that it is the fear of encroachment on civil and industrial freedom – on a man's right to choose his own trade and his own master and to make his own terms of service – that makes the opposition to military compulsion a question of principle and almost a passion with men whose devotion to their country is wholly beyond question.'[1]

At first, partly as a result of Labour opposition to conscription, skilled munitions workers were exempt[2] and, in theory, protected against the use of conscription by employers as a disciplinary weapon by a two-month period of continuing exemption after they had left munitions work.[3] This was far from watertight protection, and during 1916 the anarchic competition between War Office and Ministry of Munitions for manpower led to constant violation of the skilled men's exemption by the recruiting officers. Some employers took advantage of the unsettled position to use the threat of conscription as a disciplinary weapon.[4] This

strike weakens, the weakening process can then be hastened by prosecuting those who hold out.

(5) The foregoing policy of not necessarily using the Munitions of War Act to prosecute strikers is conditional upon one point, namely, that there should be no bargaining, either directly or indirectly, with the men while on strike, and no acceptance from them of anything but an unconditional return to work and the reference of any outstanding differences in accordance with the Munitions of War Act.'
'Summary of Dilution Programme . . .', revised 22 January 1916, in *Bev.* iii, p. 268.

[1] Quoted in M. Hamilton, *Arthur Henderson: a Biography* (1938), p. 110. See also Labour Party, *Conference Report*, January 1916, pp. 6–24.

[2] The less skilled workers were not exempted, and within weeks the Government was conscripting less skilled workers where their work could be done by women, and employers were using this as a disciplinary weapon: Cole, *Trade Unionism and Munitions*, p. 129; *Mun.* 2. 28, 13 January 1917.

[3] I.e. long enough to get a new job even if he had no leaving certificate.

[4] *MM* vi, 1, pp. 14–15; *Mun.* 5. 57, Negotiations with the ASE, 27 April, 27 September, 15 November 1916; Wolfe, *Labour Supply and Regulation,*

culminated in November 1916 in a strike of the skilled engineers in Sheffield. The Government, judging that the need for skilled workers was as yet greater than the need for trench fodder, conceded a more effective protection to the craftsmen in the shape of exemption cards to be issued through their unions. However, from the Government's point of view this was an ill-thought-out measure, and the extraordinary power it conferred on the craft unions was not allowed to stand for long. The Trade Card scheme, because it applied in the main only to the members of the craft unions, was ineffective in protecting essential workers, and, because it applied to all the members of those unions, protected many who were not essential. When, in the spring of 1917, the demand for troops, and in particular for skilled men for the technical units, could no longer be met under the existing system, the Government did not hesitate to provoke a national strike by abolishing it.[1]

In its place they introduced the Schedule of Protected Occupations, which defined the exempted categories with far more precision than the criterion of membership of a craft union had permitted. In accepting this the unions accepted in principle that skilled men could be conscripted and that this could be done quite openly as a means of direction of labour, since the categories of exemption could be altered to meet the changing balance of military and industrial necessity. Moreover, no individual workman was automatically exempted under the Schedule, which stated that 'men who have a bad record for absenting themselves from work' should not be granted exemption.[2] In the early months of 1918 the craftsman's protection was further diminished by legislation giving the Ministry of National Service the right to cancel exemptions under the Schedule without consulting the unions, and by the 'clean cut', which made all munitions workers under the age of 23 liable for conscription whatever their occupation.[3]

pp. 23, 42–3, 110, 221; *Mun.* 5. 79, 'History of the Strike', 29 August 1917. Addison is here quoted as saying: 'Half the troubles with the skilled men have arisen from some over-enthusiastic recruiting officer running in a man who really ought to have been exempted.'

[1] Cole, *Trade Unionism and Munitions*, p. 135; *MM* vi, 1, pp. 74–82; *Mun.* 2. 28, 24 February 1917.

[2] M. B. Hammond, *British Labour Conditions and Legislation During the War* (New York, 1919), pp. 128–136; *MM* vi, 1, pp. 83–4.

[3] *MM* vi, 2, pp. 39–42. Men on hull construction and repair remained exempted whatever their age.

When the Munitions Act was introduced military conscription had not yet been instituted and the idea of 'national service' was therefore rejected. One of the brave new starts of the Lloyd George coalition of December 1916 was the establishment of a Ministry of National Service under Neville Chamberlain, whose job was to determine priorities for all industries and occupations and thus prepare the way for an overall scheme of direction of labour. The scheme failed. The apparent simplicity of the national service idea was belied by the extraordinary complexity of the problems of inspection and administration raised by the attempt to control the whole manpower of the nation. Nevertheless, a number of more piecemeal efforts were made by the Government during 1918 to step up its controls over labour mobility in response to immediate emergencies.

At the end of April 1918 the War Cabinet decided to 'secure more economic use of manpower in the munitions industry by largely increasing the number of War Munitions Volunteers'.[1] Detailed proposals were worked out, including provisions to force men into the Volunteers by withdrawing their exemption if they did not join, and submitted to the Trade Union Advisory Committee at the beginning of June.[2] This aroused a storm of protest. The proposed measures were seen as an attempt to 'convert the War Munitions Volunteers scheme into a form of compulsory service'. On July 1st the Advisory Committee rejected the scheme and declined all responsibility for the consequences of introducing it. The Government 'beat a strategic retreat'.[3] During the same period, however, it had been developing, without any consultation with the unions, a parallel policy of increasing dilution by 'regulating and restricting the employment of labour', in individual firms.[4] Disguised Ministry of Munitions embargoes on a firm's right to engage skilled labour had already been used for this purpose, and during May these restrictions were extended.[5] On July 1st, the very day on which the Advisory Committee

[1] Mun. 1.8 (MC), 25 April 1918.
[2] Mun. 1.9 (MC), 14 May 1918; Mun. 1.10 (MC), 4, 10, 13 June 1918.
[3] The Herald, 13 July 1918.　　　　[4] Mun 1.8 (MC), 25 April 1918.
[5] Mun. 5. 72, Dilution Section Minutes, no. 137, 9 May 1918. An embargo had already been placed on the further employment of skilled labour at Daimler in February 1918: MM VI, 2, p. 64. Daimler was 'notorious for using numbers of skilled men for work which was quite unworthy of their skill'. Mun. 2. 28, 15 December 1917. By the end of June embargoes had been placed on 30 firms: Mun. 5. 52, memorandum on the embargo scheme, July 1918.

rejected the proposals for extending the WMV scheme, the first open embargoes were imposed on about twenty-five firms throughout the country.[1] This could only seem like a determined attempt by the Government to introduce industrial conscription by the back door.[2] 'No assurance is given that the embargo will not be extended and it is possible to suddenly find that the embargo has been extended from hundreds to thousands of firms, and that would mean that a skilled man was chained to his job and that no freedom of movement was left.'[3] The embargoes led to strikes in Coventry, Birmingham and Manchester which forced the Government to set up a Committee of Enquiry and withdraw the scheme pending its report. By the time the final report of the Committee appeared, recommending withdrawal, the war was over.

Wartime Governments never succeeded in disciplining the labour force in the image of the army; nor did they ever abandon the attempt to do so. 'With all its formlessness, with all its alarms, false starts, and retreats, the history of government labour regulation during the war is, in substance, that of an attempt to introduce controls approaching industrial conscription, but not so closely as to unite workers against the Government.'[4] In the resulting battle to resist and push back the multiform pressures of industrial compulsion the trade union officials proved less convincing generals than the revolutionaries of the shop stewards movement. Above all else, it was the shop stewards who were responsible for the major victory over compulsion – the *de facto* maintenance of the right to strike.

The capacity of any section of the labour movement to resist the wartime offensive of the state and the employers against traditional working-class rights depended in no small part on its perception of the character of that offensive. The wartime extension of the role of the state in the economy has been des-

---

[1] *MM* VI, 2, p. 65. By July 10th a further 45 firms had been drawn into the scheme: *Mun.* 5. 52, memo. *cit.*

[2] *Midland Daily Telegraph*, 20 July 1918, statement by Walter Givens, Coventry District Secretary of the ASE.

[3] *Birmingham Gazette*, 26 July 1918, statement by Birmingham and District Joint Committee of Engineering Trade Unions. As Humbert Wolfe pointed out later: 'The embargo system . . . though it was not consciously intended to take the place of the leaving certificate, might, if it had been successful, have done so.' Wolfe, *Labour Supply and Regulation*, p. 230.

[4] S. J. Hurwitz, *State Intervention in Great Britain* (London, 1949), pp. 77–8.

cribed as a 'doctrineless collectivism' which grew out of piecemeal and pragmatic responses to the urgent needs of wartime.
Scarcity was the motor of its growth:

'The economic breakwaters which, if seen as a whole, would
have caused cries of alarm, grew, like coral islands, through the
unseen activities of the industrious, but silent insects, composing
the Civil Service. Each addition to the structure was related to
some immediate necessity of incontestable urgency . . . The
most extensive and intricate scheme of state intervention in
economic life which the country had seen was brought into
existence without the merits or demerits of state intervention
being even discussed.'[1]

Tawney's characterization is misleading. It is true that 'the
controlled economy was not seen and planned as a whole',[2] and
that the fundamental determinants of the growth of state intervention were the overriding immediate demands of war. (Though
war only made such demands because of the scale and level of
technology reached by capitalist industry.) But this growth did
not occur without ideological confrontations, and, together with
the pull of immediate necessity, more generalized attitudes to the
value of state intervention certainly played their part both in the
construction of, and in the opposition to war collectivism.
Freedom versus control was a central theme of the rhetoric of
high politics during 1915–17. Indeed, within the labour movement, which played a part both in building and in resisting war
collectivism, attitudes towards the desirability of state intervention might themselves go some way to determining attitudes
to the war itself.

To many in the labour movement war collectivism appeared in
general as a progressive development, even a fulfillment of
socialist predictions: 'Thus in the hour of its supreme need does
the nation turn to the collectivist experiments urged for so many
years by the Labour movement. And the experiments are not
found wanting. They are abundantly and brilliantly vindicated.'[3]
The experience of war thus seemed to bear out the Fabian
doctrine that socialism would arise, indeed was arising, not out
of the prosecution of class struggle, but as an administrative

[1] R. H. Tawney, 'The Abolition of Economic Controls, 1918–21', *EcHR*,
1943.
[2] E. V. Morgan, *Studies in British Financial Policy, 1914–22*, p. 35.
[3] *Daily Citizen*, 5 October 1914, quoted in Marwick, *The Deluge*, p. 173.

necessity – as the only feasible response to the problems of production and distribution confronting the state. Collaboration in the war effort was to be justified as much by the opportunities apparently opened up for a policy of strengthening, radicalizing and rendering permanent a 'collectivist consensus', as by the need to defeat German nationalism. Beatrice Webb remarked acidly on the Labour leaders' decision to join the Lloyd George coalition in December 1916: 'A thorough beating of the Germans may have passed through their minds. But their main motive . . . is the illusion that the mere presence of Labour men in the Government, apart from anything they may do or prevent being done, is in itself a sign of democratic progress.'[1] But this illusion was itself encouraged by the gradualist ideology of Fabianism, and the Webbs were more responsible than most for persuading the Labour Party to base its strategic perspectives on the notion of an emergent collectivist consensus:

'Today no man dares to say that anything is impracticable. The war, which has scared the old Political Parties right out of their dogmas, has taught every statesman and every Government official, to his enduring surprise, how very much more can be done along the lines that we have laid down than he had ever before thought possible. What we now promulgate as our policy, whether for opposition or for office, is not merely this or that specific reform, but a deliberately thought out, comprehensive and systematic plan for that immediate social rebuilding which any Ministry whether or not it desires to grapple with the problem, will be driven to undertake.'[2]

Similarly, opposition to Labour's collaboration in the war effort might spring less from internationalism, than from the belief that war collectivism, far from establishing 'stepping stones to socialism',[3] was a stage in the construction of a state capitalism which would weigh even more heavily on the workers

[1] M. Cole (ed.), *Beatrice Webb's Diaries, 1912–1924* (1952), p. 73. Beatrice, however, was opposing not collaboration but collaboration at too cheap a price: '. . . there is a maddening muddle-headedness which makes them quite incapable of asking for terms for their own class before they consent to take office, and wholly blind to the distinctions between supporting the government on conditions and accepting the responsibility in advance for every plan which a majority of reactionaries may adopt'.

[2] 'Labour and the New Social Order', the 1918 manifesto of the Labour Party, written by Sidney Webb.

[3] This was H. M. Hyndman's attitude: *Justice*, 13 August, 22 October 1914.

than nineteenth-century individualism. The state, it was true, might respond to the threat of working-class revolt with palliatives in the form of excess profits duty, rent control, food rationing: but 'Labour in Chains'[1] was the essential meaning of war collectivism. The Defence of the Realm Acts suppressed basic civil liberties, the Munitions Act erected the scaffolding of industrial slavery, and the Military Service Acts threatened to constitute the walls. These features, which seemed to the state socialists regrettable but temporary wartime distortions in an inexorable 'landslide towards Social Democracy',[2] were, in the eyes of the shop stewards and their political allies, new and formidable weapons in the arsenal of the ruling class, milestones on the road to the 'servile state'.

This term had received considerable publicity in the labour movement immediately prior to the war following the publication of Hilaire Belloc's book, *The Servile State*, and was in common use on the left throughout the war years. Belloc coined the term as a description of the tendency inherent, as he saw it, in the pre-war New Liberal social legislation. Two measures in particular pointed the way. The Labour Exchange system, established in 1909, was seen to provide the state with the means of registering and recording data on each worker: 'No man, once so registered and known, can escape . . .' Lloyd George's National Insurance Act of 1911 made attendance at the Labour Exchange, and the consequent registration, compulsory for the classes of workers it covered. The Insurance Act, despite its undoubted material benefits for the workers, enabled the state, in effect, to fine a worker who declined to work at the job selected for him by officialdom. Who could tell for what purpose this machinery of compulsion would be used in the future?[3]

Belloc was not complaining of any servile implications of state intervention *per se*. His primary concern was with the question, 'On whose behalf is the state acquiring these powers of compulsion?' Here his polemic turned again those Labour Party leaders who, in the name of socialism, found it convenient to collaborate with the Liberal Government. He argued that the

---

[1] Title of a pamphlet by Philip Snowden, published in 1917.
[2] Cole (ed.), *Beatrice Webb's Diaries*, p. 18.
[3] H. Belloc, *The Servile State* (2nd ed., 1913), pp. 175–6. There is a fascinating article by George Lansbury, *Daily Herald*, 13 January 1913, in which he argues that even the provision of school meals for children had, because of its bureaucratic administration, served to bring nearer the servile state.

collectivism promoted by New Liberalism had nothing in common with socialism, but represented, rather, the use of state power in the direct service of private capital.

'What I have said . . . is that the object of the Socialist . . . is not in practice being approached; that we are not, *as a matter of fact*, coming nearer towards the collective ownership of the means of production, but that we *are* rapidly coming nearer to the establishment of compulsory labour among an unfree majority of non-owners for the benefit of a free minority of owners . . .

'[Much of the so-called welfare legislation is in fact concerned with] regulating, "running", and drilling the proletariat without trenching by an inch upon the privilege in implements, stores, and land enjoyed by the Capitalist class.'[1]

Before the war it was easy to dismiss Belloc's forebodings as melodramatic and one sided.[2] But to munition workers in wartime the servile state might well seem to have made very rapid progress indeed:

'You have to remember that for some years past there has been considerable nibbling at the individuality of the worker. During all his working hours he is merely a cipher – known by a check number. At the Labour Exchange he has a number, and when he is ill, under the State Insurance, he is also known by a number. The Munitions Act and the Defence of the Realm Act have divested him of the last shreds of individuality, and it begins to look to him as if they were gone permanently . . .'[3]

When Lloyd George introduced the Munitions Bill in the summer of 1915 was he not carrying forward the work he had begun in the establishment of compulsory National Insurance in 1911? To the young Ernest Bevin the men behind Lloyd George's wartime legislation were not the 'silent insects', the merely pragmatic civil servants of Tawney's aloof description; they were 'a sinister crowd . . . the Labour Exchange crowd, Mr Beveridge, Llewellyn

---

[1] Belloc, *The Servile State*, Preface, p. xi, and p. 129.

[2] E.g. *The Servile State* was 'a good enough description of the social ideal of Fascism. As however the principle danger sign which Belloc quoted was the passing of the Insurance Act, most people thought he was making a perverse and unnecessary fuss.' M. Cole, *Beatrice Webb* (1945), p. 111.

[3] Clyde Workers' Committee's statement to Lloyd George, published in *The Worker*, 15 January 1915.

Smith and the rest'.[1] It is not difficult to see how the Ministry of Munitions, in whose very composition big business and the 'arms ring' converged with the administrative élite of New Liberalism, could appear to those it controlled, and who were themselves entirely unrepresented on its staff, as a logical culmination of the repressive implications of pre-war social reform. 'We regard you with suspicion', said David Kirkwood to Lloyd George in December 1915, 'because every Act with which your name is associated has the taint of slavery about it.'[2]

Belloc's own solutions were reactionary – he was a declared anti-socialist who argued for a return to Catholicism and peasant proprietorship – but his acute identification of the servile tendencies of 'welfare' legislation became the common property of the progressive opponents of state socialism: industrial unionists syndicalists, guild socialists.[3] The most systematic, and, for the leadership of the shop stewards' movement, the most influential elaboration of the socialist critique of state capitalism during the war was that undertaken by the Socialist Labour Party. Like Belloc the SLP saw the pre-war New Liberal reforms as essentially repressive:

'Every reform . . . brings its own army of State despots. This is because reforms are administered, not by the workers, but by the Capitalist Government and its officials . . . The consequence is that in the same measure that reforms are passed and administered in the same ratio the workers come under the domination of the Servile State.'[4]

Not only was the demand for state welfare policies in danger of being turned against the workers, so also was the demand for

[1] Ernest Bevin, in September 1916, quoted in Beveridge, *Power and Influence*, p. 127.

[2] *The Worker*, 15 January 1916. See also J. T. Murphy in *Solidarity*, March 1917: 'The State has become the almighty power regulating and controlling the lives of all . . . The centralising process has been wonderfully rapid. From the Insurance Act the speed has been culmulative . . .'

[3] In 1911, *Clarion* endorsed Belloc's case against the Insurance Act – see issues of 16 June and 23 July 1911 – and during the first half of 1913 a vigorous debate was conducted in its columns about Belloc's book, *The Servile State*, published in October 1912. The *Daily Herald* also discussed the book at length, endorsing Belloc's attack on labour leaderships, and arguing for syndicalism as the alternative to slavery (e.g. *Daily Herald*, 7 January 1913). See also *Socialism and the Servile State: a Debate between Messrs Hillaire Belloc and J. Ramsay MacDonald, M.P.* (1911).

[4] *The Socialist*, July 1916.

state ownership of industry, nationalization. The publication of a series of articles on 'The Elements of Reconstruction' in *The Times* during August and September 1916,[1] in which piecemeal nationalization was proposed as a means of consolidating the efficiency of the capitalist economy as a whole (a measure urged in anticipation of an inter-imperialist trade war after the war), provided the SLP's paper, *The Socialist*, with an opportunity to remind its readers:

'For over thirteen years we have sought to show . . . that State Ownership was the final word in capitalist domination, that it was pregnant with sinister danger for the workers, who would become State serfs . . . The capitalist class is more than pleased with its State subjugation of Labour, and now faced with fierce commercial competition in the world's markets, it realizes that to protect Profits, the time has now come, as the SLP. prophesied, when in order to concentrate its activity against competition abroad, and to crush the growing opposition of the workers at home, Capital needs State ownership.'[2]

'The first, and, from the point of view of working class tactics, most important point to be noted is that Nationalization or "State Socialism", so far from being the method of working class progress to Socialism has become the very life blood and method of the most militant and aggressive Imperialism.'[3]

[1] These articles, which were anonymous, were subsequently published as a pamphlet with a glowing introduction by Lord Milner.

[2] *The Socialist*, September 1916. The *Times* articles also caused a considerable stir in the ILP, for which see J. R. MacDonald's articles in *Forward* during September and October 1916, and his very interesting re-evaluation of pre-war attitudes to the state in *Socialism and the War* (1917).

[3] *The Socialist*, October 1916. In *The State: its Origins and Functions*, written during 1917, William Paul, a leading SLP theorist, further elaborated this theme. The state socialism of the ILP was, he argued, no accident. It stemmed from the capture of the Party by that 'most original and by far the cleverest section of the middle-class intellectuals' – the Fabians. It was clear to the Fabians that the 'future of competitive Capitalism shows little hope of the intellectual proletariat improving their lot'. Any extension of state activity would result in 'new avenues of well paid official jobs' being opened up. Small wonder, therefore, that the 'intellectual proletarians' of the Fabian Society look upon the state as a glorified institution, 'as something destined to save the world'. 'The economic ideal of the intellectual wage-earner is a national state controlling the industry of the country in which each is rewarded according to a weird theory called the "rent of ability"'. Thus the intellectuals were using the labour movement as a vehicle for the establishment of their own Utopia – an 'intellectual despotism', in which the workers will be faced by 'a gigantic army of State-subsidized officials who will fight like tigers to maintain their status and power'.

This was the standpoint from which much of the leadership of the shop stewards' movement approached the wartime struggles. In those struggles the rank and file were brought up against an extension of repressive state power that tended to confirm their leadership's analysis of the character of war collectivism. Their revolt against the servile state constitutes the central strand of opposition to state monopoly capitalism, and to the bureaucratization of social relations associated with it, during the first major period of its growth. Much of the interest of the shop stewards' movement lies in this fact.

TRADE UNION OFFICIALDOM

Outside the shipyards and foundries, dominated respectively by the boilermakers and ironfounders, one union had a clear claim to primacy in the industry. The Amalgamated Society of Engineers (ASE) accounted for about 38% of all the organized skilled workers in the industry in 1914.[1] Recruiting predominantly fitters (60%), turners (21%) and machinists (10%),[2] its closest rivals were three smaller unions organizing these same trades. The Amalgamated Society of Toolmakers (AST) organized the most highly skilled workers. The United Machine Workers' Association (UMWA) and the Steam Engine Makers (SEM) catered both for skilled men and for some of the classes of semi-skilled workers that the ASE traditionally had failed to organize. Of the 219,000 workers organized by these four unions in 1914, the ASE had 79·8%, the SEM 8·1%, the AST 7·1% and the UMWA 5·1%.[3]

From its inception in 1851 the ASE had intended to organize all skilled workers in the industry, to eliminate 'these small and unnecessary . . . absurd and irritating institutions'.[4] In face of the progressive differentiation of the skills required by the industry, and the consequent viability of sectional craft unionism, this policy had met with little success. Its failure was given formal

1 Cole, *Trade Unionism and Munitions*, pp. 27–8.
2 ASE, *Annual Reports*, 1914–18.
3 J. B. Jefferys, *The Story of the Engineers* (London, 1946), p. 105; Cole, *loc. cit.* To its great annoyance the UMWA was sometimes treated as a semi-skilled union: *Mun.* 2. 15, 13 April 1918.
4 ASE, *Quarterly Report*, March 1893, quoted in H. A. Clegg, A. Fox and A. F. Thompson, *A History of British Trade Unions since 1889* (Oxford, 1964), p. 131.

recognition when in 1905 the ASE agreed to join the Federation of Engineering and Shipbuilding Trades, in which each sectional union, however small, had an equal voice with the ASE. Shortly before the war, however, largely as a result of the new experience of joint action in the local collective bargaining procedures, a substantial agitation for amalgamation had grown up within the engineering craft unions.[1]

Wartime pressures on the craft workers intensified the desire for closer unity, and rank and file initiative in the construction of joint organization at workshop level showed the union officials that the maintenance of their authority depended upon achieving amalgamation. Simultaneously the working alliance between the ASE and the sectional societies was severely strained. The ASE constantly claimed special treatment from the Government, both because it could be outvoted by the smaller unions in any joint action, and because in general its national officials took up a more militant stance than those of the other unions.

'Including on each occasion a number of societies little or not at all affected by the Government's proposal, the Federation has time and again been chosen by the Government as the body with which to negotiate, with the result that the societies not affected by the particular proposals concerned have either accepted the Government's plan or offered only lukewarm support . . .[2]

Eventually, in January 1918, the ASE seceded from the Federation, and at the same time launched a major new drive for amalgamation. Although the boilermakers and foundry workers remained independent, this drive succeeded in bringing the major sectional organizations of the central engineering skills into unity.

The establishment of the Amalgamated Union of Engineers in 1920 did not, however, solve the major problem of disunity in the industry. In 1914 trade unionism was still, excepting the major advances made by the Workers' Union in the Midlands, predominantly a privilege of the skilled workers in the industry. Organization among the less skilled workers in the industry expanded very rapidly in wartime. While the major craft unions grew by 76% between 1914 and 1918, the two major general unions organizing in the industry, the National Union of General

---

[1] S. and B. Webb, *Industrial Democracy* (1902), pp. 110–12; Jefferys, *The Story of the Engineers*, pp. 56–8, 163–4.
[2] ASE, *Monthly Journal and Report*, October 1917, p. 9.

Workers (NUGW)[1] and the Workers' Union (WU) grew by 216%
and 137% respectively.[2] The relationship between these unions
and the craft unions was complicated by the impact of wartime
dilution of labour and will be discussed later in that context.

The leaders of the ASE, like the leaders of the trade union
movement in general, collaborated in the war effort. Within three
weeks of the outbreak of war the trade union executives had
declared an 'industrial truce', renouncing strike action for the
duration of the war. The first major breach of this truce, the
strike of Clydeside engineers in February 1915, enabled the ASE
Executive to demonstrate its practical patriotism. In response to a
hurried request by the Government, the Executive ordered the
men back to work, and cut off strike pay; the strikers disregarded
their Executive. This established the pattern for nearly every
other wartime strike. The industrial truce was formalized, with
ASE agreement,[3] in the Treasury Agreement of March 1915.
Voluntary collaboration led, inevitably, to compulsion. The
progression is clear in the statements of Robert Young, president
of the ASE and editor of its journal. In November 1914 he wrote:
'For myself I can see no difference between German militarism . . .
and the British advocacy of conscription.' By April 1915, however, he had come to accept that only by increasing voluntary
enlistment and by maximizing productivity could the workers
establish either the right or the possibility of resisting military
and industrial compulsion. Brownlie, the general secretary of the
union, argued a similar case at the same time. It was only a short
step from here to the acceptance of both the Munitions Act and
the Military Service Acts as the unfortunate necessities of war.
As the historian of the TUC has put it, Lloyd George 'no doubt
shrewdly realized that once he had obtained the voluntary agreement of the unions for the policy adopted at the Treasury meetings, it would be difficult for them to oppose the Government's

1 The National Union of Gasworkers and General Labourers changed its
name to the National Union of General Workers in 1915. Throughout this
study, for the sake of simplicity, the union is referred to by the latter title, the
NUGW.

2 Cole, *Trade Unionism and Munitions*, p. 24. The other major union, the
National Amalgamated Union of Labour organizing mainly among platers'
helpers on the Tyne and Clyde and among less skilled iron and steel workers
in Sheffield, grew by 159% in the same period.

3 The ASE membership voted to accept the Treasury Agreement by 18,000
votes to 4,000 against. 190,000 members were entitled to vote. ASE, *Monthly
Journal and Report*, July 1915.

action in taking powers to see that the objects of the Agreement were achieved'.[1] In June 1915 the unions voted assent to the Munitions Bill before it was introduced into Parliament, thus ensuring that Labour opposition to the Bill in Parliament was minimal. The radical MP W. Pringle fought for free collective bargaining while the partriotic trade union MPS sat silent.

The argument of the collaborationists was that 'while the Unions by the Munitions of War Acts have relinquished for the time being many of the liberties and rights that have taken a generation to build up, on the other hand, they have come forward and occupied a place in the affairs of the country which will do much to consolidate and strengthen them in the future'.[2] It is true that in return for their sacrifices the Government accorded the trade union officials 'a unique and unprecedented place as the diplomatic representatives of the wage-earning class'.[3]

The Treasury Agreement earned them a National Labour Advisory Committee, representative of the Parliamentary Committee of the TUC and the Labour Party leadership which consulted with the Government on matters arising from the Agreement for the rest of the war. The Munitions Act earned them representation in the local Munitions Tribunals set up to administer the provisions of the Act, and participation in the Central Munitions Labour Supply Committee which during the autumn of 1915 drew up the regulations governing dilution. When the craft unions accepted conscription in principle in May 1917, they were rewarded with the setting up of Local Labour Enlistment Complaints Committees, with powers to interpret the application of the conscription regulations to particular cases.[4]

The ASE leadership, influenced by guild socialist notions about the gradual devolution of industrial power from a collectivist state to the autonomous organizations of the workers,[5] made several attempts to extend their footholds, particularly in relation

[1] B. C. Roberts, *The Trade Union Congress, 1868–1921* (1958), p. 278.
[2] Labour Party, *Conference Report*, January 1916, p. 56.
[3] S. and B. Webb, *History of Trade Unionism* (1920), p. 637; Cole, *Trade Unionism and Munitions*, p. 74; Roberts, *The Trade Union Congress*, pp. 276–7; *MM* IV, 1, p. 51; Addison, *Four and a Half Years*, p. 127.
[4] The value of all this was limited, however, by the fact that the individuals 'representing' the trade unions on Munitions Tribunals and Enlistment Committees were appointed by the Government rather than elected by the membership.
[5] B. Pribicevic, *The Shop Stewards' Movement and Workers' Control* (Oxford, 1959), ch. 3 *passim*.

to the administration of industry at local level. In the spring of 1915 considerable influence had been gained by local joint committees of employers, government officials and trade union representatives, especially on the Tyne. They 'came to be looked on as authorities exercising a general supervision over labour questions throughout their area'.[1] Some of the authorities saw this development in terms of initiating 'through the local Armaments Committees, a largely decentralized system of control'.[2] The establishment of the Ministry of Munitions in June, however, tended to submerge these committees in a centralized bureaucratic controlling authority within which the trade unions had very little power.

As soon as the ASE turned its attention to amending the Munitions Act, in the winter of 1915–16, the precedent of the Armaments Committees was remembered in a bid to establish at local level a counter to the centralized bureaucracy of the Ministry of Munitions in the administration of the Act. The union argued that the required changes

'profoundly affect the position of the workers, and there can be no guarantee that they will work smoothly unless the workers are allowed a hand in administering them. This shall be the chief task of the local joint committee which shall be entrusted with the task of adapting industry to the new needs and of directing its conduct under the new conditions.'[3]

But neither the Government nor the employers were any longer prepared to countenance joint committees in the localities, seeing them as a waste of time and potentially a threat to joint control exercised centrally by the employers and the state.[4] A further attempt to establish local joint committees was made during the negotiations over the extention of dilution from munitions to private work in the winter of 1916–17, but it came to nothing.[5]

---

[1] *MM* I, 3, pp. 43–53, 121–48.

[2] Cole, *Trade Unionism and Munitions*, pp. 75–7; Addison, *Four and a Half Years* pp. 98–9.

[3] Cole, *Trade Unionism and Munitions*, p. 124; *MM* IV, 1, pp. 76–8.

[4] *MM* IV, 1, pp. 79–81; *Mun. 5. 79*, Notes for the Prime Minister prior to negotiations with the ASE, 31 December 1915. The failure of the trade unions to agree among themselves on a basis of representation on the local committees also contributed to their failure to establish these local bodies: *MM* IV, 1, pp. 80–2.

[5] Cole, *Trade Unionism and Munitions*, pp. 143, 150; ASE, *Executive Minutes*, vol. 195, 11 September 1915.

Of course the union leaders retained considerable bargaining power despite the very limited character of their inroads into the formal decision-making process. And the ASE leadership was a good deal more ready to use that power than most other union leaderships. Thus it was the ASE which, by refusing to sign the initial agreement made by the other munitions unions at the Treasury, secured some of the most important concessions made by the Government in the Treasury Agreement.[1] Similarly the ASE used the dilution issue to lead the fight to repeal the worst elements of the Munitions Act during the autumn and winter of 1915. A memorandum written by Llewellyn Smith, the general secretary of the Ministry of Munitions, shows how effective such pressure could be:

'No sooner is an Agreement arrived at than it is broken, and new blackmailing conditions are proposed. The demand at the last moment for drastic amendments of the Munitions Bill as a condition of fulfilling the Agreement as to dilution already entered into is the last stage of a series of obstructive tactics, and any yielding will only be the signal for the putting forward of some fresh conditions.'

But yield they did, for '. . . we are so much in the hands of the ASE at present, [that] it would not be wise to refuse to see them'.[2]

But the ability of the trade union officials to employ 'obstructive tactics' was severely limited by their commitment to the war effort. Having accepted anti-strike legislation in the Munitions Act, the officials could hardly back up their claims with the direct threat of strike action.[3] There remained the vaguer threat that failing the required concessions the officials would find themselves unfortunately unable to control their members: 'You can take my word for it that you are on the edge of a volcano, and the officials of the Union cannot prevent an eruption taking place.'[4] But this was a two-edged weapon. In so far as they derived their power from 'uncontrollable' rank-and-file militancy, the officials

[1] I.e. promises of profit limitation; dilution *only* on war work (not commercial work); and the Government's promise to 'use its influence' to get traditional practices restored after the war.

[2] *Mun.* 5. 79, Llewellyn Smith to Beveridge, 31 December 1915; *Mun.* 5. 10, 'Amending the Munitions Bill', 31 December 1915.

[3] In February 1916 they climbed down in the test case on this issue: see below, pp. 184–85.

[4] *Mun.* 5. 57, Negotiations with the ASE, and other unions, 15 November 1916. See also Cole, *Trade Unionism and Munitions*, p. 119.

feared that power. The ASE Executive was up in arms at the first sign that the Government might recognize unofficial movements;[1] in the spring of 1916 the Government in fact used such a threat effectively to weaken the Executive's stand on dilution. When the Government suppressed the May 1917 strike the officials indicated, discreetly of course, their gratification: 'They [the ASE Executive] were, I believe, without exception, delighted that we had arrested some of the ringleaders, although they would have done their best to get them off if they had come to them for assistance . . .'[2]

The consultation accorded to the trade unions did not become secured as of right, and could be withdrawn at the convenience of the Government. In December 1916, for example, when the ASE Executive was being obstructive about the introduction of dilution on private work, the Ministry of Munitions decided 'to proceed without any further discussion with the ASE, lest they should force the issue by taking a ballot of their members, which would almost certainly result in an adverse vote.'[3] On that occasion the rank and file saved the day with the great strike movement of May 1917. A year later, however, a similar decision to revoke pledges and negotiating 'rights' previously given to the ASE – this time over conscription – was successfully carried through by the Government.

The leaders of organized labour were only recognized by the Government so long as this recognition served the Government's purposes. The trade unions had indeed become 'a part of the social machinery of the State', but only in the most subordinate capacity, and without tenure. After the war the expulsion of trade unionists from the corridors of power was almost total.[4] In the meantime the primary result of collaboration was not to extend working-class power into the state machine, but to complete the process, already well advanced before the war, by which the leaders of the organized workers were divorced from their members.

During the war the engineers occupied a position of strategic importance in the class struggle. They made the munitions; and it was, as Lloyd George said, 'an engineers' war'. Nearly a third of all wartime strike activity occurred in the engineering and

---

1   ASE, *Executive Minutes*, vol. 193, 29 February, 6 April 1916.
2   Addison, *Four and a Half Years*, p. 382.
3   *MM* VI, 1, p. 54.
4   V. L. Allen, *Trade Unions and Government* (London, 1960), pp. 30–1.

shipbuilding industries.[1] Most of the strikes were repudiated by the trade union officials, and most of them were illegal. The shop stewards' movement stood in the forefront of the battle to resist industrial compulsion, and its record of strike activity alone bears witness to its success in that battle. Leading such a struggle, against the authority of the state in wartime, must of necessity involve the movement in a political as well as a purely economic understanding of its own function and goals. Confronted by employers, state and trade union officialdom, the shop stewards' movement saw all three forces as collaborating in the construction of the servile state. It is as a revolt against this emergent servile state that the political aspect of the shop stewards' movement is primarily to be understood.

There is a further reason why the skilled engineers found themselves in the vanguard of wartime class struggle. Not only were they, as munitions workers, of primary importance to the war effort, but, in order that they should play their part adequately, their working conditions and practices required a more radical transformation than those of any other group of workers. Much of the wartime strike activity arose directly from the tensions set up by this transformation of the industry. The struggle over rationalization and dilution of labour is at least as important a part of the context of the shop stewards' movement as the struggle against industrial compulsion. And the skilled engineers' part in the dilution struggle held deeply ambiguous implications for their capacity to develop the political awareness required of them by their role in the leadership of the struggle against the servile state.

[1] *The Labour Gazette* (Board of Trade, 1914–16, Ministry of Labour, 1917–18), *passim*. Between 1899 and 1913, the number of working days lost through strike action in engineering and shipbuilding averaged only 16% of those lost in other industries: *MM* IV, 2, p. 9.

Chapter 2

The Craft Tradition

Central to any understanding of the shop stewards' movement is the fact that it was a movement of craft workers who felt their traditionally privileged position within the working class to be under the most severe pressure. Again and again in the course of this study we shall come back to search for explanations of the movement's behaviour in its ambiguous inheritance from the craft tradition.

The first principle of craft unionism was exclusiveness. The basis of the trade strategy around which engineering trade unionism had been consolidated in the 1850s and 1860s was the restriction of the supply of skilled labour, carried out firstly by limiting the ratio of apprentices to journeymen, and secondly by the restriction of traditionally skilled jobs to 'legal men' (i.e. either qualified journeymen, or – necessity forced this compromise – men who had worked five years at the trade and were paid at the standard craft rate). Whatever else may be said about the craft tradition, its central method of operation held profoundly conservative social and political implications:

'If constrained to make restrictions against the admission into our trade of those who have not earned a right by probationary servitude [apprenticeship], we do so knowing that such encroachments are productive of evil and when persevered in unchecked, result in reducing the condition of the artisan to that of the unskilled labourer, and confer no permanent advantage to those admitted. It is our duty, then, to exercise that same care and watchfulness over that in which we have a vested interest, as the physician does who holds a diploma, or the author who is protected by a copyright.'[1]

[1] ASE, *Rules*, 1864: quoted in S. and B. Webb, *Industrial Democracy* (1902), pp. 469–70.

In so far as the engineers were successful in achieving a permanent advantage for themselves they condemned those excluded to an equally permanent disadvantage. 'Between the artisan and the labourer a gulf is fixed.'[1]

The Webbs described the social implications of this 'Doctrine of Vested Interest':

'To men dependent for daily existence on continuous employment, the protection of their means of livelihood from confiscation or encroachment appears as fundamental a basis of social order as it does to the owners of land. . . . The abiding faith in the sanctity of vested interest; the distrust of innovation; the liking for distinct social classes, marked off from each other by corporate privileges and peculiar traditions . . . and the deep rooted conviction that the only stable organization of society is that based on each man being secured and contented in his inherited status in life – all these are characteristic of the genuine Conservative, whether in the Trade Union or the State.'[2]

While we have become increasingly aware of the social and political ambivalence of the mid-Victorian aristocracy of labour, and much could be said in qualification of its reputed conservatism, the Webbs' characterization remains valid in at least one essential. Royden Harrison has shown that the mid-Victorian labour aristocrats often found it convenient 'to pose as the authentic spokesmen of the working class as a whole':[3] but it *was* a pose. So long as they held to the exclusive character of their trade unionism the aristocrats could never genuinely embrace the working class as a whole, and, therefore, could never develop a politics of working-class hegemony. The economic privilege which made them the political vanguard of the working class movement itself assured that they would lead the workers corporatively, as a subordinate, and not as a revolutionary class. It is this basic non-revolutionary character of the craft tradition that poses the central paradox to be faced in evaluating the wartime shop stewards' movement. How was it that this most craft-conscious stratum, the skilled engineers, produced and sustained a militant rank-and-file movement in wartime, led by

---

1 T. Wright, *Our New Masters* (London, 1873), p. 5.
2 Webb, *Industrial Democracy*, pp. 566, 597–8.
3 R. Harrison, *Before the Socialists* (1965), p. 32.

revolutionary socialists, and seen both on the right and the left as a dramatic portent of revolution?

The phenomenon of a privileged stratum of the working class becoming, under threat of immiseration, the revolutionary vanguard of the class is not unfamiliar. Eric Hobsbawm has drawn a parallel between the role of the skilled engineers after 1914 and that of the old handicrafts in the first half of the nineteenth century.[1] Lenin too understood that high wages and a rich culture are more valuable revolutionary assets than abject poverty, and in January 1917 was predicting that the metal workers would 'represent the vanguard of the proletariat . . . in the impending proletarian revolution [throughout] Europe'.[2]

In this chapter it is argued that our understanding of this dialectic between craftsmanship and revolution has been inhibited by the historiography which stems from the Webbs, who could see nothing but conservative implications in the craft tradition. How did the exclusiveness of that tradition affect the shop stewards' pursuit of an all-grades strategy? How much did the capacity of the engineers to throw up so quickly and so spontaneously new organs of struggle when their officials abdicated industrial leadership, owe to the craftsmen's 'fanatical' devotion to local autonomy?[3] What relation existed between traditions of craft control and the revolutionary aspirations expressed in the shop stewards' movement? The answer to these questions will involve some re-examination of the mid-Victorian period when the fundamental patterns of the engineering craftsmen's practice and attitudes were formed. The bulk of the chapter, however, is concerned to identify the problems posed for the craft tradition by the structural and technological developments in the industry from the 1880s, and to show how the engineers' attempts to grapple with these problems established the conditions from which the shop stewards' movement of wartime was to emerge.

EXCLUSIVENESS

From the 1880s a technical revolution in the industry increasingly threatened the engineers' ability to control the supply of skilled labour. Larger units of production, increased specialization,

1 E. J. Hobsbawn, *Labouring Men* (London, 1968), pp. 300–1.
2 V. I. Lenin, *Selected Works* (Moscow, 1960), vol. I, pp. 831–2.
3 Webb, *Industrial Democracy*, p. 97.

greater managerial cost consciousness induced by foreign competition, the emergence of new mass-production sectors – all served to promote the development of skill-reducing machine tools and a more specialized division of labour. Manual dexterity gave way to the machine. At a time when about 90% of new members of the ASE were either fitters or turners[1] it was precisely these skills which were displaced or fragmented by the advance of the new engineering technology. Turrett and capstan lathes and particularly the automatic versions of these, made it possible for the bulk of the turner's work to be performed by a machine minder. The turner was needed only to set up the tools before the machining began. A whole series of specialized machine tools, grinders, millers, borers, etc., were developed to take over work previously performed on lathes. Based on the principle of substituting revolving tools for revolving work, a principle long applied in the drilling machine, these machines were capable of operation by semi-skilled workers. More generally, the advance of repetition production made possible an increasing formalization and simplification of the operations performed even on the more complex machines. Improved techniques in the machine shop resulted in work finished to much finer limits than had previously been possible. This threatened the fitter. 'When an article is received by the fitter correct to thousandths of an inch, it is hardly conceivable that he will mend matters with his file.'[2] Fitters could be replaced by semi-skilled assemblers. In July 1915 the editor of *Machinery* was looking forward confidently to the complete 'elimination of the fitter'.[3]

Increasingly the employer, able to hire the new class of semi-skilled workers at a considerably lower price than the craft rate,[4] was able to dispense with the versatility and manual dexterity of the old turner or fitter. The trend was revealed clearly in the progressive degeneration of apprenticeship. Apprenticeship had never been fully effective as a means of restricting entry, and the

[1] J. B. Jefferys, *The Story of the Engineers* (London, 1946), p. 127.

[2] J. W. F. Rowe, *Wages in Practice and Theory* (London, 1928), p. 92.

[3] *Machinery*, 29 July 1915. For general description of the mechanical revolution of the late nineteenth and early twentieth centuries see Rowe, *Wages in Theory and Practice*, pp. 93–103, 263–270; A. L. Levine, 'Industrial Change and its Effects upon Labour, 1900–1914' (London Ph.D., 1954); and D. S. Landes, 'Technological Change and Development in Western Europe, 1750–1914', in *Cambridge Economic History of Europe*, vol. VI (Cambridge, 1965).

[4] Rowe, *Wages in Theory and Practice*, pp. 106–9.

traditional acceptance of men who had worked five years in the trade and were earning the district rate must have acted to discourage lads from undertaking 'probationary servitude'. Since the early 1880s the union had abandoned direct attempts to limit the ratio of apprentices to journeymen.[1] Up to 1914 at least apprenticeship remained the chief route of entry into the Society,[2] but the quality of apprenticeship was visibly declining. Employers often took advantage of the very low wages payable to apprentices to exploit their labour on routine jobs, while neglecting to fulfil their obligation to instruct them in the craft. J. T. Murphy records the fight he had at the Vickers' Sheffield works to get a proper apprenticeship in the early 1900s:

'It quickly became apparent to me that unless I made a stand for myself I should become a victim of mass production. After a spell on a drilling machine and then a shaping machine I moved on to a miller. In all cases the process was simple and there was considerable repetition in it. I began agitating to be transferred to a universal miller where the work was more varied and skilled. So began the fight for variety of work and training. As soon as I felt I had mastered a particular machine and its class of work, I would politely ask Mr Graham the foreman, for a move on to another job. Politeness passed into indignant daily protests until in exasperation he would consent. In the course of a few years I worked on almost every machine in the place and on all classes of work.'[3]

The technological revolution demanded basic changes in the Engineers' strategy. Often the craftsmen, feeling that to work the new machines was beneath their dignity, refused to do so, leaving the field wide open to the 'handymen'.[4] Some justification for this attitude could be found had they sought to consolidate their surviving craft bargaining power in a tightly knit union based on a test of genuine craft skill, and been prepared to pay the price of inevitable numerical decline as the new technology spread.[5] But there was no sign of this. The policy actually adopted followed the line of least resistance: the union claimed that all jobs

1 Jefferys, *The Story of the Engineers*, p. 103.

2 *Ibid.*, p. 127. Contrast the Webbs' characteristic exaggeration of the decline of apprenticeship: *Industrial Democracy*, p. 464.

3 J. T. Murphy, *New Horizons* (1942), p. 23.

4 Jefferys, *The Story of The Engineers*, p. 142.

5 The Webbs describe the success of such a policy by the cordwinders in the boot and shoe industry: *Industrial Democracy*, pp. 417–18.

traditionally performed by craftsmen should continue to be treated as craft work and paid at the craft rate, even when the introduction of new machinery eliminated most of the skill necessary for its performance.[1] There was considerable dispute within the union over whether none but their own members should be permitted to operate the machines, the more realistic leaders understanding that the 'handymen' could not be eliminated from the industry[2] and that more success would attend the effort to enforce payment of the craft rate to whoever did the work.[3] All agreed, however, that the craftsmen should have a preferential right, against the handymen, to work the new processes.

The Engineers 'followed the machine'; and despite the employers' formal vindication in 1897–8 of their right to engage whom they chose to work the new machines, this policy was remarkably successful. Though unable to prevent the emergence of a large group of semi-skilled workers paid below the craft rate – about 20% of the workforce were semi-skilled by 1914[4] – the craftsmen were able to wring from the employers recognition that 'special consideration' should be given to the employment of displaced craftsmen.[5] By 1914 a substantial proportion of the work performed by craftsmen, at the craft rate, required little of their skill[6] – a measure of how far the engineers had succeeded in 'following the machine'.

Success held its own dangers. While the union remained (more or less)[7] an exclusive craft union in its membership policy, its defence of the standard rate rested increasingly on bluff. As the

[1] B. Weekes, 'The Amalgamated Society of Engineers, 1880–1914' (Warwick Ph.D., 1970), pp. 80–1; R. Hyman, 'The Workers' Union, 1898–1929', (Oxford D.Phil., 1968), pp. 171–2; Jefferys, *The Story of The Engineers*, p. 142.

[2] Which was the aim of the Manchester District Committee in 1906: Jefferys, *ibid.*, p. 157.

[3] Weekes, 'The Amalgamated Society of Engineers', pp. 80–81.

[4] Jefferys, *The Story of the Engineers*, p. 134.

[5] *Ibid.*, p. 157; H. A. Clegg, A. Fox and A. F. Thompson, *A History of British Trade Unions since 1889* (Oxford, 1964), p. 429; Hyman, 'The Workers' Union', pp. 171–2.

[6] The spread of piecework was partly responsible for this. Craftsmen were attracted to less skilled work by the possibility of earning well above the district rate on piece-rated repetition production. G. D. H. Cole, *Trade Unionism and Munitions* (Oxford, 1923), pp. 165–6.

[7] In 1901 the ASE had opened a section for semi-skilled workers getting over 75% of the district rate, and who had worked for two years in the trade. Until shortly before the war there was very little recruitment into this section. Jefferys, *The Story of the Engineers*, p. 166.

craftsmen accepted work on the new machines the real skill content of their work declined,[1] and they lost their ability to defend the standard rate by deploying genuine craft bargaining power. In any future conflict the skilled engineers, for the first time since the decline of the millright in the early years of the nineteenth century, risked finding themselves susceptible to large scale blacklegging.

The vast expansion of engineering production required by the war effort revealed the degree to which the genuine skill content of the craftsmen's work had declined. In a very short space of time the employers were able to import a mass of new workers, men and women, on to jobs previously the preserve of skilled craftsmen. Much of the initial dilution involved very little mechanical innovation. But wartime dilution went far beyond taking up the slack created by the craftsmen's pre-war policy. The pace of technological advance quickened under wartime stimuli and the skill requirements of the industry underwent a further proportionate reduction. In wartime there was little check on the expenditure involved in extensive dilution – the installation of new machinery, making special canteens, toilet arrangements for the women and so on. 'Even where such expenditure ultimately resulted in economic production', commented the Ministry of Munitions, 'it could rarely have been undertaken subject to ordinary commercial risks.'[2] At the same time there was an enormous advance in repetition production. 'Every factory now engaged in munitions work is more or less in the position of a bulk repetition manufacturer and can afford to utilize machinery and methods which have not previously been justified by its ordinary activities.' Dilution was advanced by the design and installation of 'special classes of machines for munitions work, machines which are characterized by unusual simplicity and strength' and thus suited for female and unskilled labour.[3] Simultaneously there was a massive development in the use of jigs and fixtures of all types to render existing machines foolproof.[4]

Between 1914 and 1921 the proportion of skilled workers in

[1] In Sheffield even shell machining had been successfully claimed as skilled work: B. Drake, *Women in the Engineering Trades* (1917), pp. 13, 16; *Mun.* 2. 27, 22 January 1916. See also R. Spicer, *British Engineering Wages* (1928), p. 92.

[2] *MM* iv, 4, pp. 14–15, 87.

[3] *Engineering Review*, February 1915, May 1916.

[4] *MM* iv, 4, p. 74.

the industry as a whole fell from 60% to 50%.[1] Undoubtedly the proportion was lower in 1918 than in 1921. In particular sectors the extent of dilution was far greater. The figures given in Table 3 relate to the autumn of 1916,[2] The category Arms and ammunition conceals the very high degree of dilution in the

Table 3 *Percentage composition of labour force, autumn 1916*

	Skilled	Semi-skilled males and females	Unskilled
	%	%	%
Shipbuilding	59	30	11
Machinery, plant, tools	49	39	12
Vehicles and aircraft	36	54	10
Arms and ammunition	30	53	17

latter. In the National Shell Factories, for example, the proportion of women employed rose from 13% in July 1915 to 73% in July 1917. In individual factories the proportion went as high as 81% (Babcock & Wilcox, Clyde) and 89% (Firth, Sheffield) by December 1916. The very high proportion of women on shell and similar work did not reflect an equivalent displacement of skilled men in these industries. In most cases the women were introduced on new plant and in new factories. Only 10% of the recorded replacement of men by women during the year following the summer of 1916 occurred in bomb, shell, fuse or gun work. 38% occurred on general machine-shop work, and a further 7% on fitting-shop work.[3] The impact of dilution on the skilled workers was therefore far greater in the heavy munitions, motor car and aircraft works than it was in the ammunition factories where dilution went furthest.

Even where skilled men were directly replaced by dilutees, there was little, if any, actual downgrading. Apart from the short period of unemployment in the autumn of 1914, there was an acute shortage of skilled men throughout the war years. Dilution was carried out under Government direction entirely as a process of upgrading: 'No person shall be employed on any work the performance of which requires less degree of skill or

[1] Jefferys, *The Story of the Engineers*, p. 134. These figures are not very reliable.

[2] *MM* vi, 3, p. 56.

[3] *MM* vi, 4, p. 62; *Bev.* v, p. 80; *Mun.* 2. 28, 25 August 1917.

usefulness than that which he or she possesses.'[1] And there was considerable room for upgrading.

Skilled turners were needed to set up the tools for dilutees and to supervise their work. 'Dilution is possible only in so far as men of sufficient skill are available to superintend for the semi-skilled labour introduced.' The craftsmen's claim to such work was not altogether secure. Even before the war some semi-skilled machinists regularly did their own toolsetting, and were even, in wartime, promoted to full-time toolsetting.[2] Already by the end of 1915 the Ministry of Munitions had discovered that unskilled men could be trained to set up and keep in order straightforward tools in four to six weeks.[3] It is not clear how far this form of dilution was carried during the war.

Dilution required an expansion of the anciliary, servicing departments of the machine shop. In November 1915, for example, the manager of the Vickers' Crayford works wrote:

'The very large size of the toolroom staff is necessitated by the current installation of new plant and will, when this is complete, be somewhat reduced, but repetition work and the dilution of skilled labour on repetition machinery invariably means a large toolroom employing for the most part the very highest skilled labour.'[4]

Expanded toolrooms were needed both to manufacture, and – since each workshop had a different range of machines to adapt to munitions production – to design the great variety of jigs and fixtures needed to simplify machine operations, to render the machines 'foolproof'.[5] Within the toolrooms themselves dilution made little progress.[6] In 1925 the president of the Engineering Employers' Federation testified to the Balfour Commission: 'The proportion of toolmakers today is enormously increased.'[7]

Probably the greater number of displaced craftsmen did not go on to toolsetting or into the toolroom, but on to a variety

[1] *MM* IV, 4, p. 79.

[2] *Bev.* iv, pp. 260–1, Report by the sub-committee of CMLSC, 10 November 1915.

[3] *Bev.* iii, p. 192, Report for the second week of the Dilution Campaign, n.d. (? December 1915).

[4] *Bev.* iv, p. 146.

[5] *Times Engineering Supplement*, June 1915; *MM* IV, 4, p. 79.

[6] *Mun.* 5. 71, 'Progress of Dilution', June 1918.

[7] *Committee on Industry and Trade*, Board of Trade, 1928, Minutes of Evidence, vol. I, p. 562.

of other jobs. Fitters, displaced by the advance of the principle of interchangeability, were needed to cope with the increased maintenance work involved in using less skilled labour. They were also needed, in a time of rapid expansion and capital replacement, to erect new machinery. In addition there was the testing and inspection of finished products, the fitting and finishing of the more complex mechanisms (e.g. machine guns, aero-engines), the experimental and design work, and even, for those who crossed the line from shop floor to office, the ratefixing and expanded costing departments.[1]

The skilled engineers remained a privileged stratum despite dilution. The effect of this was not so much to soften the anxiety caused by the threat inherent in dilution, as to enhance the craftsmen's power to take militant action against that threat. It was this combination of a very powerful bargaining position with a very strong sense of insecurity that made the engineers in wartime such an explosive force.

One reason why that force could not be accommodated within the existing structures of engineering trade unionism was that the ASE Executive never faced up to the problems posed for the traditional craft strategy by wartime dilution. Having achieved remarkable success in the pre-war policy of claiming all work traditionally performed by craftsmen as skilled work to be paid the skilled rate, the Executive was very slow to understand that this policy was bound to break down before the tidal wave of dilutees sweeping into the industry from 1915–16. While, in public, accepting the need for wartime dilution, their policy was the traditional one of insisting that the dilutee should be paid the full craft rate, even where he or she was working on only a part of the work previously performed by a skilled man. 'The ASE [policy] is that if a woman, however inexperienced and unskilled she may be, touches the most trivial part of any work, which trivial and skilled together was previously done by a skilled man, she is at once entitled to be paid the full rate of the skilled man. . . .'[2]

Dilution, which required the consent of both employers and unions, could not be pushed forward by the Government until agreement had been reached among all parties on the principles which should govern the wages to be paid to the dilutees. The

---

[1] *Bev.* iv, pp. 144–6, letter from the Superintendent at Crayford, 14 October 1915; *MM* iv, 4, p. 80; Jefferys, *The Story of The Engineers*, p. 207.

[2] *Bev.* v, p. 95, Memo. by Macassey (n.d.).

C

negotiation of these principles during 1915 and 1916 was a long drawn out and exceedingly confused process: this account is concerned only to highlight a number of relevant aspects of that process. By the summer of 1915, when the Munitions Act gave statutory force (in 'controlled establishments') to the provisions of the Treasury Agreement, a number of basic principles had been established. Skilled workers were on no account to suffer any loss of earnings as a result of dilution. Male dilutees were guaranteed 'the usual rates of the district' for the class of work performed.[1] Women's wages were covered by the vaguer guarantee that their admission into the workshops 'shall not affect adversely the rates customarily paid for the job'. It was this last provision which caused the most trouble.

So far as piecework jobs were concerned the Government was prepared to interpret the Munitions Act guarantee as meaning that (after a short and non-repeatable period of probation) women should be paid the same piece rates as the men they replaced. In the common case of there being no exact precedent for the women's work the price was to be computed so as to yield the same amount as it would have if a man had been on the job.[2] The major difficulty arose when women replaced men on time-working jobs. In an attempt to clarify the provisions of the Munitions Act during the autumn of 1915, the Government-appointed Central Munitions Labour Supply Committee approved a circular, known as L2, on women's wages. L2 laid down that women on time work customarily performed by 'fully skilled tradesmen' should be paid the full skilled rate. At the same time it established a basic minimum of 20s per week[3] for women on time work customarily done by men other than 'fully skilled

[1] There was little controversy over the wages of male dilutees. The details of their wages were agreed during the autumn of 1915 and made statutory under the January 1916 Munitions of War Amendment Act: Cole, *Trade Unionism and Munitions*, pp. 91–2, 98. These conditions would appear to have been widely observed by employers: Hyman, 'The Workers' Union', p. 204.

[2] H. Wolfe, *Labour Supply and Regulation* (Oxford, 1923). P. 280. Whether these conditions were fulfilled was in the nature of the case very difficult to determine. See *Forward*, 11 December 1915; Drake, *Women in The Engineering Trades*, p. 121. For other inadequacies of the piecework regulations see *ibid.*, pp. 20, 33.

[3] In fact rather lower since the 20s was to be paid for the normal number of hours worked in the district, and women usually worked a shorter week than men. During 1916 L2 was amended to make 20s the minimum rate for the 48-hour week normally worked by women.

tradesmen'. The ASE, which was represented on the committee which drew up L2, accepted this formula, but refused to give the go-ahead for dilution until it had been given statutory force. On 28 February 1916 L2 became law, under a provision of the Munitions of War (Amendment) Act of January, though only after the union had threatened to withdraw all co-operation if their demand was not met.[1]

Legally enforceable or not, however, L2 had a number of crucial flaws as a guarantee against cheap labour. On the one hand it made no provision for the payment of equal time rates to women replacing semi-skilled men – the 20s minimum was far below the rates earned by the semi-skilled. At no point during the war was this inadequacy of L2 put right, no doubt because the semi-skilled men and women whom it concerned lacked the economic power to force the issue. The crucial battle was fought over the wages to be paid to a woman doing work previously performed by a 'fully skilled tradesman''. The employers saw L2 as a guarantee that they would not have to pay the full craft rate to women dilutees. In very few cases was dilution simply a matter of replacement of skilled labour by less skilled. The actual content of the job, the methods of production, changed simultaneously. Consequently an employer could always argue that the nature of the work had changed, that the dilutee was not on 'work customarily done by a fully skilled tradesman' and need not, therefore, be paid the full skilled rate.[2] When L2 was issued, Alan Smith, chairman of the Engineering Employers' Federation, was confident that 'women will never be employed on the work of a fully skilled tradesman'.[3] The ASE, however, insisted on interpreting the L2 guarantee as meaning that a woman performing only a part or portion of a skilled man's work was entitled to the full skilled rate.[4] As the more sophisticated of the civil servants warned when it was drafted, L2 had not solved this question, it had merely defined the field of battle: ' "Skilled work" is not defined and will cause endless trouble.'[5]

At first the struggle revolved around the dilution scheme at the firm of John Lang at Johnstone, near Glasgow. Lang's became a

[1] ASE, *Executive Minutes*, vol. 193, 21 December 1915; ASE, *Monthly Journal and Report*, January 1916.
[2] *MM* IV, 1, p. 1; Cole, *Trade Unionism and Munitions*, p. 105.
[3] *Bev.* iii, p. 63, Beveridge to G. Askwith, 4 October 1915.
[4] *Bev.* v, pp. 83–4, Rey to Beveridge, 15 February 1916.
[5] *Bev.* iii, p. 66, G. Askwith to Beveridge, 29 September 1915.

test case because, as one of the largest machine-tool firms, it was among the first firms to try to introduce female labour outside shell and fuse works.[1] Furthermore, its owner, Provost Lang, was particularly active in promoting dilution, and his workers were particularly hostile.[2] Already in August 1915 the ASE Executive had supported the Lang's workers' resistance to dilution.[3] When L2 was accepted, the Executive instructed the men to continue to oppose dilution until the full skilled rate was paid to all dilutees whether on all or part of a skilled man's work[4] At the beginning of February 1916, with the apparent connivance of the Executive,[5] the Lang's workers struck work for a week. The ASE tried to use this strike to force the Ministry to climb down, but succeeded only in extracting a promise of further negotiations once the men had returned to work. After considerable delay the Ministry fulfilled its promise, with reluctance, and purely formally: no concessions were made on either side. At the beginning of March 1916 the deadlock between the Government and the ASE Executive over the interpretation of L2 was as complete as it had ever been.[6]

Meanwhile the real breakthrough was being made in the main Clydeside munitions factories, by the Government's Dilution Commissioners in negotiation with the shop stewards of the Clyde Workers' Committee. The fundamental principle still insisted upon by the ASE Executive was that all work once recognized as part of a skilled man's job should continue to be paid as skilled work however far the subdivision of labour or mechanical improvements had reduced the skill necessary for its operation. It was a wages strategy which made no allowance at all for the technological dynamism of the industry.

On these terms dilution was not likely to be acceptable to employers, however hard the Government pushed it: it would

---

1 Dilution extended from shells and fuses first to machine tools, since this was the main bottleneck in munitions production: D. Lloyd George, *War Memoirs*, vol. I (1938), p. 183; Cole, *Trade Unionism and Munitions*, pp. 106–7. Lang's was the largest lathe manufacturer in Britain: *Machinery*, 13 July 1916.

2 *Bev.* iii, p. 358, I. H. Mitchell, 'The Clyde Position', 21 February 1916; Wolfe, *Labour Supply and Regulation*, pp. 166–7.

3 ASE, *Executive Minutes*, vol. 192, 28 August, 11 September 1915; *MM* IV, 4, pp. 98–100.

4 *Bev.* v, pp. 83–4, Rey to Beveridge, 15 February 1916; ASE, *Monthly Journal and Report*, February 1916.

5 *Bev.* v, pp. 17–18, memorandum by Macassey, 5 February 1916.

6 C. Addison, *Four and a Half Years* (1934), vol. I, p. 177; ASE, *Executive Minutes*, vol. 193, 2, 15, 25, 29 February 1916.

'render further progress with dilution absolutely impossible'.[1] Probably this was the ASE Executive's underlying objective.

The principle accepted in the Clyde munitions factories departed fundamentally from the Executive position. Its novelty lay in a different definition of cheap labour. The Executive approached the question of dilutees' wages with the exclusive concern of preventing the employment of any cheaper class of labour in those phases of production traditionally recognized as skilled. The Clyde agreements approached the problem not from the standpoint of the wages to be paid to the dilutees *per se*, but from the standpoint of ensuring that the process of dilution should not be allowed to reduce the *overall* labour cost of production. Insistence on this was sufficient to guarantee that wartime dilution would be based, not on the employers' pursuit of *cheaper* labour, but purely and simply on the industry's need for *more* labour. The employment of dilutees as a cheaper class of labour need not be resisted, so long as, overall, the employer could not use dilution to cut his labour costs. Hence, when a dilutee worked on only a part of the work previously performed by a skilled man, a deduction could be made from the full craft rate to allow for reduced productivity. The agreement negotiated in the main Clydeside munitions factories laid down (*a*) that the women should serve a probationary period at reduced rates while they were learning the job, and (*b*) that their full rate, when doing only part of the work customarily performed by a skilled man, should be such that 'with the wages paid to the necessary supervisor and the increased wages paid to the men who now solely perform the difficult portion of the operation, will make the cost of doing the work not less than it was before'.[2]

This was to provide the basis of a solution to the problem; though not immediately. For some time the ASE Executive continued to hold out for its 'absurd interpretation of Circular L.2'.[3] So great was its obstinacy that, in spite of the Clyde muni-

---

[1] *Bev.* v, telegram from the North West Engineering Employers' Association, 8 February 1916.

[2] *Bev.* v, p. 91, memorandum by Macassey, 15 February 1916. See also ASE, *Monthly Journal and Report*, February 1916. It may be significant that early in March 1916 the NFWW concluded an agreement with Vickers that: 'When a group of workers who require the services of a separate setter-up replaces one who could do their own setting up, the wages of the setter-up are to be met by a uniform levy upon the members of the group which they serve': *Mun.* 2, 27, 11 March, 1916.

[3] Addison, *Four and a Half Years*, p. 183.

tions agreements, the Ministry was eventually forced to compromise on dilution at Lang's, agreeing to pay the full skilled rate to
dilutees on part only of a skilled man's work (provided it was a
skilled part) and with no deductions for extra toolsetting or
supervision. In return the union accepted a three-month probation period at lower rates.[1] Though the Ministry insisted that this
agreement was for Lang's only and not to be taken as a precedent
elsewhere, within weeks a very similar agreement had been
negotiated by the Dilution Commissioners on the Tyne. This
Tyneside agreement seems to have been due, not so much to the
militancy of the ASE, as to the quite extraordinary ineptness of
the chairman of the Tyneside Commissioner, Sir Corydon
Marks, MP.[2]

These successes for the policy of the ASE Executive proved to
be short-lived. In the autumn of 1916 the rival dilution schemes
were submitted by the Minister both to the Special Arbitration
Tribunal established to deal with women's wages, and to the
Committee which had originally drafted L2, and both bodies
reported in favour of the Clyde munitions agreements. Subsequently, despite continuing ASE opposition, these agreements
were made the basis of a new Ministry Order and became
statutorily enforceable for the rest of the war. A woman on 'part
or portion' of a skilled man's work – i.e. 'if she does not do the
customary setting up, or, when there is no setting up, if she
requires skilled supervision to a degree beyond that customarily
required by fully skilled tradesmen undertaking the work in
question' – was to have three-months probation at lower rates
rising to the district rate, with a deduction of up to 10 % to cover
costs incurred by the additional setting up or supervision.[3]

---

[1] ASE, *Executive Minutes*, vol. 195, 31 May, 3, 5, 6, 9, 13, 14 June 1916;
Cole, *Trade Unionism and Munitions*, pp. 111–13; ASE, *Monthly Journal and
Report*, August 1916. There was further trouble at Lang's during September
1916, because the management defaulted on the agreement and were still
paying the starting rate of 20s to women dilutees. The Ministry had to
intervene to force them to pay up. ASE *Monthly Journal and Report*, October
1916; ASE, *Executive Minutes*, vol. 195, 25 July, 27–29 September, 3 October
1916.

[2] ASE, *Executive Minutes*, vol. 195, 7, 11, 15 July 1916; Addison, *Four and a
Half Years*, pp. 175, 180.

[3] Cole, *Trade Unionism and Munitions*, pp. 113–14; Wolfe, *Labour Supply
and Regulation*, pp. 84–7, 395; *Mun.* 2. 28, 13 January 1917. The Order was
not entirely satisfactory as a guarantee against cheap labour even in the sense
intended by the Clyde munitions agreements. In particular, while the men's

Underlying the Executive's incapacity to develop a viable wages policy in the face of dilution was its continuing belief in the long-term future of craft unionism. As the war proceeded it became increasingly clear to most observers that the restoration guarantees were largely useless. As early as December 1915 *The Engineer* had spelled out the employers' determination to make the wartime innovations permanent:

'The introduction of female labour might be used so as to lead to a lowering of the rates of payment for services. The fact of the matter is not that women are paid too little but that men are paid too much for work that can be done without previous training. It is only the Trade Unions which, after the war, will stand in the way of our realizing the anticipation that we might be able to reduce our workshop costs by the employment of women . . . [If they can be brought to see the advantages] and agree to accept a lower scale of wages than skilled men, they may, by their preponderance of numbers, be in a position to defy the unions.

In face of a growing number of such statements, the Executive refused to budge from its original position: the old craft practices could be restored so long as the guarantees given in the Munitions Act were properly enforced. When the Webbs published their (anonymous) articles in *The Times* pointing to the futility of the restoration demand and proposing a new 'Industrial Charter' in its place, one Executive member was reported to have dismissed this as employers' propaganda designed to 'discredit trade unions in the public mind before the fight for restoration got under way'.[1]

The pursuit of restoration underlay the Executive's relations with the unions organizing the less skilled workers in the industry which expanded so fast during the war. The ASE had a common interest with the general unions in raising the rates paid to dilutees – though even in this an important part of the ASE motive was to establish rates so high that further dilution would become impracticable – but, so long as it was relying on post-war restoration, it had much to fear from the increasing strength and independence of the less skilled workers. The general unions

district rate formed the basis of the women's rates, the women were not paid the war bonuses granted to the men.

[1] ASE, *Monthly Journal and Report*, March 1917; Labour Party, *Conference Report*, 1917, pp. 104–5.

could hardly be expected to approach with enthusiasm the restoration of craft practices designed to perpetuate the inferior status of their members.

One method of meeting this danger was for the ASE to undertake the organization of the less skilled workers itself, and it made some effort in this direction. In 1901 a new section had been opened for semi-skilled workers getting over 75 % of the district rate, and who had worked for at least two years in the trade. Until shortly before the war hardly any members were recruited to this section, but by August 1914 it had 10,700 members, 6·1 % of the total membership of the ASE. By June 1918 this proportion had increased to 10·4 %[1] More important, however, were the union's attempts to bribe and bully the less skilled unions into subordination to the interests of the craftsmen. 'The society's relations with societies catering for unskilled workers will largely affect the restoration of pre-war conditions', ran a resolution passed by an ASE delegate meeting in 1917, 'so that working arrangements with such societies are essential'.[2] In return for the Engineers' agreement to act jointly with them in wage negotiations, the National Federation of Women Workers agreed to withdraw its members at the end of the war from any occupation claimed by the ASE.[3] A year later, in the summer of 1916, agreement was reached with the National Union of General Workers. The ASE would negotiate jointly with the NUGW provided the latter agreed not to enrol fully skilled engineering craftsmen, and to permit those of its own members 'who have become fully rated and skilled workmen' to transfer to the ASE.[4] Though the ASE did not attempt to impose any formal condition on the NUGW to collaborate in post-war restoration, the General Workers were, in fact, sufficiently subordinated to give their active support to the craftsmen in Parliament during the passage of the Restoration of Pre-War Practices Bill.[5]

Agreement was possible with the NFWW since it accepted that most of its members would be expelled from the industry after

1 Jefferys, *The Story of the Engineers*, p. 166; ASE, *Annual Reports*, 1914–18, *passim*.

2 ASE, *Annual Report*, 1917, Minutes of Recalled Delegate Meeting, January 1917.

3 Despite ASE discouragement, however, more women joined the general unions than joined the NFWW.

4 H. Clegg, *General Union in Changing Society* (Oxford, 1964), pp. 83–4; ASE, *Executive Minutes*, 8, 27 June, 13 July, 12 August 1916, 8 March 1917.

5 Hyman, 'The Workers' Union', p. 238.

the war in any case; and with the NUGW since it organized mainly labourers and women, rather than the semi-skilled men whose advance was the main potential threat to the jobs of the craftsmen.[1] With the Workers' Union, which organized predominantly this latter class, the ASE could reach no agreement. The Workers' Union would hardly be enthusiastic about permitting its own fully skilled members to transfer to the ASE, and would certainly not agree, as the NUGW eventually did, never to recruit a fully skilled man. Nor was the ASE prepared to lose control over the machinists in its own semi-skilled section by facilitating their transfer to the WU. When the craftsmen's claim to exemption from conscription re-emphasized the exclusiveness of the ASE, relations between the two unions degenerated into an open confrontation between the doctrine of vested interest and the propaganda of class unity.[2]

Though the logic of industrial development was obscure to them, the Executive could respond to the clear call of patriotic duty. '. . . throughout the protracted negotiations with the Employers' Federation and the Government's representatives with reference to the suspension of our hard won trade rights', wrote Brownlie, general secretary of the union, proudly in December 1915, 'the Executive Council fought strenuously and consistently against the innovations, and only acquiesced in them when it was demonstrated that further resistance was a menace to the national interest.'[3] Craft exclusiveness tempered by patriotic collaboration: no more ineffective policy could have been devised with which to meet the threat of dilution.

It was the shop stewards' movement that produced the most realistic response to dilution. Although based in the anxiety of craft workers faced with immiseration, the movement repudiated not only the patriotic collaboration of the Executive, but also its craft exclusiveness. Dilution was accepted as inevitable and progressive: 'a step in the direct line of industrial evolution'.[4] From the outset the pursuit of restoration was seen to be futile, and, in contrast with the Executive, whose whole position implied

---

[1] From 1917 the ASE discontinued the recruitment of unskilled workers as earnest of their desire to avoid a clash with the NUGW.

[2] Hyman, 'The Workers' Union', pp. 190–1, 228–9, 233–40; ASE, *Executive Minutes*, 1915–17, *passim*.

[3] ASE, *Monthly Journal and Report*, December 1915.

[4] *The Worker*, 8 January 1916, Muir's statement to Lloyd George on behalf of the Clyde Workers' Committee.

a ruthless purge of dilutees from the industry after the war, the shop stewards attempted to meet dilution in a way which would reconcile the interests of craftsman and dilutee. J. T. Murphy stated their standpoint with eloquence:

'The root of the matter lies in the fact that the tradesman resents any encroachment on his trade, naturally, and looks upon the labourer as his antagonist: the labourer in turn looks upon the mechanic as his antagonist, because he thinks that because he has the misfortune to be a labourer it is the will of the mechanic that he should remain a labourer. The labourers and the women have the development of machinery with them. This is a great alliance, which the mechanics of today assist by the prosecution of their everyday labour. The only solution to the problem is to frankly recognize the process and proceed to meet the situation by a determination among all the workers that these changes are not allowed to jeopardize any man of his livelihood or any man or woman of advancement.'[1]

Because their concern was with the construction of an industrial, all-grades union in the workshops – at no time did the Executive's ambitions go beyond a *craft* amalgamation – the shop stewards set out to develop a wages strategy within which the interests of all grades of workers could be protected. They saw that the Executive's obstinate insistence on the full craft rate for a dilutee performing only a part of a skilled man's work did not constitute such a policy: it could be construed only as resistance to dilution as such.

The precise formula arrived at in the Clyde munitions factories was a product of negotiations between the shop stewards and the Dilution Commissioners and cannot be represented as a simple victory for a policy freely determined by the Clyde Workers' Committee. Nevertheless there can be little doubt that the readiness of the Clyde workers to accept a less restrictive definition of cheap labour than that insisted on by their Executive owed much to the insistence of the Clyde Workers' Committee that dilution was a progressive and permanent development which could not be resisted and with which the craftsmen must come to terms. Coming to terms with dilution did not imply any complete identity of interests between craftsmen and dilutees. The craftsmen might no longer resist dilution as such, but they remained concerned to maintain their wage differential over the

1 *Firth Worker*, no. 16 (n.d.).

encroaching class of semi-skilled workers. The breach with exclusiveness expressed in the Clydeside wage agreements was by no means decisive, and the allegiance of the craftsmen to the class-conscious policies of the shop stewards' movement – most centrally to the construction of all-grades organization in the workshops – proved to be volatile in the extreme. In particular the war itself was to create a new category of privilege – exemption from military conscription. The struggles to retain exemption during 1917 and 1918 provided a sheltered refuge within which exclusive craft consciousness, weakened by the cold winds of dilution, could be nurtured and restored. In the process much of the shop stewards' movement's work of forging an alliance with the less skilled workers was undone or retarded.

Nevertheless the abandonment of the policy of 'following the machine' can be seen as marking a crucial, if not irreversible, stage in the craftsmen's rejection of exclusiveness. Thus, the pursuit of the wages policy developed on the Clyde in 1916 had much to do with the capacity of the Amalgamated Engineering Union in the long term to adapt itself to the technological dynamism of the industry and gradually expand into an all-grades industrial organization.[1] More immediately, the acceptance of dilution as irresistible was the starting point for the efforts of the shop steward leadership's attempts to inculcate a revolutionary perspective among the craftsmen. Of course there could be no short cut from craft to revolutionary consciousness.

The answer to dilution could not be revolution. First the systematic disruption of working-class consciousness implicit in the craft tradition of exclusiveness must be repaired. In its wages policy taken together with the unremitting effort to abolish inherited divisions by the construction of all-grades organization in the workshops, the shop stewards' movement revealed its rejection not only of craft exclusiveness, but also of any merely utopian revolutionary impulse of the displaced craftsmen. Revolution, if revolution was to come, could be the work only of a united working class, not the hopeless gesture of a few despairing craftsmen the price of whose loyalty capitalism was no longer willing to pay. Nevertheless the craftsmen, as craftsmen, had a specific contribution to make to the revolutionary movement. In so far as the shop stewards' movement was able to transcend the exclusiveness of the craft tradition it found itself able to release

[1] Cf. Jefferys, *The Story of The Engineers*, pp. 246–7, 241. It took, however, a second world war to complete this process.

from that tradition elements of the popular consciousness which held a profoundly revolutionary potential.

LOCAL AUTONOMY

When, in the aftermath of the lockout of 1897–8, the employers imposed a national procedure 'for the avoidance of disputes' on the Engineers, they precipitated a crisis within the union that remained unresolved until the First World War. This crisis took the form of a struggle between the Executive and the District Committees for control of trade policy, the Executive arguing that local autonomy was suicidal for the union now that the employers had the power to impose a national lockout in response to a workshop dispute. Historians of the Engineers have normally accepted this view, and, with the Webbs, condemned the rank and file for its 'fanatical attachment . . . to an extreme local autonomy'.[1] Thus for H. A. Clegg, Fox and Thompson the insistence on local control of trade policy stands condemned as an outgrowth of regressive aspirations to the unilateral regulation of the trade, of resistance to 'procedures for the collective settlement of disputes'.[2] There is an ambiguity in their use of the term 'collective bargaining' which obscures the real nature of the tradition of local autonomy and consequently of its contribution to the shop stewards' movement.

In *Industrial Democracy* the Webbs distinguished three methods of trade unionism: Mutual Insurance, Collective Bargaining and Legal Enactment. The last need not concern us; it is the relationship between Mutual Insurance and Collective Bargaining that is conceptually important here. The basic unit of nineteenth-century engineering trade unionism has been seen as the branch, organized on a local, residential basis and primarily concerned with the administration of friendly benefits designed to cover the hazards of working-class life. The humane and moralizing effects of this on the workman, so much emphasized in the propaganda of craft unionism, was incidental to its purpose. Mutual Insurance was a method: its aim was to keep out of the labour market those unfortunate craftsmen who might be tempted to work for less than the standard rate, and thus to protect the conditions of the trade.

Between 1852 and 1874 the Engineers had no formal trade

1 Webb, *Industrial Democracy*, p. 97.
2 Clegg *et al.*, *A History of British Trade Unions*, pp. 302, 471.

policy, the original objects of the Amalgamation having been formally abandoned in response to the defeat of 1851. Between 1852 and 1866 there was only one strike of any size, and no grants at all were made from the Society's Contingent Fund. In these circumstances it is clear that the Executive could exercise little leadership on trade questions; its activities being in fact largely restricted to the routine interpretation of benefit rules. Nevertheless, outside the written rules, the branches conducted the trade policy of the Society – resistance to systematic overtime and piecework, limitation of apprentices, establishment of standard rates and hours in each district – and manipulated the friendly benefits in order to achieve this aim. Basic to the operation of the method of Mutual Insurance was the use of out-of-work benefit for trade purposes. 'Should any free member be thrown out of employment *under circumstances satisfactory to the branch* to which he belongs . . . he shall be entitled to the sum of 10/- per week for 14 weeks . . .'[1]

Historians have stressed the unilateral character of the craftsman's attempts to regulate his trade. In so far as the branch made good its claim to monopolize the supply of skilled labour, and in so far as that labour was in demand, resistance to wage reductions or movements to raise wages in a particular shop could be undertaken without explicit resort to either collective bargaining or the strike. Any shop not conforming to conditions unilaterally determined by the branch could be closed to Society men and those who already worked there withdrawn and given out-of-work benefit while in search of another job. On this technique of the 'strike-in-detail' – more or less perfectly realized in practice – rested the craft unionist's aspiration to unilateral regulation.[2]

Concerned to demonstrate their respectability and that of their members, the mid-Victorian leaders of the Engineers exaggerated the degree to which the union's purposes were achieved without the use of the strike or of other forms of collective action within the workshop.[3] What has been neglected is that at no time did the Engineers' organized strength rest solely upon the branch and friendly benefits. More or less formally, organization on the job

[1] ASE, *Rule Book*, quoted by Thomas Wright, *Some Habits and Customs of the Working Classes* (1867), p. 50; Jefferys, *The Story of The Engineers*, pp. 42, 68.

[2] Webb, *Industrial Democracy*, p. 164; Jefferys, *The Story of the Engineers*, pp. 69–70; Clegg et al., *A History of British Trade Unions*, pp. 8–9.

[3] Cf. William Allan's evidence to the Royal Commission on Trade Unions, 1867.

and collective bargaining within the workshop played a crucial part in the conduct of trade policy. The principle of branch organization, based on residence, derived from the millwrights' local trade clubs of the eighteenth century. Hired to construct or service the machinery of (say) a textile mill, carrying his tools from mill to mill, the millwright was clearly in no position to organize on the job. As the engineering workshop developed, however, and the millwrights' skills were parcelled out among the specialist workmen of the 'engineers' economy', the community of the branch came to coexist with a community of the workshop, to some extent separate and distinct. The 'inner life of the workshop' provided a basis from which bargaining at workshop level was bound to occur. 'Memorials', deputations, shop meetings; the weapons of ca'canny, refusal to teach apprentices or to set up tools for handymen; joint action by members of different sectional societies, and by unionists together with non-unionists – all these forms of workshop bargaining, organization and activity were practised in mid-Victorian times.[1] The degree to which, inside the workshop, workers' influence was based upon bargaining or unilateral regulation would be difficult to determine. What is clear, however, is that to a greater or lesser degree, collective bargaining occurred inside the mid-Victorian engineering workshops, supplementing the unilateral regulation carried on by the branches and the method of Mutual Insurance.

The Webbs' categories of Mutual Insurance _or_ Collective Bargaining have tended to set up a false polarity. While neither the Webbs, nor Clegg, Fox and Thompson neglect the existence of this workplace collective bargaining, they pay scant attention to it. The very term 'collective bargaining' comes to be used exclusively to describe national or industry-wide bargaining, and autonomous or semi-autonomous bargaining practices below this level are presented as a merely 'primitive' form of that 'definite and differentiated machinery of Collective Bargaining'[2] which can only emerge at the national level. Efforts to preserve such 'primitive' forms are then easily dismissed as regressive and thereby become indistinguishable from the pursuit of unilateral regulation. The Webbs' categories obscured the potential conti-

---

[1] William Allan, _loc. cit._, Q/628, 658–60; Jefferys, _The Story of the Engineers_, pp. 9–10, 69; Wright, _Some Habits and Customs_, pp. 36–8, 83ff.; T. Wright, _Our New Masters_ (London, 1873), pp. 73–4; John Burnett, _History of the Engineering Strike in Newcastle and Gateshead_ (1872).

[2] Webb, _Industrial Democracy_, p. 179.

nuity of relatively autonomous local or workshop levels of bargaining, a continuity which the wartime shop stewards' movement was to reveal clearly.[1]

It has been common to see in the imposition of national collective bargaining by the employers in 1898 a victory (albeit one that proved very hard to consolidate) over 'the hostility of a rank and file which was still wedded to the traditions of unilateral regulation'.[2] This statement not only neglects the mid-Victorian practice of workshop collective bargaining, it also tends to obscure the development, since the 1870s, of collective bargaining at a local level. From its base in the workshops collective bargaining expanded in response both to the emergence of local employers' associations[3] and to the new militancy of the rank and file during the boom of the early 1870s. The successful negotiation of standard district rates, and the victories of the nine hours movement, despite the reluctance of the Executive to support it, established the leadership of the District Committees in trade policy. This was subsequently consolidated in the eight hours movement of the 1890s, the militant wages movements of 1896, 1902–3 and 1908, the negotiations of long-term wage contracts at district level from 1908, and the growing practice of settling district by-laws by collective bargaining.[4]

This development of local collective bargaining occurred not at the expense of workshop organization and bargaining, but in symbiotic relationship with it. The District Committees could not in fact operate their policies without more direct contact with the workshops than could be provided by the branches which elected them. From 1892 shop stewards were officially appointed by the union, responsible for card-checking, joining up new members, inspecting pay-lines, receiving complaints from

[1] As indeed was that typical feature of post-Second World War British trade unionism: the existence alongside national collective bargaining of an informal system of industrial relations operating more or less independently of union Executives and employers' associations.

[2] Clegg et al., A History of British Trade Unions, p. 471.

[3] Jefferys, The Story of The Engineers, pp. 94–5. Naturally when employers' organization was weakly developed, or disintegrated, the District Committee would not go out of its way to encourage its revival (Clegg et al., A History of British Trade Unions, pp. 140, 341; Royal Commission on Labour, PP 1893–4, xxxii, Q 23,204). This preference for bargaining with an individual employer, rather than a local association, need not be explained by any aspiration to unilateral regulation – 'divide and rule' is a basic technique of all warfare.

[4] Jefferys, The Story of The Engineers, pp. 62–3, 98–9 and passim; Weekes, 'The Amalgamated Society of Engineers', p. 74.

members and reporting back to the District Committee. By 1909 shop stewards had been appointed in most major engineering centres.[1] Militant local autonomy achieved its fullest development first on Tyneside, the main trouble spot in the ASE during the 1900s, and subsequently in Glasgow. When the Glasgow District Committee took over the Tyne's leading role shortly before the war, it did so in alliance with a vigilance committee of shop stewards. First established in 1896, this committee had sufficient independence of the branches and of the District Committee itself to initiate the first engineers' strike of the war in February 1915, and subsequently became the basis of the Clyde Workers' Committee.[2]

Shop stewards did not confine themselves to supplying information and undertaking organizational work on behalf of the District Committees. The tradition of workshop delegates serving on deputations to their employers continued, and the workshop deputation was a recognized part of the collective bargaining procedures of the industry after 1898. To an increasing extent before 1914 the ad hoc workshop deputation crystallized into a shop stewards' committee engaged in regular negotiations. This was especially so where piece work was practised since prices, negotiated job by job, could not be brought under any centralized procedure. 'The extension of piecework and the growth of the method of collective bargaining in the shops by Works Committees of stewards, have gone side by side, and it would appear that, to a considerable degree, the one is the immediate cause of the other.'[3] Thus in Manchester, where piecework was very widespread, the District Committee allowed shop committees to negotiate piece rates with the foremen, and these committees operated with considerable autonomy. Other factors promoting the development of an autonomous bargaining role for the shop stewards included the introduction of new machines – after 1898 predominantly a question for 'isolated shop tactics' – and, as the

---

[1] Clegg et al., A History of British Trade Unions, Pp. 431–2; G. D. H. Cole, Workshop Organisation (Oxford, 1923), p. 9; Jefferys, The Story of The Engineers, p. 165.

[2] R. Croucher, 'The A.S.E. and Local Autonomy, 1898–1914' (Warwick M.A., 1971). Mr Croucher shows that the shop steward system was more fully developed before the war on the Clyde than on the Tyne.

[3] Ministry of Labour, Works Committees, 1918, p. 7. Between 1886 and 1906 the proportion of Engineers on piecework increased from 5% to 27·5%. Jefferys, The Story of The Engineers, p. 129.

influence of scientific management made itself felt on the shop floor, the growing number of disputes over workshop discipline.[1]

In the light of this analysis the tradition of local autonomy appears a very different phenomenon from that presented by the Webbs. Far from being an excrescence of unilateral regulation and the method of Mutual Insurance, it represents the mainstream of the development of collective bargaining from its pre-1870 workshop origins. In operating this policy the members were not resistant to enhancing the power of the Executive to encourage and co-ordinate trade movements. Thus the 1892 delegate meeting, concerned to promote national co-ordination of the eight hours movement, created a representative Executive, in place of the old Central Branch, and appointed full-time Organizing District Delegates responsible not to the District Committees but directly to the Executive. But they would not permit the power of initiative in trade policy to be taken from the best organized and most militant districts where they thought it belonged.[2]

Having no right under rule to control trade policy, and knowing that no delegate meeting would willingly revoke local autonomy, the Executive, after 1898, attempted to gain control 'by the gradual acquisition of authority through the working of the centralized bargaining system' imposed on the union after the lockout.[3] In a situation where the employers refused to permit the extension of national collective bargaining to cover issues of vital concern to the membership – the machine question, the closed shop – and where those agreements that were negotiated, for example the Carlisle Agreement on the introduction of the Premium Bonus system, and the 1907 agreement on hours, were highly unfavourable to the members, such a strategy was hopeless.[4] The Executive proved unable to secure the material benefits from the national collective bargaining procedure which alone could have reconciled the rank and file to the loss of

[1] *The Story of the Engineers*, pp. 139, 157, 159.

[2] *Ibid.*, pp. 136–7; Weekes, 'The Amalgamated Society of Engineers', pp. 22–3. This devotion to local autonomy earned the epithet 'fanatical' when in 1896, following unpopular Executive intervention in wage disputes in Belfast and the Clyde, the delegate meeting removed the Executive's power to call off a strike without first balloting the strikers: Webb, *Industrial Democracy*, p. 97.

[3] Weekes, 'The Amalgamated Society of Engineers', p. 245.

[4] *Ibid.*, ch. 5; Jefferys, *The Story of the Engineers*, pp. 152ff.; Clegg *et al.*, *A History of British Trade Unions*, p. 430.

initiative and the inevitable delays and compromises involved in national bargaining. All attempts by the Executive to interfere with local autonomy were, in this situation, met by further restrictions on the power of the Executive.

The first major conflict occurred when the Clydeside engineers struck against a wage cut in 1903, and it set the pattern for subsequent trials of strength between local autonomy and the Executive. The Executive, believing that the reduction was inevitable, suspended the District Committee, negotiated a settlement over the heads of the strikers, and forced them back to work by cutting off strike pay. The membership reacted strongly. The Final Appeals Court overruled the Executive on strike pay – throughout these years the Appeals Court regularly overruled 40–50% of Executive decisions – and in the Executive elections the next year all four candidates up for re-election were defeated by relative unknowns. The 1904 delegate meeting took steps to reinforce local autonomy. Similar conflicts occurred in 1906–7 with the Manchester and Erith District Committees when they refused to accept centrally negotiated agreements.[1]

In defending local autonomy the members were not, as we have seen, resisting collective bargaining as such, nor were they primarily concerned with the defence of conservative practices on the machine question against more progressive Executive policies: most of the major conflicts were over straightforward wage and hours issues. The vitality displayed by the tradition of local autonomy after 1898 was rooted in the members' refusal to be bound by the highly unfavourable Terms of Settlement, and, most significant for the future, in resistance to the increasingly apparent corollary of national collective bargaining – control by a collaborationist oligarchy. Looking to the operation of the machinery of national collective bargaining to enhance their power within the union, the full-time officials, both at national and (to a lesser extent) at local level, came increasingly to act as 'peace agents and mediators'[2] rather than as organizers and leaders, and to see in rank-and-file militancy not the basis of their power but a threat to their authority. Frank Rose writing in 1909 expressed an opinion that was, with justice, to become very widespread by the outbreak of war: 'By slow, almost imperceptible

[1] Jefferys, *The Story of The Engineers*, p. 167; Weekes, 'The Amalgamated Society of Engineers', pp. 215ff.; Croucher, 'The A.S.E. and Local Autonomy', pp. 13–39.

[2] Jefferys, *The Story of The Engineers*, p. 164.

degrees, trade union officialism has become a profession, and its members a social caste. A distinct interest, growing curiously apart from the general interest of the rank and file, and drifting more and more widely away from democratic sentiment and practice, has evolved.'[1] This tendency was revealed for all to see in the course of the greatest of the pre-war disputes, the Tyneside strike of 1908. The strike, against a reduction in wages, was opposed by the Executive. Unable, under rule, to prevent the Newcastle District Committee from paying strike benefit, the Executive did its best to weaken the strike by forbidding the Manchester District Committee to levy funds in support, by suspending some of the strikers for issuing 'inflammatory leaflets', and by generally harassing the District Committee. When George Barnes, the general secretary, visited Newcastle to address mass meetings of the strikers, he was greeted with storms of abuse and the clearly expressed opinion that he should go home and leave the conduct of the dispute to the local strike committee. Barnes, deciding that the moment had come to settle the issue of Executive control of trade policy once and for all, demanded that the Executive summon a delegate meeting to increase its own power. The Executive, knowing full well that the delegate meeting would do just the reverse, refused, and Barnes resigned complaining bitterly that the Tyneside militancy represented 'an undemocratic feeling in the trade unions which worked out in the direction of the mistrust of officials and officialdom'.[2]

One possible solution to this deadlock lay in the development of democratic institutions within the union capable of formulating a national trade policy and exercising effective rank-and-file control over the execution of that policy. From 1910–11 a reform movement emerged in the ASE, partly under syndicalist influence, committed to the establishment of an annual policy-making delegate meeting and the democratization of the Executive by establishing two-year non-renewable terms of office for its members. The existing delegate meeting met infrequently and was exclusively concerned with rule making, a very cumbersome and indirect method of deciding policy. The 1912 delegate meeting, while not accepting this programme in its entirety, went some way towards meeting the Reform movement's demands, replacing national by district election of Executive Councilmen

[1] F. Rose, *Stop the Strike* (1909), p. 9.
[2] Jefferys, *The Story of The Engineers*, p. 167; Croucher, 'The A.S.E. and Local Autonomy', pp. 39–70.

(thus strengthening their ties with and loyalty to a particular constituency) and referring the issue of an annual policy-making meeting to the branches for further consideration. They further instructed all members of the Executive to stand for re-election, as they were obliged to do under the terms of the National Insurance Act of 1911 to become an approved society for the administration of state insurance funds.

This mild attack on 'officialdom' provoked an extreme reaction. Refusing to accept the decisions of the delegate meeting, the existing Executive attempted to nullify them by referring a number of controversial side issues settled at the delegate meeting to a ballot vote. The ballot vote went against the delegate meeting's decisions on these issues, and the Executive recalled it, instructing it to think again about its whole policy. The delegate meeting, its power threatened by the unconstitutional action of the Executive, unanimously refused to re-open any of its previous discussions and insisted on the collective resignation of the Executive. When the appointed day arrived, 1 January 1913, the old Executive sat tight in the offices of the union. Only by breaking through the wall from an adjoining house and evicting them from the premises by force was the delegate meeting, still in session, able to re-establish its authority. The delegates then appointed an ad hoc Executive which arranged for the election of a new Executive in accordance with the new rules of the Society.

That this miserable exhibition of organization degeneracy did little to solve the constitutional problems of the union, was illustrated by the still more bizarre events that followed. The new Executive, composed entirely of new men, many of them straight from the workshop floor, balloted, as they were pledged to do, on the continuation of the Terms of Agreement, and were instructed by a vote of 26,000 to 5,000 to end them forthwith. They did so; leaving the union powerless in face of a united Employer's Federation. Within months provisional Terms of Agreement, the York Memorandum, containing the most marginal improvements, were negotiated, and the membership voted assent. It was clear, that the problems for trade union government consequent on the development of national collective bargaining could not be solved simply by rejecting the latter.[1]

During the war the idea of a policy-making delegate meeting was accepted by the union. The expansion of national bargaining

[1] Weekes, 'The Amalgamated Society of Engineers', pp. 308ff.

with employers and Government, over dilution in 1915–16, over wages from early 1917, together with the growing difficulty of restraining the rank and file from independent action, forced the national leadership of the union to take the initiative in establishing some forum for consultation with representatives of the members on policy questions. In December 1915, to reinforce its efforts to persuade the Government to accept the Society's amendments to the Munitions Act, the Executive called a national conference of District Committee representatives and full-time officials. Though this was ruled unconstitutional by the Final Appeals Committee, the delegate meeting subsequently changed the rules to allow the Executive to call national conferences to consider policy questions when it so desired. In 1918 this advance was formalized in the establishment by rule of an annual policy-making National Committee representative of the branches, and this innovation was carried over into the constitution of the AEU when it was formed a year later.[1]

The historian of the Engineers has argued that this constitutional innovation 'prepared the ground for a solution to the problem of democracy within the Society' and ensured 'that the officials were fully in touch with the feelings and opinions of the membership in the workshops'. Underlying the change, he argued, was the wartime development of 'a national policy approach to all problems' on the part of the membership, an approach which 'finally triumphed over the local and provincial outlook . . . For good or ill, the membership realized that on the main issues of wages, working conditions and the rights of trade unions, purely local struggles were a thing of the past.'[2]

Written in 1945, this judgement now seems unduly optimistic. While the AUEW, in part, no doubt, because of the existence of its National Committee, is certainly among the most democratic trade unions in Britain, its membership – possibly to a larger degree than any other union – is deeply involved in the semi-autonomous machinery of shop stewards' committees, combine committees, unofficial strikes, etc., and not notably amenable to Executive control. A union large sections of whose membership claim and exercise an initiative in policy and action quite independently of and frequently in defiance of Executive control, can hardly be seen as having 'solved the problem of democracy'

[1] Jefferys, *The Story of the Engineers*, p. 190; ASE, *Monthly Journal and Report*, January, November 1916, May 1917.
[2] Jefferys, *The Story of The Engineers*, p. 189.

in trade union government. In the light of these post-Second World War developments, the growth of workshop organization after 1914, and the effective strengthening of militant rank-and-file initiative against a collaborationist Executive would appear to be at least as important a development as the centralizing trend emphasized by Jefferys.

Workshop organization grew, in wartime, out of the disintegration of the traditional wage structure of the industry. It is true that the war promoted national bargaining over wages, as in the dilution negotiations of 1915–16 examined earlier. Inflation too contributed to this development. In February 1915 a Committee on Production was set up. Intended simply to report on the reasons for the shortage of munitions, it rapidly developed into an arbitration court, allowing employers and unions to bypass the lengthy and drawn-out procedures established in 1898. When arbitration was made compulsory in July 1915, it was to the Committee on Production that the unions were directed to take their claims. Throughout the war the chief argument for wage rises was the rising cost of living, and as this was a national phenomenon, trade union officials from each locality tended to present exactly the same arguments. Apart from the duplication of effort involved, this procedure encouraged a wage drift based on inter-local comparisons which the Government was concerned to prevent. From February 1917, therefore the case for a general rise was considered automatically every three months by the COP and, in the meantime, no general local advances were permitted except in exceptional low paid districts.[1]

This picture of a wartime trend towards greater centralization in wage determination is, however, misleading. While the establishment of the national framework for dilution of course required national negotiations, no dilution could actually take place without detailed negotiations at workshop level, nor could workshop agreements be enforced except by continuing pressure at that level. Moreover, both inflation and dilution gave rise to tensions in the wages structures of individual shops and factories which tended to promote an enormous expansion of wage determination at workshop level.

Because the leading criterion of the Committee on Production's general wage awards was the rising cost of living, flat rate awards were granted to all grades. This narrowed the time-honoured

<hr />

[1] Cole, *Trade Unionism and Munitions*, pp. 157–62; *Mun.* 2. 27, 8 April 1916; Lord Askwith, *Industrial Problems and Disputes* (1920), p. 410.

differential between craftsmen and labourers,[1] and was itself a source of tension if only because the craft rate was lagging well behind the rise in prices.[2] Other factors, associated with dilution, intensified these tensions, in particular the tendency for the earnings of semi-skilled pieceworkers to exceed those of the skilled timeworkers.

'Before the war it was, on the whole, far easier for a skilled man to earn a high piecework balance beyond the time rate of wages on the simpler than on the more intricate part of his work, and he relied largely on getting enough of this simpler work to compensate for the loss of earnings on that which required the greater skill.'[3]

When that 'simpler part of his work' was taken over by the dilutee the craftsmen's earnings were threatened. The Munitions Act guaranteed no loss of earnings to the skilled men replaced by dilutees, but the enforcement of this guarantee created new difficulties. As William Weir pointed out in January 1916, men released by dilution tended to go from piecework into the tool-rooms, on to heavy gun work or the installation of machinery in new factories. On these jobs they could only be paid time rates. To pay them as much as they had earned as pieceworkers would only serve to disrupt the wages structures of the departments into which they were transferred.[4] Nor was this the end of it.

In order to combat restriction of output on piecework, the Munitions Act (as amended in January 1916) laid down that no reduction in piece rates could be made as a result of increased output. Although this guarantee was by no means foolproof it did lead to a very considerable rise in output. Prior to the war the fear of price cutting had led to the systematic restriction of output, ca'canny, which had 'often more than neutralized the incentive to increased output which the piecework system was designed to provide'.[5] Now, there was a 'general and quite remarkable speed-up made possible by guarantees against price-

[1] By July 1918 labourer's rates were 113% up on July 1914; skilled rates had risen by only 73%. Between July 1914 and April 1919 labourer's rates increased from 59% to 76% of the skilled rate. A. L. Bowley, *Prices and Wages in the United Kingdom, 1914–1920* (Oxford, 1921), pp. 131, 125.

[2] *Ibid.*, pp. 106–7.

[3] Cole, *Trade Unionism and Munitions*, pp. 165–6.

[4] *Bev.* iii, p. 23, 'Definite Sources of Weakness of Ministerial Position', W. Weir, 18 January 1916.

[5] Cole, *Workshop Organisation* p. 59.

cutting', and a consequent rapid rise in the earnings of piece-workers.[1] By the early months of 1916 the enhanced wages of semi-skilled pieceworkers on shell work had become a standing grievance with the skilled workers who supervised them, set up their machines, made their tools, and did the more difficult parts of the work. In many cases these earnings exceeded those of the skilled men.[2] This grievance could not easily be put to rights. In the summer of 1916 the Committee on Production granted a series of local increases to timeworkers alone.[3] The stability achieved was both temporary and partial. On the one hand pieceworkers' earnings continued to rise as output increased, thus once again closing or inverting the differential with the earnings of skilled timeworkers. By the summer of 1917 the unrest of the skilled timeworkers was again acute.[4] On the other hand pieceworkers' earnings were by no means universally high. In Glasgow in October 1916: 'While many men employed on munitions are earning greatly enhanced wages the majority of our members working on piecework [in the loco shops] are practically on pre-war rates.'[5] Consequently many pieceworkers were quite unfairly differentiated against by the award and the Committee on Production was forced to return to giving equivalent percentage increases to pieceworkers.

As the disequilibrium could not, apparently, be dealt with by general awards, the Committee turned from the autumn of 1916 to a policy of encouraging special grants to the skilled timeworkers in those firms 'whose vital interest it was to keep them contented'.[6] In a situation of rising prices and full employment this was occurring spontaneously in any case. Such compensatory increases to skilled timeworkers – lieu rates – were frequently paid as a bonus on output. 'The majority of National Projectile Factories', reported the Labour Department of the Ministry of Munitions

---

[1] *Mun.* 2.27, 1 January 1916; Cole, *Trade Unionism and Munitions*, p. 116.

[2] As early as November 1915, that was seen as a leading cause of unrest: *Mun.* 2.27, 1 November 1915. The high earnings of the semi-skilled also upset the 'unskilled', many of whom (boilermen, cranemen, furnacemen, etc.) were in fact too skilled to be promoted. It would take longer to train substitutes for their work than to train machine operators (*Mun.* 2.28, 3 November 1917).

[3] Engineering Employers' Federation, *Wage Movements, 1897–1925* (1926), *passim.*

[4] Cole, *Trade Unionism and Munitions*, p. 167.

[5] ASE, *Monthly Journal and Report*, October 1916.

[6] Lord Askwith, *Industrial Problems and Disputes*, p. 427.

in December 1916, 'are now working on a system of piecework for machinists with a bonus on output to other employees who assist production indirectly.'[1]

The payment of lieu rates was designed to eliminate the troublesome disequilibrium between time and piece earnings, but it achieved this at the expense of hitching all earnings on to the inflatory piecework wagon. Attempts were made to find a more satisfactory solution. Many managements came to prefer an overall collective bonus on output to any form of individual piecework, possibly supplemented by individual bonuses to machinists who exceeded the norm. Such schemes had the advantage that the bonus paid need not vary proportionally with output, as under piecework systems, but could taper off the proportional gain to the workers as output rose.[2]

An alternative method of containing wage inflation was the Premium Bonus system, whose acknowledged objective was 'to obviate the necessity of ratecutting by so arranging the piecerates that the workmen could never earn excessive wages'.[3] Instead of a price being fixed for each job, a standard or basic time was fixed. For each hour the worker saved in the operation of the job he was paid some proportion over his hourly rate. The most widespread system, the Rowan premium bonus system, was constructed so that earnings could never reach double time, and the increase in earnings slowed down as the worker increased his speed. During the war this system was extended particularly on the Clyde, where it had originated as an American import in the late 1890s, and at the Vickers works in Barrow.[4]

One further method of combating the disruptive effect of the disequilibrium between time and piece wages, was to press for the extension of piecework to as many skilled men as possible. In January 1917 the newly established Ministry of Labour, under John Hodge, pressed the union Executives to accept a general extension of pieceworking. As a panacea this was ineffective,

[1] *Mun.* 2.27, 9 December 1916.

[2] G. D. H. Cole, *The Payment of Wages* (1918), pp. 44, 46; *Mun.* 2.27, 18 March 1916; *Mun.* 2.28, 10 February, 4 August 1917.

[3] *Mun.* 5.82, 'Payment by Results', 1919.

[4] Jefferys, *The Story of The Engineers*, p. 130; Levine, 'Industrial Change and its Effects upon Labour', p. 371. The Premium Bonus system was described by D. Schloss, *Methods of Industrial Remuneration* (1898), pp. 49–50, 53, 58, 137–40; Board of Trade, *Labour Gazette*, Arbitration and Conciliation Cases, May, June, August, December 1916, January 1917; ASE, *Monthly Journal and Report*, May 1916, January, April 1917.

since the majority of skilled unions remained opposed to piece-work on principle.[1] At local level, however, the campaign had some success, particularly in Manchester, where piecework had been accepted by the ASE far earlier than in other districts. In the autumn of 1917 a general movement at workshop level for a 25% increase in skilled time rates was countered by the employers, with Ministry encouragement, by the introduction of schemes of payment by results – with considerable success.[2]

The relatively simple traditional wages structure, based around a craft district rate, was thus replaced by a far more complex system built into which was a significant gap between rates, determined at district or national level, and actual earnings, determined on the shop floor in bargaining over piecework and bonuses. As early as the autumn of 1915 the district rate was becoming a safety net for the less fortunate skilled workers, applying only in the less well-organized firms. It was vanishing beneath a welter of bonus schemes, merit rates, 'guaranteed time rates', and so on.[3] As the earnings rates gap widened, the importance of workshop organization naturally increased relative to that of the District Committees in the system of wage deter-mination. Within each locality a firm or group of firms became recognized wage leaders. In West London, for example, by January 1916:

'CAV and the Gramophone Company [Hayes] vie with each other for highly skilled men, and it appears to be not uncommon for an employee of Vandervell [CAV] to go to the Gramophone Co. and receive a higher rate of wages and then to return to Vandervell where he will receive a further increase.'

This is what the Munitions Act was designed to prevent and prosecutions were in fact undertaken in West London.[4] But the same effect was achieved simply by the wartime emergence and consolidation of a distinct arms sector in each locality composed of large, well-organized firms, employing the highest skilled labour, reluctant to face delays on important and very profitable

1 Cole, *Trade Unionism and Munitions*, pp. 166–7. Askwith disapproved on the grounds that Hodge based his views solely on his own experience in the steel industry, and that no one really knew how advantageous it would be to extend piecework generally in engineering: Lord Askwith, *Industrial Problems and Disputes*, p. 422.
2 *Mun.* 2.28, 9 June, 6 October, 3 November 1917.
3 *Mun.* 2.27, 25 September, 9 October 1915.
4 *Ibid.*, 6 November 1915, 1 January 1916.

contracts and able to offer the highest pay in order to maintain peace and production within their works. To the general instability of the wages structure was added the driving force of a new super-aristocracy of toolmakers and maintenance workers who exploited their indispensability and their mobility – their skills, being of a general nature, were far more transferable than those of the semi-skilled production workers – to bid up wages in defiance of the Act.[1]

None of the Government's measures was successful in eliminating the 'skilled timeworkers grievance', which remained a major determinant of the Ministry's wages policy. The unanimity of the reports of the Commissioners of Industrial Unrest in the summer of 1917 in finding that the disparity between the earnings of skilled timeworkers and those of semi-skilled pieceworkers was a major cause of unrest, helped to persuade the Government to award a $12\frac{1}{2}\%$ bonus to all skilled timeworkers in October 1917. Far from settling the question, this award triggered a veritable earthquake in the wages structure.[2] A year later another Government committee reported that the problem was as bad as it had ever been: 'a striking difference exists in many cases between the earnings of certain sections of skilled timeworkers and those men and women employed on systems of payment by results who entered their occupations since the beginning of the war as dilutees'. In the opinion of this committee, the problem was insoluble.[3]

The 'skilled timeworkers' grievance' was one intractable problem within an emergent structure of wage payment and wage determination characterized by a general chronic instability. The central aspect of this instability was the earnings-rates gap, which generated constant wage pressure at workshop level. Out of that activity workshop organization grew. This provided local autonomy with a greatly strengthened basis in the workshops. Despite constant effort by employers and government the earnings-rates gap and the associated power of workshop organization could not be eliminated. There was only one panacea which could eliminate the inbuilt wage inflation, and that was not practicable in wartime. When mass unemployment returned after the war, on a scale larger than ever before, the weakness of a wages

[1] E.g. in London, *Mun.* 2.27, 23 September 1916; in Coventry, *Mun.* 5. 329, 'Time, Wages and the Skilled Time Workers' Problem' (n.d.).
[2] See below, pp. 243–47, 252–54.
[3] Ministry of Munitions, *Report of Committee on Labour Embargoes*, 1918.

structure based on the piling of bonus upon bonus at workshop level, and dependent on workshop power for its maintenance, rapidly became apparent. Under conditions of full employment, however, the new wages structure greatly strengthened the power of decentralized workshop initiatives at the expense not only of the centralized power of the Executive, but also of the District Committees. At the same time as it was strengthened, therefore, the tradition of local autonomy was superseded by the new autonomy of independent rank-and-file organization, in which the workshops, not the District Committee, played the leading role.

In building up local autonomy against the centralizing initiatives of the Executive, militant Engineers were not expressing regressive aspirations to unilateral regulation: they were staking out positions for the future. In place of Jeffery's picture of a linear advance of a 'national policy approach', a dualistic perspective seems more appropriate to describe the wartime experience, in which activity and power pass simultaneously upwards to the Executive and downwards to the workshops. The concentration of power at the base of the union tended both to reinforce the tradition of local autonomy, and to transform it. More than ever before the power of initiative in trade policy passed to the localities, but in place of the old alliance of District Committee and workshop organization this power was now increasingly vested in workshop organization itself, co-ordinated, if at all, on a local basis and operating independently of any constitutional organ of the union, District Committee included. Out of this wartime experience came a new tradition of independent rank-and-file organization which, despite its virtual destruction during the depression of the inter-war years, has at the present time become probably the central structural feature of engineering trade unionism in Britain.

G. D. H. Cole, in his study of workshop organization, saw the independence of that organization from trade union control simply as a product of the failure of conservative officials to recognize the new needs created by the war. Reviewing the post-war decline of workshop organization, he confidently predicted its revival, when full employment returned, as an 'integral part of the machinery of Trade Unionism'.[1] We know better: workshop organization revived, but, despite very substantial efforts in that direction, the machinery of trade unionism has proved unable to contain it. Shop stewards' committees are often as autonomous

[1] Cole, *Workshop Organisation*, p. 75.

in exercising their powers as they were in the First World War. The independence of militant sections of the rank and file from national trade union control, whether exercised in the nineteenth-century tradition of local autonomy or in the tradition of workshop organization which replaced it, appears not as an immaturity, but as a permanent feature of engineering trade unionism.

The growth of independent workshop organization was not in itself evidence that the craftsmen had transcended the limitations of economism, or acquired revolutionary aspirations. The refusals of workers to be bound by the terms negotiated on their behalf by national or local trade union officials, their sporadic forays beyond the limits of industrial (or, in wartime, state) legality, may be of the greatest inconvenience to capitalism, but they do not, in themselves, herald its downfall. The indisciplined behaviour of the price of labour is a symptom only of the anarchy of capitalist production, not of the awakening of the revolutionary army. The wartime growth of workshop organization represented, as J. T. Murphy pointed out with fine revolutionary scorn, no more than a 'scramble in the ash heaps of industrialism for piecework and bonuses'.[1] Nevertheless, it was workshop organization that provided the base – in a number of localities – for the growth of the Workers' Committees, local delegate bodies based in the workshops, led by revolutionary socialists and committed to the revolutionary goal of workers' control of production.

CRAFT CONTROL

Apart from local autonomy, the craft tradition had a further positive contribution to make to the shop stewards' movement. The attempts of the nineteenth-century Engineers to exercise control over various aspects of managerial prerogative – the types of machine used, the manning of machines – have been considered above in the context of their concern with the material rewards of work: 'control as a bulwark of wages'.[2] But the craftsman's attitude towards his work was not merely an instrumental one: despite capitalism, and in defiance of the arid logic of the cash nexus, work continued to have its spiritual rewards. Craft controls had been built and tenaciously maintained not only in defence of material interests, but also as a means of resistance to the reduction of craft labour to commodity status.

[1] *Solidarity*, March 1917.
[2] C. Goodrich, *The Frontier of Control* (New York, 1920), p. 20.

The craft worker always retained something of the creative psychology of the producer.

However great the divide between the engineering craftsman and his labourer, however strong the craftsman's apparent acceptance of the bourgeois ideology of laissez-faire, self-help, his aspirations remained an implicit fundamental challenge to capitalist rationality. This is how the Engineers' Executive in the peaceful mid-50s protested their innocence of any antagonism to the employers: 'It is not intended . . . to damage their interests, but rather to advance them, by elevating the character of their workmen, and proportionately lessening their own responsibilities.'[1] Inherent in craft unionism was the desire to 'lessen the responsibilities' of the employer: to limit and encroach upon managerial prerogatives. Each of the great lockouts of 1851, 1897–8 and 1922 was fought explicitly in defence of managerial prerogatives, seen, by the employers, as the front line of bourgeois hegemony. In 1897 the employers claimed to be defending the community against a band of socialist desperadoes who were out 'to obtain entire control of the workshops of England' and to dispossess the capitalists.[2] In 1851 they had fought 'a system of dictation and espionage' which 'projects the propagandism of new and dangerous principles of social and political economy which, if suffered to invade the rights of capital . . . will ultimately prostrate all liberty of action, and freedom of contract and exchange . . . and revive, in its most invidious and incongruous form, the ancient monopolies of trade corporations, and the exploded theories of exclusive property, or vested interest in the practice of the skilled handicrafts'.[3]

This subversive character of nineteenth-century craft control was concealed in large degree from the Engineers themselves. In 1851, as in 1897–8, the Engineers stood upon their vested interest, their right to dispose of their skills as they wished. Craft skill, they argued, was as much their property as the employer's establishment, business and capital were his.[4] The class fears of the employers were dismissed as propaganda, and this dismissal has been largely followed in subsequent standard accounts, which, in emphasizing the unilateral character of trade policy,

---

[1] S and B. Webb, *History of Trade Unionism* (1920), p. 208.

[2] Weekes, 'The Amalgamated Society of Engineers', p. 97.

[3] *Trade Societies and Strikes*, Report of the Committee on Trades' Societies, 1860 (New York, 1968), pp. 195, 197.

[4] *Ibid.*, p. 189.

operated by the branch from outside the workshop, have tended to neglect the specific contribution of the community and organization inside the workshop to mid-Victorian engineering unionism.

The workshop, as one would expect, was a source of ceremony and social ritual. Thomas Wright, 'the Journeyman Engineer', writing in the late '60s describes some of these: initiation rights to which newly bound apprentices were subjected; 'footings' (standing drinks for one's workmates) exacted, in some shops, on every conceivable occasion; all the small acts of generosity.[1] Wright's description of the ritual of 'ringing in' is worth quoting:

'On the occasion of his marriage . . . he receives his ovation in the shape of what is technically called "a ringing in". The men and boys in the shop stand, hammer in hand, around boilers, plates of iron suspended from beams, or anything else that comes handy that will give out a good ringing sound when struck. The arrival of the subject of the demonstration is duly announced by the scouts; all stand to their posts, and the instant he enters the shop strike up producing a thundering peal. The ringers in each shop, having rung him through their particular department, follow him as he passes out of it, until the whole body of them are assembled in his own shop, and then the peal reaches its grand climax. As many as five or six hundred men, all skilled in the use of the hammer, all hammering their best on high or sharp sounding material . . . continue for five minutes, and then the proceedings are wound up with a hearty cheer.'[2]

Apart from special occasions, the normal social intercourse of the workshops occurred around the breakfast stoves on the shop floor, or in the workshop dining and reading room. But it did not cease during working hours: carefully and systematically the men preserved an area of existence in the workshop protected from the encroachments of the employer, outside the wages contract. Even in the employer's time a humane environment could be constructed. Wright describes the first job of the new apprentice, taught to him in all probability before he is even told the names of the tools – 'keeping nix':

'Keeping nix, consists in keeping a bright look-out for the approach of managers or foremen, so as to be able to give

---

[1] Wright, *Some Habits and Customs of the Working Classes*, pp. 87ff.
[2] *Ibid.*, pp. 99–100.

prompt and timely notice to men who may be skulking, or having a sly read or smoke, or who are engaged on "corporation work" – that is work of their own. The boy who can keep nix well – who can detect the approach of those in authority, while they are yet afar off, and give warning to those over whose safety he has been watching, without betraying any agitation, or making any movement that might excite the suspicion of the enemy – will win the respect of his mates; he will be regarded by them as a treasure, a youth of promise.'[1]

Even at this rudimentary level the autonomy of the workers in the workshop could represent a real threat to managerial control, particularly when, from the 1880s onwards, the employers felt the need to tighten up that control. 'Ringing in' can scarcely have been a custom popular with 'scientific' managers. Over and above the techniques of preserving a small area of freedom within the discipline of the factory, typical of any workshop community, the engineering craftsman was justly famed for his resistance to supervision on the job itself. Craftsmen have always claimed that it is impossible to supervise their work – 'the workmen, as a rule, know their trade sufficiently well to be able to evade the task-master'[2] – and in proportion to the skill content of the work this was probably true. Examples of resistance are legion. The best example known to the writer is apocryphal (though none-the-less evidence for that) and was told to him by an engineer in North London who remembered it as one of the first pieces of shop wisdom imbibed during his apprenticeship. The story runs: 'There used to be a craftsman in this shop who always came to work with a piece of chalk in his pocket. When he arrived each morning he would at once draw a chalk circle on the floor around his machine. If the foreman wanted to speak to him he could do so as he wished, so long as he stayed outside the circle. But if he put one foot across that line, he was a dead man.'

Underlying such stories is a profoundly non-instrumental attitude towards the practice of the craft. Inside every engineering craftsman lay the ideal type, derived from the old millwright, of the man who is hired to do a job, and to do it from start to finish without interference from his employer. For the craftsman the exercise of his labour power was not divorced from personality:

---

1 Wright, *Some Habits and Customs of the Working Classes*, p. 85.
2 *Royal Commission on Labour*, PP 1893–4, xxxii, evidence of William Glennie, Tyneside District Secretary of the ASE.

the practice of his trade was a condition of his personal fulfilment. Typical of descriptions of craft pride is a passage from the trade journal *Machinery* in 1915:

'. . . he is engaged in tasks where the capacity for original thought is exercised; he has refined and critical perception of the things pertaining to his craft. His work creates a feeling of self-reliance . . . he lives a full and satisfying life; neither hypocrisy nor real malice can exist side by side with skill or in an atmosphere where real skill is respected.'[1]

The rationalization and standardization of production techniques associated with dilution both before and during the war involved a direct assault not only on the economic security but also on the self-respect of the craftsman. It threatened his independence in the workshop and his pride in his work. Traditionally the craftsman worked from drawings of the job to be done, preparing the tools he could see to be necessary, and setting them up on a machine in a pattern appropriate to the machining involved. In December 1915 a trade journal pointed out:

'In the old days when the workmen were divided into two classes, the skilled and the unskilled, it used to be a matter of pride on the part of all skilled . . . operators to have a few tools ground by themselves to their own special shapes and angles; these tools they kept jealously locked away in their toolchests or cupboards. When they wanted renewals, it was a case of spending half an hour or so in the blacksmiths shop superintending the forging; then another half hour or so at the grindstone, from which they returned to their neglected machines with their faces glowing with that sense of satisfaction engendered by a man's pride in his own skill.'[2]

The connecting thread of these activities was that it was the worker who made 'the final choice of the operative details by which the job is to be done, and to some extent of the tools he is to use'. The ability of the workman to make these decisions was a very large part of his expertise – it was the 'brain work' involved in the job that distinguished his talent from mere dexterity.[3]

Apostles of scientific management had long claimed that modern

[1] *Machinery*, 23 September 1915.
[2] Alfred Herbert Ltd., *Monthly Review and Stock List*, December 1915.
[3] *Times Engineering Supplement*, November 1916.

D

engineering production could dispense with craftsmanship: 'their essential principle was that the machine man should not exercise any discretion at all'.[1] Though ideologues exaggerated, the trend was clear. New jigs attached to lathes and other machines turned skilled work into almost foolproof machine minding. Improved gauges, which dispensed with the need for fine judgment in machining work to precise limits, 'made the turning of a piece of work to a given size quite a simple operation, requiring more patience than skill'.[2] High speed steels, introduced from the 1890s, made it possible to supply more accurate cutting tools, which could only be spoiled by permitting the craftsmen to touch them up to their own liking on the hand grinder, and to define precise instructions for the speed at which the efficiency of each tool would be maximized in relation to different materials and operations. 'Speed and feed' tables replaced the experienced judgement of the craftsman.[3]

When unchallenged, craft pride was, in the words of the Webbs, a source of 'the "gentle" nature – that conjunction of quiet dignity, grave courtesy and consideration of other people's rights and feelings'.[4] When challenged, however, either by a tyrannical foreman in the 1850s, or, more to the point, by the emergence of mass production techniques and scientific management before and during the war, the pride of the craftsman rendered him hypersensitive to every increase in industrial discipline, to every tightening of social control. The fact that wartime dilution threatened not only the economic security of the craftsmen but also spiritual values that lay at the heart of their world outlook goes some way towards explaining the ferocity of their militancy, and their readiness at least to tolerate a leadership which publicly attached revolutionary goals to this militancy. More specifically, the non-instrumental tradition of craft control played a powerful part in making the engineers the most tenacious opponents of the wartime growth of the servile state. The craft basis of the movement could hardly be more clearly revealed than it is in the way the Scottish shop steward leaders chose to present their argument for the necessity of a revolutionary seizure of power at the end of 1919:

[1] *The Engineer*, 1903, quoted in Levine, 'Industrial Change and its Effects upon Labour', p. 403.

[2] *Engineering Review*, March 1916.

[3] Levine, 'Industrial Change and its Effects upon Labour', p. 361.

[4] Webb, *History of Trade Unionism*, pp. 571–2.

'Under the guise of "scientific management" the Capitalists are introducing into industry schemes for dividing operations, and making the labour of the workers more automatic. The result of this tendency is to deny the worker responsibility, rob him of initiative, and reduce him to the level of some ghastly, inhuman, mechanical puppet. The Capitalist idea of more "automatic" workers is bound to conflict with the workers' aspirations for greater responsibility, greater initiative and democratic control of industry. The two are absolutely incompatible. . . . The struggles of the Capitalists to impose their ideal on the workers will be met by the workers increasing their effort to get rid of the tyranny that is crushing them . . . Today the worker is merely a living tool . . . It is against this industrial degradation that the workers are beginning to struggle . . . The Servile State or Industrial and Social Democracy? That is the choice that circumstances are presenting to the workers.'[1]

The argument is not that the craft tradition contained any spontaneous aspiration to working-class hegemony, to the abolition of wages slavery. Not only would this be to neglect the central role of politics, of socialist and syndicalist propaganda, in spreading ideas of workers' control, it would also be to forget that exclusiveness of the craft tradition which necessarily limited its political horizons. The argument is, rather, that the tradition of craft control, embodying as it did a tenacious resistance to capitalist rationality – 'the Capitalist ideal' – provided a more fruitful soil for the growth of revolutionary aspirations to workers' control than would the more purely instrumental attitude to work characteristic, for example, of a semi-skilled production-line worker in a modern car factory.

The shop stewards' movement developed out of a situation in which the alienation of trade union leadership from the rank and file under the impact of national collective bargaining was greatly intensified by the collaboration of the trade union Executives in the war effort. Consequently the rank and file had to construct their own defences, independently of their officials. Full employment gave them the power to do this, and the immediate problems of dilution and the emergent wages structure dictated that work-

[1] J. R. Campbell and W. Gallacher, *Direct Action* (Glasgow, 1919), pp. 5–7, 30; cf. Campbell in *The Worker*, 29 March 1919; and see the very similar tone of the Clyde Workers' Committee's statement to Lloyd George of Christmas 1915, above p. 45.

shop organization, rather than the older tradition of local autonomy, would be the basis on which they built. The very fact of the engineers' militancy in wartime, of their confrontation with employers and the state, tended to push them to the forefront of the political struggle of the working class as a whole. In so far as they led that struggle they directed it, as we shall see, against the growth of the servile state, and into channels productive of solutions to the problems posed for labour and for socialism by the emergence of state monopoly capitalism, solutions very different from those that, in the Labour Party, held the centre of the stage. The revolt of the engineers was deeply rooted in a craft tradition that was itself disintegrating under the impact of war. Aspects of that tradition held back, and were ultimately to cripple, the political development of the shop stewards' movement. What is, however, far more remarkable is the reserve of creative revolutionary energy revealed in the old aristocracy of the engineering workshops during these final years of its power. Only through the narrative of the wartime growth and activity of the shop stewards' movement can that energy and creativity be appreciated.

Part Two

Wartime Struggles

Chapter 3

The Clyde Workers' Committee:
Origins and Policy

The shop stewards' movement originated on the Clyde. In the strike launched in February 1915, over a wage demand for 2d an hour, J. T. Murphy was to see the decisive 'transition from pressure on the executives to action in spite of the executives'.[1] Not only did this, the first significant strike of the war, at once establish the Clyde as the leading militant centre; it also represented the first move towards independent rank-and-file action based on organization at workshop level. The Clyde Workers' Committee, set up in October 1915, acknowledged its origin 'in the last big strike of February 1915. [It was] probably the best organized strike in the annals of Clyde History. . . .'[2]

The claim for 2d an hour was first put to the employers in December 1914 on the expiration of a three-year wage pact. During the prosperous years of 1911–14, the engineers' wages had remained static, while prices and wages in comparable trades rose.[3] But the demand represented more than a desire to catch up: it was a wage-leading demand. Put forward in the ASE branches from the spring of 1914, it horrified the local officials: 'An engineer's rise is a farthing an hour, not twopence.'[4]

[1] J. T. Murphy, *Preparing for Power* (1934), p. 111.

[2] Clyde Workers' Committee, leaflet (? November 1915), in *Bev.* iii, p. 95.

[3] *MM* iv, 2, pp. 36–7; Amalgamated Society of Engineers, *Monthly Journal and Report*, April 1915.

[4] D. Kirkwood, *My Life of Revolt* (1935), p. 88. Success in this claim – totalling 9s per week – would have put the Clyde engineers far ahead of other trades. The Glasgow district rate was only a few pence (per week) below the national average, and only 2s 9d below the Sheffield rate, the highest in the country. *Sixteenth Annual Abstract of Labour Statistics*, 1914, LXXX, 301. A. L. Bowley, *Prices and Wages in the United Kingdom, 1914–1920* (Oxford, 1921), p. 127.

The demand reflected an exceptional militancy among the Glasgow engineers. For years they had followed the Tyne in wage movements, and the Tyne had been the leading trouble spot in the ASE.[1] But in the months immediately preceding the war it was from the Clyde that demands for a closed shop agreement threatened to cause a national lockout.[2] The Glasgow ASE had already recognized the shop stewards organized in a vigilance committee as a local force independent of the branches.[3] Workshop organization was emerging as an autonomous bargaining force in several of the leading engineering firms, including Weir of Cathcart and the Beardmore works at Parkhead, and was very much in the minds both of militant trade unions and of their employers.[4] The inroads into the powers of management in the shops had become so serious, said the general manager of Weir's in 1916, that 'had the war not intervened, the Autumn of 1914 would probably have seen an industrial disturbance of the first magnitude'.[5] The disturbance was not long delayed. Late in December 1914, the employers turned down the claim for 2d an hour. The Glasgow District Committee on the ASE reacted strongly calling on its members to refuse to sell their labour to the employers under $10\frac{1}{2}$d per hour. The vigilance committee of the ASE shop stewards met unofficially and despite the pleading of William Brodie, the full-time Organizing District Delegate, an overtime ban was decided on a most unanimously. By January 15th the Beardmore works at Dalmuir were imposing the ban, and by the 28th all the principal Glasgow firms were involved. Under pressure from the Employers' Federation, who threatened to break off all negotiations on the claim, the Executive convened an aggregate meeting in Glasgow on February 7th to get the ban called off. But 'the District Committee . . . failed in

[1] H. A. Clegg, A. Fox and A. F. Thompson, *A History of British Trade Unions since 1889* (Oxford, 1964), p. 438; G. Askwith, *Industrial Problems and Disputes* (1920), p. 374.

[2] ASE, *Executive Minutes*, vol. 189, 1, 9 September 1914; EEF, *Decisions of Central Conference, 1898–1925* (1926) North-West, 10 July 1914; W. Gallacher, *Last Memoirs* (London, 1966), p. 59.

[3] ASE, *Executive Minutes*, vol. 190, 3 December 1914; Labour Party, *Report of the Special Committee . . . to inquire into . . . the Deportations . . .* (1917), p. 12.

[4] Author's interview with Mr H. McShane; G. D. H. Cole, *Workshop Organisation* (Oxford, 1923), p. 30; T. Bell, *Pioneering Days* (1941), p. 106. For pre-war organization at Parkhead see below, p. 149.

[5] J. C. Richmond, 'Some Aspects of Labour and its Claim in the Engineering Industry', *Glasgow University Enigneering Society*, 1916–17 (1917), p. 6.

their duty [of] in any way assisting the representatives of the EC and the object of their mission, and the meeting enthusiastically declared against calling off the ban'.[1]

Up to this point the militancy was reflected by the Glasgow District Committee. On February 16th, a dispute at G. & J. Weirs (Cathcart), over the employment of American engineers at specially high rates, led to a strike of 2,000 men.[2] This strike spread rapidly through the whole district around the issue of the 2d claim. The District Committee backed down at once, expressing their 'entire disapproval' of the strike, and ordering the men back to work. At an aggregate meeting in the 18th, the district officials supported the Executive's attempt to get the men back, though without success. Four days before the strike broke out the Employers had made a 'final' offer of ¾d, which the officials accepted pending a ballot in the district. The offer was rejected by a 10 to 1 majority. The result of a ballot on the strike itself was a foregone conclusion. Consequently the District Committee declined to hold such a ballot until the men resumed work. Meanwhile the branches were instructed not to pay strike benefit.[3]

Deprived of official leadership, the strike was nevertheless remarkably solid. A local paper commented:

'In no previous strike has there been such a surprising display of solidarity as in the present dispute. Even where tempting offers have been made to sections of the strikers, and where in one case the full demand was conceded at the very start of the strike, the men have resolutely declined to divide their forces, and all along they have contended that no one will start work until all have been satisfied.'[4]

The strike lasted two weeks, from Tuesday, February 16th, to

[1] ASE, *Executive Minutes*, vol. 190 *passim; MM* IV, 2, p. 37; ASE, *Monthly Journal and Report*, February 1915; ASE, *Branch Minutes*, Coatbridge, 8 February 1915.

[2] The fact that in January 1915 William Weir, the owner, had issued a pamphlet urging his workers to give up their restrictive practices may also have had something to do with the strike. The pamphlet was entitled *Responsibility and Duty*. W. J. Reader, *Architect of Air Power, William Weir, 1877–1959* (1968), p. 38.

[3] *MM* IV, 2, p. 37; Gallacher, *Revolt on the Clyde* (London, 1936), pp. 38–40; ASE, *Executive Minutes*, vol. 190, 25 February, 10 March 1915; *Glasgow Herald*, 18, 19, 25, 26 February 1915. Inevitably, the Executive was overruled by the Final Appeals Court: ASE, *op. cit.*, vol. 192, 23 August 1915.

[4] *Daily Record and Mail*, 2 March 1915.

Wednesday, March 3rd. Within four days of the first walkout at Weir's, 10,000 Glasgow engineers (including members of the major sectional unions) from at least twenty-six factories were on strike—about two-thirds of the total number of skilled engineers in Glasgow.[1] Only in the last few days of the strike did their solidarity begin to crumble.

Such solidarity was not achieved without organization. On February 18th a Central Labour Withholding Committee was formed – so named in order to avoid trouble under DORA. As more firms joined the strike this Committee was accepted as the leadership.

> 'Every morning mass meetings were held in the areas and the discussions and decisions of the previous day's committee meetings were reported. Every afternoon and evening the committee was in session, taking reports from the areas and considering ways and means of strengthening and extending the strike . . . The organization and contacts between the factories and the areas and between the areas and the centre was almost perfect.'[2]

The CLWC was composed in the main of the ASE shop stewards who had previously met together in the officially recognized local vigilance committee.[3] Although most of these shop stewards did not represent fully fledged workshop organizations, the leading group within the CLWC came from those factories which had

---

[1] Board of Trade, *Labour Gazette*, March 1915; *The Herald*, 6 March 1915; *Glasgow Herald* and *Daily Record and Mail, passim;* B. Drake, *Women in the Engineering Trades* (1917), p. 127. There is no evidence to support Gallacher's claim, first made on p. 10 of his pamphlet *Direct Action* (1919) and repeated in *Revolt on the Clyde* (1936), p. 51, that the unskilled workers struck in sympathy.

[2] Gallacher, *Revolt on the Clyde*, pp. 43, 47. This description is confirmed by A. MacManus writing in the March 1916 issue of *The Plebs*. There were important precedents for this type of strike organization on the Clyde. The 1897–8 lockout had been run by lockout committees consisting of delegates from the federated workshops on Clydeside, and, in 1903, strike delegates in Glasgow had created an alternative structure to the District Committee which took over control of the strike when that Committee tried to call it off. The similarity with 1915 is remarkable: 'On May 9th, there were meetings of Strike Committees representing the different shipyards in dispute throughout the upper reaches of the Clyde, and arrangements were made between them to meet every morning after breakfast, and to report as a combined organization.' R. Croucher, 'The A.S.E. and Local Autonomy, 1898–1914' (Warwick M.A., 1971), pp. 29–30.

[3] Labour Party, *Report of the Special Committee . . .*, p. 12.

already established workshop organization as a bargaining force – James Messer, the secretary, from Weir; William Gallacher, the chairman,[1] from Albion, David Kirkwood[2] and Tom Clark from Parkhead.[3]

On Friday, February 26th, ten days after the strike had broken out, the Government intervened, demanding a return by Monday, March 1st, and offering arbitration by the Committee on Production. The Executive, after a last-minute attempt to get the Employers to negotiate while the strike was on, informed the Government, 'we are prepared to assist . . . in every possible way in securing immediate resumption of work pending arbitration proceedings'. Over the weekend the local and national officials of the union, and various Government officials, mounted a large-scale campaign to get the men back to work, with a liberal application of threats and bribes – the men would get strike pay if they went back, strikes would be made illegal and arbitration compulsory if they did not.[4] This barrage hardly weakened the hold of the CLWC. On Sunday Executive and district officials failed to convince a meeting of 500 ASE shop stewards that the Government's instruction to return to work should be obeyed and the offer of arbitration taken up.[5] When the ASE and Government officials put their arguments to the rank and file on Monday, only two out of seven local meetings decided to return. One of these was the outlying area of Johnstone, eight miles west of Glasgow. In the other, Renfrew, the decision was disregarded by the workers in the largest local factory, Babcock & Wilcox.[6]

[1] Gallacher, who was a brassfounder, records that he handed over the chair to an ASE man during the strike to disarm ASE prejudice against the 'brassies' which threatened the unity of the strike: *Revolt on the Clyde*, p. 47.

[2] Kirkwood later grossly exaggerated his own role in the strike: *My Life of Revolt*, p. 91. Gallacher makes no mention of him and even implies that he took no part in the leadership of the strike: *Revolt on the Clyde*, p. 63.

[3] Gallacher, *Revolt on the Clyde*, p. 43; *The Herald*, 16 October 1915. It is not clear how far workshop organization was established at Albion by this point; Gallacher claims to have been established as 'the leader of the workers in the factory' by the outbreak of war: Gallacher, *op. cit.*, p. 17.

[4] *Glasgow Herald*, 27 February, 1, 2 March 1915; *Daily Record and Mail*, 27 February 1915; ASE, *Executive Minutes*, vol. 191, 26 February to 3 March 1915.

[5] *The Herald*, 6 March 1915. The report of this meeting in the *Glasgow Herald*, 1 March 1915, asserted that the shop stewards decided to recommend a resumption on the Government's terms. This seems unlikely.

[6] *Glasgow Herald*, 2, 4 March 1915.

The CLWC maintained its hold over the rank and file. While recognizing that arbitration was far from being an undisguised blessing – 'our experience of arbitration in the past has not been very satisfactory' – they were also aware that they could not hold out indefinitely. Consequently they recommended the workers 'to resume work on Thursday, working the usual 54 hours per week on day shift, and 60 hours on night shift, with no overtime until our demand is granted. If the 2d is not conceded by Tuesday, March 9th, we immediately set up a "stay-in-strike".' This was put to six local meetings on Tuesday, March 2nd, and gained an overall majority of nearly 2,000 in a vote of about half the 10,000 strikers. The great majority of the strikers stood by this decision and did not go back until Thursday.[1]

The CLWC had not succeeded in establishing itself as a permanent local shop stewards' committee. As soon as the men were back in the factories its authority evaporated. The overtime ban was partial from the start, and the stay-in-strike never materialized.[2] After the Employers had refused to make any further offer the ASE put the question of whether to go to arbitration to the vote. The result confirmed the Executive's authority with a large majority for arbitration. When the COP awarded a war bonus of 1d and 10% on piece rates, there was no attempt to renew the strike. The Executive could 'express its disappointment' with the award, without any fear that its words would be translated into action by its members.[3]

In the concluding days of the 2d an hour strike, a general separation of the more from the less militant engineers had taken place. The central Goven and Finneston area voted by a large majority against the CLWC's resolution on the Tuesday, and by and large went back to work the next day. Where the Committee's resolution was passed and the resumption delayed until the Thursday, the backbone of militancy was to be found – in Dalmuir, Scotstoun and Parkhead.[4] This separation was significant: it was from these same militant areas that the CWC emerged in the autumn of 1915. The location of these leading sectors corresponds very closely with certain structural divisions

[1] *Daily Record and Mail*, 2, 3, 5 March 1915.

[2] *Ibid.*, 6 March 1915; *Glasgow Herald*, 5 March 1915; G. D. H. Cole, *The Payment of Wages* (1918), p. 24.

[3] ASE, *Executive Minutes*, vol. 191, 6 March; Board of Trade, *Labour Gazette*, May 1915; *Glasgow Herald*, 25 March 1915; *MM* IV, 2, p. 41.

[4] *Glasgow Herald*, 3, 4 March 1915; *Daily Record and Mail*, 3, 4 March 1915.

within the Glasgow metal industries. These divisions help to explain many of the problems which the Clydeside militants were to meet in their attempt to establish permanent local rank-and-file organization.

The relatively diverse industrial structure of the Clyde included a large clothing and textile industry, a food, drink and tobacco manufacturing industry, and a large group of dock workers. But it was the metal industries, employing 29% of the occupied population which dominated the city. Since the 1870s shipbuilding and marine engineering had been the most dynamic sector of the metal industries, directly employing, by 1921, over a third of their workers. This dynamism was pivotal to the development of the engineering industry as a whole.[1] A handful of firms dominated both shipbuilding and the marine engineering sector. Four of them – John Brown (Clydebank), Harland and Wolff and Fairfield (Govan), and Yarrow (Scotstoun) – employed 20,000 workers, perhaps half the total, in 1915. There were many smaller shipbuilding and marine engineering firms, clustering particularly in the central Govan-Finneston area. In addition there were two large independent marine engineers. Babcock & Wilcox (Renfrew) was said to be the largest manufacturer of ships boilers in the country and employed 5,000 workers in 1915. G. & J. Weir (Cathcart) made hydraulic and other equipment for naval use. In 1915 it employed at least 2,000 engineering workers as well as many others in other trades.[2]

Other important sectors were forge and foundry work, employing 10%, and iron and steel manufacturing, employing 6·5% of the metal workers in 1921. Locomotive manufacture was dominated by the North British Loco. Co. which had 8,347 workers in its three works (two in Springburn, one in Govanhill) in 1914.[3] Two railway companies also had works in Springburn.[4] Structural

[1] *Census of Scotland* (1921), Industry Tables. The area dealt with combines the census areas of Glasgow, Clydebank and Dalmuir. See also R. H. Campbell, *Scotland since 1707* (Oxford, 1965), pp. 231, 288.

[2] 'Report on Labour in Controlled Establishments', in *Bev.* v, p. 76; *Glasgow Herald*, 3 August 1915; *The Shipbuilder*, January 1915; Glasgow Chamber of Commerce, *Handbook* (1919), p. 163; *Daily Record and Mail*, 19 February 1915; Bell, *Pioneering Days*, p. 106.

[3] W. R. Scott and J. Cunnison, *The Industries of the Clyde Valley during the War* (Oxford, 1924), p. 113.

[4] The St Rollox works of the Caledonian Railway Co., and the Cowlairs works of the North British Railway Co.

engineering, and in particular bridge building, was of importance, dominated by Sir Wm. Arrol (Parkhead), and electrical engineering, with $3 \cdot 2\%$ of the workers in the industry in 1921, was relatively well developed in Glasgow, primarily because it served the needs of the shipyards.[1] But the vital sector, counterposed to the dominance of the shipyards, was the munitions industry.

Prior to the war there was only one arms firm in Glasgow – Beardsmore's at Parkhead and Dalmuir. Originating as Parkhead Forge in 1842, it began to produce armour plate in the 1860s. In the 1880s it was manufacturing steel plate for locomotive and gun production as well as for warships, but it employed only a small number of engineers in addition to its iron, steel, forge and foundry workers. Subsequently it developed on the classic pattern of the arms firms. In 1900 it bought Napier's shipyard at Dalmuir, and was soon 'able to undertake the whole work of completing war vessels without subletting any contracts for constructional materials'.[2] In 1902 half its ordinary share capital was bought by Vickers, from whom Beardmore had earlier secured a large loan. Vickers' aim in this quasi-merger was to prevent Beardmore from expanding into arms manufacture. Despite this the first gun was completed at Parkhead in 1909, and subsequently one of the largest and most up to date gun shops in the country was laid down there. By 1918, 9,000 workers were employed at Parkhead; Dalmuir had 8,000 in 1915.[3]

Up to 1914 Beardmore's expansion into ordnance work had made little inroad into the domination of the Glasgow metal industries by shipbuilding. At the beginning of 1915 Glasgow was firmly in the grip of the Admiralty, and the only firms on munitions work apart from Beardmore and its subcontractors were 'a few subcontractors of English firms'.[4] But from August 1915, under Government pressure, the munitions industry began to penetrate Glasgow engineering. William Weir of Weir (Cathcart) – itself an Admiralty contractor – was appointed Director of Munitions of Scotland, his job being to carve out

[1] Glasgow Chamber of Commerce, *Handbook*, pp. 164–5; Campbell, *Scotland since 1707*, p. 244; Scott and Cunnison, *The Industries of the Clyde Valley*, p. 92.

[2] Glasgow Chamber of Commerce, *Handbook*, pp. 152–3; Bell, *Pioneering Days*, p. 29; Kirkwood, *My Life of Revolt*, pp. 78–9.

[3] J. D. Scott, *Vickers; a History* (1926), p. 49; Glasgow Chamber of Commerce, *Handbook*, pp. 152–3; Kirkwood, *My Life of Revolt*, pp. 78–9; *Mun.* 2. 15, 11 May 1915; *Vanguard*, November 1915.

[4] Scott and Cunnison, *The Industries of the Clyde Valley*, p. 93.

an area in the metal trades to be devoted to munitions production, while taking care not to tread on the toes of the shipbuilding firms.[1] Shell production was the easiest sector of the munitions industry to develop in firms not accustomed to munitions work. Already, in the last months of 1914, Babcock & Wilcox, the marine boilermakers of Renfrew, had been given a contract for shell.

By December 1916, shell production had made a very deep inroad into the dominance of the shipyards in the Glasgow metal industries, penetrating both marine and railway engineering and employing 11,000 workers in the main factories alone. But this figure should not be taken at its face value: 6,196 of the workers alone were women, new to the industry and unlikely to be more than a temporary wartime acquisition. Only 1,261 were the skilled engineers, forge and foundry workers on whom the Glasgow engineering industry was based.[2]

More central, from our point of view, to the growing importance of the arms industry was the development of the gun, tank and aircraft manufacture, all of which involved a high degree of skilled engineering labour. Beardmore's gun production expanded from its origin in 1909. By 1915 guns were also produced in the Dalmuir works, 400 men working in the gun mounting department alone. Beardmore spawned sub-contracts for gun work to large firms like Weir, N.B. Loco. Co., Lang (Johnstone), and to smaller general engineering firms like Meechan (Scotstoun) and Harney (Govan) – the latter being in September 1917 'almost wholly on gun work'.[3] In 1915 Beardmore also took over the abandoned works of the Arrol Johnstone Motor Car Co., at Paisley, and converted them to the manufacture of machine-gun components and aircraft engines. Apart from Beardmore, only one other arms firm – the Coventry Ordnance Works (Scotstoun), jointly owned by Cammell-Laird and John Brown – established itself in Glasgow during the war, again producing guns.[4] Apart from gun manufacture, many large firms in Glasgow also took up other varieties of munitions work, like tank manufacture at

[1] *MM* ii, 2, pp. 131–2.

[2] 'Report on Labour in Controlled Establishments', *Bev.* v, p. 79.

[3] Scott and Cunnison, *The Industries of the Clyde Valley*, p. 114; Gallacher, *Revolt on the Clyde*, p. 106; ASE, *Monthly Journal and Report*, October 1917; *Glasgow Herald*, 6, 10 January and 1916.

[4] 'Cases and Rules etc. alleged to restrict output' (7 September 1915), in *Bev.* iii, p. 162; *Machinery*, 24 June 1915; *MM* x, 1, p. 84; H. W. Macrosty, *The Trust Movement in British Industry* (1907), p. 44.

N.B. Loco. Co., and especially aircraft. Weir organized many, of the shipbuilding firms into producing the wooden frames while Beardmore (which had produced aero engines prior to the war), Weir itself, the North British and other firms, fitted and engined them.[1]

The larger firms in the new engineering industries were also drawn into the orbit of the arms firms. Albion (Scotstoun) was the only remaining motor car firm in Glasgow by 1914. It specialized in commercial vehicles, and during the war produced these for army use, as well as engaging in munitions work. The largest scientific instrument firm, Barr & Stroud (Anniesland), had grown up since the 1890s on the basis of supplying range finders to the War Office. And the huge Singer's Sewing Machine works at Clydebank – it employed 10,000 people in 1918 – applied its mass production techniques and its experience of female labour to the problems of shell and fuse production during the war.[2]

Some idea of the overall impact of the munitions sector on the Clyde metal industries can be gained from an analysis of the ASE branch membership figures during the five years 1914–19 (see Appendix, p. 338 below). There was a close correspondence between the location of the munitions factories and the location of the most rapidly expanding ASE branches. In the East End, dominated by Beardmore's factory at Parkhead, ASE membership grew by 258 %. In Scotstoun and Anniesland, the home of Barr and Stroud, Albion, the Coventry Ordnance works, Meechan – all deeply engaged in munitions work – it grew by 166 %. On the other hand, in the whole central area of Glasgow – Govan, Partick, Finneston – dominated by shipbuilding and marine engineering firms the ASE grew by only 53 %. These areas between them accounted for over half the ASE membership in Glasgow. The correspondence carried through the rest of the district, though less strikingly and with some exceptions. The areas dominated by the munitions firms were the most militant areas in the February 1915 strike. They were also the areas on which

1 Scott and Cunnison, *The Industries of the Clyde Valley*, p. 114; J. Cunnison and J. B. Gilfillan, *The Third Statistical Account of Scotland* (Glasgow, 1958), pp. 218–19; *MM* XII, 1, p. 55.

2 Scott and Cunnison, *The Industries of the Clyde Valley*, pp. 93, 96, 108–9, 208; Campbell, *Scotland since 1707*, pp. 244–6; Bell, *Pioneering Days*, p. 73; Drake, *Women in the Engineering Trades*, p. 29; *Glasgow Herald*, 20 March 1915.

the Clyde Workers' Committee was to be based. According to the ASE branch membership figures, these areas accounted for no more than 20 % of ASE members in 1919. There is no direct evidence that this 20 % of engineering workers worked in munitions firms, but it seems unlikely that the coincidence between the location of an expanding munitions sector and the location of the fastest-growing ASE branches could be explained in any other way.

The figure of 20 % of the ASE membership thus provides a (very crude) indicator of the basis of support immediately available to the CWC. It is clear from the outset that one of the chief problems facing the militant rank-and-file movement in Glasgow would be that of extending its influence beyond the sector of its origin, into the much less expansive, but much larger, sector dominated by shipbuilding and marine engineering.

After the 2d an hour strike the CLWC did not altogether disintegrate, despite the failure of its 'stay-in-strike' policy. 'Two or three members of the old Labour Withholding Committee . . . kept in touch with one another . . .' ready, when the appropriate issue arose, to call the rank-and-file movement into being.[1] For a time it seemed that the moment had come early in June 1915, when a Parkhead shop steward by the name of Marshall was jailed for assulting a fellow-worker allegedly in order to enforce restrictive practices on shell work. But the ASE officials were able to get Marshall released, and the moment passed.[2]

Within days of Marshall's trial, however, the Munitions Act became law. It was the impact of this on the Clyde and the impotence of the trade union officials in the face of it, which eventually led to the formation of the Clyde Workers' Committee. Although the Glasgow Munitions Tribunal was relatively mild in its administration of the Act, the employers' use of their increased power was largely beyond its control. The Tribunal might protest strongly about employers suspending men without granting them leave certificates, but it could no nothing to penalize management or compensate the men in these cases. There was in fact no penalty for the refusal of a leaving certificate,

---

[1] *The Worker*, 29 January 1916.
[2] *Forward*, 3 July 1915, 1 January 1916; *Vanguard*, October 1915; Gallacher, *Revolt on the Clyde*, pp. 62–3; ASE, *Executive Minutes*, vol. 192, 18, 29 June, 13, 16, 22 July, 6 August 1915.

however unreasonable.[1] More important, when strikers came before the Tribunal, they found it extremely difficult to grasp the full import of compulsory arbitration and the illegality of strikes.[2] They had struck over what they considered to be a genuine grievance, and they wanted this grievance discussed in court. The chairman could not allow this. 'The reasons for going on strike matter nothing under this Act. Men may have a grievance or not. He had nothing to do with that. The Act stated "thou shalt not strike". They had deliberately disobeyed this command, and they must take the consequences.'[3] The result of the Munitions Act on the Clyde was greatly to enhance the disciplinary powers of the employers – managers and foremen becoming 'more dictatorial in their treatment of the men'.[4]

Matters came to a head over the prosecution of some strikers at the Fairfield shipyard (Govan). Since the passing of the Munitions Act the Fairfield management had added a particularly aggressive tone to its longstanding inefficiency.[5] On 26 August 1915, 430 shipwrights struck over the dismissal of two men for slacking. The management had marked the dismissed men's leaving certificate with the cause for their dismissal. This was seen by the men as an attempt to revive the unpopular system of character notes which had previously operated on Clydeside. Twenty-six of the strikers were tried on September 3rd, and seventeen men, all shop stewards, were fined £10 each, with a penalty of thirty days in jail if they failed to pay within three weeks. Intimidated, the strikers returned to work the next day.[6] Since their officials were unsympathetic, some of the convicted men approached the Govan Trades Council, declaring their intention of going to prison rather than admitting their guilt by paying the fine. On September 14th, Henry Hopkins, secretary of this body, wrote to Lloyd George urging him to reduce or remit the fines. The Govan Trades Council issued a circular to

[1] ASE, *Monthly Journal and Report*, October 1915; *Glasgow Herald*, August–November 1915, *passim*.

[2] When strikers were first threatened with heavy fines, the men in the courtroom laughed increduously: *Glasgow Herald*, 3 August, 4 September 1915.

[3] Govan Trades Council, circular (?September 1915), in *Bev*. iii, p. 76.

[4] *MM* iv, 2, p. 61.

[5] Barttelot to Beveridge, 11 September, 1915, in *Bev*. iii, p. 4; C. Addison, *Four and a Half Years* (1934), pp. 142–3; *Glasgow Herald*, 3 August 1915.

[6] Board of Trade, *Labour Gazette*, 4 September 1915; *MM* IV, 2, pp. 50–4; *Glasgow Herald*, 4 September 1915; *Forward*, 18 November 1915.

its members urging them to send up resolutions demanding the remittance of the fines and the abolition of the Munitions Act: 'Has the fear of the DORA and the Munitions Act affected the rank and file as it has apparently affected its leaders? Are we to remain passive, or are we to protest and offer resistance to coercive Acts of Parliament.'[1]

The initiative taken by the Govan Trades Council evoked widespread sympathy among the Clydeside workers. 'You find resistance to the Act, and a determination to cripple and crab it, exalted into a principle of belief, and tenaciously held and publicly preached by workmen who judged by conventional standards, are honest, industrious operatives, are elders of the Kirk and have their boys fighting at the Front.'[2] Already on September 12th, at a meeting of the shop stewards' vigilance committee, officially summoned by the Glasgow District Committee and chaired by David Kirkwood, a resolution had been carried demanding that the Executive secure the abolition of 'the Slave Clauses' of the Act. It was further decided to convene a meeting of representative shop stewards for Saturday, October 2nd. The District Committee endorsed this resolution and forwarded it to the Executive, who, well aware that 'many of our members are almost in revolt at being bound over to one employer', despatched Brownlie, the general secretary, to the Clyde. On Thursday, September 30th, Brownlie faced the rank and file. A request by the shop stewards for David Kirkwood, Tom Clark (Parkhead) and James Messer (Weir) to be allowed to speak was refused. In the event Brownlie was howled down and a resolution demanding the repeal of the Act carried.[3]

The leading group of the old CLWC saw their moment and seized it. On Saturday, October 2nd, the unofficial meeting of delegates from many of the trades in the Glasgow engineering and shipbuilding industry met under Kirkwood's chairmanship, and decided to set up a 'strong representative committee . . . [to] organize the prevailing opposition to the operation of the Act, and [to] arrange for a General Meeting of the Allied Trades to be held in Glasgow at an early date'. The organization which emerged called itself the Clyde Trades Vigilance Committee.

---

[1] Govan Trades Council, *op. cit.; MM* IV, 2, p. 54.

[2] Memorandum by Macassey, 18 December 1915, in *Mun.* 5. 73.

[3] *Forward*, 18 September, 9 October 1915; *Glasgow Herald*, 12 October 1917; ASE, *Executive Minutes*, vol. 192, 1 October 1915; ASE, *Monthly Journal and Report*, October 1915; *MM* IV, 2, p. 55.

It was this Committee which fused the purely ASE-based militancy represented by Kirkwood with the broader trend represented by Gallacher and Messer.[1] At the beginning of October, *Vanguard*, a local revolutionary paper, wrote:

'At the moment, in the Clyde Area, the officials are discredited and count for little, the real leaders of the men are to be found in the workshops. In many shops on the Clyde, vigilance committees, composed of delegates from each of the trades in the shop, have been formed, and have already many times demonstrated their usefulness . . . Then the vigilance committees are linked together in a central committee which contains most of the most trusted men of the labour movement in Glasgow.'

On October 6th three recalcitrant shipwrights were jailed. Immediately preparations for a strike were made at Fairfields and other Govan works. Government officials panicked. Most of the morning, wrote Addison in his diary on Monday, October 11th,

'was taken up with threatened labour trouble on the Clyde. It was difficult to disentangle the facts from the excited comments of Weir and our representative there [Paterson] . . . One big employer was bursting with a desire to arrest a lot of people, but he could not mention anybody who ought to be arrested except one man against whom there was no evidence. His suggestion was the proclamation of Martial Law . . .'[2]

Isaac Mitchell, the Board of Trade official who had negotiated with the unofficial leaders in February 1915, was sent to enquire. On the 13th two wires reached the Ministry. One from Mitchell said that the position was critical, and urged the appointment of a Commission of Enquiry. The other, from the Govan Trades Council, read: 'Fairfields shipwrights demand release of three shipwrights from prison by Saturday [17th]; failing which we cease work.' Mitchell was instructed to announce that an enquiry into the shipwrights' grievances would be held at once.[3]

The next day the local trade union officials stepped in to avert disaster. Through the Central Board of the Clyde Shipyards

---

[1] *Forward*, 9 October 1915; *The Herald*, 30 October 1915; *The Worker*, 29 January 1916; *Glasgow Herald*, 14 April, 1916, 12 October 1917.

[2] Addison, *Four and a Half Years*, p. 135.

[3] *MM* IV, 2, p. 56.

Joint Vigilance Committee – a body composed entirely of local union officials[1] – they issued a leaflet proclaiming the enquiry a victory for their pressure, and strongly advising against 'drastic action'. 'You may rest assured that everything possible will be done to establish our claims.' But they had lost their powers to charm. When the enquiry opened on Friday 15th, Lynden Macassey, one of its members, was immediately convinced that the strike called for the next day would be effective. Rushing back to London, he tried to persuade a meeting at the Ministry late that night to release the shipwrights. It was the only possible way, so he thought, of averting a strike. The shipwrights were not released; but something was cooked up by that late night consortium. Saturday's press gave a strong impression that they had been released and the strike was thus averted. The unofficial Clyde Trades Vigilance Committee met but, under the prevailing impression that the men had been released, they took no action.[2]

This manoeuvre only brought the Government a few days. On October 21st the Committee of Enquiry issued a preliminary report. They sympathized, but had no power to recommend the release of the shipwrights. At this point the officials refused to have anything more to do with the enquiry, and called a meeting of the Executive Committee for Saturday, October 23rd. This meeting sent off a curious telegram to London. The shipwrights should be released, it read, 'with a view to restoring the confidence of the workers and promoting the harmonious feeling among all classes in the country, which is so essential if our hopes and aspirations in this grave national crisis are to be realized'; and then added, 'we demand an answer within three days'. The rhetoric of industrial truce was thus brutally shattered. It was Gallacher, who attended the meeting as an official of his union, who had moved the final phrase. The next day the unofficial committee met, heard Gallacher's report, and, presumably, decided to await the results of the officials' telegram. On Wednesday, October 27th, in London, an arrangement was reached by which the officials were (secretly) to pay the fines,

[1] The constitution of this Committee is described in Ministry of Labour, *Industrial Reports, No. 2, Works Committees*, (1918). According to Arthur MacManus this body had been defunct since the outbreak of war and was revived at this point in the hope that the rank and file would confuse it with the unofficial body: *The Plebs*, March 1916.

[2] 'Threatened Clyde Strike', 16 October 1915, in *Mun. 5. 79*; *The Herald*, 23 October 1915; *Forward*, 23 October 1915; *Glasgow Herald*, 15, 16 October 1915.

and Lloyd George to release the shipwrights. They had already served two-thirds of their sentence. The leaders of the unofficial movement felt they had allowed themselves to be bamboozled by the Government and the trade union officials. The moment for independent action had passed unexploited.[1] The rank-and-file initiative, moreover, had remained with the Govan Trades Council – itself too geographically limited a body to lead effectively – and had not been grasped by the unofficial committee.

Underlying this was the uneven impact of the Munitions Act on the Clyde, in those early months. It fell hardest on the shipyards, but left the central core of militancy – the engineers in the arms firms – virtually untouched. No member of the ASE or of its close allies among the small engineering unions had come before the Munitions Tribunal for striking, though three short strikes were settled without prosecutions. The engineering employers had learned the lesson of February 1915, and they were wary of provoking their workers.[2] As David Morton, a Glasgow ASE militant, wrote a year later:

'Owing to the fact that the shop stewards were linked together, and had already proved that they had the men in the workshops behind them, prepared to take action if necessary, the Act was lightly administered in the Clyde Area. In fact, while members of the ASE in every other district of the country were groaning under the slave clauses of the Act, the Clyde district, as far as engineers were concerned, was practically free.'[3]

Nevertheless it was the Fairfield case that mobilized the unofficial committee, and the Clyde Workers Committee was able to claim that 'it was through the "powers that be" getting to know that the Committee was again at work, that ultimately forced the release of the three shipwrights'.[4] Moreover, two days before the case was finally settled the workers in one of the key militant factories won a resounding victory in their first encounter with the Munitions Act. Bridges, an ASE shop steward at Weir,

---

[1] MM IV, 2, pp. 58–60; Gallacher, Revolt on the Clyde, pp. 64–6; Vanguard, November 1915.

[2] Glasgow Herald, August–October 1915, passim; 'Reports on Strikes and Lockouts to 13th November, 1916', in Bev. ii, p. 99.

[3] Trade Unionist, October 1916.

[4] Clyde Workers' Committee, leaflet (? November 1915), in Bev. iii, p. 95. This was not an unrealistic claim. Macassey had feared trouble from this source on 15th October: 'Threatened Clyde Strike', loc. cit.

was to be prosecuted under the Act for 'interfering with a non-society fitter'. A shop meeting was called, and decided to strike if he was found guilty. The tribunal tried to postpone the case, but on Monday, October 25th Bridges turned up with 300 engineers, and insisted that the case be heard. The charge was withdrawn, to cheers from the 'unruly crowd', and jubilant shouts for the payment of Bridges' expenses.[1] This victory gave the unofficial committee the fillip it needed. Even *Forward*, the ultra-cautious paper of the local ILP, could not help observing the contrast between the victory of direct action at Weir's, and the miserable prevarications of the officials in the Fairfields case.[2] At the end of October the unofficial committee re-established itself on a more permanent basis, published a general statement of its aims, and found itself a new name – the Clyde Workers' Committee.[3]

The Clyde Workers' Committee originated in the failure of the union Executives, or District Committees, to place themselves at the head of the militancy of a section of the Clydeside engineers. From the Fairfield's case the more militant of the engineers learned that if the Munitions Act was to be opposed root and branch, it must be opposed by an organization and leadership able to act independently of the official trade union structures. The February 1915 strike had taught them that this organization, to be effective, must be a delegate organization based directly in the factories. Out of this experience the militants formulated and clearly expressed, for the first time, the principle of independent rank-and-file organization which was to constitute the basis of the shop stewards' movement.

'We will support the officials just so long as they rightly represent the workers, but we will act independently immediately they misrepresent them. Being composed of Delegates from every shop and untrammelled by obsolete rule or law, we claim to represent the true feeling of the workers. We can act immediately according to the merits of the case and the desire of the rank and file.'[4]

[1] *Glasgow Herald*, 26 October 1915; *Vanguard*, November 1915.
[2] *Forward*, 30 October 1915.
[3] *The Herald*, 30 October 1915; *Vanguard*, November 1915. According to MacManus the new name was adopted in order to distinguish the unofficial committee from the recently revived Clyde Shipyards Joint Vigilance Committee: *The Plebs*, March 1916.
[4] Clyde Workers' Committee, leaflet (? November 1915), in *Bev*. iii, p. 95.

From October 1915 until April 1916, when the Committee was smashed by the Government, 250–300 delegates met every weekend in a hall in Ingram Street, Glasgow. In addition to the ASE shop stewards who had formed the basis of the Labour Witholding Committee there were delegates from many of the other engineering and shipbuilding trades. There were delegates from the mines, the railways, from the co-operative workers, and at least one schoolteacher.[1] The Committee had no written constitution,[2] and the statement quoted above – *delegates* from *every* shop – represented more an aspiration than established fact. 'You could represent a minority in the Shop just the same as a majority even though the minority was one.' It seems probably that outside a few major arms firms the delegates represented minority militant groups rather than established workshop organization. In practice the Committee fully recognized this position: each delegate would say who, if anyone, he was representing when he spoke.

The day-to-day work was done by 'a small leading committee' elected at the delegate meeting and meeting two nights a week.[3] Two things characterized this leading group. Its members were all shop stewards at one or other of the arms firms which had led the February 1915 strike and were to remain the backbone of the Committee through 1915–16. And they were all socialists.

The Independent Labour Party, by far the largest socialist organization on the Clyde, was of no great importance in the shop stewards' movement. Only two of the leaders of the CWC, Messer and Kirkwood, belonged to it, and neither of them was of any importance in the party hierarchy. James Messer, a shop steward at Weir and secretary to the Committee, was primarily an organization man and appears to have contributed little to the development of the Committee's policy.[4] David

---

[1] *Ibid.;* Gallacher, *Revolt on the Clyde*, p. 58; *Glasgow Herald*, 14 April 1916.

[2] A minute book was kept, but this was 'lost' by James Messer, the secretary, when the authorities arrested him in March 1916: Labour Party, *Report of the Special Committee* . . ., pp. 12–13. The constitution reproduced in Scott and Cunnison, *The Industries of the Clyde Valley*, p. 210, probably dates from the winter of 1918–19.

[3] Labour Party, *Report of the Special Committee* . . ., pp. 13–14; Gallacher, *Revolt on the Clyde*, p. 58.

[4] D. M. Chewter, 'The History of the Socialist Labour Party of Great Britain from 1902–1921' (Oxford B. Litt., 1964), p. 154; Gallacher, *Revolt on the Clyde*, p. 58; Labour Party, *Report of the Special Committee* . . ., p. 19.

Kirkwood[1] had been weaned from the Socialist Labour Party by John Wheatley[2] at the outbreak of war. Curiously, though Kirkwood left the SLP over its failure to adopt a clear anti-war stance, he was by the winter of 1915–16 a bitter opponent of the revolutionary anti-war movement.[3]

Assiduous attempts were made to build up David Kirkwood as the leading figure in the rank-and-file movement,[4] but although convener at the largest factory in Glasgow he was far from being the Committee's leader. Parkhead, under Kirkwood, was on more than one occasion the weakest link in the militants' chain, and Kirkwood, older than the other leaders and far more the labour aristocrat than the revolutionary, accepted neither the authority nor the policy of the Committee.[5] In this he was in tune with his party, whose associated paper, *Forward*, was consistently hostile to the CWC's claim to independence of established trade union authority.[6] So intent was the editor, Tom Johnston,[7] on avoiding any unpleasantness with the authorities that he consistently refused even to report strike actions for fear that this might be interpreted as subversive of 'the military defence of the country'.[8]

It was from the revolutionary parties to the left of the ILP

[1] David Kirkwood (1872–1955). Had worked at Parkhead since 1910. Subsequently a member of the ILP National Administrative Committee and MP for Dumbarton, 1922–51. Created Baron Kirkwood of Bearsdon in 1951.

[2] John Wheatley (1869–1930). Son of Irish labourer, miner until aged 24, small grocer, journalist. In 1912 started successful publishing business. Joined ILP in 1908. Founded Catholic Socialist Society in Glasgow. Glasgow City Council, 1910–20, for Shettleston ward, where many Parkhead workers lived. MP for Shettleston from 1922 until his death. Minister of Housing in 1924.

[3] Gallacher, *Revolt on the Clyde*, p. 27; Kirkwood, *My Life of Revolt*, pp. 114, 125.

[4] Cf. Gallacher, *Revolt on the Clyde*, p. 127: 'The whole apparatus of the I.L.P. including *Forward*, was brought into play to boost him. Soon all others were forgotton; Kirkwood, the deportee was established.' For earlier ILP boosting of Kirkwood, see *Forward*, 21 August 1915.

[5] Bell, *Pioneering Days*, p. 98.

[6] *Forward*, 13 March 1915, 1 April 1916.

[7] Tom Johnston (b. 1882). Inherited printing business and founded *Forward* as a commercial enterprise in 1906. Editor for 27 years. The paper, while it served the Glasgow ILP was not controlled by it. Johnston later sat as MP for various Scottish constituencies. Secretary for Scotland, 1941–5.

[8] *Forward*, 6 March 1915, 5 February 1916, 26 January 1918. See for discussion of *Forwards*' wartime policy in general, T. Brotherstone, 'The Suppression of the *Forward*', *Bulletin of the Scottish Society for the Study of Labour History*, No. 1, May 1969.

that the CWC drew the bulk of its leadership.[1] The Socialist Labour Party had been founded in 1903 as a split from Hyndman's Social Democratic Federation. Wedded to an industrial unionist socialism inspired by Daniel De Leon and James Connolly, the SLP was to be the major political influence on the shop stewards' movement, and, subsequently, contributed most of the leading cadre of the British Communist Party. Though very small, the SLP membership had always been concentrated in Scotland, and it is probable that it was the larger of the two Marxist parties on the Clyde at this time. The other, the British Socialist Party, was the successor of the SDF which had been badly weakened in Scotland when the SLP was formed.

More than any other socialist organization in Britain, the British Socialist Party was torn apart by the First World War. Hyndman and the 'Old Guard' of established leaders came out in full support of the war and a bitter struggle ensued between an entrenched leadership which clung tenaciously to the apparatus of the Party, and a growing internationalist movement among the membership. The struggle was not resolved until Easter 1916, when, faced with an overwhelming internationalist majority at the first national conference since war broke out, the Hyndmanite faction walked out taking the party's paper, *Justice*, with them. They established a new party, unfortunately named the National Socialist Party. The dominant tendency among the BSP internationalists was a 'centrist' opposition led by E. C. Fairchild, who held to the view that working-class actions against the war must wait upon the reconstruction of the second international.

On the Clyde, however, the leadership of the anti-war section of the BSP fell to John Maclean,[2] a schoolteacher who adopted a consistently revolutionary defeatist position on the war. Maclean had joined the SDF in 1903 at the time of the SLP breakaway. In the pre-war years he had become figure well known on the Clyde and in the Lanarkshire coalfield, for his anti-militarist agitation and his classes in Marxist economics. From the outbreak of war he preached a revolutionary defeatist line at the factory gates

[1] The history of the revolutionary parties during these years has been written by W. Kendall, *The Revolutionary Movement in Britain, 1900–21* (1969). For a pertinent critique of his treatment see J. Hinton, Review of Kendall, in *Bulletin of the Society for the Study of Labour History*, no. 19, Autumn 1969.

[2] John Maclean (1879–1923). Schoolteacher, M.A. Led anti-war agitation in Glasgow. Soviet Consul for Scotland, 1918. Jailed 1915, 1916, 1918. Left BSP in 1920, and declined to join Communist Party.

and in the streets – an activity which required very great courage in the early years of the war, and which would have been physically impossible outside Clydeside where the ordinary workers were uniquely tolerant of such heterodox opinions. Maclean and his 'first lieutenant', James MacDougall – bank clerk, revolutionary orator and tutor in 'industrial history' – were accepted as frequent contributors at the weekly delegate meetings of the CWC. During the autumn of 1915 the Glasgow BSP issued a monthly paper, *Vanguard*, clearly controlled by Maclean, whose columns reveal a very close association with the CWC. The main basis of BSP influence in the Committee, apart from Maclean's general reputation as an agitator, appears to have been the Weir factory at Cathcart. Both Maclean and MacDougall were members of the Pollockshaws branch of the BSP. Weir's was the nearest sizeable factory and the branch concentrated its attention there. The only Weir shop steward who was actually a member of the BSP was a young man named Harry McShane, later to become famous as the leader of the Scottish unemployed workers' movement between the wars. But other senior stewards – John Smith, the convener, Robert Bridges, the man unsuccessfully hauled before the Munitions Court in October 1915, and James Messer who was in the ILP – were deeply influenced by John Maclean and attended his economics classes in 1917.

William Gallacher, chairman of the Committee, was a member of the BSP and 'a disciple of John Maclean'. At the Albion Works, where by 1912 he was 'the recognized leader', it was with a group of SLP militants that he had built up the organization, and this closeness with the SLP was probably reinforced by a trip to America in 1913 where he came into direct contact with the sources of SLP doctrine. When in December 1915, Maclean and the SLP fell out over the policy to be followed by the Committee, Gallacher had no hesitation in siding against his erstwhile master.[1]

Apart from Gallacher, Kirkwood and Messer all the other leaders of the CWC were members of the Socialist Labour Party. Johnny Muir,[2] convener at Barr & Stroud (Anniesland), the

[1] Based on information in Kendall, *The Revolutionary Movement in Britain, passim*, and Gallacher, *Revolt on the Clyde, passim*. William Gallacher (1881–1965), Executive member of United Brassfounders Union. Joined SDF in 1905. Subsequently founder member of Communist Party, and MP for West Fife, 1935–50.

[2] John Muir (1879–1931). Jailed in April 1916. Subsequently joined ILP and became MP for Maryhill in 1922. Parliamentary secretary to the Ministry

leading theorist of the Committee during 1915–16 and editor of
its paper, *The Worker*, had been editor of the SLP paper, *The
Socialist*, until Christmas 1914. Arthur MacManus,[1] shop steward
at Weir (Cathcart) and later at Beardmore's works at Dalmuir,
one of the most able members of the leading group of the Committee, succeeded Muir as editor of *The Socialist*. At the age of
twenty-one MacManus had been a leader in the abortive SLP
attempt to organize the Singer's works at Clydebank on dual
unionist lines. The mass victimization which followed the defeat
of this attempt – 400 militants were sacked – helped to establish
a network of SLP and SLP – influenced shop stewards throughout
the Clyde, a network which was undoubtedly to play an important
part in the organization of the CWC.[2] Tom Clark, treasurer of
the Committee and a shop steward at Parkhead, was another
leading SLP agitator: 'Glasgow's greatest declaimer', wrote
Gallacher from the safe distance of the 1930s, 'of De Leon's
petty bourgeois phantasies'.[3]

For many years Glasgow had been the centre of revolutionary
propagandist activity in Britain. Both the SLP and the John
Maclean group in the BSP laid heavy emphasis on educational
work. The SLP's influence was felt, typically, through the education classes which, year after year, turned out more 'worker-
tutors'. Small groups of SLP members, trained in these classes,
ran mealtime discussion circles in many of the Clydeside factories,
instilling the principles of Marxism and the ideas of Industrial
Unionism and distributing revolutionary literature. Simultaneously, John Maclean filled large halls with Clydeside engineers
for lectures on Marxist economics. Through these educational
activities, a politically conscious vanguard of workers considerably larger than the membership of the revolutionary groups was
created on the Clyde. Nevertheless the groups remained minute.

of Pensions, 1924. Later, general secretary of the Workers' Educational
Association.

[1] Arthur MacManus (1889–1927). Elected president of Shop Stewards'
and Workers' Committee Movement in August 1917. First president of
British Communist Party. MacManus' oratory was 'like the firing of a
Gatling gun. After an emotional outburst and hanging on for the next word
and sentence, it was not *er, er, er*, but *the, the, the* unity of the workers is
vital in the struggle.' G. Hodgkinson, *Sent to Coventry* (1970), p. 45.

[2] Bell, *Pioneering Days*, p. 75; *The Socialist*, October 1910, April–July,
December 1911; *Forward*, 10 February 1917; Cole, *Workshop Organisation*,
p. 34.

[3] Gallacher, *Revolt on the Clyde*, p. 27.

The dominant faction, the SLP, had about a hundred members in Glasgow in 1915.[1]

The CWC represented for its leaders a dramatic breakthrough from propagandist policies to leadership in a genuine mass movement. Leadership, however, raised unfamiliar problems: problems which long immersion in the abstract clarities of propaganda had not equipped the revolutionaries to solve. The CWC sprang from a sectional grievance and rested on a narrow base. It developed, however, in a broader context of unrest. At different moments during the autumn and winter of 1915–16, anti-war politics, the fight for free speech, the struggle over rents and the fight against conscription became the main immediate focus of activity for revolutionaries on the Clyde. The history of the Clyde Workers' Committee in this period is in large measure the history of the unsuccessful attempts by the revolutionaries at its helm to make connections between the narrow economic concerns of the skilled munitions workers and these other struggles, to discover a way of tapping the revolutionary possibilities of a mass movement of craft workers threatened by the onrush of dilution in wartime.

The difficulty they would face in this task was illustrated from the outset. Shortly after the CWC was formally established a new convulsion seized Clydeside. Yet again the militant workers in the munitions factories who had led in February failed to take the initiative. One of the hoariest legends about the CWC is that it led the rent strike of the autumn of 1915.[2] The origin of this legend appears to be Gallacher's account in *Revolt on the Clyde*.[3] 'From far away Dalmuir in the West, from Parkhead in the East, from Cathcart in the South and Hydepark in the North, the dungareed army of the proletariat invaded the centre of the city ... leaving the factories deserted, shouting and singing.' In its combination of verve and inaccuracy, this passage is typical of Gallacher's account as a whole. According to the Ministry of Munitions' records not one of the factories referred to by Gallacher struck work. Agitation over rent rises due to acute housing shortage had been growing since the beginning of 1915.

[1] Chewter, 'The History of the Socialist Labour Party', pp. 2, 23, 25–8, 101, 129, 131; Bell, *Pioneering Days*, pp. 38, 55, 57; Gallacher, *Revolution on the Clyde*, p. 24, 51.

[2] E.g. B. Pribicevic, *The Shop Stewards' Movement and Workers' Control* (Oxford, 1959), p. 27.

[3] *Op. cit.*, pp. 54–5.

The situation was worst in the Govan and Fairfields wards, where, by October 1915, rents were 12% to 23% up on the July level.[1] During the summer of 1915 *Forward*, the ILP weekly paper, reported a whole series of rent strikes, growing in volume towards the autumn.[2] The movement was particularly strong in Govan where a women's housing committee led by a previously unknown housewife, Mrs Barlow, organized constant propaganda meetings (including factory gate meetings), rent strikes and physical resistance to evictions. Early in October a large demonstration of women lobbied the Town Council with banners reading: 'Our Husbands, sons and brothers are fighting the Prussians in Germany. We are fighting the Prussians of Partick!', and there was a threat of strike action from the Parkhead Howitzer shop if evictions took place.[3] When Isaac Mitchell came to enquire into the Fairfield case on October 11th, he reported threats of a general strike against evictions.[4] By October 30th a general rent strike was in progress.[5] The climax came on November 17th, when to overcome physical resistance to evictions the factors (landlords agents) summoned eighteen tenants before the Small Debts Court, intending to get the increased rent impounded from their wages at source. A demonstration of women outside the Court was joined by all the men from five Govan, Partick and Whiteinch shipyards, and the Coventry Ordnance works in Scotstoun.[6] The other munitions factories were represented, if at all, by deputations. Up to 15,000 people surged around the court house. Inside a deputation from Dalmuir, where several of the summoned tenants worked, met the Sheriff:

'You hear the voice of the people out in the street. That is the workers of the upper reaches of the Clyde. These men will only resume work in the event of you deciding against the factors; if you do not, it means that the workers on the lower reaches will stop work tomorrow and join them.'[7]

[1] *MM* IV, 2, pp. 103–4; Glasgow Trades Council, *Minutes*, 21 April 1915.
[2] This agitation had been launched by the ILP secretary of the Glasgow Labour Party's Housing Committee: Kendall, *The Revolutionary Movement in Britain*, p. 115.
[3] *Vanguard*, November 1915; *Forward*, 9 October 1915; *Workers' Dreadnought*, 16 October 1915.
[4] *MM* IV, 2, p. 55.   [5] *Herald*, 30 October, 6, 13 November 1915.
[6] Fairfield, Henderson, Stephen, Harland & Wolff, Barclay Curle: *Mun*. 2. 27, 20 November 1915; *Mun*. 5. 346, 'Clyde Rent Strike' (n.d.).
[7] *Vanguard*, December 1915; *Trade Unionist*, December 1915; *The Herald*, 20, 27 November 1915; Gallacher, *Revolt on the Clyde*, p. 55.

Legal niceties tumbled before the blast, and the Sheriff did as he was told. The next day the Government announced in the Commons that a Bill to limit rents to their July 1914 level would be introduced. On November 25th it received its first reading.[1]

Undoubtedly the CWC drew confidence from the strike. Six weeks later, when the struggle against the Munitions Act appeared to be reaching a new peak, the movement was strengthened by the feeling 'that as they got the better of the Government over rents, by intimidation, they will be able to do the same thing over the Munitions Act'.[2] But the rent issue arose most acutely in Govan and Partick, and in so far as its leadership came from the industrial workers, it came not from the leading arms firms, whose workers were not so badly affected, but from the shipyards of Govan which had led in the Fairfield case. The rent strike may well have been the Clyde Workers' greatest victory of the war,[3] but the CWC as such had nothing whatsoever to do with it. John Maclean was bitterly critical of the Committee's failure to take the lead in the rent strike. It is probably that the Committee, little more than two weeks old when the rent strike reached its climax, considered it more important to consolidate policy on the issues immediately facing the skilled munitions workers on whom it rested than to attempt to lead in a struggle which did not directly concern the bulk of its supporters. The first few delegate meetings of the Committee were, therefore, primarily taken up with the 'academic discussions and futile proposals'[4] which, despite the impatience of John Maclean, are always a necessary part of policy making.

Dilution was the central issue facing the CWC. The Munitions Act was seen as designed to 'furnish the employers with a machine which would shatter to its foundations the whole fabric of trade union liberties and customs'.[5] From the start the CWC identified 'the scrapping of trade union rules' as the foremost change in the war. It set itself to make good the failure of the

[1] *MM* IV, 2, p. 105. Allan Clinton has pointed out that agitation in other areas as well as Glasgow, notably Woolwich and Coventry, was important in winning rent control in 1915: 'Trades Councils during World War I', *International Review of Social History*, 1970, pt. 2.

[2] *Mun.* 5. 70, 'Notes from the Intelligence Officer in Glasgow' (? January 1916).

[3] Murphy, *Preparing for Power*, p. 118.

[4] *Vanguard*, December 1915.

[5] *Mun.* 5. 73, 'Memorandum on Clyde and Tyne', by Macassey, 10 December 1915.

officials 'to grasp the significance of these changes, and . . . to formulate a policy that would adequately protect the interests of the workers. . . .'[1]

Until the end of 1915, outside shell work, mere negative resistance to dilution had been a very successful policy on the Clyde.[2] In the shipyards dilution did not seem possible at this stage in any case.[3] In the arms sector, where dilution was possible, it was the resistance of the skilled workers which had prevented its advance. The open skirmishes as at Weir in April and May 1915 and at Dalmuir in September,[4] were less important than the employers' generalized fear of provoking trouble after the engineers had demonstrated their power in the 2d per hour strike. In May William Weir wrote: 'The position has become so difficult that an employer has really to consider whether he should or should not take on Government work of a new nature . . . in case he involves himself in labour difficulties which will affect his entire normal business.'[5] In December 1915, W. Rowan Thompson, president of the local Engineering Employers' Association, 'voicing the views and experiences of the majority of large engineering employers in this district', pointed out that 'no employer is going to imperil the continuity of his work, or run the risk of a stoppage [by introducing dilution] . . . as long as the Trade Unions are permitted to flout the Government's instructions'.[6]

The formation of the CWC coincided with two events which showed that the policy of mere negative resistance was no longer adequate. On October 25th the Bridges case at Weirs was dismissed. Although in this instance the workers had won, the fact that Weir had brought the case at all indicated a new aggressive

[1] Clyde Workers' Committee, leaflet (? November 1915), in *Bev.* iii, p. 95.

[2] Dilution on shell work was very well advanced on Clydeside. There was little rank-and-file objection to this form of dilution since shell work was new to Glasgow and therefore (a) the employment of women did not involve the direct replacement of men, (b) it could be expected to disappear after the war. *MM* IV, 2, p. 49; Scott and Cunnison, *The Industries of the Clyde Valley*, p. 98.

[3] 'Intelligence Report', 26 October 1915, in *Bev.* iv, p. 212; *Mun.* 2. 27, 13 November 1915; Mun. 5. 73, 'Memorandum on Dilution of Labour', by Patterson, 18 December 1915.

[4] *Glasgow Herald*, 21 May 1915; ASE, *Monthly Journal and Report*, April, November 1915; *Machinery*, 6 May 1915.

[5] *Glasgow Herald*, 21 May 1915.

[6] *Mun.* 5. 73, 'Memorandum on Dilution of Labour', by Patterson, 18 December 1915.

tone among the engineering employers. Three days later the
ASE Executive accepted L2 and L3 in principle and during
November William Brodie, the district delegate, explained the
circulars to meetings throughout the Clyde, urging the members
to accept dilution on the terms laid down in these agreements.[1]
In these circumstances it was clearly necessary for the revolutionaries to face up to the task, neglected by the trade union
officials, of 'formulating a policy that would adequately protect
the interests' of the craft workers by whom the Committee had
been formed.

This was no easy task. For years the SLP had denounced the
craft unions and the craftsmen as 'the blue blood of the working
class. . .'.[2] Now they were faced with the problem of devising a
policy acceptable to a rank-and-file movement largely based on
those same aristocrats.[3] The policy they produced was presented
by John Muir to a meeting of the Committee in December 1915.[4]
The initial step, and in the circumstances the most important
and courageous step, was explicitly to reject the protective reflex
of the craftsmen, hostility to dilution as such. 'We regard
[dilution] as progressive from the point of view that it simplifies
the labour process, makes labour more mobile, and tends to
increase output. In short it is a step in the direct line of industrial
evolution.' Both mere resistance, and the Executive's dependence
on the guarantees of post-war restoration were shown to be
worthless policies in the light of this analysis. But what was to
be put in their place?

The Committee was clear that no policy of accepting and
negotiating the introduction of dilution could hope to succeed
which permitted the dilutees to be played off against the craftsmen.
In the long term, the obvious answer was to do away with sectional
trade unionism altogether: 'The *ultimate aim* of the Clyde
Workers' Committee', wrote Gallacher in January 1916, 'is to
weld these unions into one powerful organization that will place
the workers in complete control of the industry.' More immediately, control over dilution could best be achieved by building

[1] ASE, *Monthly Journal and Report*, December 1915; ASE, *Executive Minutes*, vol. 192, 28 October 1915.

[2] *The Socialist*, May 1911.

[3] '. . . it must not be thought that the rank and file are socialists. The Committee was formed to stem the onslaught on the privilege won by organised labour in the past.' *The Socialist*, April 1916.

[4] Gallacher, *Revolt on the Clyde*, pp. 60–1; published in *The Worker*, 15 January 1916.

E

up an all-grades organization in the workshops, thereby reconstructing the trade union movement from the base upwards.[1] But
the threat of dilution was an immediate one, and must be met by
the organization which already existed within the workshops, or
which could be improvised in a few weeks. Here the leaders of
the Committee encountered one of their most crucial problems.

The general unions had never been strong in Scotland. Despite
successes in Singer's, and among female shell workers, the
unions had made little headway among the unskilled workers in
the major munitions firms,[2] and this weakness was reflected in
the workshop organization on which the CWC rested. At the
largest of the arms works, Parkhead, for example, the shop
stewards' committee was still, during the early months of 1916,
only representative of the engineering craft unions. Kirkwood's
success in 'overcoming craft jealousies' did not extend beyond
craft workers. Although, from the summer of 1915, the women
shell workers at Parkhead had been 100% organized in the
NFWW, the craftsmen were not in a position to rely on the
women's organization to prevent women being used as cheap
labour. The organization of the women had largely been the
work of the ASE shop stewards. When the latter were annihilated
in the spring of 1916, this 'most fully organized and most vigorous
body of women shell workers in the district' rapidly disintegrated.[3]

Faced with the urgent problem of dilution the CWC had to
formulate a policy which was based on the real *craft* strength of
its members, rather than on the powerful all-grades organization
which existed as yet only as an 'ultimate aim'. The difficulty was
that the defence of craft unionism by craft unionists alone against
the threat inherent in dilution was all too likely to submerge
the long-term aim of replacing craft by industrial organization.
The revolutionaries attempted to break out of this vicious circle
by adopting an ambitious programme of nationalization and

[1] *The Worker*, 29 January 1916. See also *Bev.* v, pp. 38–9, 'C.W.C. Scheme
for Dilution of Labour' (February 1916).
[2] Thus for the Workers' Union: 'efforts at the major munitions firms
yielded disappointing results'. R. Hyman, 'The Workers Union, 1898–1929'
(Oxford D.Phil., 1968), p. 115. The other general unions had even less success: see J. Hinton, 'Rank and File Militancy in the British Engineering
Industry, 1914–1918' (London Ph.D., 1969), pp. 160–2.
[3] Labour Party, *Report of the Special Committee* . . ., p. 7.; Kirkwood, *My
Life of Revolt* pp. 87–8; Scott and Cunnison, *The Industries of the Clyde*,
pp. 215–16; *Forward*, 12 June 1915; Drake, *Women in the Engineering Trades*,
p. 129.

workers' participation in management: 'that all industries and national resources must be taken over by the Government – not merely "controlled", but taken over completely – and organized labour should be vested with the right to take part directly and equally with the present managers in the management and administration in every department of industry'. And Muir added: 'I have used the word "demand" advisedly, as this is no propagandist statement. It is our fixed decision to force this matter to an issue.'

When Muir put this policy to the Committee, no one challenged the irresistibility of dilution. But the demand for nationalization and workers' participation in management raised a storm of argument. Peter Petroff,[1] Maclean's closest associate, launched an attack on the policy in the course of which, apparently, he implied that Muir was an *agent provocateur*. Gallacher, formerly a member of the Maclean group, sided with Muir and, as chairman, expelled Petroff from the meeting. This ended the Maclean group's participation in the CWC and left the SLP in control. There is no direct record of the debate, but its content can be reconstructed from other sources. Petroff concentrated his attack on the issue of the war. The SLP after some confusion during the first months had come down firmly in opposition to the war. On the CWC, however, their members, and particularly John Muir – who was known to be 'soft' on the war – pushed a line of neutrality. Whatever its members might say as individuals, the Committee itself was neither for nor against the war: it was concerned only to defend the workers against the threats to their organization brought about by the war. To John Maclean such 'neutrality' was hypocritical and a betrayal of socialism.[2] The dilution policy would give this betrayal concrete form. The

[1] Peter Petroff, a Russian, was jailed for his role in the 1905 revolution. He escaped, and reached Britain in 1907. He became a prominent member of the London SDF. In 1915 he joined Maclean on the Clyde. Interned for his anti-war activities, he was deported to Russia after the February Revolution, where he became, for a time, a Soviet diplomat. In January 1916 a local Munitions official informed his superiors about 'Peter Petroff, a Russian socialist of a very dangerous type. The easiest thing to do with Petroff is to have him repatriated, when, from all that I am told, he will be shot within 24 hours of landing in Russia': *Bev.* iii, p. 111, Paterson to Llewellyn Smith, 17 January 1916.

[2] Gallacher, *Revolt on the Clyde*, pp. 59–62; interview with Mr H. McShane, Chewter, 'The History of the Socialist Labour Party', pp. 125–7; *Glasgow Herald*, 14 April 1916; Kendall, *The Revolutionary Movement in Britain*, pp. 111–12.

workers in question were, after all, munitions workers. They had a responsibility not only to themselves but also to the soldiers being killed in a war whose continuance the munitions workers facilitated in their everyday work. 'If the Clyde Workers took part control of the munitions work they would thus accept part responsibility for the War.'[1]

Neither side in this quarrel adopted an altogether satisfactory position. Viewed as an attempt, against all the odds, to maintain a principled internationalist stand, John Maclean's opposition to the SLP policy is unimpeachable. But it was a gesture, not a policy. It would be wrong to see in it proof of his unique capacity 'to unite revolutionary ideology with a practical programme'.[2] Maclean had no programme to offer the Committee on the immediate practical problem that they faced: how to deal with dilution. Had he succeeded in persuading the Committee's leadership to take a consistent revolutionary defeatist stand – to refuse to do anything that might facilitate munitions production – the practical problems of the Committee would have been no nearer solution. There is nothing to suggest that the Clydeside munitions workers would have fought in open opposition to the war effort. In the circumstances any attempt to lead them into battle under a revolutionary defeatist banner, in so far as it evoked any responses at all would probably have degenerated into a stubborn and reactionary craft battle against dilution as such.

If John Maclean's standpoint was remote from the real possibilities of the Committee, the SLP policy, despite its admirable insistence that dilution as such could not be fought, represented a very confused and inadequate attempt to come to terms with those possibilities. There was no novelty in the policy of nationalization and workers' participation in management. This had been widely canvassed by the Guild Socialists through the columns of *The Herald* and other papers, and on Clydeside, by

---

[1] *Mun.* 5. 70, extracts from the suppressed issue of *Vanguard*, 30 December 1915. Gallacher claims that 'despite trouble over Petroff' there was no cooling off between himself and Maclean: *loc. cit.*, pp. 67, 115. But Gallacher fails to mention the real cause of the quarrel with Petroff, and his whole account is most improbable. McShane says that Maclean attacked Gallacher publicly on the war issue, just as he did Kirkwood. Cf. Kirkwood, *My Life of Revolt*, pp. 114, 118.

[2] Kendall, *The Revolutionary Movement in Britain*, p. 108 and *passim*. In general Kendall overestimates the degree to which Maclean was a revolutionary *leader*, as against an educator and propagandist.

both the ILP and the BSP.[1] It is, however, surprising – and evidence of the general disorientation experienced by sectarians when faced with sudden and unexpected prospect of mass leadership – that the SLP, which had always opposed nationalization as a tyrannical capitalistic device, should now demand it.

What was new was Muir's transformation of the argument from a propagandist point into a negotiating stance over the issue of dilution. For the CWC leadership, 'forcing this matter to an issue' became the central task of the Committee. 'The SLP section declare that they would not strike for anything short of this.'[2] This single-minded concentration on the dilution policy had fatal implications for the development of the CWC as a revolutionary vanguard on the Clyde. At this stage dilution was being proposed as an urgent measure only in the munitions factories. It is not surprising therefore that when during January 1916 John Maclean and his associates attacked the CWC as a pro-war and selfish body which was demanding nationalisation only for the munitions industry, the allegation, though untrue, should have embarrassed the Committee's leaders.[3] Whatever they might say in justification, it remained a fact that their policy was only of direct relevance to the munitions workers. Taken at face value the dilution policy committed the munitions workers, alone in any position to negotiate about dilution, to enter a fight to blackmail the Government into effecting a social revolution relying entirely on their own resources. Instead of the political vanguard trying to use its position in the leadership of the rank-and-file movement to broaden that movement out beyond a militant section of the labour aristocracy, the vanguard was proposing to bring the entire weight of the class struggle to bear on that section alone. While they were right to see the skilled engineers, in war conditions, as the key section of the workers, they were quite wrong to assume that this section was so strong that it had no need to draw other sections into the struggle. As J. T. Murphy later commented, Muir's policy was 'either window-dressing propaganda, or a complete over-estimation of the power and extent of the influence of the Clyde Workers' Committee'.[4]

[1] Cole, *Workshop Organisation* (Oxford, 1923), pp. 90, 92; *Forward* 29 May 1915; *Vanguard*, October, December 1915.

[2] *Mun.* 5. 70, extracts from suppressed issue of *Vanguard*, January 1916.

[3] *Ibid.* The embarrassment of the CWC leadership is clear from their repeated denials of the charge. See *The Socialist*, February 1916; *The Worker*, 8 January 1916.

[4] Murphy, *Preparing for Power*, p. 121.

However inadequate the CWC's policy on dilution, at least it had a policy. This gave it a great advantage, initially, over the trade union officials, an advantage which it rapidly put to use. On December 20th Lloyd George announced that he would visit the Tyne and the Clyde to put the Government's case on the urgent need for dilution to the workers.[1] The arrangements for his visit to the Clyde were botched. Originally, a meeting was arranged with the officials of the Allied Trades for the evening of Thursday, December 23rd. At the last moment this was postponed to the Saturday, Christmas Day, so that Lloyd George could tour the factories first. The resentment of the trade union officials at being treated in such an offhand manner gave the CWC a chance to capitalize on the situation. The CWC, meeting on the night of Thursday, December 23rd, adopted a two-pronged strategy to force Lloyd George to meet them. First, when Lloyd George toured the factories the following day, the shop stewards were to refuse to meet him and refer him to the CWC. Gallacher and Muir toured the factories ahead of him to make sure this decision was applied. The policy failed at Parkhead, where Kirkwood could not resist the opportunity of giving the Minister a piece of his mind. But Lloyd George was kept out of Weir's and thereby forced to abandon his other projected visits. Concealing his humiliation he rushed off to Houston to christen a new filling factory – 'Georgetown'.[2]

Second, a rather disingeneous attempt was made by the CWC to get control of the meeting on Saturday. Gallacher, making the fullest use of his dual position as chairman of the CWC and an official delegate of his union on the Allied Trades, persuaded the latter, at its meeting on the Thursday evening to refuse to have anything to do with the projected meeting for Lloyd George on the Saturday. Two reasons were given for this decision. On the one hand the short time allowed would make it impossible to get a representative meeting. On the other hand it was decided that before any future conference with the Minister a meeting

---

[1] *The Times*, 21 December 1915. Lloyd George's visit was the result of pressure by Henderson and Brownlie. Labour Party, *Report of the Annual Conference*, 1917, pp. 106, 108.

[2] Glasgow Trades Council, *Minutes*, 22 December 1915; *The Worker*, 8 January 1916; *The Socialist*, February 1916; Gallacher, *Revolt on the Clyde*, pp. 79, 85–6; D. Lloyd George, *War Memoirs* (1938), pp. 187–8; *Mun. 2. 27*, 25 December 1915; *The Herald*, 1 January 1916. The date of Lloyd George's visit to the factories is the 24th, as shown by the official report, not the 23rd as given by *The Herald* and Gallacher.

of trade union officials and shop stewards should be convened to formulate a policy on dilution. In the ensuing flap, while Henderson vainly tried to get the officials to rescind their decision, the CWC managed to get the tickets for the meeting from Sam Bunton, the local district secretary of the ASE. Bunton was trying to help Lloyd George, and failed to understand that the last thing the Minister wanted was a meeting controlled by the CWC. On the morning of Friday, December 24th, the news reached Lloyd George that the CWC had control of the meeting. He gave way at once and arranged to meet the CWC leaders that evening. Having successfully forced Lloyd George to climb down, the CWC leaders took the opportunity to present him with their dilution policy in its entirety. In reply, the Minister contented himself with: 'It would be a revolution, and you can't carry through a revolution in the midst of war.' But he did agree to allow Muir to make a statement at the next day's meeting.[1]

These were the origins of the celebrated meeting in the St Andrew's Hall on Christmas Day, 1915. The meeting served as an important morale-booster for the CWC: 'Seldom has a prominent politician, a leading representative of the Governing Class, been treated with so little respect by a meeting of the workers. It is evident that the feeling of servility towards their masters no longer holds first place in the minds of the Clyde workers. . . .'[2] About 3,000 delegates attended, and gave Lloyd George a noisy reception, particularly towards the end when it became apparent that Muir was not going to be given time to speak.[3] The meeting was given exaggerated importance by the Government's ill-conceived and badly managed attempt to censor reporting of it. The press was excluded from the meeting and a misleading official statement issued. *Forward*, which carried a detailed report of the meeting and of Lloyd George's speech, was suppressed.[4] Ironically it was money collected from the authorities in expenses for delegates who attended the St Andrews Hall meeting that enabled the CWC to launch its own paper.

[1] *The Worker*, 8 January 1916; *The Socialist*, February 1916; Gallacher, *Revolt on the Clyde*, pp. 79, 81–97.

[2] *Vanguard* supressed issue in *Mun. 5. 70*.

[3] Kendall, *The Revolutionary Movement in Britain*, p. 122 suggests that the disruption was entirely the work of John Maclean and his comrades, and that the SLP did its best to quiet the meeting down. In light of the explanation given above this seems at best a half-truth.

[4] Brotherstone, 'The Suppression of the *Forward*', gives a full account of this.

The first issue of *The Worker* appeared just in time to publish the story for which *Forward* had been suppressed.[1]

Having demonstrated their contempt for Lloyd George and the Government the CWC was left with a deep sense of foreboding. Already it was clear that the dilution policy was a non-starter so far as the Government was concerned. In that case the Government was bound to go on to the offensive. 'Every effort will be made to crush us', warned Gallacher. The shape of the offensive soon, so the CWC leaders thought, made itself clear. On January 5th, after weeks of rumour, Asquith introduced the first Military Service Bill in the Commons. Gallacher saw this as the direct result of Lloyd George's humiliation on the Clyde.[2] Persuasion had failed; conscription was the big stick. There was widespread agreement on the Clyde (and elsewhere) that the introduction of conscription was not dictated by immediate military necessity, but rather by the need for 'the military control of industry and consequently the abolition of the functions of our trade unions'.[3]

The concern of the CWC with the issue of conscription possibly explains how, in the first week of January, the first prosecution of a group of Glasgow munitions workers for striking was carried through without any attempt to organize sympathetic action on a large scale. Forty men from the gun-mounting shop at Dalmuir were prosecuted for their part in a stay-in-strike at the end of December after their shop steward had been sacked in connection with a dispute over the arrangements made for delegates to attend the St Andrew's Hall meeting on the 25th. The authorities feared trouble. The Chief Constable, fearing widespread strike action if the verdict went against the men, enquired as to how soon he could get a large body of military reinforcements if they were needed to 'overcome the mob at once and completely get them in hand'. The local intelligence officer kept his finger on the pulse: 'Gallacher, one of the biggest agitators from Paisley, was up at the trial making a great row . . .'

---

[1] Gallacher, *Revolt on the Clyde*, pp. 99–100. The circulation of *The Worker* increased from 9,000 to 15,000 before it was in turn suppressed at the beginning of February: *Daily Record and Mail*, 14 April 1916.

[2] *The Worker*, 8 January 1916; *The Socialist*, January 1916; *Mun.* 5. 70, BSP leaflet, 'Clyde Workers' Beware' (? December 1915).

[3] CWC resolution, quoted in Gallacher, *Revolt on the Clyde*, p. 116. See also Glasgow Trades Council, *Minutes*, 3 January 1916; *Mun.* 5. 70, BSP leaflet *cit.*

But, in the event, the steward was shown to have been in the wrong – he had sworn at the management – and the convictions were accepted with no further protest.[1] One SLP militant writing in retrospect saw this as 'the test case . . . the first real challenge by the employers to the shop steward system'. In his opinion the result of inaction was disastrous. 'The Dalmuir case was allowed to pass unchallenged, although the men on the Clyde were waiting for a lead to smash the now hated Munitions Act. The psychological moment had come, the CWC had failed to give a lead, and the employers recorded another victory.'[2] Whatever the explanation of the Committee's inactivity – is it possible that the obscenity with which the Dalmuir worker had defended his rights *did* make it difficult to fight for him? – the fatally narrowing effects of Muir's dilution policy, and the Committee's 'refusal to fight for anything less than this', became very clear in the struggle over conscription during January 1916.

The December issue of *Vanguard*, dealing with 'The Conscription Menace', had called on the workers to use the political strike to prevent conscription. 'The only weapon we can use today is the strike. We urge our comrades to be ready to use that weapon to prevent the coming of absolute chattel slavery.' At first it seemed that this policy had been fully endorsed by the Committee. 'Workers of the Clyde', wrote Gallacher in the first issue of *The Worker*, 'you must prepare for action. When this loathsome enemy of Freedom raises its head you must *strike* and *strike* to kill.' To 'drive from office the gang of incompetent, blundering, reactionary lawyer-politicians, who are being lashed into action by Northcliffe and his yellow Press', alliances with other sections of the workers would be needed, and the CWC was well aware of this. Gallacher spoke of alliances with the Tyneside engineers, the miners and the railwaymen. MacManus went to Derby, others to Merseyside, Tyneside and Woolwich. At the end of January a detailed plan of campaign for an alliance with the miners of Lanarkshire and Fifeshire was outlined in *The Worker*.[3] But nothing came of these efforts. All that was

[1] *Glasgow Herald*, 6 and 10 January 1916; *Mun.* 5. 70, 'Notes from the Intelligence Officer in Glasgow'. The Government did not push its luck. When the men failed to pay their fines, no attempt was made to collect them. *The Herald*, 22 January 1916.

[2] *Trade Unionist*, October 1916, 'Reminiscences of the Clyde Struggle', by D. Morton. J. T. Murphy also took this line: *Preparing for Power*, p. 121.

[3] *The Worker*, 8 and 29 January 1916. Gallacher claimed later that 'Early in January, 1916, Bruce Glasier came to Glasgow and had a meeting . . . with

achieved by way of mounting joint action against conscription was a large demonstration on Glasgow Green which the CWC organized jointly with the local Trades Council, the ILP and other political groups. There the action finished. The Trades Council would have nothing to do with strike action.[1]

In the fight against conscription the CWC had a chance to broaden its base among the Clydeside workers. Well aware of the need to do this, it nevertheless failed. Underlying this failure was the continuing commitment of the CWC to Muir's dilution policy. Two quite distinct elements appeared in the CWC propaganda against conscription. On the one hand, it talked of a last-ditch struggle in defence of democracy: 'The whole British constitution is in the melting pot . . . The next few weeks may decide the fate of democracy.' On the other hand the struggle was seen exclusively in terms of the dilution policy. At Christmas, Muir had told Lloyd George that if his policy were adopted, 'the coming fight on conscription would be avoided, because conscription would be absolutely unnecessary'. Conscription was seen purely as a weapon which the Government would use to tighten its control over the workshops, for the specific purpose of imposing dilution. Hence a policy designed to meet the threat of dilution, and argued out and popularized in terms of that threat, was simply switched to meet the conscription threat. The relevance of the CWC's proposals continued, therefore, to be limited to the skilled engineers in the munitions works who alone were faced with the threat of dilution. The nearest thing the CWC had to an ally in the industrial field, the Glasgow Trades Council, despite its co-operation over conscription, never even debated, let alone approved, the CWC's 'only alternative to Industrial Conscription'.[2]

During 1915 a rank-and-file movement had been built on the Clyde prepared to act independently of the trade union officials. In forcing a Cabinet Minister to consult with its leaders over the heads of the trade unions the Committee had proved its ability to do so. Though narrowly based in an arms sector which accounted for no more than 20% of the skilled engineering

the leaders of the Clyde Workers' Committee. He begged us to do something to stop conscription.' *Revolt on the Clyde*, p. 115.

[1] Glasgow Trades Council, *Minutes*, 3, 19 January, 9 February 1916; *The Herald*, 20 November, 22 January 1916. In December 1915 the Workers' Union in Glasgow was reported to have threatened strike action if conscription was introduced: *Trade Unionist*, December 1915.

[2] *The Worker*, 8, 15, 29 January 1916.

workers in Glasgow, the movement had been persuaded by the revolutionaries who led it to issue a quasi-revolutionary challenge to the Government over dilution and conscription. Moreover it had done so in such a way as to make the establishment of any wider class unity in the struggle over conscription even more difficult than it need have been. The Government did not fail to respond to the challenge, and when it did so it was able to exploit the weaknesses of the Committee to devastating effect.

Chapter 4

The Clyde Workers' Committee: the Dilution Struggle

The launching of the Government offensive to force through dilution was made public in a statement by Asquith on 21 January 1916. He referred to the delays that had occurred in effecting dilution under the Munitions Act and announced the Government's intention of pushing ahead with dilution without permitting any further delay 'on any ground whatever'.[1] To give effect to this special Commissioners were to be despatched at once to the most important districts. On January 24th three Dilution Commissioners arrived on the Clyde, and from that day the CWCs stand on dilution began to disintegrate. The first priority of the Government was to break through the purely craft resistance to dilution typified by the workers at Lang's, Johnstone, and by the ASE Executive. Nevertheless the undermining and subsequent destruction of the Committee was by no means merely an incidental effect of the Government's dilution campaign. The aim of destroying the CWC had been clearly understood in advance, and the methods to be used prepared in broad outline. The CWC was recognized as a danger to the war effort and to the maintenance of social order quite independently of its desire or capacity to obstruct dilution. It was, in fact, only after dilution was well under way on the Clyde, and conservative craft resistance had been effectively broken, that the authorities mounted their premediated offensive against the Committee itself.

The first mention of the CWC in the Government papers on 24 November 1915 was unequivocal: 'To obtain a reasonably smooth working of the Munitions Act, this committee should be

[1] HC Debates, 5s., vol. 78, cols. 765–6.

smashed.'[1] On November 30th Beveridge, at the Ministry of Munitions, advised that the signatories to the CWC's first leaflet, Gallacher and Messer, be prosecuted under DORA. However, Lloyd George's decision to visit the Clyde altered the situation, and the idea was dropped. The problem remained.[2]

By January the Clyde situation had sorted itself out into two major problems. On the one hand there was the urgent need to speed up the advance of dilution. It seemed unlikely that this could be achieved without provoking a large strike. On the other hand something had to be done about the CWC, preferably the removal of the leaders from the area under DORA. But this also seemed likely to provoke a big strike.[3] One big strike was preferable to two. In a letter to the Ministry of Munitions on January 17th, Paterson, the labour officer on the Clyde, outlined the position. After listing 'the gentlemen whose removal from the Clyde district for an indefinite period would go a long way towards helping production', he continued:

'I am afraid that the removal of almost anyone of these men . . . would at once cause a big strike.

'When a strike takes place, it is desirable that the Government should have the best case possible to present to the public. Ultimately it will be forced to give some reasons for the removal of these men, and it would then have to be disclosed that action had been taken on general statements, unsupported by real evidence of a convincing nature.

'A very much cleaner [sic] issue would be a strike against the enforcement of the dilution of labour, as the Government there would be in the position of asking the skilled men of the country to allow their skill to be used to best advantage, and the public opinion would be overwhelmingly against the men.

'If, therefore, definite orders for the dilution of labour are to be given, I think it would be better to delay consideration of the question of removing any men out of the district.'[4]

[1] *Bev.* iii, p. 94, Barttelot to Third Sea Lord, 24 November 1916.
[2] *Ibid.*, pp. 96–104, various notes on the CWC leaflet.
[3] *Ibid.*, p. 224, memorandum by J. B. Adams, 15 January 1916; *Mun.* 5. 70, 'Notes on the Suppression of *Forward*', by Beveridge, 6 January 1916, and 'Notes from the Intelligence Officer in Glasgow', (n.d.); *Mun.* 5. 73, 'Memorandum on the Clyde and Tyne', by Macassey, 18 December 1915.
[4] *Bev.* iii, p. 111. The men listed by Paterson were Kirkwood, Gallacher, Messer, Muir, MacManus and Clark. John Maclean and Peter Petroff were also mentioned. Within three months every one of these men had been imprisoned or deported from the area.

The Ministry was indeed preparing to give definite orders for dilution, and it anticipated truble. To meet this a detailed scheme for introducing dilution and contingency plans to deal with strike action were to be prepared. Preparation was seen as all important: 'Plans must be laid very carefully as to the whole procedure in order that the thing may be carried out on well thought out lines, quickly and firmly, so as to give no time for opposition to be engineered.'[1] The job was given to William Weir, Director of Munitions for Scotland and part-owner of Weir's of Cathcart. The choice of Weir was significant. He had long been the leading exponent within the Ministry of the 'hard' line. While the Munitions Act was being prepared, he had vociferously backed in-industrial conscription, arguing that the Government should act with 'the arbitrary justice appropriate to wartime', taking over from management when the workers got out of control, and placing works under military law if necessary. In August 1915 he was made Director of Munitions for Scotland. In the same month Lloyd George had pledged to the employers that if the trade unions threatened a strike against dilution, 'the whole influence of the Government must be brought to bear upon it'. During the ensuing months, as the Lang's case dragged on, Weir tried to hold the Minister to his word. Exasperated by difficulties over dilution at his own works in Cathcart, Weir was spoiling for a fight. In October he had written to Addison accusing the Ministry of 'want of sincerity'. 'Every delayed decision of the nature I give shows to the working man that the State – or rather its leaders and advisers – are not in earnest. The effect of this is unrest and ferment in the shops . . .' In December, before Lloyd George visited the Clyde, Weir submitted another memorandum, reiterating his previous arguments. He pointed out that from the beginning of the war the Government had negotiated and compromised with the trade unions. 'The fallacy was the belief that bargaining was necessary . . . the bargaining spirit becomes rife. The actual position was that the men would have loyally done whatever the country required of them, if the position had been clearly put to them, as they have done as soldiers.'[2] By January, support for the tough line was general. On January 15th a

---

[1] *Bev* iii, p. 222, letter from Rey to Lloyd George, 18 January 1916.
[2] *Glasgow Herald*, 21 May 1915; W. J. Reader, *Architect of Air Power, William Weir, 1877–1959* (1968), pp. 39–45; *MM* ii, 2, pp. 131–2; *Mun.* 5. 73, 'Memorandum on Dilution of Labour', by Weir (n.d.).

memorandum approved by representatives of both Vickers and Armstrong-Whitworth argued:

'It is my view, and I have suggested it to others in the industry, and it is backed by the biggest employers who are having trouble in this connection, that dilution in cases where there is obstruction should be taken out of the hands of the employers altogether and that it should be done by the Ministry. I mean to say that employers should be relieved of all responsibility in this matter and that the Ministry should accept it and all that it involves.'[1]

Weir was the man for the job.

The scheme Weir prepared and submitted to Lloyd George on January 18th was the basis for the scheme that was finally adopted after a week of intensive discussion involving several Ministries.[2] Three Commissioners were to be sent both to the Clyde and the Tyne, where they would check that the dilution schemes already prepared by leading munitions firms were suitable. Having done this, the Commissioners would arrange to meet the shop stewards' committee, together with management, at the firm in question. The workers would be informed of the scheme and given two days in which to consult with the management further on the scheme, though any refusal to acquiesce in dilution at all would be ignored.[3] On the third day, whatever issues had been raised in consultation, the scheme in its final form would be carried into force.

In the event of a strike the immediate reaction would be to provide 'police and military protection to all who are willing to work' to make sure, if necessary by injunction, that trade union funds were not used to support the strikers; and to 'deport and bring to trial under DOR Regulations any persons inciting to strike'.[4] Further measures would depend on the size of the

---

[1] *Bev.* iii, pp. 267–8, memorandum by J. B. Adams, 15 January 1916.

[2] C. Addison, *Four and a Half Years* (1934), pp. 161–3; *MM* ii, 2, p. 134; *Bev.* iii, pp. 167–8, 'Summary of Dilution Programme as based (with modifications) on Mr. Weir's memorandum', 22 January 1916. Except where otherwise stated the following section is based on this document.

[3] Weir's original memorandum also provided that 'A shorthand writer should be in attendance and any expression of open resistance or obstruction on the part of any individual should be carefully noted with the name of the man concerned.' In the event of a strike these men were to be the first to be arrested. *Bev.* iii, p. 231.

[4] This quotation is taken from a handwritten outline of the scheme by Sir Hubert Lewellyn Smith, permanent secretary of the Ministry: *Bev.* iii, p. 218.

strike. The strikers themselves (as distinct from their leaders who would already have been deported from the area) could only be prosecuted if the strike were a small one. A large strike would 'have to be left to take its own course',[1] though, once it started to weaken, 'the process can then be hastened by prosecuting those who hold out'. Finally the condition of withholding the use of the Munitions Act in such a case was that there should be 'no parleying or negotiation with the strikers, either directly or through the Labour Advisory Committee'.[2]

On the 20th Lloyd George told a friend, Lord Riddell, that he expected serious trouble. 'He intends to take a firm line and would rather have a six weeks' strike now than later on.'[3] To put this programme into effect three Dilution Commissioners were despatched to the Clyde on 24 January 1916. The Commission was chaired by Lynden Macassey, K C, who had been a member of the Commission of Enquiry in the autumn, and who was an experienced industrial arbitrator. The other two members were Isaac Mitchell, who had risen from the shop floor via the secretary-ship of the General Federation of Trade Unions to become an Assistant Industrial Commissioner at the Board of Trade, and Sir Thomas Munro, county clerk of Lanarkshire and a figure of local weight and influence.

The most carefully planned operation is bound to need adjustments when put into action. The first stumbling block encountered by the Commissioners when they arrived on the Clyde was the attitude of the employers. Before Lloyd George's visit Weir and the local Engineering Employers' Association had been at pains to point out that, due to the Government's vacillation, 'the interest in dilution has largely evaporated so far as the employers are concerned'.[4] Now that the Government was prepared to be tough it was assumed that the employers 'were both ready and able forthwith to accept dilution'.[5] They were

[1] This was in conformity with the view put forward by Beveridge in his 'Notes on the Suppression of *Forward*' of 6 January 1916, *Mun.* 5. 70.

[2] Lewellyn Smith, *Bev.* iii, p. 218. Weir had proposed immediate prosecution however large the strike, and the repeal of the Trades Dispute Act if any attempt were made to spread it sympathetically. The scheme eventually adopted moderated his proposals on these and other points. They did not weaken their central repressive intention.

[3] Lord Riddle, *War Diary* (1933), pp. 150–1. This is confirmed in *Cab.* 23. 7, 24 July 1918.

[4] *Mun.* 5. 73, 'memorandum on Dilution of Labour', by Patterson, 18 December 1915.

[5] *Bev.* v, p. 14, memorandum by Macassey, 5 February 1916.

not. Most of the firms which had schemes prepared, had omitted to make the necessary provisions for starting women workers – separate lavatory and mess facilities, forewomen, etc. More important, the majority of employers were still unprepared to accept dilution. This was not, now, because they feared trouble from the men, Rather, having as yet little faith in the value of women workers, they were reluctant to lose scarce skilled labour to other firms. (The transfer of skilled labour to those shops where it was most essential was a stated aim of dilution.)[1]

It was immediately clear to the Commissioners that any precipitate forcing through of dilution, as laid down in their instructions, would at once provoke 'a more or less general strike on the Clyde against the *principle* of dilution'. A general strike could not be fought out to a satisfactory conclusion so long as the employers were in two minds about dilution. It was therefore decided that in order both to convince the employers of the value of dilution, and to break up the 'rigid opposition' to dilution among the men: 'our right procedure was to convert and persuade the men in say half-a-dozen of the principal establishments to the principle of dilution, then arrange a scheme for each establishment thoroughly effective and efficient in all its details, get it started and from time to time thereafter fix and adjust the minor inequalities that emerge . . .' Problems about the detail of wages 'arise very quickly and acutely within a few days after the scheme's commencement and if not immediately disposed of may lead in one hour to a strike'. 'To avoid that', Macassey went on, 'I have made it a condition of each scheme that a Joint Shop Committee be formed of Employers and Shop Stewards to discuss and adjust any difficulties in regard to the working out of dilution.'[2] This policy met with rapid success. Within a week dilution schemes were in operation at Parkhead and Weir's. During the second week Dalmuir and Yarrows followed. For the first month or so the Commissioners main foothold was Parkhead, where 338 women and 268 men – nearly half the total dilutees on the Clyde – had been started by the end of February. The next largest inroads were Dalmuir (237), Weir (108), and Halley's Industrial Motors (105).[3] During the next six months

---

[1] *Bev.* iii, pp. 14–15; *MM* IV, 4, p. 91; *Bev.* iii, p. 357, 'The Clyde Position', by I. H. Mitchell, 21 February 1916.

[2] *Ibid.*, p. 357; *Bev.* v, pp. 14–15, memorandum by Macassey, 5 February 1916.

[3] Addison, *Four and a Half Years*, pp. 163–8; Labour Party, *Report of the*

the pace of dilution remained fairly steady, though the proportion of women introduced increased. By August 1916, 10,021 dilutees had been introduced, 9,000 of them women. The great majority were on general engineering work in the munitions firms and the marine engineering departments of the shipyards. 7,436 skilled engineering workers on the Clyde had been transferred to new jobs as a result of dilution by August.[1] This was a major industrial upheaval.

Success in getting dilution under way, however, by no means changed the Commissioners' intention of smashing the CWC. The confrontation had merely been postponed. On February 9th, for example, Macassey was writing: 'I have for some days been convinced that the only way to handle the situation is to strike a sharp line of cleavage' between loyal workers and the CWC hard core.[2] Munro agreed with this perspective. The other Commissioner, Issac Mitchell believed at this time that it would be better to concentrate the attack on the more conservative workers. But he was equally concerned to 'split the men into sections.'[3] Two opportunities arose for the Commissioners to put into effect the repressive policy outlined in their instructions, during their first weeks on the Clyde. The first, the strike against dilution at Lang's (Johnstone), was unsuitable both because at that time (February 2nd–7th) the policy of conciliation was working well in the main Glasgow firms, and because the dispute was essentially one between the ASE Executive and the Government. To escalate the strike by deporting its leaders would be unlikely to provoke the CWC out on to the necessary limb. The Committee had little influence at Lang's, a machine-tool works at Johnstone, seven miles west of Glasgow, and was uneasy about the narrow craft outlook revealed by the strike.[4] Direct repressive measures against the Clyde Workers' Committee seemed more likely to precipitate the crisis.

Already, on January 1st, *Forward* and John Maclean's paper

Special Committee . . . to inquire into . . . the Deportations . . . (1917), p. 10; *Bev.* v, pp. 17–18, memorandum by Macassey, 5 February 1916; *Mun.* 5. 73, 'Dilution on the Clyde', 1 March 1916. By this date, 1,337 dilutees had been introduced in 10 factories. Negotiations were under way for the introduction of a further 886 dilutees in 30 factories.

[1] *Mun.* 2. 27, 29 April, 5 August 1916.

[2] *Mun.* 5. 73, memorandum on the 'Industrial Situation on the Clyde', 9 February 1916.

[3] *Bev.* iii, p. 357, 'The Clyde Position', 21 February 1916.

[4] *Bev.* v, p. 18, memorandum by Macassey, 5 February 1916; *Bev.* iii, 355–8, 'The Clyde Position', by I. H. Mitchell, 21 February 1916. Mitchell wanted to escalate this strike but was overruled by the other commissioners.

Vanguard had been suppressed, possibly in order 'to warn the troublemakers on the Clyde that the government's tolerance was at an end'.[1] 'Halls let for meetings have been cancelled by the score, and even where meetings have been held, summonses against the speakers have been issued and fines imposed.'[2] Leading members of the Committee complained of being constantly followed by detectives.[3] Once the Committee's stand on dilution had been broken, and agreements were being successfully pushed through in the major Clydeside factories, repression was stepped up. On February 2nd the police raided the Socialist Labour Press, broke up the machinery, and suppressed the forthcoming (fifth) issue of *The Worker*. There was no immediate strike, so the authorities had time to consider whether to follow up the suppression with the arrest of those most closely involved in the production of the paper. On the evening of Monday, February 7th, Gallacher, Muir and Walter Bell, the printer, were arrested. The next day they were charged under DORA and refused bail. John Maclean was arrested on the same day.[4]

This new offensive provoked an immediate and massive response. Within eighteen hours strikes had broken out at Weir, Albion, Barr & Stroud, Coventry Ordnance Works and Dalmuir. Up to 10,000 workers downed tools.[5] Under this pressure the court changed its mind about bail and the Committee's leaders (though not John Maclean) were released on the morning of February 9th. At this point Macassey saw his opportunity to 'strike a sharp line of cleavage'. By the morning of the 9th some of the workers

[1] T. Brotherstone, 'The Suppression of the *Forward*', *Bulletin of the Scottish Society for the Study of Labour History*, no. 1, May 1969, p. 16. But see also I. S. McLean, 'The Labour Movement in Clydeside Politics, 1914–24' (Oxford D.Phil., 1971), ch. 5.

[2] *The Plebs*, March 1916.

[3] *The Herald*, 26 February 1916. Compare Weir's original scheme, which provided for 'a careful watch by detectives on the actions of members of the CWC, and a few others specified on a private list [Scotland Yard men] . . .': Bev. iii, p. 232.

[4] *Mun.* 5. 73, report from Rey, 7 February 1916; *Glasgow Herald*, 4, 8 and 9 February 1916. Technically *The Worker* was suppressed because of an article entitled 'Should the Workers Arm?' That the authorities were not greatly concerned with technicalities is clear from the fact that the article in question firmly opposed insurrection and argued for peaceful Industrial Unionism.

[5] *Mun.* 2. 27, 12 January 1916; *Mun.* 5. 73, memorandum by Macassey, 9 February 1916; *The Plebs*, March 1916; ASE, *Executive Minutes*, vol. 195, 9 February 1916. It is possible that partial stoppages also occurred in some other factories: *The Herald*, 19 February 1916.

were returning, and more were expected to go back on the 10th. Those that remained out, demanding the unconditional release of the arrested men, could be assumed to be the hard core of the trouble makers. The deportation of the agitators would catch the Committee disunited and enable the Government to break it up without further trouble[1] At the last moment, however, the hunter was deprived of his prey. The leadership, seeing the weakness of the strike, called it off, and, at some cost to their own prestige, persuaded the more obdurate strikers to return to work.[2] For the time being the Committee survived, though its paper was gone and the threat of a long prison sentence hung over the heads of Gallacher and Muir. Within two months the Commissioners had returned to the offensive and successfully smashed the Clyde Workers' Committee.

Before *The Worker* case arose the Committee had already suffered a major defeat over dilution. When the Commissioners arrived the CWC's first reaction had been to attempt to force them to negotiate centrally by mounting a policy of non-co-operation at factory level. This was an instantaneous failure, since their first visit on January 24th was to Parkhead, where Kirkwood agreed to meet them. Parkhead had always been a weak link in the CWC chain. At Christmas Kirkwood had nearly sabotaged the attempt to force Lloyd George to meet the Committee by agreeing to meet him separately at Parkhead. Later, in *The Worker* strike, Parkhead failed to come out. When Kirkwood met the Commissioners and they made it plain that he had forty-eighty hours in which to formulate his conditions for the introduction of dilution, it was not to the CWC leaders that he turned for help, but to John Wheatley.[3] The unreliability of Parkhead as a CWC base was rooted in the peculiar combination of militancy and paternalism which characterized workshop organization as it had developed at Parkhead.

Beardmore's Parkhead Forge was a family firm with strong paternalistic traditions. Its mushroom growth since the 1880s had

1 *Mun.* 5. 73, memorandum by Macassey, 9 February 1916. The final sections of this document are missing from the PRO, but the drift of the argument is clear, and is fully collaborated in Mitchell's report of February 21st.

2 *The Herald,* 19 February 1916; *Forward,* 19 February 1916; *Trade Unionist,* October 1916; J. T. Murphy, *Preparing for Power* (1934), pp. 121–2.

3 W. Gallacher, *Revolt on the Clyde* (1936), pp. 102–3; Labour Party, *Report of the Special Committee . . .,* p. 9; D. Kirkwood, *My Life of Revolt* 1935), pp. 115–18.

undermined 'the old patriarchal conditions' – the crucial events in this being the expansion into gun work in 1909, when, for the first time, the firm took on a large contingent of skilled engineers.[1] By 1914 the ASE and AST were the two largest unions in the works. Under Kirkwood's leadership the Parkhead engineers built up strong workshop organization in the years before the war. By 1914 they were strong enough to enforce a closed shop. The Beardmore paternalism, previously anti-union, asserted itself in a refusal to permit the local ASE delegate to be party to this agreement. Sir William Beardmore intended to maintain a direct relationship with 'his own' engineers, without any interference from 'outside'.[2]

Kirkwood was peculiarly fitted to lead the shop stewards in Parkhead. He was an older man than the other shop steward leaders on the Clyde and his motivation was far more than of a labour aristocrat than of a revolutionary socialist. He was also a born snob, as the stories of his great pride in his association with Sir William indicate.[3] The peculiar dependence of workshop organization at Parkhead on the personal relationship between Kirkwood and Beardmore is best revealed in Kirkwood's own words:

'I had the free run of the works. If a man got into trouble with his foreman, he would come to me and I would see the foreman. If a foreman got into trouble with his manager, he would come to me and I would see the manager. If a manager got into trouble with the firm, he would come to me and I would go to Sir William. I suppose that no other man had held quite such a peculiar position in any great works as I had at the end of 1915.'[4]

Kirkwood, writing in 1935, no doubt exaggerates; but the exaggeration is true to form and there is ample evidence to suggest that he held this same inflated opinion of his own importance at the time. This dependence of workshop organization at Parkhead on the Beardmore-Kirkwood relationship tended to cut the

[1] T. Bell, *Pioneering Days* (1941), p. 29; Kirkwood, *My Life of Revolt*, pp. 78–9; ASE, *Monthly Journal and Report*, July 1917; Glasgow Chamber of Commerce, *Handbook* (1914), p. 153.

[2] ASE, *Quarterly Report*, June 1915, Kirkwood's election address; *MM* IV, 2, pp. 39–40; Labour Party, *Report of the Special Committee . . .*, pp. 7, 11, 12, 17; *Forward*, 21 August 1915.

[3] Bell, *Pioneering Days*, p. 98; R. K. Middlemass, *The Clydesiders* (1965), p. 74; interview with Mr H. McShane.

[4] Kirkwood, *My Life of Revolt*, p. 100.

workers off, not only from the local officials but also from the rank-and-file movement. The organization at Parkhead would not submit to outside discipline from whatever source.

In agreeing to meet the Commissioners Parkhead broke the front – as it had done in agreeing to meet Lloyd George at Christmas. In so doing it precipitated the collapse, factory by factory, of the CWC's position on dilution. The CWC leadership was thrown into confusion by the débâcle. While all their attention had been focused on the threat of conscription, the offensive had suddenly materialized from an unexpected quarter. The SLP policy had been too craft-oriented to lay the strategic foundations for a revolutionary movement; too revolutionary to serve as the tactical response of a craft movement to dilution.

It was not only John Maclean and his group who had declined to accept Muir's dilution policy. Although they made less noise about it, this was also true of Kirkwood and his allies in the ILP. For this section the argument for workers' participation revolved solely around the need for the skilled workers to have a say in the introduction of dilution if a flood of cheap labour was to be avoided.[1] The demand for nationalization had, from the start, left them cold. It is this attitude that explains the position of leadership in the rank-and-file movement gained by Kirkwood and John Wheatley for a couple of weeks at the end of January 1916.[2]

While the CWC leadership was forced to recognize the failure of Muir's dilution policy, Kirkwood and the ILP section remained unalarmed. The Commissioners' recognition of workshop organization to negotiate grievances arising out of dilution appeared

[1] *Forward*, 1 January, 5 February 1916; Kirkwood, *My Life of Revolt* p. 118; Labour Party, *Report of the Special Committee . . .*, p. 17.

[2] The role of Kirkwood and his mentor Wheatley in the CWC has been overestimated both by Marwick in *The Deluge* (1967), pp. 75–8, and by R. K. Middlemass in *The Clydesiders* (1965), pp. 66–7. Both Gallacher, *Revolt on the Clyde*, pp. 126–7, and Bell, *Pioneering Days*, p. 98, testify that Wheatley's undoubted influence over Kirkwood (see for example, Kirkwood's *My Life of Revolt*, p. 82) was used to draw him away from the CWC leadership. It is true that Wheatley did retain sufficient influence with Gallacher and Muir for them to pay attention to his views during the deportation crisis (Gallacher, *op. cit.*, p. 107) but Marwick's claim that he was 'the political genius in the background' is certainly unfounded. Middlemass is probably a great deal nearer the truth in his assertion that Wheatley used his influence to 'undo the extremists' (*op. cit.*, pp. 68, 72). The present writer is, however, unaware of any materials that could shed adequate light on Wheatley's motives.

as a victory for their policy. This is what they had meant all along by workers' control. The Parkhead agreement, written, at Kirkwood's request, by Wheatley, was welcomed by Patrick Dollan, the industrial correspondent of *Forward*, as admitting 'the principle of control by the workers for the first time in an industrial agreement'.[1]

From the standpoint of the SLP leadership of the Clyde Workers' Committee the Parkhead agreement represented a resounding defeat for 'the principle of workers control'. It involved the abandonment of their dilution policy, the collapse of the Committee's attempt to force the Commissioners to recognize and negotiate with the Committee as a whole, and it engendered a bitterness against Parkhead in the other major strongholds of militancy that was to be instrumental in the defeat of the movement two months later. The original Parkhead agreement was badly formulated and had to be rapidly revised. Nevertheless the Kirkwood-Wheatley initiative marked a crucial phase in the development of the characteristic strategy of the shop stewards' movement.[2] While, for the time being, it undercut the revolutionary implications of that strategy, in the long term, after the defeat on the Clyde the principles established at Parkhead helped to clear the ground for the development of revolutionary politics in the national shop stewards' movement on a far more realistic basis than that provided by John Muir's dilution policy.

The preamble of the Parkhead agreement accepted the need to obtain increased output through dilution, as Muir had done, and asserted that the only concern of the workers was to prevent the introduction of cheap labour 'under the cloak of patriotism'. In an attempt to secure this the most important clause of the agreement laid down: 'That the income of the new class of labour be fixed, not on the sex, previous training or experience of the worker but upon the amount of work performed, based on the rates presently obtaining for the particular operation.' 'The amount of work performed' was not a concept which could easily be applied to timework, however, so the agreement had the major weakness of applying only to pieceworkers, and going, therefore, no further than the regulation already accepted by the Government.[3] This problem was solved during the next few days, probably after talks between the Parkhead and Weir's shop

---

[1] *The Herald*, 5 February 1916; Kirkwood, *My Life of Revolt*, pp. 115–18.
[2] See above, pp. 68–69, 74–75.
[3] Gallacher, *Revolt on the Clyde*, p. 104. See above, p. 66.

stewards. By February 2nd a new clause had been added to the Parkhead agreement, subsequently applied generally on the Clyde, to the effect that the dilutee 'should be paid after a period of probation, such a rate of wages as, with the wages paid to her necessary supervisor and the increased wages paid to the man who now solely performs the difficult portion of the operation, will make the cost of doing the work not less than it was before'. 'Dilution', wrote Macassey, 'is for the purpose of increasing output and not of reducing labour costs.'[1]

In accordance with the Commissioners' promise of consultation, the agreement also provided for the formal recognition of workshop organization, already recognized in practice at Parkhead.

'That a committee appointed by the workers be accepted by the employers, with power to see that this agreement is loyally carried out. Failing agreement between employer and the committee, the matter be referred to a final tribunal mutually agreed.' This raised greater problems than the wages clause. As a guarantee of joint consultation on the problems arising from dilution it was clear enough. But it was vague on the vital issue of the convener's right to move around the works to check how the agreement was operating, his 'powers to see'. And it neglected altogether to specify that the Committee should have any control over transfers of skilled men arising out of dilution.[2]

Within two weeks of the collapse of their previous dilution policy the Clyde Workers' Committee leadership accepted the breakaway agreement at Parkhead as a basis for the reconstruction of the Committee as an influence in the dilution negotiations. On February 12th P. J. Dollan, a leading figure in the Glasgow ILP and chief Glasgow correspondent for *The Herald*, reported: 'The Clyde Workers' Committee, acting in conjunction with the shop stewards, have evolved a dilution of labour scheme applicable to the whole Clyde area, and copies of this scheme are being sent to every workshop affected by dilution.' The preamble was the same as the one Wheatley had drafted for the Parkhead agreement, and all the original Parkhead clauses were incorporated. It is not clear, however, how far the Committee as a whole had fully grasped or accepted the principle, accepted by the shop stewards at Parkhead, Weir and other factories, of permitting

[1] *Bev.* v, p. 91, memorandum by Macassey, 15 February 1916; ASE, *Monthly Journal and Report*, February 1916; *The Herald*, 5 February 1916.
[2] Gallacher, *Revolt on the Clyde*, pp. 103–4.

less than the full skilled rate to be paid to dilutees to allow for their inexperience, the extra supervision they required, etc. Moreover the concern displayed for safeguarding the prospects of apprentices[1] clearly reflected the continuing strength of craft motivations in the Committee.

The provision for recognition of workshop organization contained in the Parkhead agreement was reiterated in the Committee's proposals, but further clauses were added to remove its inadequacies.

'7. To ensure successful working of this Scheme it is advisable that a Committee representative of each Department be appointed in every Shop, same to be consulted on all questions of Transfer, etc.

8. In case of transfer, that no one who has been active in the interests of the men in the shop be transferred against his will.

9. (a) Everyone who enters a shop as a result of dilution *must* be organized in some Union to be decided by the Shop Committee.'

Finally the Committee insisted, as it had done prior to the Parkhead agreement, on central negotiations with the Dilution Commissioners and did its best to prevent any 'further dilution ... until this agreement is accepted'.[2] For the SLP leadership this was a rearguard action. Nevertheless it had considerable immediate success.

By the middle of February, when James Messer submitted the programme to the Commissioners and demanded negotiations, he could claim to be representing twenty-nine shops and yards on the Clyde.[3] Already, on February 9th, Macassey had reported the CWC had been

'spurred into fresh activity . . . Its tentacles are now fairly widespread and are growing . . . The outstanding feature of the position is that the Official Trade Unions in the District are in many works now wholly unable to speak for their members. Agreements arrived at between the Commissioners and the local Trade Union Officials or even the shop stewards in the

[1] Clause 12c of the scheme demanded: 'That every second diluted Unit should be an apprentice of three years standing and to receive the district rate'.

[2] *The Herald*, 19 February 1916.

[3] Labour Party, *Report of the Special Committee . . .*, pp. 15–16.

works are promptly repudiated by the members at the instigation of the emissaries of the CWC.'[1]

Two weeks later Mitchell wrote: 'The Committee initiates its own programme; lays down its own policy; submits, through the shop stewards in the various shops, their own demands, and issue, privately, their own orders, including decisions to strike, to enforce these demands.'[2]

The Commissioners had no intention of coming to terms with the Clyde Workers' Committee. From its inception the Commission had 'made it a stated matter of policy to refuse under any circumstances to recognize organizations other than the official unions'[3] This was not an easy policy to sustain. The Commissioners were well aware that their dilution campaign had to be forced through as much against the opposition of the ASE Executive as of the Clyde Workers' Committee. They were not above playing off the one against the other. Thus by the middle of March Macassey had 'inspired the ASE Executive with a real fear of what would happen to themselves if we recognized the Clyde Workers' Committee', and this threat was being used in negotiations at a national level.[4] In the event, however, the Commissioners' close relationship with the local ASE officials proved a more effective way of undermining the Executive's stand. While the ASE Executive was holding out against anything less than full skilled rates for dilutees, the Commissioners found two invaluable allies on the Clyde, William Brodie, the Organizing District Delegate of the ASE, and Sam Bunton, the Glasgow district secretary.[5] Brodie and Bunton had been in favour of meeting Lloyd George at Christmas 1915, when other officials had refused.[6] During the succeeding month they had done their best to convert the other local ASE officials to dilution. Their

[1] *Mun.* 5. 73, memorandum on the Industrial Situation on the Clyde, by Macassey, 9 February 1916.

[2] *Bev.* iii, p. 355, 'The Clyde Position', 21 February 1916.

[3] *Mun.* 2. 27, 5 August 1916.

[4] Addison, *Four and a Half Years*, pp. 182–3; Mun. 5. 73, memorandum by Macassey, 9 February 1916. The Executive, of course, was adamant in its opposition to the recognition of the unofficial committee: ASE, *Executive Minutes*, vol. 195, 9 February 1916.

[5] *Bev.* v, p. 16, memorandum by Macassey, 5 February 1916; *Bev.* iii, pp. 355–6, 'The Clyde Position', by Mitchell, 21 February 1916. According to Mitchell, the Glasgow District Committee was itself split almost 50–50 between support of Bunton and the Workers' Committee.

[6] Gallacher, *Revolt on the Clyde*, p. 83.

main concern was that dilution negotiations should not be left to management and workers in individual firms, but should take place under the centralized control of the District Committee. In effect this would mean putting the fate of the militant minority in the local movement who were threatened by dilution into the hands of the relatively passive shipbuilding workers to whom dilution was not, as yet, a pressing issue. As soon as they arrived on the Clyde, before visiting Parkhead, the Commissioners met Brodie and Bunton and formed a close alliance with them, thereby guaranteeing that the dilution negotiations would not undermine their authority.[1] This alliance survived the succeeding weeks, despite the efforts of the ASE Executive to break it.[2]

On February 26th Macassey firmly refused Messer's demand for negotiations. Both sides knew that the stage was now set for a final confrontation. Macassey and Munro expected the conflict to break out when Gallacher and Muir were convicted on *The Worker* charges. Mitchell expected it to arise from a renewed outburst at Lang's.[3] Arthur MacManus anticipated a crisis either over the dilution scheme, or over the application of the Military Service Act.[4] In fact it was trouble at Parkhead that provided the occasion for the crisis. Again, as in January, the Committee was caught by surprise.

Since the conclusion of the dilution agreement, relations at Parkhead had deteriorated. The initial cause of this was the introduction of soldiers into the shell department. More important, however, was Beardmore's sudden decision, at the end of February, to revoke the right previously granted to Kirkwood as convener of the shop stewards to move freely about the works. This right had long existed in practice, but, as we have seen, was not adequately guaranteed in the dilution agreement. On paper, therefore, Beardmore was within his rights, but no adequate reason was ever given for his sudden decision to revoke Kirkwood's power in the plant.[5] Possibly Beardmore and the Com-

[1] *Bev.* iii, pp. 302–53, Minutes of a Conference on Dilution, Glasgow, 21 January 1916; ASE, *Monthly Journal and Report*, February, March 1916; B. Drake, *Women in the Engineering Trades* (1917), pp. 130–1.

[2] *Mun.* 5. 73, Notes for Lloyd George on negotiations to be held with the ASE, 11 February 1916; Addison, *Four and a Half Years*, p. 174.

[3] *Bev.* iii, p. 355, 'The Clyde Position', 21 February 1916.

[4] *The Plebs*, March 1916.

[5] Scott and Cunnison, *The Industries of the Clyde Valley during the War* (Oxford, 1924), pp. 225–6; Labour Party, *Report of the Special Committee . . .*, pp. 11, 20, 22, 37. The revocation of Kirkwood's privileges may have been the

missioners had already decided that this was to be the attack on the CWC. After two weeks of negotiations the Parkhead engineers finally decided to strike, 1,000 of them coming out on March 17th. The Commissioners were informed, but succumbed to a strange paralysis and made no attempt to settle the dispute in its early stages. On the 21st the strike spread to the North British Diesel Engine works at Scotstoun, where the men were given gun work belonging to Parkhead, and on the 23rd to the gun shop at Dalmuir, for the same reason.[1] Late on the 23rd Macassey finally set the wheels in motion. He wired the Ministry of Munitions, recommending 'that we should deport the whole of the CWC'. Addison tried to stem the tide, but on Friday, March 24th 'after various frenzied telegrams from the Commissioners, recommending first one thing and then another, we decided that . . . we would agree to the deportation of certain leaders'.[2] The next day, a Saturday, Kirkwood and two other Parkhead stewards were arrested. Two other CWC leaders, Messer and MacManus, who worked at Weir's which was not even on strike, were also arrested, and all five deported from the area. The deportations provoked an immediate extension of the strike.

On Monday, March 27th, some of the engineers at Weir's came out, and the rest followed the next day. More men struck at Dalmuir, and the engineers at the Coventry Ordnance Works and two other firms also came out. Finally, on Wednesday, March 29th, Gallacher got the Albion workers out. Two more Parkhead stewards were deported, including Tom Clark, and three more from Weir's. Immediately the deportations started posters were put up threatening the strikers with prosecution under DORA and the Munitions Act, and promising that no action would be taken against workers who returned to work at once. On Thursday, March 30th, thirty men from three leading factories on strike were prosecuted under the Munitions Act and

result of a management revolt against the master-servant paternalism of the Beardmore/Kirkwood partnership. Kirkwood's son suggested this in an interview shortly before he died in 1970. I am grateful to Mr Iain McLean of the University of Newcastle for this information.

[1] Labour Party, *Report of the Special Committee* . . ., pp. 18–26, 43, *Glasgow Herald*, 30 March 1916. Compare the inactivity of the Commissioners on this occasion with their previous practice: 'On the mere suggestion of a strike, I am down on the spot, at all hours of the day and night.' *Bev.* v, p. 17, memorandum by Macassey, 5 February 1916.

[2] Addison, *Four and a Half Years* . . ., pp. 184–5.

fined £5 each. In the final days of the strike rumours, no doubt inspired, of the impending declaration of martial law circulated through the district.[1]

The Government used its emergency powers further to prevent any direct press reporting of the strike until March 30th, and meanwhile it put out its own version of events. On the 28th Addison made a statement on the general circumstances of the strike, in which he sought to present it as 'a systematic and sinister plan' operated by the CWC, to blackmail the Government into repealing the Munitions Act and the Military Service Act by bringing out men 'engaged upon the production of a particular heavy gun and gun-mounting for which we are receiving the most urgent demands'.[2]

The Commissioners could not have chosen a better issue on which to attack the CWC. The strike was small and partial even in the firms which did come out. At its peak (March 29th–30th) there were probably not more than 4,500 workers on strike, compared with at least 10,000 in the strike of February 1915.[3] The CWC leaders cannot have been unaware that this was the general offensive against the Committee which they had anticipated ever since Christmas 1915, but they were reluctant to resist. Within hours of the first deportations the Committee met.

'So keen was the indignation that a motion was submitted that the CWC should declare a strike in the Clyde District. The Chairman, William Gallacher, ruled this motion out of order as it was against the accepted aims of the CWC. This aim was the building of an industrial organization in the engineering industry. The members of the committee could inform their fellow workers in the shop where they worked as to what happened at the Forge, but beyond this the CWC had no jurisdiction. No further discussion about the possibility of a strike took place at the meeting.'[4]

[1] Labour Party, *Report of the Special Committee* . . ., pp. 18–19; *Mun. 5. 79*, Papers re Clyde strike, March 1916; *Glasgow Herald*, 27, 30 March, 1, 3 April 1916; *The Socialist*, April 1916.
[2] HC Debates, 5s., vol. 81, cols. 564–6. Ths fiction appears to have been dreamed up by Macassey – see L. Macassey, *Labour Policy – False and True* (1922), p. 79. It was entirely refuted by Gallacher and Muir in their statement of 30 March, *Glasgow Herald*, 30 March 1916.
[3] Labour Party, *Report of the Special Committee* . . ., p. 18; Board of Trade, *Labour Gazette*, May 1916.
[4] Quoted in Murphy, *Preparing for Power*, p. 123.

What lay behind this timidity was not, as might appear, a doctrinaire industrial pacifism, but rank-and-file hostility towards Parkhead.[1] Indeed, Gallacher and Muir issued a statement to the press on March 30th which disassociated the Committee from the Parkhead strike and emphasized that 'the shops in which the president and other officials of the Committee are employed find that dilution is working smoothly and without a hitch'.[2] The cwc had not recovered from the fragmentation caused by the collapse of its original, ill-considered policy on dilution.

The extent of this fragmentation is illustrated by the attitude of the workers at Barr & Stroud. When Muir, the convener, was arrested on *The Worker* charges on February 7th, the Barr & Stroud workers struck. Subsequently a dilution agreement was negotiated. So smoothly did this agreement work that at Muir's trial in April his managing director could testify: 'As Convenor of shop stewards he exercised his influence for the good, and his employers had every confidence in him . . . He had also done his best to carry out the scheme for the dilution of labour.'[3] Satisfied with their agreement, the Barr & Stroud workers looked with disdain and hostility on the troubles at Parkhead. Not only did they not strike in sympathy but also a large majority of them voted (according to a report in the *Glasgow Herald*) to repudiate 'the frantic effort of a small percentage of the workers to retard by strikes' the production of munitions.[4] To the extent that the workers elsewhere shared these views it is not surprising that the cwc leaders accepted defeat.

After the first wave of deportations on the 25th other shops came out. But Gallacher and Muir were now the only influential leaders who remained. Aware that they were beaten, and perhaps afraid of the repercussions of too militant a stand on the outcome of their impending trials, they accepted Wheatley's advice to go at once to London to try to save the situation by negotiations. With the help of the Fabian Research Department they contacted Addison (Lloyd George was in France) and pressed for the lifting of the deportations and the general extension of the recognition

[1] Cf. Gallacher, *Revolt on the Clyde*, p. 107: 'Parkhead had broken the front. Parkhead could take the consequences. Such was the situation we were facing.'

[2] *Glasgow Herald*, 30 March 1916.

[3] 14 April 1916. When he came out of jail nine months later, Muir was immediately reinstated at Bərr & Stroud: Gallacher, *Revolt on the Clyde*, p. 138.

[4] *Glasgow Herald*, 1 April 1916.

agreement in force at Barr & Stroud. They had some success until Lloyd George came rushing back from France and put a stop to it. 'If I had gone to see the factory committees at several of the other factories', Gallacher commented later, 'instead of trying a piece of "clever" intriguing in London, the situation might have been saved.'[1]

After Gallacher and Muir returned from London, on the 30th, no further efforts were made to extend the strike. This, in itself, revealed most clearly the isolation of the CWC from the broader labour movement on the Clyde. Friday, March 31st, saw the culmination of a wage movement involving all trades in the engineering and shipbuilding industry on the Clyde, which had been going on since November 1915. The unions had asked for a 2d an hour rise. Refused by the employers, they were also turned down by the COP, not because they had no case, but because the Government had instructed the COP to issue no general awards. Infuriated by this parody of arbitration, the local officials called a demonstration during working hours for Friday, March 31st. 5,000–10,000 workers attended, and a resolution was passed threatening strike action for the wage rise if the Government did not at once take measures to reduce food prices.[2]

Lesser grievances had led to strike action a year earlier, and the militant shop stewards had taken the lead thereby creating the basis on which the CWC was founded. Now, however, the movement was decapitated. The most powerful and militant sector of the Glasgow metal workers, the skilled engineers in the munitions works, had become in the CWC so involved in their private struggle over dilution that they had no energy to spare to give a lead in the wage movement. That movement therefore petered out in official fulminations.[3] Nor did the CWC make any attempt to develop sympathetic action in support of the dilutees when the

[1] Gallacher, *Revolt on the Clyde*, p. 111; HC Debates, 5s., vol. 81, cols. 989–1002; *Glasgow Herald*, 28, 30 March 1916; M. Cole (ed.), *Beatrice Webb's Diaries, 1912–24* (1952), p. 58; W. Gallacher, *Last Memoirs* (London, 1966), p. 85; A. J. P. Taylor (ed.), *David Lloyd George: A Diary by Frances Stevenson* (1971), p. 105.

[2] *Mun.* 5. 81, memorandum by Sir George Gibb, 21 February 1916; *Glasgow Herald*, 5, 22, 24 February, 9 March, 1 April 1916.

[3] Cf. *The Herald*, 8 April 1916: 'Perhaps some of our readers will ask why the men returned. The answer is to be found largely in the fact that the great mass of Clyde Workers are more interested in wages than in freedom. The deportations of the nine shop stewards failed to excite as much interest as was aroused by the refusal of the Committee on Production to grant an extra 2d. per hour.'

Glasgow Trades Council committed itself to supporting direct action, and the March 31st demonstration turned into a protest against the deportations.[1] The CWC had given up the struggle; it had no further action to propose.

The return started, at Weir's, on March 30th, and on Sunday, April 2nd the strike committee handed over its authority to the District Committee, the CWC. By April 4th the resumption was general, though a few of the most determined strikers stayed out till the 6th. The militant sector, isolated and defeated, abdicated its leading role in favour of a District Committee on which it was a minority, and through this to the local officials who were in cahoots with the Commissioners' plans to smash the rank-and-file movement. On April 14th a further batch of strikers were prosecuted for their part in the strike and fined from £5 to £25 each. The same day, in Edinburgh, Gallacher and Muir were sentenced to a year in jail on *The Worker* charges.[2] They were released, with remission, in February 1917, but the ten deportees did not get back to Glasgow until the summer of 1917. It was eighteen months before the shop stewards' movement was re-established on the Clyde.

Previously accepted accounts of the Government's activity on the Clyde during the early months of 1916 have greatly exaggerated the conciliatory aspect of the dilution campaign.[3] Conciliation there was, as for example in the Commissioners' willingness to recognize workshop organization for the purpose of negotiating dilution agreements; but the repressive aim of smashing the Clyde Workers' Committee was always present in the authorities' intentions.[4] An examination of the official papers leaves little reason to doubt the accuracy of William Weir's evaluation of the Government's role: 'It was obvious that no

[1] Glasgow Trades Council, *Minutes*, 29 March 1916; *Glasgow Herald*, 1 April 1916. James Maxton and James MacDougall were both arrested and subsequently imprisoned for urging down-tools action at this rally.

[2] Addison, *Four and a Half Years*, p. 188; *Glasgow Herald*, 1, 3, 4, 6, 14 April 1916; Labour Party, *Report of the Special Committee . . .*, p. 18.

[3] See for example, G. D. H. Cole, *Workshop Organisation* (Oxford, 1923), p. 50.

[4] Some were more conciliatory than others. Christopher Addison, for example, was always a moderate, and was far from happy at his own implication in the proceedings: 'I can assure you', he told Brownlie a month afterwards, 'that it was just as objectionable to me as it was to you; we disliked it intensely. I do not think myself that I have been associated with anything I hated doing more'. *Mun.* 5. 57, Minutes of a conference with the ASE, 27 April 1916.

substantial degree of dilution could take place without involving some repressive action . . . This was foreseen in the approved scheme, provided for in my report, and, when the trouble came, action was taken on repressive lines. . . .'[1]

The Committee was easy prey for the Government. Narrowly based in an arms sector that employed only about 20% of the skilled engineers on the Clyde, militancy could not easily be developed beyond the protective reflex of a threatened aristocracy, and this difficulty was intensified by the lack of organization among the less skilled workers whose co-operation was essential if dilution was to be positively controlled, not merely resisted. By the end of 1915 the revolutionary movement on the Clyde was split between the impossibilist revolutionary defeatism of John Maclean, and the tortuous self-deceptions involved in the SLP dilution policy. The Committee failed to transcend the objective limitations of its original base, to become an effective vanguard for the local working class as a whole. Even the revolutionaries could not escape entanglement in the protective reflexes of the craftsmen, and it was a narrow and self-isolating path that they cut through the turmoil on the Clyde.

It would be wrong, however, to pass a merely negative judgement. Despite great objective difficulties and great confusion among the leadership, the Committee did succeed in initiating a quite new type of local independent rank-and-file organization based in the workshops and the shop steward system. The Government could smash the Clyde Workers' Committee, but not the idea that it embodied. Indeed the deportations, by forcing several of the leaders to find work in other munitions centres, helped to spread the idea. What was done on the Clyde in the winter of 1915–16 made possible the subsequent national development of the rank-and-file movement.

[1] Weir to Montague, August 1916, quoted in Reader, *Architect of Air Power*, p. 54.

F

Chapter 5

The Origins of the
Sheffield Workers' Committee

Before the shop steward movement collapsed on the Clyde, developments were already under way which would lead to the formation of the Sheffield Workers' Committee in the winter of 1916–17.

'It is too often forgotten that it was Sheffield which led in the improvement of organization and which gave birth, in the writings of J. T. Murphy, to the only thought out shop stewards' philosophy and proposals for a complete national structure, and it was in Sheffield were the movement achieved some of its most notable successes.'[1]

Sheffield was the only centre apart from Glasgow to maintain a fully developed Workers' Committee for any length of time. Effectively it shared the national leadership of the movement with the Clyde. In many respects the swc was a more successful body than its Scottish counterpart. In particular it was far more integrated into the local labour movement as a whole.[2]

Underlying the strength of the swc was the cohesiveness of the local engineering industry in which it was based. The metal industries of Sheffield, which employed nearly half the occupied population in 1921, were divided into two distinct sectors. The heavy trades – steel, arms and machinery – were located on the

[1] J. Mendelson and S. Pollard, *Sheffield Trades and Labour Council, 1858–1958* (Sheffield, 1958), p. 71.

[2] All the important leaders – Ted Lismer, Jack Murphy, Walt Hill, Ev. Rayner – held official positions on the Trades Council at some time during the war. Lismer was chairman of the Allied Trades in 1917.

level ground in the valley of the Don, running in a belt north-eastwards from the city centre towards Rotherham. The light trades – cutlery and small tools – with less need for flat ground or transport facilities, spread over the hills to the south and west of the city centre.[1] The firms in these two sectors were distinct, as were the workers: not forgers and grinders but razor forgers, scissor grinders, etc., were the skilled workers of the light trades.[2] For our purpose it is only the heavy trades which are important.

Within the heavy trades the dominance of the arms firms was more clearly marked in Sheffield than in any other munitions centre. All but one of the traditional arms firms had originated from Sheffield steel firms.[3] In 1911 there were 38,379 workers in the heavy metal trades, in 1921 65,724. In 1919–20 Pollard estimates a peak of about 70,000 workers.[4] Against this we have the figures for the arms firms in November 1916 (Table 4).[5]

Table 4   *Employment in Sheffield arms factories, November 1916*

Vickers	10,807
Hadfield	10,805
Cammell-Laird	5,097
⎰ Firth	5,500
⎱ Brown*	3,497
	35,706
Firth NPF	6,579
Hadfield NPF	2,568
	44,853

* Since 1903 Brown had held a controlling interest in Firth: *100 Years in Steel* (T. Firth & J. Brown Ltd., Sheffield, 1937), p. 16.

About 45,000 workers were employed by the five arms firms in November 1916, over two-thirds of all the workers in the heavy

[1] Census of England and Wales, 1921, Industry Tables; P. Abercrombie, *Sheffield, A Civic Survey* (Sheffield, 1924), p. 15.
[2] C.f. S. Pollard, *A History of Labour in Sheffield* (Liverpool, 1960), pp. 202ff.
[3] Armstrong-Whitworth, originating in Newcastle, was the exception.
[4] Pollard, *A History of Labour in Sheffield*, pp. 269, 334–5.
[5] *Bev.* v, pp. 76, 79, 'Report on Labour in Controlled Establishments'. The Firth figure is estimated from 1914 and 1918 figures of 3,000 and 8,000 respectively. A. C. Marshall and H. Newbold, *The History of Firths* (Sheffield, 1924), p. 101.

metal trades. What proportion of the *engineering* workers in Sheffield were employed in the arms firms, it is impossible to say. Steel manufacture, forge and foundry work bulked large in the activities of these firms. During the war, however, engineering work, especially the production of guns and of shells, expanded very fast. Vickers increased its output of guns nearly ten times. Hadfields took up the higher (engineering) stages of gun manu- facture for the first time.[1] Two National Projectile Factories were set up during the war, and this, together with the expansion of the arms firms' own shell shops, further increased the number of engineering workers employed. In July 1915 the industrial correspondent of the *Sheffield Daily Telegraph* reported:

'Lathes and machine tools for shell turning are being installed at the large works as rapidly as they can be obtained. The appearance of numerous machine shops in the East End marks quite a new departure in local industry, and before the end of the war Sheffield promises to be an engineering centre of some consequence.'[2]

In 1911 there were only 5,000 skilled engineers in Sheffield, 13% of the workers in the heavy trades. By 1921 this number had doubled, to 10,463 and the proportion risen to 16%[3] A large part of this expansion was probably accounted for by the expan- sion of the arms firms into engineering work.

Those engineers not in the arms firms nevertheless tended to work in trades closely tied to those firms. Davy Brothers, with 700 workers in March 1916, made steel manufacturing plant for the arms firms; Brightside Foundry and Engineering Co. made, among other things, heating and ventilating plant for them. The electrical engineering industry had emerged in great part from the electrical repair shops of the arms firms. Heavy electrical machinery was produced for the rolling mills, and 'the local industry has taken an important part in the application of electricity to warships',[4] presumably via the three arms firms

1 Sheffield and Rotherham Chambers of Commerce, *Industrial Sheffield and Rotherham* (Sheffield, 1919), p. 142.

2 *Sheffield Daily Telegraph*, 31 July 1915.

3 Census of England and Wales, 1911 and 1921. The skills taken were turner, fitter, toolsetter and machineman.

4 Sheffield and Rotherham Chambers of Commerce, *Industrial Sheffield and Rotherham* p. 151–2 and *passim*.

engaged in shipbuilding.[1] During the war the one local representative of the motor car industry, the Sheffield Simplex Motor
works, was drawn into shell and aero-engine production. In
addition, there was the usual mass of smaller engineering firms,
mostly, during the war, under sub-contract to the armament firms
on shell work.[2] The Sheffield engineering workers were thus
drawn together by the local industrial structure, rather than
fragmented, as on the Clyde. Not only did they work together,
they also lived together. In 1918 only two of the fifteen ASE
branches were located outside the East End residential areas on
the hills overlooking the Don valley. Two-thirds of the members
belonged to branches located within a mile of Firth Park.[3] The
isolation of a militant section from the engineering workers as a
whole was therefore far less likely to occur in Sheffield than on
the Clyde. For the same reason, the need for a rank-and-file
movement independent of the local trade union machinery was
much less acute. The SWC was only set up when the ASE District
Committee could no longer stretch trade union rule to accom-
modate militancy. Throughout its career the SWC was to work
closely with the District Committee, the leading members
serving in both an official and an unofficial capacity.

The first steps towards independent rank-and-file organization
were taken late in 1915 as a direct result of dilution. Dilution
was probably never so extensive in the Sheffield engineering
shops as on the Clyde, because the very heavy nature of much
of the work involved made it unsuitable for female labour.[4] In
November 1916, for instance, there were still no women working
at Brown and only about 300 (2·7%) at Hadfield.[5] There was a

[1] Cammell-Laird (Liverpool), J. Brown (Clyde), Vickers (Clyde and
Barrow).

[2] Sheffield and Rotherham Chambers of Commerce, *Industrial Sheffield
and Rotherham*, pp. 161–2, 191ff.; Pollard, *A History of Labour in Sheffield*,
p. 269; *Mun* 1.7 (MC), 21 March 1918; *Mun.* 2. 25, 9 October 1915; *Machinery*,
1 October 1914; *MM* II, 2, p. 157; *Sheffield Year Book* (Sheffield, 1916 and
1918).

[3] Branch membership figures in ASE, *Monthly Journal and Report;* addresses
of branch secretaries in Fabian Research Department, *Gazetteer of Trade
Union Branches* (1918).

[4] *Sheffield Daily Telegraph*, 24 July 1915, 19 February, 11 March 1916. Not
until 1918 was any concerted attempt made to introduce women into the
heavier branches of the trade, and then it met with 'the most stern opposition'
from the skilled engineering unions: ASE, *Monthly Journal and Report*,
June 1918.

[5] *Bev.* V, p. 76, 'Report on Labour in Controlled Establishments', November 1916.

limit to the amount of male dilution that could occur, the upgrading of unskilled workers tending to create an acute shortage of strong labourers. However, dilution on shell work was exceptionally important in Sheffield. Shell making was a traditional Sheffield industry, and had been recognized prior to the war as a skilled trade.[1] Moreover, the new shell factories were not, as on the Clyde, seen as temporary wartime phenomena, but were expected to remain after the war. The pressure for dilution on shell work was no new thing to the Sheffield engineers. During the armaments boom of 1913 the upgrading of semi-skilled labour had become a major grievance with the local ASE.[2] By the beginning of 1915: 'Cheap labour . . . [was] being employed in all our shops in considerably increasing numbers.' From the summer of 1915 women workers began to be introduced on shell work,[3] and in the early months of 1916, under Government pressure, the pace was intense. The biggest impact was at Firth where, in April 1916, 800 men on shell work were replaced by women – most of these men, however, were semi-skilled.[4] In the same month Firth opened a National Projectile Factory at Templeborough employing about 80 % women. By November the proportion had risen to 90 %, the highest in the country. Female dilution was also very extensive in Cammell-Laird – 35 % by November 1916. 12·5 % of the workers at Vickers were women by the same date.[5]

The most acute problem caused by dilution for the skilled workers was not the threat of cheap labour, but rather the reverse. Less skilled pieceworkers on shell work were earning far more than the skilled men who supervised them, set up their tools and maintained their machines.[6] At the same time the opportunities for the skilled men transferred from shell work to earn high wages were limited because piecework was exceptionally

---

[1] *Sheffield Daily Telegraph*, 4 November 1916; *Mun*. 2. 27, 22 January, 5 February 1916; B. Drake, *Women in the Engineering Trades* (1917), pp. 13, 16.

[2] ASE, *Monthly Journal and Report*, August–November 1913, June 1916.

[3] *Sheffield Guardian*, 5 February, 14, 21 May, 4 June 1915.

[4] ASE, *Monthly Journal and Report*, February 1916; *Sheffield Daily Telegraph*, 19 February, 1 March 1916.

[5] *Mun*. 2. 27, 27 May, 4 November 1916; *Mun*. 2. 28, 10 February 1917; *MM* VIII, 11, p. 145; *Bev*. v, p. 79, 'Report on Labour in Controlled Establishments'.

[6] *Mun*. 2. 27, 22 January 1916; C. Addison, *Four and a Half Years* (1934), p. 176; *Sheffield Daily Telegraph*, 26 February 1916.

rare in the district (Table 5).[1] Together with the rocketing cost of living, long hours and overwork, and hostility to dilution itself, this had created widespread discontent by the beginning of 1916.

Table 5 *Percentage of skilled workers on payment-by-results, 1906*

	Turners %	Fitters %
Sheffield	17	12
Glasgow	37	24
Tyne	31	26
National	39	30

The authentic tone of this discontent was caught by an old militant, interviewed thirty-five years later:

'As a result of the demand for munitions and dilution, men came in and were put on repetition jobs. They smashed the machinery. Nothing mattered, only their huge wage at the week-end. The skilled men had to keep the machinery going, and all for the weekly daywork rate. This was the trouble. We said we were entitled to something apart from the ordinary daywork rate.'[2]

In November 1915 the local Allied Trades applied for a 10s rise. The ASE had attempted to limit this claim solely to the skilled timeworkers, but not surprisingly, the joint body turned this down. Since the District Committee itself was tied to the Allied Trades in the wage movement, an unofficial Day-Workers' Committee was set up in the ASE to press the skilled time-workers' grievance. At this stage the Committee was essentially a pressure group within the Allied Trades, and one which represented an extreme craft exclusiveness. In January 1916 the employers turned down the Allied Trades' claim. The Day-Workers' Committee, believing that the ASE Executive would not press the matter, sought to make direct contact with the Ministry of Munitions.[3] In the normal course of events the

---

[1] *Report of an enquiry by the Board of Trade into the Earnings and Hours of Labour of Workpeople of the United Kingdom in 1906*, pt. IV, 1911, lxxxviii, 1.

[2] W. Moore, *Verbatim Report of a Discussion between Veteran Engineers in Sheffield* (1953), p. 9; Addison, *Four and a Half Years*, p. 190; *Mun.* 2. 27, 22 January 1916; ASE, *Monthly Journal and Report*, February 1916.

[3] Engineering Employers' Federation, *Wage Movements, 1897–1925* (1926); *The Herald*, 17 June 1916; *Mun.* 2. 27, 29 January, 5 February 1916; Moore, *Verbatim Report*, pp. 2, 8, 9; ASE, *Monthly Journal and Report*, February 1916.

Ministry would have had nothing to do with an unofficial body of this kind. Addison however thought he could solve the Sheffield problem by tying the dayworkers' earnings to piecework earnings – a kind of local lieu rate. Though initially he hoped to negotiate this with the ASE Executive, the latter's stand on dilution made this impossible. Consequently Addison went behind their backs, and agreed to meet a deputation from the Day-Workers' Committee on March 1st.[1] This meeting appears to have paved the way for the conclusion in March 1916 of local agreement on dilution with the ASE District Committee.[2] Subsequently the Day-Workers' Committee petered out, though not before persuading the local ASE to secede from the Allied Trades in the next wage movement and to put in a bigger claim for the skilled timeworkers alone.[3] By its success in initiating negotiations with the Ministry the Committee may have encouraged ideas of independent rank-and-file activity. It also created 'a nucleus of local organization which asserted itself with much force subsequently'.[4]

Within weeks of the secession of the ASE from the Allied Trades, the District Committee decided to launch a systematic campaign 'to ensure that in every department there shall be fully accredited representatives of the men, empowered to take action on their behalf and recognized as part and parcel of the Union's machinery'.[5] This was the first attempt by an ASE District Committee to come to terms with the wartime boom in workshop

[1] Addison, *Four and a Half Years*, pp. 176, 178; *Mun.* 2. 27, 4 March 1916; Moore, *Verbatim Report*, p. 2. Addison got into considerable hot water over this with the ASE Executive who were as adamantly opposed to recognizing the CWC: *Executive Minutes*, vol. 193, 29 February, 6 April 1916. Addison's agreement to meet the Sheffield Committee must have made more convincing Macassey's threat to recognize the CWC unless the Executive climbed down on L2, and may even had been a tactical manoeuvre in that game.

[2] *Mun.* 5. 73, *Dilution of Labour Bulletin*, November 1916. There is no record of the content of the agreement. The Ministry's enquiry into the grievances of the Sheffield dayworkers which reported at the end of March asserted that the issue had become a national one and should be dealt with at national level: *Mun.* 2. 27, 1 April 1916. What really happened therefore remains something of a mystery.

[3] *The Herald*, 17 June, 1 July 1916; *Mun.* 2. 27, 27 May 1916; Engineering Employers' Federation, *Wage Movements, 1897–1925*.

[4] *Mun.* 5. 329, 'Time, Wages and the Skilled Time Workers' Problem' (n.d.).

[5] *The Herald*, 14 October 1916, 20 January 1917; J. T. Murphy, *Preparing for Power* (1934), p. 126; J. T. Murphy, *New Horizons* (1942), p. 45; Moore, *Verbatim Report*, p. 1.

organization. The Sheffield rules for shop stewards extended their role from dues collection, recruiting and reporting grievances to include negotiation with the management, though this was of course restricted by the Procedure for Avoidance of Disputes. Any failure to agree at shop floor level had to be taken up to national level through Procedure before strike action could legitimately be taken.[1] Launched in the midst of a campaign against the Munitions Act and conscription,[2] the drive to elect shop stewards 'went like wildfire. The rank and file knew they were divorced from the officials and that the officials were linked with the Government so far as the war was concerned. The rank and file wanted to express themselves and this was their medium.'[3] By November 1916 about sixty shop stewards had been elected. Underlying this success was the advance of dilution. Because the details of dilution could only be negotiated at workshop level even the most conservative trade unionists were forced to recognize the urgent need to elect shop stewards. By the autumn of 1916 a local Engineering Shop Stewards' Committee had been formed to link up the shop stewards in different factories.[4] Though still subject to trade union rule and limited to the ASE, this Committee provided the basis from which an independent rank-and-file movement could be launched.

Dilution provoked a response which laid a foundation for the Sheffield Workers' Committee, but did not, in itself, lead to its creation. The Day-Workers' Committee was essentially a temporary revolt against the Allied Trades, and not the basis for permanent local independent rank-and-file organization. The shop steward system, until the autumn of 1916, flourished as a means of negotiating dilution, but it remained under District Committee control. Dilution proved a less explosive issue in Sheffield than it had in Glasgow. The Day-Workers' Committee expressed the intense irritation of skilled craftsmen whose own standard of living was falling because of rising prices, while a

[1] *The Herald*, 14 October 1916; Moore, *Verbatim Report*, p. 1. These rules were approved by the ASE Executives.

[2] The shop steward leaders figured prominently in these campaigns: Sheffield Trades and Labour Council, *Minutes*, 5, 12 October, 30 November 1915, 4, 18 January, 7, 21 March 1916; ASE, Sheffield No. 12 Branch, *Minutes*, 8 October 1915, 10 March 1916; *Sheffield Daily Telegraph*, 26 August 1916.

[3] Moore, *Verbatim Report*, p. 2.

[4] J. T. Murphy in *The Socialist*, 10 July 1919; Murphy, *New Horizons*, p. 45; Moore, *Verbatim Report*, p. 1; *Mun.* 5. 54, 'Notes on the Shop Stewards' Movement', 29 May 1917.

bunch of incompetent newcomers earned unheard-of wages on simple operations that the craftsmen were no longer permitted to perform. It did not express the acute anxiety of the labour aristocrat who feared for his future because the dilutees were an unorganized mob, an incoming tide of cheap labour. Underlying this was the fact that the less skilled workers were a good deal better organized in Sheffield than they were in Glasgow. The Workers' Union and the NAUL had about 2,000 members each in the East End by 1918 – though a substantial proportion of the latter's membership was in iron and steel manufacture rather than engineering. But the largest of the general unions in the Sheffield engineering industry was the NUGW, with 7,000 members in the East End by 1918, and most of these worked in the foundries and engineering shops. In August 1916, for example, 4,000 members attended a meeting of its engineering section.[1] It was also the chief general union organizing women dilutees. When not in one of the general unions, women were organized by the NFWW whose membership grew from 350 before the war to 5,000 by 1918.[2]

It is impossible to make any precise quantitative comparison with other areas because what figures there are for organization of less skilled workers in engineering are seldom more than informed guesses. A very rough estimate shows, however, that in 1918 there were two ASE members for every less skilled worker organized in Glasgow, and two organized less skilled workers for every ASE member in Sheffield engineering shops.

This high level of organization among the less skilled workers in itself constituted an important guarantee against cheap labour. From the outset the general unions understood their common interest with the craftsmen, as the NUGW organizer made clear in February 1915: 'Now that the war is forcing labourers into competition with the skilled artisans it is essential that the wages

[1] I am grateful to Dr R. Hyman, University of Warwick, for the Workers' Union figures. See also Fabian Research Department, *Gazetteer of Trade Union Branches; Sheffield Guardian*, February 1915; *The Labour Gazette* (Board of Trade, 1914–16, Ministry of Labour, 1916–18), 'Arbitration and Conciliation Cases', *passim;* Pollard, *A History of Labour in Sheffield*, pp. 220, 234; *Sheffield Daily Telegraph*, 21 August 1916.

[2] Pollard, *A History of Labour in Sheffield*, p. 271; *Sheffield Guardian*, 23 July 1915. The acceptance of the women as equal partners in the local labour movement was symbolized by the election of their leader, Mrs Wilkinson, to the Trades Council Executive in 1918, and her subsequent appointment as its first woman president: Mendelson and Pollard, *Sheffield Trades and Labour Council*, p. 74.

paid to labourers shall approximate more closely to those paid to skilled artisans.'[1] Moreover the Sheffield craftsmen themselves had already, before the war, taken definite steps to meet the problems created by dilution, and thereby prepared the ground for a relatively smooth expansion of dilution in wartime. In 1912 the ASE had negotiated a local agreement on the work, status and pay of semi-skilled machinists, and at the outbreak of war the recognized rates for machinists, at 83–88% of the district rate were probably the highest in the country.[2] The ASE and its satellite unions continued this activity throughout the war. In August 1917 an agreement was reached with the local Engineering Employers' Association which put the top grades of machinist, millers and borers on to the full district rate. Planers, slotters and shapers increased their rate from 90% to 92% and drillers from 76% to 82%. Not only were rates negotiated for the semi-skilled, but agreement was reached on 'the promotion of men on the lesser paid to the higher paid machines', and a system of apprenticeship was arranged for the machinemen. 'We have been able to place these workmen', commented the district delegate of the ASE, 'on a much surer footing; and we hope have safeguarded the position of this branch of the trade for the future.'[3]

While the ASE, along with the other skilled engineering unions, devoted a great deal of time and energy to establishing minimum rates for semi-skilled workers, it actually had very few machinist members.[4] Evidently the chief concern was not so much to improve the rates of this small section of their membership, as to establish a recognized rate for the dilutees, members of other unions or no union, who threatened to undercut the craft workers' rates. The craft unions themselves enforced the local agreement on managements in respect of dilutees, and, more important, the existence of this agreement presumably made it easier for the general unions to push up the wages of their members.[5]

This wages strategy, like the Clydeside dilution agreements of February 1916, might be seen and intended in two quite different

[1] *Sheffield Guardian*, 5 February 1915.
[2] Millers, slotters, shapers and planers got 88%, while machinists got 83–88% and drillers 76%: 'Wage Advances During the War', F. Ellison, n.d., in *Moore Collection;* Pollard, *A History of Labour in Sheffield*, p. 236.
[3] ASE, *Monthly Journal and Report*, September 1917.
[4] *Ibid.*, 1914–18, Branch Returns.
[5] Board of Trade, *Labour Gazette*, Arbitration and Conciliation Cases, 1914–18, *passim*.

ways. On the one hand it could reflect an Industrial Unionist commitment, a desire to open up the union to all grades of workers. On the other hand it could be intended as a means of underpinning craft privilege by a more realistic approach to the problems created by the technological dynamism of the industry than the head-in-the-sand policy of 'following the machine'. In the latter case, while the strategy would help to make dilution acceptable to the craftsmen, this acceptance would not represent any conscious abandonment of craft status. That this was the case in Sheffield seems clear from the failure of the ASE, despite its machinists' policy, to recruit any large number of semi-skilled workers, and from the intensity of the craft-consciousness reflected in the Day-Workers' Committee. The Sheffield engineers accepted dilution, but they were still a very long way from rejecting the pursuit of craft privilege.

The leading group of militants in Sheffield differed from their counterparts on the Clyde in that there had been, before the war, no equivalent ferment of revolutionary propaganda and ideas. The workers of the East End of Sheffield were solidly committed to labour politics and returned a Labour MP in 1909, but (perhaps therefore) there was no local SLP branch and no John Maclean to enliven the BSP.[1] The leaders of the Sheffield movement served their political apprenticeships in the Amalgamation Committee movement, of which Jack Murphy[2] had been the secretary since its foundation in the spring of 1914. Murphy had 'resigned himself to engineering' only after his early ambition to enter the civil service had been cut short by an accident which made him prematurely the chief bread winner of the family. He remained studious, however, and achieved the not inconsiderable

[1] Pollard, *A History of Labour in Sheffield*, pp. 197–201.
[2] J. T. Murphy (1888–1966). ASE. At Vickers from 1902 to 1918. Tool-turner. Secretary of the Sheffield Amalgamation Committee and Daily Herald League before the war. Sheffield Trades Council Executive member, 1916–17. Leader of Sheffield Workers' Committee and leading theorist of national shop stewards' movement, for which see *The Workers' Committee* (1917), *Compromise or Revolution* (1918), a chapter in A. Gleason, *What the Workers Want* (1920), *Preparing for Power* (1934), *New Horizons* (1942) and numerous articles in *Solidarity*, *The Socialist* and other revolutionary papers. Joined Socialist Labour Party in late summer of 1917. Stood as SLP candidate for Gorton in general election of 1918, polling 1,300 votes. Founder member of Communist Party and a leading member until his resignation in 1932. Suspect among some of the Sheffield workers who remember him as 'an intellectual'.

feat of reading Marx, Connolly and others 'for hours at a stretch' while turning propeller shafts and gun barrels at the Vickers Brightside works. The size of the work was an advantage since it effectively hid him and his reading matter from the view of the foreman as he walked down the centre of the shop.[1] Both Murphy and Ted Lismer[2] became leading figures in the national Amalgamation Committees movement, and played an important part in persuading the movement to fuse with the shop stewards. Ev. Rayner, another of the Sheffield leaders, stood for the ASE Executive in July 1915. In his election address he declared:

'I am rather doubtful over standing for the EC now we have compulsory arbitration, because I have no wish to be a benefit administrator or depriver. Delegate Meetings should in future be held at the Treasury, where they nullified all previous ones . . . Vote for me if you like, but I would remind you that votes unless followed by actions are futile, or put another way, "to follow is weak, to lead encourages weakness in others".'[3]

The 'syndicalist socialism' of Connolly, Mann and *The Miners' Next Step* formed the ideological base from which this group approached the industrial problems of wartime. Later Murphy claimed that even before the war he was developing the idea of carrying the struggle for Industrial Unionism into the workshops:

'Shortly before the war it had occurred to me that while we were waiting for the amalgamation of the unions, something could be done with the machinery of the shop steward system. My idea was that all the trade unionists in any shop should have shop stewards, who should form themselves into a committee to represent the workers in that shop regardless of the trade unions they belonged to and thus make the first step towards uniting the unions.'[4]

[1] *Solidarity*, February, April 1914. For a short time in 1913 he was secretary of the Herald League in Sheffield: Murphy, *New Horizons*, pp. 24, 31–2, 36.
[2] Ted Lismer. Guild socialist and member of Amalgamation Committee Movement. Member Steam Engine Makers. 1917–18 chairman of Official Joint Board of engineering trade unions in Sheffield. Leading activist on Trades Council throughout the war; first elected to Trades Council EC in July 1913, vice-president in 1918. President of Sheffield Workers' Committee in 1919. Joined Communist Party. Organizing secretary of RILU in 1920–3.
[3] ASE, *Annual Report*, 1915. Rayner was born in 1882. He was on the Executive of the Trades Council, 1916–17.
[4] Murphy, *New Horizons*, pp. 44–5.

This claim is unconfirmed. What is certain however is that through the experience of the Day-Workers' Committee and of war conditions in general the leading group was able to introduce to the workshops the idea of building an independent rank-and-file organization on the model of the Clyde Workers' Committee.

It was over the issue of the conscription of skilled workers that the Sheffield Workers' Committee came into being, in November 1916. Throughout the summer of 1916 the local ASE had been harassed by the constant conscription of its members. 300 call-up papers had been dealt with by the district delegate by the end of August. Although, in all these cases, the men were released, this was wasting a great deal of time and irritating the District Committee. The fear that conscription would be used as a disciplinary weapon by the employers was never far from their minds. In October 1916 a fitter at Vickers, Leonard Hargreaves, was conscripted into the army, having missed the chance to appeal because the firm had withheld the papers that would have secured his discharge. The 'connivance' of the firm with the military authorities appeared to realize the fears of industrial conscription.[1]

The Hargreaves case was put to the ASE Executive, but no response was forthcoming. On Sunday, November 5th, the District Committee called a mass meeting, attended by 3,500 workers. At this meeting the District Committee, feeling its freedom to act restricted by 'legal commitments', gave way to the shop stewards' committee. (In fact the leaders of the shop stewards were all on the District, so the change was more formal than real.) The meeting passed a resolution: 'That in the event of the military authorities attacking our members for military service a down tools policy will be adopted.' The Hargreaves case was characterized as 'a deliberate violation of the pledges given' to the skilled men, and strike action was threatened if he were not returned within a week. Jack Murphy, secretary of the Engineering Shop Stewards' Committee, forwarded this resolu-

[1] ASE, *Monthly Journal and Report*, July, September 1916; *Mun 5. 57*, Negotiations with the ASE, 15 November 1916. Similar cases had occurred in Coventry a few months earlier: *Mun. 5. 57, idem*, 27 September 1916. Sir William Clegg, chairman of the local Munitions Tribunal and a much hated figure, was later to exacerbate the trouble by advising Firths to 'make representations to the military authorities in cases where young men were systematically loosing time': *Sheffield Daily Telegraph*, 11 November 1916.

tion to the ASE Executive and on the 9th to the Prime Minister.[1]

The Sheffield workers were well aware of what they were up against, and the efforts of the militants to perfect the shop steward organization now 'developed like magic': 'Active workers in Sheffield had been striving for months in the autumn of 1916 to get stewards elected in the shops, and had managed to get about sixty. In a week or ten days prior to the November strike the number rose to more than 300.'[2] In addition, the transfer of authority to the unofficial committee facilitated the broadening of the Committee from the ASE to involve members of other skilled unions, many of whom had attended the mass meeting of the 5th.[3] In conditions of press censorship – the first mention of the trouble in the local press occurred when it was virtually over – special attention had to be given to informing workers in other centres of what was going on. Delegates were appointed at the mass meeting to visit all the leading munitions centres and try to arrange for joint action.[4]

The Executive did not get round to asking the District Committee for further details of the Hargreaves case until Tuesday, November 14th, the day before the strike was due to start. But this faint sign of activity came too late. On the 15th a mass meeting decided to strike the next day. The ASE had telegraphed that they were to put the case before the Man-Power Board that day, but the workers were not inclined to accept any vague offers. They resolved to stay out until Hargreaves was returned to Sheffield in person. This resolve was realistic. A few hours

[1] Murphy, *New Horizons*, pp. 49–50; *MM* VI, 1, p. 29; telephone message from Mr Chuffy, the Chief Industrial Officer in Sheffield, on 15 November 1916.

[2] *The Socialist*, 10 July 1919. See also Murphy, *New Horizons*, p. 50.

[3] Moore, *Verbatim Report*, p. 7. According to the figures in the Fabian Research Department's *Gazetteer of Trade Union Branches* (1918) the UMWA, AST and SEM had about 2,000 members in 1918, compared with about 5,600 in the ASE.

[4] *Mun. 5. 57, idem.* Gavigan, the ASE district secretary, and the only local official conspicuously opposed to the shop stewards' movement, told Mr Chuffy 'that his men are all joining the No Conscription Fellowship as a result of the Mass Meeting on November the 5th. Two men chosen were from the Fellowship to go to the Clyde to get further members, two to go to London and Coventry, two to Manchester and two to Liverpool.' As the militants themselves recalled the occasion the delegates did not go to recruit for the NCF but, of course, to organize sympathetic strike action on the Hargreaves question: Moore, *Verbatim Report*, p. 4; Murphy, *New Horizons*, p. 50. They were successful only in Barrow, which came out on Saturday, November 18th: *MM* VI, 1, p. 37.

after the mass meeting the ASE Executive telegraphed again to say that Hargreaves was being released. In fact they had been misled. It was not until the strike had started that the War Office was eventually bullied into releasing him.[1]

12,000 men – probably the complete membership of all the skilled engineering unions in Sheffield – came out on the evening of Thursday, November 16th. 'In the annals of the war', commented the History of the Ministry of Munitions, 'no strike showed so few signs of indecision or half-heartedness.' The strikers stayed out until Hargreaves – despatched at once to Sheffield through the intervention of a leading local employer, Sir Robert Hadfield – had been presented to them at a mass meeting on the Saturday. The rapid victory of the strike, however, was due not only to its solidity, but also to the Government's readiness to give way on this issue. The local official of the Ministry of Munitions, hoping that 'some of the men might be dealt with in a similar manner as those on the Clyde', had made a list of 'a certain number of people who are working at the National Projectile Factory'.[2] But tough measures were not taken. Negotiations for the Trade Card scheme were already under way, favoured by the Ministry of Munitions, and the main result of the strike was to tip the balance in an interdepartmental tussle, forcing the War Office to toe the line. 'For the time being', commented Murphy, 'the shop steward committee became the dominant authority.' Early in January 1917 it reorganized itself as the Sheffield Workers' Committee, giving formal recognition to its unofficial character and to the allegiance of skilled workers other than those in the ASE.[3]

The strength of the unofficial movement in Sheffield reflected the dominance of the arms firms from which it sprang in the local industrial structure. The Sheffield militants were not, like their Glasgow counterparts, isolated from the engineering workers in general, and they had no difficulty in controlling the District Committee. At the same time the confusions between the craft response to dilution and revolutionary politics which so weakened the early Clydeside movement were not repeated in Sheffield, partly because dilution was not such an explosive issue and partly because Sheffield possessed no equivalent to the

---

[1] *MM* VI, 1, pp. 36–7; Addison, *Four and a Half Years*, pp. 262–3; telegrams in *Moore Collection*.

[2] *Mun. 5. 57, idem; MM* VI, 1, pp. 37–8; Moore, *Verbatim Report*, pp. 4–5.

[3] Murphy, *Preparing for Power*, pp. 132–3; Moore, *Verbatim Report*, p. 1.

revolutionary vanguard on the Clyde. While the movement in Sheffield was strong, it was, as much as on the Clyde, a movement of craft workers. The issue of conscription which precipitated the rank-and-file movement centred on craft privilege just as much as the issue of dilution, and, as the strike movement of May 1917 was to show, the Sheffield engineers were as concerned to protect their privileges as craftsmen anywhere. Before dealing with this strike, however, attention must be given to the development of the rank-and-file movement before the spring of 1917 in three other munitions centres.

Chapter 6

Woolwich, Barrow and the Tyne: the Significance of Failure

Apart from Glasgow and Sheffield there were three other centres in which munitions production in the traditional sense – i.e. excluding the motor car/aircraft complex – most clearly predominated. In none of these centres, Woolwich, Barrow or the Tyne, did the shop stewards' movement ever exist as a permanent and effective organization. Workshop organization with full bargaining rights developed, or had already developed before the war, in Woolwich and Tyneside (though not in Barrow). But strong local Workers' Committees, based directly in the workshops and able to act independently of the local official trade union structures, did not emerge. Consequently the revolutionary left which in other munitions centres was able to achieve real leadership among the mass of the engineering workers, remained more or less isolated and powerless. An analysis of the causes of failure in these areas throws further light on the causes of success elsewhere. The three centres can be dealt with conveniently at this point since the main developments in rank-and-file organization all took place prior to the strike movement of May 1917.

There is one obvious, if apparently paradoxical, factor underlying the failure of the movement in all three centres: each was the site of one of the three largest munitions works in the country (Table 6).[1] Because these works were so large they tended to

Table 6   *Employment in the giant munitions works, November 1916*

	Labour force in Nov. 1916
Woolwich Arsenal	68,000
Vickers, Barrow	33,107
Elswick and Scotswood, Tyne	57,630

[1] *Bev.* v, p. 76, 'Report on Labour in Controlled Establishments', November 1916; *MM* viii, 2, p. 16.

employ the great majority of the engineering workers in the area. In so far as the local Workers' Committees emerged simply from the need to link up the rank and file in different factories outside the official machinery of the unions, there was relatively little reason why it should have emerged in any of these centres.[1] This alone, however, is quite insufficient to explain the different characteristics of militancy, and the differing degrees of independence assumed by rank-and-file militancy in the three centres.

WOOLWICH

Woolwich Arsenal, the largest works in the country, was 'a bewildering range of factories and departments, occupying an area of about $3\frac{1}{2}$ miles long by $2\frac{1}{2}$ miles wide, with about 150 miles internal railway track'.[2] At the outbreak of war it employed 10,868 workers. By the beginning of 1915 this had already more than doubled. It reached its peak – 74,467 – in May 1917, and by August 1918 employed 65,462 workers. Nearly a third of these were employed filling shells. Of the rest, the most important sections were those listed in Table 7.[3] Dilution was launched in

Table 7 *Employment in Woolwich Arsenal, 1918*

Laboratories (bombs, cartridges, fuses, shells, mines)	12,986
Small arms ammunitions	9,720
Gun carriage dept.	5,538
Gun dept.	3,828

[1] The two Vickers works in Crayford and Erith constituted another such area. Because the workers here caused little trouble during the war, they left little mark in the official records. In November 1916 the two factories employed:

	Total	Women
Erith (Ordnance)	9,543	24·2%
Crayford (Small arms)	5,083	17·2%

Bev. v, p. 76, *op. cit.*
There is no positive evidence of fully-fledged workshop organization at any time during the war at either factory, though it may have existed. Though the factories were out in the May 1917 strike (*MM* vi, 1, p. 111; *MM* xi, 5, p. 12), and the Erith workers staged a one-day strike over the food question in February 1918 (*Solidarity*, March 1918), there was certainly no effective local rank-and-file movement. The only other notable militant outbreak occurred in the summer of 1916 at Crayford when five chargehands were sacked. The strike was short lived. ASE, *Executive Minutes*, 26, 27 July 1916; *MM* xi, 5, p. 11.

[2] D. Lloyd George, *War Memoirs* (1936), pp. 470–1.
[3] *MM* viii, 2, p. 17.

the summer of 1915 with a hamhanded attempt to put semi-skilled men on toolsetting and toolmaking, provoking furious resistance.[1] Subsequently, however, dilution proceeded smoothly. Women were introduced from the autumn of 1915, and on a larger scale, in the early months of 1916. By May 1917 a third of the workers in the Arsenal were women, and a further boost during the summer of 1918 brought the number up to 28,000, 44% of the total. Most of these women worked on shell and ammunition, though there were about 1,150 (30%) in the gun factory.[2] The smoothness with which dilution was introduced probably reflects the fact that already, before the war, the skilled workers had built up a shop stewards' committee and gained recognition for it.

In March 1916 there were over 6,000 skilled engineering workers in the Arsenal, most of them members of the ASE.[3] These men held a unique position in the union. Though within the London District, they were, in practice, largely outside the normal trade union machinery. As Government employees they were outside the collective bargaining procedures of the industry. Instead they had their own procedures within the Arsenal. Since November 1912 a Royal Arsenal Shop Stewards' Committee, representative of the skilled engineers, had been recognized by the management. By July 1917 there were between 110 and 130 shop stewards in the various departments, meeting together regularly once a month. They elected an Executive of seven members which conducted all negotiations with the management.[4] Cutting through the red tape which tradition and the War Office had imposed on the Arsenal, they had gained direct access to the highest levels of management. 'There was no beating about the bush with managers, shop managers or foremen: they went directly to the Supervisor or the Chief Supervisor as required.'[5]

[1] Lloyd George, *War Memoirs*, p. 185; *Bev.* iii, p. 157, 'Cases and Rules etc. alleged to restrict output', September 1915; ASE, *Monthly Journal and Report*, October 1915.

[2] *MM* VIII, 2, p. 17; only 0·4% of the workers in the gun carriage department were women.

[3] *Mun.* 5. 79, memorandum by Raven, 16 February 1916; *Woolwich Pioneer*, 17 March 1916.

[4] *Mun.* 5.53, Deputation from Woolwich Shop Steward Committee to the Ministry of Munitions, 18 July 1917. In addition there was a separate Dilution Committee consisting of 24 representatives, each provided with office facilities by the management. At least one of these was always on the Shop Stewards' Executive.

[5] *Woolwich Pioneer*, 19 November 1915.

The ASE Executive fully accepted this position, allowing the Arsenal Shop Stewards' Committee considerably more autonomy than it would normally allow a District Committee.[1] The less skilled workers were not unorganized, the Workers' Union in particular having a powerful hold in the Arsenal.[2] But the Shop Stewards' Committee made no effort to extend its organization to the less skilled. There was, in fact, great bitterness between the two sections. In July 1914 the dismissal of a skilled man for refusing to work with non-union labour led to a strike in which the labourers came out with the craftsmen – 'drawing together all the ranks of labour for a common end'.[3] This unprecedented demonstration of unity was rapidly followed by 'the first joint wages movement ever' in the London District, in which the Allied Trades negotiated jointly with the WU and the NUGW, though they failed to force the Employers' Federation to give formal recognition to the latter.

This alliance survived into the next wage movement. In April 1915 the unions put in jointly for a 6s rise, and were eventually granted 4s by the Committee on Production. The Arsenal workers, outside the industry's procedures, then had to negotiate the rise separately with the War Office.[4] They did so as a united movement, and when, in August, the authorities attempted to split the men by offering the rise only to the skilled men and machinists, the Allied Trades officials, 'to their eternal honour', decided to stick out for the all-round increase. The front was broken however by the Arsenal Shop Stewards' Committee, which, when these negotiations were reported to it by Tom Rees,[5] the ASE district secretary, threatened strike action if the rise was not

[1] Mun. 5. 53, op. cit.; G. D. H. Cole, Workshop Organisation (Oxford, 1923 p. 18.

[2] Workers' Union branches catering solely for the Arsenal

	Dec. 1914	Dec. 1915	Dec. 1916	Dec. 1917	Dec. 1918
Woolwich 1	3,030	13,190	11,930	8,420	13,850
Woolwich 8	—	—	—	—	510

I am grateful to Dr R. Hyman, University of Warwick, for these figures. See also Woolwich Pioneer, 21 May, 17 August 1915.

[3] Woolwich Pioneer, 1 January, 20 August 1915; 18 May 1917; Sheffield Guardian, 7 August 1914; G. Askwith, Industrial Problems and Disputes (1920), pp. 356–7.

[4] Woolwich Pioneer, 23 April, 4 June, 6, 13 and 17 August 1915.

[5] Tom Rees (b. 1878). Fitter. Founded Woolwich Arsenal Shop Stewards' Committee. By 1914 elected full-time London district secretary. Influential in developing shop steward system under District Committee control throughout London district. Early in 1917 he accepted a job with the Ministry of Munitions.

immediately granted to skilled men. The leaders of the less skilled workers were deeply shocked: 'I cannot believe that the men whom I know as shop stewards in the ASE were aware of the true facts. If they were, their action means the end of all combination. We have been praying and waiting for years to knock off this sectional unionism.' Rees, who was also the honorary secretary of the Shop Stewards' Committee, replied: 'We decided that we could not wait until tinker, tailor, saddler and a lot of other people got the rise . . .' Jack Sheppard, a member of the Shop Steward Executive, and an Industrial Unionist, argued that until industrial unionism had been realized every section must look after its own interests. Asked whether, as a socialist, he should not stand by 'the lower section of society and for those chaps who are not organized', he replied:

'In my opinion people who will not organize are not worth looking after. If they care to stop in the mire they are in, that is their business. I am only prepared to help those people who help themselves. Consequently I do not stand to help those who constitute the biggest enemy – the unorganized mob.'

The labourers stuck out for their rise, and were eventually paid, but the hostility between the two sections remained. In May 1917, when the skilled engineers in the Arsenal came out in the national strike movement, the Workers' Union justified its refusal to come out by the 'betrayal' of 1915.[1]

Because the struggle for recognition and the struggle to regulate dilution did not go hand in hand at Woolwich, the onset of dilution did not have the radicalizing effect on the outlook of the skilled workers which it had, to a greater or lesser degree, elsewhere. Nevertheless there was reason to believe that the Arsenal, with its unique experience of workshop organization, might act as a base from which the independent rank-and-file movement could be launched in the London area. Economically it was not isolated, many London engineering firms doing sub-contract work for the Arsenal.[2] Nor were its workers cut off from the concerns of the mass of engineers in private industry. After Woolwich had participated in the May 1917 strikes, partially caused by the

[1] *Woolwich Pioneer*, 17 and 27 August, 3, 17 September 1915, 18 May 1917; *The Times*, 19 May 1917.
[2] *Bev.* i, pp. 86ff., 'Armament Workers Survey,' 15 January 1915.

Government's attempt to introduce dilution on commercial work, the Arsenal convener, J. E. Mills,[1] pointed out:

'Several of my colleagues and many of these men were in official positions of the local Executives of the Unions and District Committees, and they still maintain touch with the Districts they come from . . . On a National question it is impossible to imagine that Woolwich should remain as a local factory unaffected by any problems which concern the whole trade, because at least 80 % of the men have come off commercial work and are going back on commercial work if there is half a chance.[2]

The local activists saw Woolwich as the base from which a London Workers' Committee could be launched.

Anticipating events on the Clyde a Trade Union Rights Committee had been formed in London immediately after the passing of the Munitions Act in July 1915. This Committee had no direct base in the workshops, but represented a broad front of activists in the BSP, the Herald League, the Amalgamation Committee movement and other organizations. It was in contact with the militants on the Clyde, and a section of its manifesto was quoted in the CWC's first leaflet. By January 1916 the Committee had made some inroads among the Woolwich workers. A campaign was undertaken to popularize the CWC's programme of workers' participation in management as a condition of dilution or conscription, and a meeting of 200 workers 'of all grades' was persuaded to pass a resolution of support for the CWC. On the basis of this members of the Trade Union Rights Committee launched a London Workers' Committee at the end of January 1916.[3] As soon as the authorities got wind of 'hostile campaigning . . . by a few men who are circulating in the shops all kinds of wild documents, for which somebody is paying . . .', they sent the police to raid the Trade Union Rights Committee offices and impounded the propaganda material being used at Woolwich.[4] This action appears to have nipped the movement in

---

[1] Mills (d. 1951) was a member of the British Socialist Party, and the son of the chief inspector of the Western Australian Water police. In 1920 he entered parliament as MP for Dartford, which he represented 1920-2, 1923-4, and 1929-31.

[2] *Mun.* 5. 53, *op. cit.*

[3] *Woolwich Pioneer*, 13 and 20 August 1915, 21 January 1916; *Trade Unionist*, January and March 1916; *Bev.* iii, p. 95; *The Worker*, 22 January 1916; interview with Mr Frank Jackson.

[4] C. Addison, *Four and a Half years* (1934), p. 163; interview with Mr Frank Jackson.

the bud so far as Woolwich was concerned, and the London Workers' Committee, though it survived until 1919 when J. T. Murphy, acting for the National Administrative Council of the shop stewards' movement, reconstructed it, merely served to reinforce London's reputation as the home of paper committees.[1] Meanwhile the militancy on which, in January, the agitators had tried to base the London Workers' Committee, burnt itself out within a month in a trial of strength between the Government and the ASE Executive.

In November 1915 the London District Committee instructed their members at the King's Norton Metal Company to strike to enforce the raising of night-shift rates to the level prevailing in the district. The men would not come out, on the grounds that such action would be illegal. Subsequently, with the approval of the Executive, the men's leaders were fined for breach of trade union discipline, and on 7 February 1916 were forced to strike under threat of expulsion. A week later the day-shift men were also called out.[2] This was a quite untypical case in which the Executive was openly behind an illegal strike, and without the support of the men concerned. The Government at once took action, summonsing Tom Rees, the London district secretary, under DORA. This complicated the issue because Rees, who had previously worked at Woolwich, had been 'the moving power and brain' behind the establishment of the Royal Arsenal Shop Stewards' Committee.[3] By February 16th the Arsenal shop stewards had decided to call a strike if Rees was convicted. The Government was prepared to take a tough line and risk a strike 'otherwise we may as well abdicate to the ASE'.[4] Arrangements were made for 'military protection for the Arsenal, for trams, trains and for the streets of Woolwich', and for the replacement of the strikers by conscripted engineers working under military discipline. When Rees was indicted on the 19th, hundreds of Woolwich engineers left work to attend the court. Rees, however, was not convicted, and the threats from Woolwich were never put to the test. Under intense pressure from the Government, the ASE Executive agreed to rescind the fines and the District Committee's strike order and submit the claim to arbitration –

---

1 *Solidarity*, August–October 1919.

2 ASE, *Executive Minutes*, vol. 193, 9, 18 November, 14 December 1915, 25 January 1916; *Mun.* 5. 79, 'The Rees case', 18 February 1916.

3 *Woolwich Pioneer*, 19 November 1915.

4 Addison, *Four and a Half Years*, pp. 175–6.

which eventually went against the union. In return Rees was discharged.[1]

Subsequently, apart from their participation in the May 1917 strikes, the Woolwich engineers caused no serious trouble for the Government. So far as the evidence goes, it would seem that the Royal Arsenal Shop Stewards' Committee failed to provide the basis from which a London Workers' Committee could be launched partly because of the unique position that the Woolwich engineers occupied outside the normal collective bargaining procedures. Its own early experience of building workshop organization could not be generalized, for it did not share the problems of engineering workers in general. Moreover the fact that workshop organization was established so early made the impact of dilution less radicalizing in its effects than it was elsewhere. Able to control dilution through their own machinery the skilled workers could afford to maintain a contemptuous superiority towards the less skilled, an outlook which, of course, would further impede the learning of political lessons implicit in the struggles they undertook.

BARROW

Barrow was a small and isolated industrial centre largely devoted to the metal industries. In 1911 there were 12,600 metal workers, nearly half the occupied population.[2] Vickers was expanding very rapidly in the immediate pre-war years, and employed about 19,000 workers by September 1914. Of these the great majority were employed on engineering work (Table 8).[3] An embryonic workshop organization was first stimulated and then frustrated

Table 8 *Employment in Vickers, 1915–16*

	Nov. 1915	Nov. 1916
Shipbuilding	4,731	6,235
Engineering	21,178	26,872

[1] *Trade Unionist*, March 1916; ASE, *Executive Minutes*, vol. 193, 20 February, 15, 21 March 1916; *Mun.* 5. 79, memorandum by Raven, 16 February 1916.

[2] *Machinery*, 10 September 1914.

[3] *Mun.* 2. 27, 6 November 1915; *Bev.* v, p. 76, 'Report on Labour in Controlled Establishments', November 1916. Its growth probably stabilized around this point – the engineering works was no bigger a year later: *Mun.* 2.28, 17 February 1917.

by the dilution negotiations. Lyndon Macassey, fresh from the Clyde, introduced dilution during the summer of 1916 with considerable difficulty – there was a six-day strike of 7,000 engineers at the end of June – and in consultation with delegations from the shops. In the final agreement however the shop stewards were not recognized. Instead, special Permanent Committees were set up to negotiate dilution, their members appointed by the District Committees rather than elected on the shop floor. Not surprisingly these were treated with suspicion by the workers.[1]

The reluctance of the firm to recognize the shop stewards, and the failure of the workers to force them to, was probably due to the fact that the local District Committees, working closely together through a Joint Board, themselves largely fulfilled the role of workshop organization. The trade union movement in Barrow represented very little besides the Vickers workers, and the officials could therefore concentrate almost exclusively on their problems. The local officials had, in fact, proved their ability to contain tendencies towards independent workshop organization in Vickers before dilution ever became an issue. As early as 1897 shop stewards were being elected in the Vickers works, and from the outset their activities were closely controlled by the District Committee to which they reported and which convened quarterly shop steward meetings. The Barrow works had been one of the first in the country to introduce the Premium Bonus system, and the District Committee had laid down a precise procedure for dealing with grievances arising out of the working of the system, a procedure which prevented the shop stewards from doing more than reporting to the District. At no stage was the District Committee prepared to concede or press for negotiating rights for the shop stewards.[2]

During the war a number of factors operated to push the Barrow workers into building up their workshop organization independent of the official trade union movement. Presumably because of the importance of Vickers in both centres they were in close touch with the Sheffield engineers. In November 1916 Barrow had been the only centre to come out, under the leadership of the shop stewards, in sympathy over the Hargreaves issue.[3]

[1] ASE, *Executive Minutes*, vol. 195, 31 May, 3, 14, 20, 27, 29, 30 June, 4, 11 July 1916; *Mun.* 2. 27, 1 July 1916; *Mun.* 2. 28, 16 June 1917.

[2] B. Weekes, 'The Amalgamated Society of Engineers, 1880–1914' (Warwick Ph.D., 1970), pp. 9–11; G. D. H. Cole, *The Payment of Wages* (1918), pp. 137–40.

[3] *MM* VI, 1, p. 37; J. T. Murphy, *Preparing for Power* (1934), p. 131.

The precedent served them in good stead. Early in February 1917, when a similar case arose in Barrow, the men 'remembered resolutions passed at the time of the Sheffield strike' and threatened to place the matter 'in the hands of the shop stewards' unless the man in question was released from the army within seven days. On the sixth day he was returned.[1] Such militancy tended to carry the Vickers workers beyond the confines of official action. Simultaneously the formation, by the spring of 1917, of a 20–30 men Shop Stewards' Executive, representing members of all the unions in Vickers, put them beyond the collective control of the skilled unions who alone were represented on the Joint Board.[2]

The crisis came over the Premium Bonus system. Since October 1916 the firm had allegedly been systematically cutting time allowances. The Joint Board, not prepared to take (illegal) strike action, had proved unable to do anything about this. Consequently leadership passed to the shop stewards. On 21 March 1917 a strike broke out, and within two days 8,000 men were out. After a promise of arbitration by the Ministry of Labour the craft union Executives condemned the strike and instructed the men to return. A few days later the Engineering Employers' Federation added a promise of a composite conference to settle the dispute and to set up special machinery 'for dealing with grievances between the Employer and the men'. Clearly the issue of recognition of the shop stewards played a leading part in the strike. The men were adamant, voting after a week on strike by an overwhelming majority to stay out until a settlement was reached on the issue of rate cutting.[3]

Alarmed by the extent and solidity of the strike the ASE Executive took the unprecedented step of moving en bloc to Barrow. Neither the Joint Board nor the District Committee would agree to recommend resumption in the face of the men's declared determination to stay out. 'It is on the carpets [*sic*]', one District Committee member said, 'that there will be no District Committee.' Eventually the Executive was forced to meet the Shop Stewards' Executive, with whom they arranged to address a mass meeting on Saturday, March 31st. They were

[1] *Solidarity*, March 1917.
[2] *Cab*. 23. 2, 2 April 1917; ASE, *Executive Minutes*, vol. 197, 20 March 1917.
[3] *Ibid.*, 21, 23 and 26–28 March 1917; ASE, *Monthly Journal and Report*, April 1917; *Mun.* 2. 28, 24 March, 7 May 1917; *North West Daily Mail*, 24, 27–29 March 1917; *MM* VI, 1, p. 62.

shouted down and derided. Nevertheless the strike was beginning to weaken. Another ballot gave a reduced majority for staying out. Over the weekend while the Executive issued veiled threats of repressive action, the shop stewards, in consultation with the Mayor, began trying to find an acceptable compromise. At this first sign of weakening the Government stepped in. On Monday, April 2nd, notices were posted threatening the strike leaders under DORA. Simultaneously – for the Government were afraid that repression would lead, in the short term, to an extension of the strike – the Ministry of Labour offered to meet a deputation from the shop stewards once the men had returned to work. These measures broke the strike. A few men drifted back on Tuesday, and the rest voted, by a small majority, to go back the next day.[1]

The March 1917 strike represented the high point of shop steward power in Barrow. In the subsequent settlement new machinery for negotiating grievances arising out of the Premium Bonus system was established. Although the Organizing District Delegate of the ASE saw in this 'the strains of democratic idealism' recognition was still withheld from the shop stewards. Before an individual workman could get his grievance taken up by a shop representative, he was subjected to 'persuasion' both by his own rate fixer and by the chief rate-fixer. If he managed to keep his end up through this, the case was referred to an appeals committee consisting of two representatives of the firm and two specially elected departmental representatives of the man's trade. Sectionalism was thus built into the machinery. Failing agreement by this committee, the matter was simply referred to the directors for decision. At no point did the agreement recognize the shop stewards, or permit access to higher management even by a committee specially elected to deal with the grievances arising out of the Premium Bonus system.[2]

For some months after the March strike the Vickers shop stewards remained a threat to the authority of the Joint Board. They brought Barrow into the national strike movement in May, and during June led a movement of opposition to the Permanent Committees set up in the dilution agreement. Despite Govern-

[1] ASE, *Monthly Journal and Report*, May 1917; ASE, *Executive Minutes*, vol. 197, 29–31 March, 1 April 1917; *Cab.* 23. 2, 26 March, 2 April 1917; *Mun.* 2. 28, 7 May 1917; *North West Daily Mail*, 31 March, 2, 4 April 1917.
[2] ASE, *Monthly Journal and Report*, May 1917; Cole, *The Payment of Wages*, pp. 137–40.

ment fears this did not result in strike action.[1] Subsequently the rank-and-file movement was limited to a 'real rebel element . . . composed of zealous and intelligent men . . .', which, failing to capture the Vickers Shop Steward Executive, eventually formed a Barrow Workers' Committee.[2] But this was never able to achieve a position of mass leadership.

In Barrow independent rank-and-file organization did not emerge because its precondition, recognized workshop organization, was never established. The failure of workshop organization to acquire negotiating rights at Vickers meant that no unofficial organization based on the shop stewards could hope to rival the authority of the Joint Board, except at moments when the workers were actually on strike. The ability of the local Joint Board of skilled engineering trade unions and the Vickers management to contain the very strong pressures towards functioning workshop organization, which arose out of both dilution and the Premium Bonus system, is most easily explained by the fact that Barrow was a company town. In the absence of competition between local employers, craft unionism in Barrow developed in a quite exceptionally centralized form. The one-to-one relationship between Vickers and the Joint Board prevented the full development of that direct democracy of the workshop which had such explosive results elsewhere.

THE TYNE

Tyneside was the most important gap in the development of the shop stewards' movement. It is also the most difficult to explain. Certainly the local industrial structure was an inhibiting factor. Like the Clyde this was a shipbuilding centre, nearly two-thirds of the local metal workers working in the shipyards or marine engineering shops. Unlike the Clyde, however, the counterveiling munitions sector consisted almost entirely of the single giant arms factory at Elswick. By 1914 about 20,000 people, out of the 48,000 metal workers on the Tyne, were employed by Armstrong-Whitworth. During the war this proportion increased as local labour migrated to Elswick, attracted by the high wage-level. By November 1916 there were 47,938 workers at Elswick and a further 9,692 in the adjacent shipyard.[3] The very dominance of

[1] ASE, *Monthly Journal and Report*, April, June 1918; *Mun.* 2. 28, 2, 16 June 1917.

[2] *Solidarity*, March 1917, May 1918.

[3] Census of England and Wales, 1911 and 1921, Occupation Tables;

the single arms firm would tend to make the establishment of a local Workers' Committee unnecessary. However, there were other engineering works, particularly the marine engineering departments of the shipbuilding firms, where the level of militancy was high, and unofficial links did develop between the militants in these firms and those at Elswick which could have formed the basis of local independent rank-and-file organization. Thus the industrial structure alone cannot explain why the engineers did not come out in the May 1917 strike; why in November 1917 attempts to set up a Workers' Committee met with 'acrimonious' rejection;[1] and why in March 1919 the shop steward movement was still 'of a very elementary character. True there are a number of sectional shop stewards' Committees, confined to their respective Trade Unions, but Committees of the type of the Clyde Workers' Committee do not exist.'[2]

The failure on the Tyne was emphasized by the fact that before the war it had been one of the leading militant districts in the country. The beginnings of the Engineering Employers' Federation had been created here in the battle over dilution at Elswick in the mid-1890s. For the first ten years of the century the north-east coast had been 'the main trouble spot' in the ASE: 'It was the men of the North East Coast who refused to compromise.'[3] A rule-book shop steward system had been developed early on the Tyne, and after the lockout a strong unofficial movement, dominating the ASE District Committee, had emerged. In 1908 a seven-month strike in defence of the district rate was led by the District Committees in defiance of Executive instructions to return to work. It was the Tyneside engineers' insistence on local autonomy in the conduct of trade policy that finally precipitated George Barnes' resignation from the union's general secretary-ship. The strike was, however, defeated, and in 1910 the Tyne accepted a five-year wages pact. Even before the war broke out the leadership of militancy had clearly passed from Tyneside to Clydeside.[4] In the autumn of 1915 the unrest over the Munitions

H. A. Mess, *Industrial Tyneside: a Social Survey* (1928), p. 40; *MM* I, 3, pp. 61, 122; *Bev.* v, p. 76, 'Report on Labour in Controlled Establishments', November 1916.

[1] *Mun.* 2. 28, 3 November 1917.

[2] *The Worker*, 8 March 1919. See also *Solidarity*, June 1918.

[3] H. A. Clegg, A. Fox and A. F. Thompson, *A History of British Trade Unions since 1889*, vol. I (Oxford, 1964), pp. 38, 161, 163, 342, 438.

[4] R. Croucher, 'Local Autonomy in the Amalgamated Society of Engineers, 1898–1914' (Warwick M.A., 1971), pp. 39–71.

Act was seen as 'little and evanescent' compared with that on the Clyde.[1] Nonetheless the dilution crisis was exceptionally bitter and long drawn out on the Tyne. This crisis must be closely examined to see why it produced workshop organization with full negotiating rights at Elswick but not a Tyneside Workers' Committee.

The employment of women on shell and fuse work was already recognized at Elswick prior to the war, and from the first month of the war dilution on shell and fuse work went ahead with little difficulty.[2] But the first attempt to dilute skilled work outside this sphere, in February 1915, met with determined resistance. A mass meeting of the skilled engineers, called by the shop stewards, threatened strike action if cheap labour was introduced. During March the matter was settled at a local conference. The workers' claim was accepted, and it was agreed that whatever class of labour was employed on the work in question the full district rate would be paid. To enforce this 'representatives of the skilled workers should be allowed to inspect both the credentials of the new workers engaged and the work actually done by them'. This was the first time the shop stewards were recognized at Elswick.[3] By November 1915 this agreement had developed into full *de facto* recognition of the bargaining rights of a joint shop steward committee representing members of the ASE and other craft unions in the plant.

On November 5th 1915 the Elswick management undertook to suspend any further dilution pending the conclusion of an agreement on the general introduction of dilution. Within a week a dispute had arisen over an alleged extension of dilution, leading to a boycott of certain work by the skilled men. The management (and the Ministry of Munitions who were consulted) declined to force this to an issue as long as the more general scheme was under negotiation. But when, on December 4th, the management's scheme was put to the stewards they turned it down flat. The management gave up, insisting that the Government take over

[1] *Mun.* 5. 73, memorandum from Macassey on Clyde and Tyne, 18 December 1915.
[2] B. Drake, *Women in the Engineering Trades* (1917), p. 13; Jefferys, *The Story of the Engineers* (London, 1946), p. 174; *MM* I, 2, p. 17; *Bev.* i, p. 359, Discussion on the possibility of increasing the production of shell (? June 1915); Mun. 2. 27, 16 October 1915.
[3] G. D. H. Cole, *Trade Unionism and Munitions* (Oxford, 1923), pp. 66–7; ASE, *Monthly Journal and Report*, March, May 1915.

responsibility for introducing dilution, 'for [the men] are in an obdurate mood'.[1]

While the Ministry of Munitions prepared its offensive on dilution, militancy accumulated at Elswick. It is possible that at this point there was some liaison with the CWC. A meeting called by 'the shop stewards' committee' (probably the Elswick committee) was held on January 12th

'to discuss the EC's action as to the Dilution of Labour. It was decided this question was not a matter for the officials to deal with, but for the rank and file of the Trade Unions concerned to settle. An endeavour is being made to bring London and Glasgow centres into line with the Tyne. I expect that Delegates from those centres will attend a mass meeting it is proposed to hold within the next fortnight.'[2]

This attitude was carried into practice when a further dispute over dilution arose the next week. On January 19th a deputation of toolsetters in the shell factory (members of the UMWA) met the management, and refused 'to follow ordinary procedure and allow their case to be taken up by their official locally and centrally'.[3] When the mass meeting reassembled on Sunday, January 23rd, it resolved to resist dilution until the Government passed a measure which would ensure a return to pre-war conditions after the war.[4] By the time the Dilution Commissioners arrived on the Tyne at the end of January, therefore, the makings of an unofficial movement had emerged at Elswick. But it did not survive, and the Government had no need to use repressive methods on the Tyne. The main reason for its failure to develop further was probably the very generous terms offered by the Tyne Commissioners. On the one hand the dilutees were guaranteed the full rate of those they replaced, with no deductions as on the Clyde for extra supervision, etc. On the other hand, female dilution was kept to a minimum, and restricted to the simpler, automatic machines. Consequently, though 633 women

[1] *Bev.* iv, pp. 353–6, 'Dilution at Elswick, Report by Mr. Kaylor', 7 December 1915; *Bev.* iii, pp. 181–6, (a) a letter from West to Beveridge, 29 November 1915, (b) notes on meeting held in Mr Brackenberg's office, 25 November 1915, (c) Beveridge to Llewellyn Smith, 27 November 1915; *Mun.* 2. 27, 15 January 1916.

[2] *Bev.* iii, p. 294, note (n.d.). See also *The Worker*, 29 January 1916.

[3] *Bev.* iii, p. 298, report on a meeting at Elswick, 19 January 1916; *ibid.*, pp. 295–6, jottings with reference to this meeting (n.d.).

[4] *Mun.* 2. 27, 29 January 1916.

had been introduced under the scheme at Elswick by mid-March, the north-east coast remained (after Wales) the least diluted area in the country.[1]

Though dilution caused further trouble on the Tyne, this did not again threaten to lead to a breakaway from the official trade union structure. But trouble on the wages front did. The Tyne was a low wage area, the 1914 district rate, at 37s, being 1s 3d below the Clyde and 4s below Sheffield.[2] Up to the end of 1916, the wartime increases awarded on the Tyne totalled 7s, the norm for the country as a whole. At first the Tyne engineers were content to try to make up for their low district rate by pushing up earnings at workshop level. But the introduction of the Committee on Production's national arbitration scheme in the early months of 1917 forced the issue. In November 1916 the ASE and other craft unions had put in for a 6s increase. The employers made no offer. In other areas claims submitted at this date were allowed to drop in view of the national 5s award operative from 1 April 1917, but on the Tyne the unions stuck out for the settlement of their 6s claim over and above this award. They were putting the committee's undertaking to level up the rates in low paid districts to the test.[3]

On 28 February 1917, 'very stormy' mass meetings were held during working hours at Newcastle, Jarrow and South Shields to demand the 6s advance. They resolved to strike on March 8th if a satisfactory settlement had not been reached by then. When the employers agreed to a composite conference to be held on March 16th the strike threat was postponed. The conference was unsuccessful, and three days later the men at Elswick came out on strike. The next day engineering workers in many of the leading shipyards on the Tyne followed. This, the only large strike on the Tyne during the war, involved 12,000 men (the whole membership of the ASE) and lasted for six working days. The District Committee had been associated with the threat to strike, but the strike itself was unofficial, and the strikers resisted

[1] *Forward*, 12 February 1916; *Bev.* v, pp. 98–102, letter from Corydon Marks to Lloyd George, 10 March 1916; *Mun.* 2. 27, 4 and 11 March, 1 July 1916.

[2] *Sixteenth Abstract of Labour Statistics of the United Kingdom*, 1914, PP lxxx, p. 301.

[3] *Mun.* 5. 73, *op. cit.*, *Mun.* 2. 27, 25 September 1915, 10 June, 7 October 1916; *Mun.* 2. 1, 18 September 1915; Engineering Employers' Federation, *Wage Movements, 1879–1925* (1926); ASE, *Monthly Journal and Report*, February 1917.

G

Executive instructions to return. They did not go back until they had exacted a promise from the Minister of Labour that the COP would consider the case within seven days. On the 26th the COP met and awarded 2s over and above the national award. Whatever unofficial links between the Tyneside firms were involved during the strike these were not subsequently developed. For the rest of the war things remained quiet on the Tyne.[1]

The importance of the prior development of workshop bargaining to the success of the shop stewards' movement in Glasgow and Sheffield is demonstrated by the experience of the revolutionaries in Barrow who, in the absence of such a development, failed in their attempt to construct a genuine Workers' Committee. The degree to which the Workers' Committees arose in reaction to the restraints imposed by national collective bargaining on workshop and local militancy is revealed by the case of Woolwich, where, because the Arsenal was outside the national procedural agreements and consequently unimpeded by the attempts of national or district union officials to impose conformity to these agreements, little antagonism developed between the shop stewards and the official union machine. In Barrow and Woolwich the capacity of the union to contain wartime militancy was clearly related to the overwhelming predominance of a single munitions plant in each area.

In both Woolwich and Barrow the early pre-war development of shop stewards' organization on an official basis goes some way to explain the failure of the revolutionary shop stewards' movement to establish itself during the war. This may also be true of the Tyne. From the outset, in the nine hours strike of 1871 the District Committee had evolved in close partnership with delegates elected in the workshops.[2] The Tyne may be a case where militant local autonomy was so strong a tradition that, instead of laying a basis for independent rank-and-file organization, it could act as a substitute for it. A comparative study of the Clyde strike of 1903 and the Tyne strike of 1908 would appear to confirm this, revealing that rank-and-file organization in the workshops capable of functioning independently of the District Committee was far less advanced before

[1] ASE, *Monthly Journal and Report*, March and April 1917; *Mun.* 2. 28, 3, 10, 24 March, 7 April 1917; ASE, *Executive Minutes*, vol. 197, 21, 22, 27 February, 8, 17, 19–21, 26 March 1917.

[2] J. Burnett, *A History of the Engineers' Strike in Newcastle and Gateshead* (Newcastle, 1872), pp. 7, 28.

the war on the Tyne than on the Clyde.[1] However true this is some part of the explanation of the failure of a Tyne Workers' Committee to emerge must also be sought in the fact that both in the dilution struggle and, later, over wages, militancy was rewarded with success before it could develop forms of organization which would carry it beyond the confines of the official trade union structures. In particular, the exceptionally favourable terms under which dilution was carried through on the Tyne may help to explain why the sudden disintegration of traditional craft security in 1915–16 did not create opportunities equivalent to those on which the revolutionaries of Glasgow and Sheffield were able to capitalize.

[1] Croucher, 'Local Autonomy in the Amalgamated Society of Engineers', pp. 67–8, 82–5. The explanation of this difference, however, remains for the time being a mystery.

Chapter 7

The May Strikes

The strike movement of May 1917 was the largest of the war, involving 200,000 engineering workers over a period of more than three weeks. One-and-a-half million working days were lost in all. The strike began in Manchester at the end of April, flared through forty-eight towns up and down the country over the next few weeks, and ended during its fourth week.[1] Two Government decisions were responsible for precipitating the outburst: the decision to abolish the Trade Card scheme, and the decision to extend dilution to private work. Though the strike was formally defeated, and the Trade Card scheme was abolished, the Government's Bill to introduce dilution on private work was subsequently dropped. The strike took the shop stewards' movement into the centre of the political stage, thus preparing the way for its head-on collision with the Government over the continuation of the war in January 1918. At the same time, because of the issues over which it was fought, it tended to reinforce the craft character of the movement, and thus to prefigure its final defeat in the crisis of January 1918.

The Trade Card scheme, signed in November 1916 during the Hargreaves strike in Sheffield, and operative from February 1917, guaranteed exemption from military service to all members of the craft unions on munitions work. By April the Government was convinced of the need to abolish it, and to substitute a more flexible Schedule of Protected Occupations. They had little option in the matter, as Christopher Addison, Minister of Munitions since the formation of Lloyd George's Cabinet in December, explained to the Engineering Employers:

[1] *MM* vi, 1, p. 119.

'the exigencies of the War Office were such that we had to do it during May, whether we were ready or not . . . The military exigencies of the situation dictated it, and we had to make the best of it . . . We had to let the thing go in May in order that certain men outside the categories of the schedule could be called up during May.'[1]

When Addison first proposed the Schedule of Protected Occupations to the craft unions on April 3rd they were adamant in their demand for the retention of the Trade Card scheme. The ASE called a special delegate conference towards the end of April which demanded that no skilled men should be called up until all dilutees of military age had been taken. The Executive, pressed by this meeting, issued a veiled threat of national strike action, and forced the Government to postpone the introduction of the Schedule for a week to May 7th while they took a ballot of the members. On May 5th, after a series of frantic conferences with the ASE Executive – 'the most wearisome and patience-racking I have ever experienced' – the Government apparently agreed to give a written guarantee that no skilled man should be taken before the dilutees of military age had been called up. In return the union accepted the Schedule.[2]

Addison's patience had been racked in vain. By May 5th, strikes had already broken out over the issue of dilution on private work. Deadlock on this question had been reached several months earlier when, in December 1916, the Government decided 'to proceed without any further discussion of the matter with the ASE, lest they should force the issue by taking a ballot of their members, which would almost certainly result in an adverse vote'.[3] After allowing the matter to rest for some months the Government, without further consultation with the unions, introduced an amending Bill to the Munitions Act to push through dilution on private work. This was at the end of March 1917. The need for more skilled men on munitions work was now urgent due to the offensive on the Western Front, and these men could only come from private work. By hook or by crook the Government intended to transfer the necessary skilled labour on to

---

[1] *Mun.* 5. 79, 'History of the Strike', 29 August 1917.
[2] *Ibid.; MM* vi, 1, pp. 95–108; C. Addison, *Four and a Half Years* (1934), pp. 364–71, 374.
[3] *MM* vi, 1, p. 54.

munitions work.[1] But if this were done without simultaneously extending dilution to the private trades the latter would be crippled. 'Dilution is the only means by which private industries can be maintained in such a state that they can recover after the War and compete against foreign trade.'[2]

The decision to extend dilution to private work, even more than the threat to abolish the Trade Card scheme, flew in the face of previous Government pledges to the engineers. Clearly trouble was to be expected. The strikes on the Tyne and in Barrow gave ample warning to the Government. On April 6th Lloyd George drew the attention of his Cabinet to 'a very considerable and highly organized labour movement with seditious tendencies, which was developing in many industrial centres'. But, for the time being, the Cabinet remained content to try to undermine the influence of the 'violent anarchists' by removing 'genuine and legitimate grievances'.[3] This was hardly compatible with their concern to press the issues of conscription and dilution.

The strike originated in Lancashire, the heart of the textile engineering industry. Textile engineering was the largest sector of the metal industries not extensively absorbed into munitions work. In May 1915, for example, only 4,000 of the 11,000 ASE members in Manchester were employed on munitions work, and the largest arms firm in the area, Armstrong-Whitworth at Openshaw (with 7,000 workers by 1917), was small by the standards of other areas. Consequently the problem of dilution on commercial work was more acute in Lancashire than anywhere else in the country. It had first been proposed in September 1914, and attempts to introduce it during 1916 met with vigorous opposition.[4]

Twedales and Smalley, a textile engineering firm near Rochdale, precipitated the crisis of May 1917. In March they sought to transfer women dilutees from an expired shell contract to their commercial work. When 500 craftsmen refused to teach the women, the firm sacked them and took on blackleg labour. From the beginning of April the Rochdale District Committee was backing the locked-out men, and the ASE Executive took up

[1] *MM* vi, 1, pp. 57, 79–82.

[2] G. D. H. Cole, *Trade Unionism and Munitions* (Oxford, 1923), p. 147.

[3] *Cab*. 23. 2, 6, 13 April 1917.

[4] *Bev*. iv, p. 212, Intelligence Report, 26 October 1915; *Machinery*, 19 September 1914, 13 May 1915; *MM* vi, 1, p. 109; *Mun*. 2. 27, 4 March, 22 July 1916.

their case, demanding that the Government prosecute the firm. The Government was reluctant to prosecute, and the firm would not respond to milder pressures. On April 29th, after a month of waiting, the Rochdale District Committee threatened to call out all its members in the district unless the Government had taken action by May 3rd. While the Government continued to prevaricate, an unofficial movement in Manchester seized the reins from the Rochdale officials. On April 30th the national strike movement was launched in Manchester.[1]

A Manchester Workers' Committee had been founded in April 1916, within a week of the Clyde deportations,[2] but as an effective mass force the Manchester shop stewards' movement originated in a wages movement during the winter of 1916–17. In September 1916 the skilled engineering unions put in for a 9s rise and the equivalent on piece rates. The COP handed out the 3s award to timeworkers only which it had already given in Coventry, Sheffield and other centres. But this award had been designed to deal with centres very largely on war work, where the pieceworkers were earning far more than the district rate. In Manchester, where a high proportion of skilled men were relatively low paid pieceworkers in textile engineering shops, the award caused a furore. On December 2nd, 2,000 engineers struck. At a mass meeting they called for a clear definition of the award – not believing that the pieceworkers had been omitted – and threatened a general local strike if a reply did not reach them the same day. Instead of an answer, they received a hasty deputation from the ASE Executive who succeeded in getting them back to work.

The opportunity had been used, however, to set up a Strike Committee, which remained in being after the return to work. Two months later there was still no settlement of the piece rate question, and the Committee again threatened a general strike. This was averted by the extension, on February 27th, of the 3s flat rate increase to the pieceworkers.[3] Meanwhile a broader Joint Shop Stewards' Committee, successor to the Manchester Workers' Committee, had been formed late in 1916, under the

---

[1] *Mun.* 2. 28, 7 April 1917; *MM* VI, 1, pp. 103–5. When the Government eventually did prosecute the firm the Rochdale men were the first to return to work: *ibid.*, p. 114.

[2] *Trade Unionist*, June 1916; *The Socialist*, January 1917.

[3] ASE, *Executive Minutes*, vol. 196, 2, 4, 5, 13 December 1916; Engineering Employers' Federation, *Wage Movements, 1897–1925* (1926), *passim; Mun.* 2. 28, 24 February 1917.

leadership of George Peet[1] and William McLaine,[2] both members of the BSP, with the aim of extending workshop organization and linking up the various unions in the shops. Peet was in contact with Murphy, and it was probably under the influence of the Sheffield movement that the shop stewards' movement got under way in Manchester. In March 1917 these two unofficial bodies appear to have merged to form a Joint Engineering Shop Stewards' Committee. This committee was a large part of what Lloyd George had in mind when he spoke of the growth of 'a highly organized labour movement with seditious tendencies'. It was characterized by the local ASE district secretary as an attempt to 'overthrow the recognized leaders and place the executive power in the hands of the shop stewards'. On April 22nd the Joint Engineering Shop Stewards' Committee decided to arrange a workshop ballot on a call for sympathetic strike action with the Rochdale engineers. At the same time it declared its intention of taking independent action if the officials failed to maintain the Trade Card scheme. The ballot went in favour of strike action and on the 29th the Committee called the men out. As from May 5th, the strike became operative against the withdrawal of the Trade Card scheme as well.[3]

By Saturday, May 4th, the strike had spread beyond Manchester to at least eighteen other towns in Lancashire, and involved about 60,000 workers. Over the whole period of the strike these accounted for something like half the total working days lost. From Monday, May 7th, new forces came in daily. Sheffield and Rotherham struck on that day, the 15,000 workers involved losing about 225,000 working days by the end of the strike, one-sixth of the total. On the 8th, 30,000 Coventry engineers came out, but most of them returned the next day and the remainder on Monday, May 14th. Birmingham failed to come out

[1] George Peet (b. 1884). Fitter. Stood for election as ASE assistant general secretary in 1916–17. Secretary National Administrative Committee of shop stewards' movement from foundation in August 1917. Member BSP. Joined Communist Party.

[2] William McLaine (1891–1960). ASE, BSP, frequent contributor to *The Call*. Wrote BSP pamphlet *Trade Unionism at the Crossroads*, October 1917. On National Administrative Committee of shop stewards' movement. Lecturer Scottish Labour College, 1919–20. Central Committee member of Communist Party in 1920. Later left CP, became assistant general secretary of AEU, and historian of early engineering trade unionism.

[3] ASE, *Quarterly Report*, March 1917, G. Peet's election address; *Mun.* 2. 28, 17 March 1917; *Mun.* 5. 79, *op. cit.; The Socialist*, January 1917; *MM* VI, 1, pp. 110, pp. 110–11.

altogether, as did Glasgow and the Tyne. By the end of the week, Saturday, May 12th, the strike was general in and around London. As the strike spread the need for some sort of national co-ordination became acute. Direct press reporting of the strike was forbidden until its third week. Rumours abounded. The strikers in one area had little accurate idea of their support elsewhere. Postal and telegraphic communications were likely to be intercepted. Teams of motor-cyclists – first used in the Hargreaves strike five months earlier – were used by the strikers to transmit information from one area to another. But this too had its drawbacks, if only because, as the official history commented, it tended 'to dissipate the energies of the more forcible and influential leaders'. In any case rushing around on motor-bikes was no sufficient answer to the increasingly hard line taken by the Government. On May 9th, two days after Sheffield had joined the strike, the Government threatened to take 'effective action against those responsible for instigating the strikes', and on the 11th posters were issued to the centres of disaffection calling on all loyal citizens to resume work. The strike leaders were threatened under DORA with sentences up to life imprisonment.[1]

For some months before the May strikes a national committee of the Workers' Committee movement had, in theory, been in existence. The smashing of the CWC in the spring of 1916 spread deportees into several industrial centres, and with them the ideas and experience of the shop stewards' movement. Arthur MacManus settled in Birkenhead and was active promoting the formation of a Workers' Committee.[2] A committee had already been formed in London and during the spring and summer others were formed in Manchester, Edinburgh and elsewhere.[3] In June the *Trade Unionist* reported: '. . . committees are being formed up and down the country and an effort is being made to arrange a conference from all parts'. Eventually in November, a couple of weeks before the Hargreaves strike broke out in Sheffield,

[1] *MM* VI, 1, pp. 109–14; *Mun.* 2. 28, 19 May 1917; Addison, *Four and a Half Years*, p. 378. The Government had leaflets printed, purporting to be from Wilhelm II, and Hindenburg, and headed 'Engineers on Strike. Kamerads. Greetings and Thanks . . .' For some reason these were never used. W. Kendall, *The Revolutionary Movement in Great Britain* (1969), p. 370, quoting *The Herald*, 22 December 1917.
[2] *Mun.* 2. 28, 17 March 1917; *Forward*, 10 June 1916; T. Bell, *Pioneering Days* (1941), p. 125. The Birkenhead Workers' Committee was already underway before MacManus arrived in the area: ASE, *Monthly Journal and Report*, March 1916.   [3] *Mun.* 2. 27, 18 March, 8 April 1916.

MacManus managed to get together militants from a variety of centres, including Clydeside, Barrow, Manchester and London. The meeting, held in the BSP's Hyndman Hall in Manchester, elected Sam Bradley as national secretary and MacManus as chairman, decided to issue a manifesto (closely modelled on the first leaflet of the Clyde Workers' Committee), print membership cards, and charge 1d per week membership fee. It was, however, very unrepresentative in character – there was at this point no genuinely mass-based Workers' Committee in existence in any locality – and little seems to have come out of it apart from a call for a second national meeting to be held at Easter 1917.[1]

When the second conference assembled in Manchester on May 5th–6th, the national strike was already in progress. The meeting made no attempt to assume direction of the strike,[2] probably because the urgent need for some form of ad hoc national committee representative of the day-by-day extension of the strike movement prevented serious consideration being given at this point to the task for which the conference had been summoned, the establishment of a permanent and properly constituted national body. It was presumably this meeting, however, which convened the national conference of strike delegates which met in Derby a few days later, on Saturday, May 12th. From Derby they proceeded to London, where, on the 15th, a new conference was convened 'to deal with the work of organizing and co-ordinating the districts affected and to decide on a common line of action'.[3] One hundred delegates from thirty-four different districts duly assembled at the Fellowship Hall, Walworth, and remained in permanent session for the next three days. They exchanged information about the progress of the strike, producing a 'Daily Bulletin' of news from the localities.[4] Their main purpose was not, however, to extend the strike, but to open negotiations for a settlement. 'I am a delegate on a committee to stop the strike', said George Peet, secretary of the Manchester Committee, after his arrest,[5] William Gallacher, who visited London early in the week, wrote later: 'My impression

---

[1] *The Socialist*, January 1917; J. T. Murphy, *Preparing for Power* (1934), pp. 145–6.

[2] Murphy, *ibid.*, pp. 136–7.

[3] *Manchester Guardian*, 14 May 1917. The London District Committee of the ASE seems to have been instrumental in convening this conference: ASE *Executive Minutes*, vol. 197, 16 May 1917.

[4] *MM* VI, p. 114; ASE, *Executive Minutes*, 16 May 1917; *Sheffield Daily Telegraph*, 19 May 1917.   [5] *Sheffield Independent*, 19 May 1917.

was that they hadn't their hearts in the strike and would not be at all displeased if something happened to call it off.'[1] This timidity reflected not only fear of the Government's threats, but also the weakening of the strike in its original stronghold, Lancashire. The Government's strong words had given heart to the local ASE officials in Manchester, who repudiated the strike and its leaders on Saturday, May 12th, and called for a return to work by the Monday. On the same day a mass meeting of the Oldham ASE decided by a large majority to go back. From Monday, May 14th, the return began in Lancashire, and half the Manchester strikers were back by the 15th when the Walworth conference assembled. Their power was slipping away, and from the start the Manchester delegates at Walworth argued for an immediate resumption and a face-saving settlement.[2]

On the first day the Walworth delegates attempted to open negotiations with the Ministry of Munitions, but were rebuffed by Christopher Addison who wrote that he would only meet them if asked to do so by the ASE Executive.[3] On the second day the conference sent a delegation to the ASE head office to demand that the Executive 'go with them to the Government re dilution on private work, and also as a secondary consideration, the retention of the Trade Card', and claiming the right to negotiate and make a settlement on behalf of the strikers. The Executive, which had only admitted the deputation after a long debate, listened with mounting irritation. After further debate they wrote to the Walworth conference that they could not allow 'representatives from an unauthorized conference to take part in negotiations and conclude an agreement upon a question which affects the whole society'. In the early stages of the strike the unofficial leaders had rejected the trade union Executives out of hand. On May 10th, for example, George Peet had wired the Ministry of Munitions: 'Joint Engineering Shop Stewards'

---

[1] W. Gallacher, *Revolt on the Clyde* (1936), pp. 146–7. See also *MM* VI, 1' pp. 114, 117.

[2] *MM* IV, 1, p. 113; *Manchester Guardian*, 14 and 15 May 1917; *Mun. 2.* 28, 19 May 1917; ASE, *Executive Minutes*, 15 May 1917. The strike was also weakened in the Midlands when Derby and Coventry decided to return over the weekend.

[3] *MM* VI, 1, p. 114. This policy was confirmed by the Cabinet on the 16th: 'The Government should adhere to its policy of recognising only the constituted authority of the Trade Unions, and that no deputation from the shop stewards' should be received except at the request of the executive of the Union.' *Cab.* 23. 2, 16 May 1917.

Committee repudiates any interference by the official executives of the workers in the present dispute.' The refusal of both the Ministry and the Executive to permit them to negotiate now led to a precipitate climb down from the original position. On the third day the Walworth conference despatched a new deputation to the Executive, which coolly informed the disbelieving Councilmen that they had never claimed the right to negotiate with the Government or to settle the matter on behalf of the men. This, they said, was 'a misunderstanding on the part of the Executive'. Instead, William McLaine and E. Airey, the leader of the Sheffield delegation at Walworth, insisted that the purpose of the strike had been to support the Executive in its difficult negotiations, not to challenge its authority. All the strike leaders claimed was the right 'to place the position of the rank and file before the Government and demonstrate that the EC was right. Having done that the conference was done. They would then report back to the conference, and get back to the districts and report.'

This statement represented a considerable retreat from the position taken earlier by George Peet and the Manchester shop stewards. But it was not capitulation. The Walworth delegates still refused to accept the right of the Executive to settle the strike, insisting that any agreement negotiated by it must be submitted to a ballot vote of the men on strike. As to what would happen if the ballot vote went against the Executive the strike leaders were vague, but menacing: 'The further course of action we are unable to state but will be determined on by the majority opinion in each locality. Through what channels it may be put into operation, we cannot at the moment say.'[1]

Had the Executive and the Ministry agreed to this procedure, and the Walworth delegates dispersed back to the provinces, the strike might well have gained in strength. Despite some weakening in Lancashire and the Midlands the strike was far from dead. In Sheffield and London it remained solid, and on the very day when the return started in Manchester, the Liverpool and Birkenhead engineers came out. On the 16th the strike spread to electrical workers in London, and attempts were made to stop the power stations in Manchester and other centres. On the 17th Dave Ramsay[2] and W. F. Watson were sent to Glasgow from Walworth,

1 ASE, *Executive Minutes*, 11, 16, 17 May 1917.
2 David Ramsay. Pattern maker. Member of the SDF, and later, SLP. Treasurer for Executive of Amalgamation Committee movement, and

hard on the heels of the pessimistic Gallacher, to try to persuade the Clyde to come out. Faced with this continuing escalation of the strike the Government intervened sharply, While the Walworth deputation stated their new terms to the Executive at Peckam Road on the morning of May 17th, warrants were issued for the arrest of ten of the strike leaders.[1]

The Executive, privately informed that the arrests were about to take place, immediately suspended its discussions with the Walworth delegates, adding mysteriously; 'Circumstances have arisen which have made it impossible for Council to reply to the request put by their deputation.'[2] Police raided the Walworth conference and confiscated correspondence and documents relating to the strike. At about 6 o'clock the Executive learned that seven of the ten wanted men were safely under lock and key at Bow Street.[3] Delighted by this news they at once got in touch with the Walworth conference in order to press home their advantage.[4] The arrests and the raid had completely intimidated the Walworth delegates. Having appointed a third deputation to settle matters with the Executive the conference broke up and dispersed. Next day agreement was reached with the Executive along the lines previously suggested by the strike leaders, but with one crucial modification: 'That we request the Executive Council to attend with us at the Ministry of Munitions in order to state our case and then immediately return to our districts telling them we have carried out our mandate and *advising them to return to work*, leaving the matter with the Executive Council. . . .' The pill was slightly sweetened by the assertion that it would only be considered binding on the delegates when they had

subsequently for National Administrative Committee of shop stewards' movement. Worked full time for shop stewards' movement from 1919 as London organizer. Shop steward delegate to second congress of Comintern in Summer 1920.

[1] *MM* vi, 1, p. 115; W. F. Watson, *Watson's Reply* (1920), p. 24. The Government had earlier put off arresting the strike leaders in order to give the King and Queen, who were visiting the north-west, the opportunity of awing the strikers back to work: C. Addison, *Four and a Half Years*, p. 379; *Mun.* 5. 79, 'History of the Strike', 29 August 1917; B. Thompson, *The Scene Changes* (1939), p. 366.

[2] ASE, *Executive Minutes*, 18 May 1917.

[3] *MM* vi, 1, p. 115; Addison, *Four and a Half Years*, p. 382; *Sheffield Daily Telegraph*, 19 May 1917; *Sheffield Independent*, 19 May 1917.

[4] 'The A.S.E. Executive were, I believe without exception, delighted that we had arrested some of the ringleaders . . .': Addison, *Four and a Half Years*, p. 382.

'received assurances of no further arrests, of no victimization and in regard to releases'.[1]

The negotiations took place on Saturday, May 19th. At first the Walworth delegates insisted on the release of the arrested men as a precondition of negotiations, but 'in a few minutes' the Executive smoothed out this 'misunderstanding'. For two hours they stated their grievances over the withdrawal of the Trade Card scheme and the Dilution Bill, while Addison listened 'sympathetically'. They criticized, not the Executive who 'have tried to do what they could', but the Government who 'have checkmated them and held them off'. 'They knew that their executive had all along opposed the [Dilution Bill], but it was unable to make its opposition effective. They felt therefore that constitutional practice must go by the board. There is no power behind the elbow of constitutional practice today, and force has got to be met with force.' Having achieved their main aim of 'strengthening the hands of our executives', the strike delegates withdrew, leaving the Executive to negotiate the settlement.

The final settlement was agreed between Addison and the ASE that afternoon, and ratified by the Prime Minister. The Walworth delegates were committed to 'advising the men to return to work at once', and to 'using their best endeavours' to prevent unconstitutional action in the future. In return the Government undertook, not to withdraw the charges against the arrested men, but merely to have them released pending trial. Guarantees were also given that no more men would be arrested and that there would be no victimization in Government and controlled establishments during the return to work. Neither of the major issues over which the strike had been fought were so much as mentioned in the agreement. Subsequently the arrested men were released, and the charges dropped, but only after they had all signed a statement drafted by the authorities: 'I undertake to adhere to the agreement arrived at on Saturday, 19th May, between the Minister of Munitions and the Executive Committee of the ASE acting at the request of the unofficial strike committee.'[2] At national level the route had been, formally, complete.

But the Walworth delegates had ceased accurately to reflect the spirit of the rank and file in the country. In many areas the

[1] ASE, *Executive Minutes*, 18 May 1917 (author's italics).
[2] *MM* VI, 1, pp. 116–18; *Four and a Half Years*, p. 385; Bell, *Pioneering Days*, p. 125, claims that MacManus did not sign. This is not confirmed from other sources.

arrests stiffened the resolve of the strikers, and they refused to return until, on Wednesday, May 23rd, the charges against their leaders were withdrawn. In Sheffield, despite dissensions among the leaders of the strike, most of the men remained out until the 24th. Many of the London strikers stayed out, and the ETU insisted on separate negotiations with the Ministry of Munitions before advising a return on the 23rd. The Liverpool and Birkenhead engineers stayed out. Over the weekend on which the national settlement was made three new areas, Barrow, Crewe and Leeds, joined the strike in protest against the arrests.[1] The real strength of the strike was not reflected at Walworth. One has to go back to the provinces to see it. From May 14th, when the Manchester engineers had started to go back, Sheffield had been the leading centre of the strike. Sheffield was also the area where the shop stewards' movement was most developed. The significance of the strike for the development of that movement is most clearly revealed in Sheffield.

The Sheffield Workers' Committee had been formed, following the success of the Hargreaves strike, in January 1917. During the Barrow strike of March–April 1917 it had made great efforts to get the men out in sympathy, but the Premium Bonus system was unknown to the Sheffield workers, and the additional grievance against Sir William Clegg, chairman of the local Munitions Tribunal (the 'Tzar of Sheffield'), proved insufficient provocation.[2] At the end of April 1917 the SWC was in touch with the Joint Engineering Shop Steward's Committee in Manchester and the workers were 'ready to strike at any moment'. The Sheffield strike was launched, not by the SWC but by the ASE District Committee. On Sunday, May 6th, the District Committee called a mass meeting which decided to strike and to 'get in touch with other districts'. On the Monday 10,000 men came out in Sheffield and a further 5,000 in Rotherham. The men were under the impression that the strike was official, despite Executive instructions to the contrary, and the District Committee confirmed the impression. The district secretary, W. R. Gavigan, though he had been prominent in the Day Workers' Committee of 1915–16,

---

[1] Addison, *Four and a Half Years*, p. 386; *MM* VI, 1, pp. 118–19. There was even a rumour on the 19th that the Triple Alliance was holding meetings in Lancashire, and other areas, to arrange for a general strike if the arrested men were not released: *Mun.* 2. 28, 19 May 1917.

[2] *Mun.* 2. 28, 24 March, 7 April 1917; W. Moore, *Verbatim Report of a Discussion between Veteran Engineering Workers in Sheffield* (7953), p. 4.

was now vigorously opposed to the militants. On the second day of the strike he bombarded the Executive with telegrams, urging them to take action against the District Committee. 'DC still running strike – men under impression strike official – important you should act forthwith as I can do nothing.' 'Mass meeting today – if Committee suspended prior to or during meeting moral effect enormous – something must be done.' The Executive was at first reluctant to take action, preferring to use the strike as a bargaining counter in its negotiations with the Government, but late that day it accepted Gavigan's pleas and decided to suspend the Committee.[1]

Gavigan had misjudged the situation. The mass meeting responded to the Executive's action by re-electing the District Committee en masse as a strike committee. On Friday, May 11th, Gavigan went to London to arrange details for the election of a new District Committee with the Executive. But the old District Committee would not accept suspension. O. C. Harbinson was appointed unofficial district secretary and he wired the Executive demanding that all communications be sent to him. On May 12th the Executive replied: 'Council has suspended Sheffield DC, and can only recognize Bro. Gavigan as District Secretary, and EC instruct you at once to cease acting as alleged District Secretary.'[2] Having made its point the Executive gave up any attempt to intervene in Sheffield, refusing, despite Gavigan's pleas, to convene a mass meeting to explain the position. It was now up to the Government to deal with the Sheffield rebels.

When the District Committee was suspended, the leadership of the strike passed into the hands of a joint committee consisting of the thirty-six re-elected members of the District Committee and over a hundred delegates to the SWC. There was considerable overlapping between the two committees, Harbinson, Gillam, Ev Raynor and Stanley Burgess all being members of both.[3] Stanley Burgess, a shop steward at Vickers, president of the district, and a member of the SWC leadership, was elected chairman of the Joint Strike Committee. On Monday, May 14th, the Committee called a mass meeting where delegates, led by E.

---

[1] *MM* VI, 1, p. 110; *Mun.* 5. 79, 'History of the Strike', 29 August 1917; ASE, *Executive Minutes*, 7, 9 May 1917; Moore, *Verbatim Report*, pp. 2, 5.

[2] Telegram, in *Moore Collection; Sunday Chronicle*, 20 May 1917, cutting in *Moore Collection;* ASE, *Executive Minutes*, 11 May 1917.

[3] *Sheffield Independent*, 21 May 1917. J. T. Murphy was sick and on holiday throughout the strike: *New Horizons* (1942), pp. 56–7.

Airey (another SWC leader) were appointed to the Walworth conference.[1]

The strikers had a great sense of their own power. A shop steward at Hadfields remembered arming his pickets with 'big, thick sticks' after the police had attacked a group of strikers. Later he had an interview with the Chief Constable.

' "Will you tell me, Mr. Sweeting, how it is that your men went out armed yesterday?"
' "Is it really necessary."
'He said: "Yes".
' "Well, don't you know that the strongest line of defence is to be prepared to attack."
'They never attacked us again after that.'[2]

The mass meeting on Wednesday, May 10th was 'hot with the spirit of revolt. The tone of the meeting was distinctly for compelling the Government to "show their hand" before work is resumed, the leaders obviously being of the opinion that they are masters of the situation.'[3] On the same day a member of the suspended District Committee told a reporter: 'We have been told time and time again that this is a machine war, and we say that we are the people to say who shall do the skilled mechanics work and who can be spared for the Army. Our position is the same as that of the doctors and lawyers.'[4] 'Don't take me, I'm in the ASE', yelled the strikers more succinctly.[5]

Powerful though they felt, the strikers were faced with an extremely hostile public. Press headlines and editorials, and savage attacks by local dignatories could be shrugged off as emanating from the class enemy. Angry crowds of wounded soldiers were less easy to disregard.[6] Most important, however, was the hostility of the less skilled workers forcibly unemployed during the strike. 'Doctors and lawyers', indeed! When the SWC had been formed at a mass meeting in January 1917, a decision had been taken to extend workshop organization from the craft workers to all grades and to women. But despite the invitation of some representatives of the less skilled workers to

---

[1] Moore, *Verbatim Report*, p. 6; *Sheffield Daily Telegraph*, 15 May 1917; *MM* VI, 1, p. 114; Murphy, *New Horizons*, p. 70.
[2] Moore, *Verbatim Report*, pp. 1, 6.
[3] *Sheffield Independent*, 17 May 1917.
[4] *Sunday Chronicle*, 20 May 1917, cutting in *Moore Collection*.
[5] Moore, *Verbatim Report*, p. 7.
[6] *Sheffield Independent*, 22 May 1917.

this meeting the SWC still represented only the craft workers in
May 1917. Whatever the aims of the unofficial leaders, the
development of the unofficial movement in the Day Workers'
Committee and the Hargreaves strike had been largely motivated
by the struggle to defend craft privileges. Murphy claims that
some unity was built up between skilled and less skilled workers
during 1916, but admits that in the early months of 1917 this was
destroyed.[1] The issues that concerned the skilled engineers – the
abolition of the Trade Card scheme and the extension of dilution
to private work – put them in direct opposition to the members
of the general unions. The Trade Card scheme, by limiting
exemption from conscription to members of the craft unions,
fused craft privilege with protection. The bitter resentment of the
general unions to this preferential treatment of the 'aristocracy
of labour' had been important in enabling the Government to
abolish the Trade Card scheme.[2] Nor could the less skilled
workers be expected to fight to prevent the extension of dilution
to private work, since it was only through dilution and the
abrogation of the craft apprenticeship restrictions that they could
hope to rise in their trade.

The less skilled workers hung around outside the mass meetings
of the skilled engineers waiting for news of a resumption. Some
of them thought of holding their own mass meeting to condemn
the strike, though nothing came of it. The wounded soldiers
egged them on, inventing a cruel parody of the craftsmen's
slogan;

> 'Don't send me in the Army, George,
>   I'm in the ASE
> Take all the bloody labourers,
> But for God's sake don't take me.
> You want me for a soldier?
> Well, that can never be –
> A man of my ability,
> And in the ASE![3]

Public hostility of this character could not fail to demoralize the
strikers. From Wednesday, May 16th, when news of the de-

---

[1] A. Gleason, *What the Workers Want* (New York, 1920), p. 190; Moore,
Verbatim Report, p. 1.

[2] *MM* VI, 1, pp. 97–9; R. Hyman, 'The Workers' Union, 1898–1929'
(Oxford D.Phil., 1968), pp. 234–5.

[3] *Sheffield Independent*, 18 May 1917.

generation of the strike in Lancashire, and of the rejection of the Walworth conference's request for negotiations with the Government must have reached Sheffield, 'there was a feeling that something would happen before the end of the week, either from a police or military source . . . the conversation of many of the more active spirits in the strike movement clearly indicated that they lived in anticipation, or apprehension of a sharp turn in the course of events'. The arrest of Stanley Burgess and Walt Hill (president of the District Committee and chairman of the SWC, respectively) came as no surprise. The Strike Committee decided on Friday to continue the strike. Together with the delegates representing the rump of the Manchester strikers, they pledged themselves to enter into no negotiations to end the strike until all the arrested men were released.

It was not the arrests, but the capitulation of the Walworth conference that weakened the Sheffield strike. The settlement was concluded in London on Saturday, May 19th. The next day, for the first time during the strike, the District Committee members met independently of the workshop representatives of the SWC. Two leading militants who sat on both committees were away, successfully persuading the Leeds engineers to come out. They heard the report of their Walworth delegate, E. Airey, who kept to his agreement with the authorities and, after 'many ups and downs and doubts and fears' decide to recommend resumption on Monday morning. Even the *Sheffield Independent* admitted that this decision was unpopular with the rank and file, who were extremely suspicious of the national settlement. When Gillam and Raynor returned from Leeds on Sunday evening they immediately took control of the situation, addressing a spontaneous gathering of 2,000 strikers from the steps of the ASE Institute. Repudiating the 'autocratic' action of the District Committee – no mass meeting had been called since the arrests and the settlement – the meeting decided to call a mass meeting the next afternoon at which the men could decide for themselves when they would resume work. Throughout Sunday night the SWC worked to prevent a resumption in the morning. Where strikers could not be informed in time or pickets mounted, militants went into the factories as if returning to work and 'brought out many of those who had returned to their duties'.

The mass meeting decided not to resume until after the trial on Wednesday, and then only if the arrested men were 'unconditionally released', and the SWC leaders did their best to put this resolution into effect. Although the discord among the leadership caused some weakening after the weekend, two-thirds of the strikers stayed out until Thursday morning.[1]

The strike movement of May 1917 was a massive battle in defence of craft privilege. In the history of the shop stewards' movement to this point a central paradox has been apparent: the contradiction between the revolutionary aims of its leaders, and the craft motivation of its rank and file. The May strikes served to confirm the latter. Before May the leaders had made considerable progress in breaking down the craftsmen's exclusive resistance to dilution, most obviously on the Clyde. The allegiance of the craftsmen to such policies was, however, extremely precarious. They would grasp at the slightest opportunity to rescue something from the shipwreck of their traditional strategy without abandoning its essential feature – exclusiveness. The cold winds of dilution had begun to force a transcendence of exclusiveness: but the war itself threw up a new category of privilege. The struggle for exemption from military service did more than anything else to undo or to retard the shop steward leaders' work of constructing an alliance with the less skilled workers and inculcating a revolutionary perspective among the craftsmen. Had the May 1917 outburst represented the high point of the movement's development, as it did represent the high point of its actual strike power, it would be difficult to see in the movement anything but the unresolved paradox between craft consciousness and a leadership composed of revolutionaries. But May was not the climax. Before looking at the progress of the unofficial movement during the final eighteen months of the war, however, some attention must be given to the attempts made during that period to 'officialize' workshop organization.

[1] Moore, *Verbatim Report*, p. 3; *Sheffield Independent*, 19, 21, 24 May 1917; *MM* VI, 1, p. 112.

Chapter 8

The Midlands: Recognition
and Emasculation

The strike wave of May 1917 alerted the Government to the power of the unofficial movement. One of its less publicized reactions can be seen in the Ministry of Munition's attempts to promote the structural adaptation of engineering trade unionism to the new forces of workship organization generated by the war. In order to restore the authority of the moderate trade union officials amongst a rank and file that had turned towards unofficial and subversive leadership, the inadequacies of the official organizations had to be corrected. From the spring of 1917 the Labour Department of the Ministry of Munitions made it policy to press for 'the constitution of officially approved workshop committees, with functions more or less defined, [which] would help to check the more revolutionary tendencies of the shop steward movement by bringing it into an ordered scheme'.[1]

George Barnes, once general secretary of the ASE and now a Minister in Lloyd George's Government, argued the same case in the union journal:

'Unions must give shop committees a recognized place in their organization . . The shop stewards and shop committes had generally been kept at arms length by the elected authorities of union, a fact which accounted for a good deal of union troubles. They had to fight for recognition from their own unions as well as from the employers . . . Whole-hearted recognition on the part of the unions would get rid of part, at all events, of industrial unrest . . . and . . . shop stewards would cease to be mere

[1] *MM* vi, 1, p. 32.

irresponsible promoters of mischief and become partners and fellow workers for industrial order.'[1]

In these efforts the Ministry received little help or encouragement from the Executive of the ASE, which throughout 1917 maintained its stubborn refusal to recognize the fact of workshop organization as a power within the union. The Executive's alarm at the growth of the unofficial movement took the form of a rigid insistence on the observance of rule, an insistance that grew more strident as – following the mass strike of May – it grew more absurd: 'There appears to be in existence a great misapprehension in the minds of our members in regard to the functions of a shop steward. Therefore it is necessary to quote the rule . . .'[2] This repressive policy was not entirely without success.

In Manchester the local officials consolidated their victory over the Joint Engineering Shop Stewards' Committee in the last days of the May strikes by launching a campaign of persecution against the unofficial leaders. 'They were going so far as to watch their members very carefully', the district secretary boasted to a Ministry official in August 1917, 'and if they were connected with the shop stewards' movement, they were waiting for an opportunity to get these men out of the unions.'[3] This crudely aggressive policy appears to have succeeded in crushing the unofficial Committee by the winter of 1917.[4] The probable explanation of this success is that in Manchester the defeat of dilution on commercial work removed the major threat to the labour aristocracy. Dilution on munitions work had never been an issue of sufficient importance in Manchester to provide a focus for local rank-and-file organization.[5] While the skilled

[1] ASE, *Monthly Journal and Report*, August 1917, pp. 53–4.

[2] *Ibid.*, June 1917, p. 16. See also April, pp. 11–12; ASE, *Executive Minutes*, vol. 198, 26 May, 11 June, 5 July, 28 August 1917. The workshop committees posed a real threat to the existing trade union officials. At a conference with the Ministry of Munitions in Glasgow in October 1917, one ASE delegate 'expressed a fear that, if shop committees were given excessive powers, they would amalgamate and virtually overthrow the unions. This, he said – and the other delegates agreed with him – would be the "nucleus of industrial unionism" and should be avoided.' *Mun.* 2. 28, 20 October 1917.

[3] *Mun.* 2. 28, 4 August 1917. See also *Solidarity*, July 1917.

[4] *Mun.* 2. 28, 15 December 1917. See also *ibid.*, 3 November, 8 December 1917; *Mun.* 5. 56, Reports on the Industrial Situation as viewed by Labour, October 1917.

[5] During the early years of the war, when dilution was advancing most rapidly, it had given rise to no more than a few isolated strikes in Manchester: *Bev.* iv, p. 276, Intelligence Reports, 11 November 1915; *Mun.* 2. 27, 18 March,

workers fought with vigour for wage increases at factory level during the autumn of 1917, and workshop organization in Manchester boomed,[1] they permitted the only body capable of co-ordinating and focussing the power of this workshop movement to collapse. The fragmented wages struggle was not, in itself, sufficient to generate independent rank-and-file organization at local level, or to sustain that organization once it had been formed for other purposes.

The Ministry's best and most constructive allies, however, were in Coventry where the local officials set out to undermine the unofficial movement and to deny the leadership of workshop organization to the revolutionary Worker's Committee, by bringing workshop organization under the control of a reformed local trade union structure. It was the activity of this movement in Coventry that led, in December 1917, to the first national agreement on the powers of shop stewards in the industry. Although this agreement, which the ASE eventually refused to sign, was ineffective, it nevertheless laid a foundation for the recognition of shop stewards within the bargaining procedures of the industry that took place in the agreements of 1919 and 1922. Equally important, as a measure of the effectiveness of the containment policy, the revolutionaries who associated themselves with the Workers' Committee movement were effectively isolated from the mass of the workers in Coventry.

Because it never succeeded in capturing the leadership of any significant proportion of the engineering workers, the Coventry Workers' Committee was primarily a propagandist body. 'The agitators', wrote the local Munitions official in May 1917, 'were more of the ultra-socialist and pacifist type than of the shop steward type'.[2] In fact the Committee was dominated by the

17 June 1916. It seems likely that dilution was not pushed very hard. In January 1917 the Openshaw works of Armstrong-Whitworth, with only 12% of its workers women or boys, was the least diluted gun factory in the country: *Mun* 2. 28, 17 February 1917. The exception to this observation was the local machine tool trade, where considerable trouble arose out of dilution between October and January 1916: *Bev*. iv, pp. 322–3, Intelligence Reports, 25 November 1915; *Mun*, 2. 27, 20, 27 November 1915; *Mun*. 2. 25, 2, 30 October 1915; ASE, *Executive Minutes*, vol. 193, 16 November 1915, 22, 25 January 1916. In no area of the country, however, did machine tool workers play an important part in building independent rank-and-file organization, possibly because they were traditionally the most conservative craft workers.

[1] *Mun*. 2. 28, 9 June, 6 October, 3 November 1917.
[2] *Mun*. 2. 28, 12 May 1917.

SLP. William Paul, 'a redoubtable lecturer on the economics of Karl Marx' and editor of *The Socialist*, who at this time was based in Derby, appears to have been instrumental in establishing the Coventry movement.[1] Tom Dingley, the best known leader of the movement, was a member of the SLP, and secretary of the local branch of the IWW.[2]

The Hotchkiss works where the movement first took hold belonged to a French machine-gun firm which set up in Coventry early in 1915. It is probably significant that the unofficial movement was based in a new and untypical firm, the great majority of Coventry engineering firms being associated with the motor car industry. Machine gun manufacture employed an exceptionally high proportion of skilled labour, both on production and in the toolroom.[3] The Hotchkiss toolmakers were noted as local wage leaders, and it was in the toolroom that the movement first asserted itself. It spread rapidly to the fitting shop, where Dingley worked, and after a strike for recognition in April 1917, this shop remained its main stronghold. After several defeats it was finally destroyed by wholesale victimizations in the spring of 1918.

From the start the unofficial movement was opposed by the local trade union officials of the Coventry Engineering Joint Committee (CEJC). Early in April 1917, 500 Hotchkiss workers came out on a one-day strike for recognition of their shop committee. In reply to enquiries from the employers the CEJC denounced the strike and advised them 'to ignore absolutely the self-called Shop Committee'. The local Employers' Association gave similar advice, fearing that recognition would lead to a 'general shop stewards' movement' throughout the district. Faced with deadlock and the threat of renewed strike action after seven days, the Ministry of Munitions intervened and persuaded the firm and the CJEC (both of whom were unwilling) to set up a representative shop stewards' committee at Hotchkiss under strict trade union control. The militants boycotted this committee (which was

---

[1] *North Western Daily Mail*, 24 May, 1917; *Mun.* 5. 54, 'Notes on the Shop Stewards' Movement', 29 May 1917; A. Gleason, *What the Workers Want* (New York, 1920), p. 203.

[2] *Mun.* 2. 28, 10 November 1917. The branch had 60 members in December 1917: *Mun.* 5. 56, Intelligence and Records Section Report.

[3] *MM* XI, 4, p. 15; Coventry Chamber of Commerce, *Year Book*, 1920, advertisements. Hotchkiss was also exceptional in not being a controlled firm until late in the war, presumably due to its French ownership: *MM* XI, 5, p. 24; *Mun.* 1.9, 24 May 1918.

consequently acceptable to the management), and maintained their own unrecognized committee in the fitting shop.[1]

Defeated at Hotchkiss the nascent shop stewards' movement had a chance to establish itself during the crisis of the May strikes. They did succeed in getting 30,000 workers out on May 8th, but the CEJC responded by calling a mass meeting on Sunday the 11th and persuading it to condemn the strike. The majority had gone back after two days, and the remainder returned after the mass meeting. The two foremost leaders of the unofficial movement, Dingley and Neil Cassidy (who worked at the Coventry Ordnance Works), were later arrested along with the strike leaders in other areas, but there was no further outbreak of strike action.[2] Subsequently the Coventry Workers' Committee maintained only a shadowy existence, represented at national conferences but unable to establish effective leadership locally.

The success of the local officials in getting the men back to work and keeping them there was made possible by the unique vigour of their reaction to the crisis. A huge meeting attended by 15–20,000 workers passed the official resolution urging 'that only a policy which concentrated the influence and organization of the trade union movement would affect any good result'. Further meetings were to be held and a policy formulated 'for the remedying of grievances in the future'. After the arrests, the Coventry ASE members were prepared to leave matters in the hands of the Executive and 'await developments'. The other main union in Coventry, the Workers' Union,[3] spoke with a more militant voice. Their reaction to the arrests was one of 'getting all the machinery into order for the purpose of coupling up all the societies so that if there is a conviction against the strikers everything will be in readiness for a down tools policy'.[4] It was

[1] *Mun.* 2. 27, 1 April 1917; *Mun.* 2. 28, 14, 21 March, 14 April, 10 November 1917; *MM* VI, 11, p. 33; Ministry of Labour, *Works Committees* (Industrial Reports no. 2, 1918), p. 87.

[2] *MM* VI, 1, pp. 112–14; *Midland Daily Telegraph*, 14, 19 May 1917.

[3] The Workers' Union was nearly twice the size of the ASE in Coventry, even discounting its women workers, having 8,590 members in December 1916 against 4,033 in the ASE (*Monthly Journal and Report*, January 1917; I am grateful to Dr R. Hyman for the Workers' Union figures). This numerical predominance of the general union in Coventry was partly mitigated by the Toolmakers' who, exceptionally, had nearly as many members as the local ASE (Coventry Trades Council, *Annual Report*, 1913; *Midland Daily Telegraph*, 23 July 1918). Nevertheless, the Workers' Union was extraordinarily important in Coventry.

[4] *Midland Daily Telegraph*, 14, 21 May 1917.

the fusion of these two tendencies which led the CEJC, during the summer of 1917, to transform itself into a body representative to some extent of workshop as well as branch organization.

Underlying, and in some respects explaining, the exceptional vigour of the Workers' Union in this crisis was relative the modernity of the engineering industry in Coventry. In contrast to the areas where the Workers' Committee movement successfully took root, Coventry belonged to the technologically advanced sector of vehicle and aircraft production. Developing from the bicycle boom of the 1880's and 90's, the vehicle industry had come, by 1911, to employ directly 58 % of the metal workers in Coventry, most of them in motor car factories. There was no iron and steel or other primary metal manufacture in the town, and the bulk of the remainder of metal workers (a further 25 %) worked in general engineering firms. Most of these were direct offshoots of the car industry, making electrical instruments, mechanical components, and so on. The motor car industry was in the forefront of engineering technology and employed an exceptionally high proportion of male semi-skilled workers. Because of the vagaries of census classifications I have no direct evidence of this. But the figures in Table 9 applying to the closely connected general engineering factories make the point sufficiently.[1] The critical breakthrough of dilution, which in the more

Table 9. *Percentage composition of labour force in general engineering, 1911*

	Sheffield %	Glasgow %	Coventry %	National %
Skilled and labourers	84	81	55	82
Semi-skilled	16	19	45	18

traditional engineering centres of the north was to occur in 1915–16 and to throw up the revolutionary shop stewards' movement, had occurred already in Coventry before the war broke out.

[1] J. A. Yates, *Pioneers to Power, the Story of the Ordinary People in Coventry* (Coventry, 1950), p. 51; Coventry Chamber of Commerce, *Year Book,* 1920, pp. 50–6; Census of England and Wales, 1911, Occupation Tables. It was not until after 1914 that the employment of women became accepted in the motor car factories. In 1911 only 2·7% of those employed in the Coventry car factories were women. The cycle factories employed a high proportion of women.

It was on the basis of this uniquely high proportion of semi-skilled workers that the WU had developed in the Midland car factories.[1] By 1914 its strength and dynamism compared favourably with that of the local craft unions. Nationally the years of the pre-war labour unrest were explosive years for the growth of the WU. The crucial moment of its establishment in Coventry came in a wage movement of 1912–13. In November 1912 the WU put in for a rise of labourers rates from 4½d to 6d an hour, and rather smaller rises for semi-skilled grades. The employers refused to touch it. In May 1913 the union brought out its members in three of the largest motor car factories and the 6d was granted. Rises for semi-skilled grades followed. By co-ordinating the various degrees of skill – 'the highest paid members came out in support of the lowest paid' – the WU had made itself a powerful force in the motor car factories. Quite how powerful it was is demonstrated by the size of the rise achieved. Labourers rates were increased from 59 % to 71 % of the district rate. (And subsequently, to 1918 at least, they never fell below 70 %)[2] In other areas the traditional level of labourer's wages, between 50 and 60 % of the district rate, was not disturbed until the impact of state intervention in wage determination and cost of living based bargaining made itself felt during the war.[3] Moreover, by 1913 many of the higher grades of semi-skilled workers, probably organized by the WU, were already receiving the full district rate.[4]

The dominance of the WU, rather than any other general unions in Coventry, was of particular significance. The WU was the most militant and ambitious of the less skilled unions. It did not limit itself to recruiting only the less skilled, but went out for all grades. Naturally the advance of dilution strengthened its hold on the higher grades as non-apprenticed members became skilled workers. And in this the WU was especially successful in the

[1] R. Hyman, 'The Workers' Union, 1898–1929' (Oxford, D.Phil., 1968) p. 186; E. J. Hobsbawn, *Labouring Men* (London, 1964), pp. 189, 192.

[2] Engineering Employers' Federation, *Wage Movements, 1898–1925* (1926); Coventry Trades Council, *Annual Report*, 1914; Yates, *Pioneers to Power*, p. 52. See also Hyman, 'The Workers' Union', pp. 181–2.

[3] A. L. Bowley, *Prices and Wages in the United Kingdom, 1914–1920* (Oxford, 1921), p. 129. For traditional differentials see J. W. F. Rowe, *Wages in Practice and Theory* (London, 1928), p. 49; Hobsbawm, *Labouring Men*, pp. 291–2, 346.

[4] Coventry Trades and Labour Council, *Annual Report*, 1914.

Midlands. The operation of the Trade Card scheme during the early months of 1917 excluded workers outside the craft unions from exemption however skilled they were. The most militant reaction to this, on the part of the less skilled workers, came from Wolverhampton, Birmingham and Coventry where the WU demanded inclusion in the scheme, and threatened strike action to secure it.[1] Evidently in these areas the WU was exceptionally concerned to look after the interests of its skilled members.

But the exceptional strength of the less skilled workers in Coventry is most clearly shown in the reaction of the workers to dilution. Normally it was the craft workers who led the struggle to prevent dilution being used to introduce cheap labour. In Coventry the WU vied for this leadership, as one important example indicates. In the autumn of 1916 there was considerable trouble over dilution at the Coventry Ordnance Works. Under pressure from the Admiralty, the firm sought to solve its problems by getting certain skilled workers conscripted – a procedure which was not unusual in the months before the Hargreaves strike.[2] While the skilled workers affected took no militant action, the WU, whose members the dilutees were, brought them out in October for the full skilled rate. The local organizer, George Morris, was prosecuted under DORA and given a 'stupid and vindictive' sentence which was subsequently annulled. Throughout the strike and prosecution the ASE and the Coventry Trades Council gave full support to the WU, but clearly it was the general union which was leading the craft unions in response to dilution in this event.[3] In February 1918 a writer in the employers' journal *Industrial Peace* grasped the significance of the George Morris prosecution: 'The successful issue of this agitation heightened the prestige of the militant section of the Workers' Union, and when the Rank and File movement obtained a footing in the town it had either to fill a subordinate role or to enter into an alliance with the Workers' Union.'[4]

Workshop organization, as it developed in Coventry, was not as in other centres intimately bound up with the struggle of the old labour aristocracy against the threat to its existence implicit

[1] *Mun.* 2. 28, 7 April 1917; Hyman 'The Workers' Union', p. 236.

[2] *Mun.* 5. 57, Minutes of a conference between officials of the Ministry of Munitions and the A.S.E, 27 September 1916.

[3] *Mun.* 2. 28, 28 October 1916; *Birmingham Gazette*, 29 November 1917; ASE, *Monthly Journal and Report*, December 1916; Glasgow Trades Council, *Minutes*, 27 December 1916.

[4] *Industrial Peace*, February 1918, p. 23.

in dilution. The exceptional pre-war development of semi-skilled grades in the Coventry engineering factories, and, more important the organization of these grades by the Workers' Union, had gone far to transforming the traditional relations of the craftsman with the other workers in the industry. Despite continuing conflicts of interest between craftsmen and the semi-skilled, the successes of the Workers' Union effectively filled that gulf beneath the labour aristocrats, whose existence in other areas occasioned the terror with which they responded to sudden and large-scale dilution. Because already well advanced, dilution was a less urgent, less important, and less politicizing question for the skilled engineers in Coventry than in the centres of more archaic technology. Moreover the influence of the Workers' Union in the local trade union movement's response to wartime dilution would tend to restrain any lurch towards politics. Dilution to the less skilled workers was pure gain. Though it might require a militant industrial spirit to grasp the opportunities presented, this militancy had none of the political overtones which rose from the choice forced on the craftsman between the pursuit of a craft or a class strategy. The revolutionary shop stewards' movements did not succeed in establishing itself in Coventry because the integrity of the traditional labour aristocracy, whose wartime disruption threw up the movement in other areas, was already thoroughly undermined before the war begun.

When during the summer of 1917 the CEJC sought to formulate its policy for 'concentrating the influence and organisation of the trade union movement' it did so in defiance of the national trade union officials. The immediate response of the local ASE to the May crisis was to set about 'an internal reconstruction of the Society', convening monthly meetings of the Midlands Division District Committees to co-ordinate action.[1] This initiative, taken without the approval of the Executive which feared anything that might tend towards a fortification of local autonomy, was intended to

'put the shop stewards' movement on a proper basis. There will have to be a frank recognition of shop stewards by the employers in order that minor questions can be settled immediately they arise, and thus prevent the irritation caused by delay. On the

[1] ASE, *Monthly Journal and Reports*, June 1917; ASE, *Executive Minutes* vol. 198, 5 July 1917.

other hand the shop stewards must be in all matters of principle and policy under the direct control of the local committees of the union.'[1]

The scheme of organization eventually established gave ultimate local power to the official District Committees acting jointly through the CEJC. Power remained based, therefore, on the relatively inadequate democracy of the branches and was not transferred, as in the Workers' Committees, to the more direct democracy of the workshops. The shop stewards could not call a district meeting on their own initiative – it was up to a joint committee to call meetings of the departmental and works conveners when necessary. Although at least one leading member of the CEJC saw it 'as the first practical step towards that complete amalgamation we all so ardently desire',[2] its structure perpetuated the practical autonomy of the individual unions. They called meetings of their own shop stewards to discuss matters of CEJC policy at least as often as the CEJC summoned general shop stewards' meetings. As Murphy was to point out: 'The retention of the identity of the individual union in the larger class organisation means that we provide, and maintain in the organization centres round which can gather elements of discontent and reaction, which can easily break away . . .'[3] At workshop level Industrial Unionism was further advanced .The shop stewards were elected without regard to which union they belonged to and ratified by the CEJC. Departmental and works committees were established on the same non-sectional basis.[4]

Having launched this scheme of organization during the summer of 1917, the CEJC sought to get it recognized. Their shop steward rules were formulated quite independently of the employers, but the Committee did not treat them as a basis for negotiation. They demanded their complete acceptance. Early in October 1917 the scheme was submitted to the local Employers Association for their approval. They referred it to the Engineering Employers' Federation and took no further action.[5] If the rules

[1] George Ryder, 'The Organising District Delegate', in the *Birmingham Gazette*, 21 May 1917. See also ASE, *Quarterly Report*, March 1918, election address of Walter Givens, Coventry district secretary.

[2] ASE, *Quarterly Report*, March 1918, election address of Walter Givens.

[3] *Solidarity*, August 1917.

[4] G. D. H. Cole, *Workshop Organisation* (Oxford, 1923), pp. 139–41.

[5] *Midland Daily Telegraph*, 30 November 1917, employers' statement on the origins of the strike.

were to be accepted at local level the CEJC would have to take more militant action.

The basis for militant action developed rapidly during the autumn of 1917. 'The air is very highly charged here', wrote the local Ministry official at the beginning of October, 'and very little will cause a great blaze.' General local strike action was narrowly averted on two occasions during October, once over evictions and once over the conscription of skilled men. The food shortage was acute. Apparently the Government was calculating Coventry's food supplies on the basis of its pre-war population, making no allowances for the influx of munitions workers. Since May 1917 the local trade unions had been committed to securing full government control of food supplies, the equal distribution of food, and a 50% reduction in prices. In November matters came to a head. The Government offered an enquiry, but too late. Over the weekend of November 17th–18th nobody worked in Coventry. A deputation of trade unionists, employers and local councillors went to London on the Friday to put their demands to the Government, and on Saturday a 'huge procession of trade unionists', organized jointly by the Trades Council and the CEJC, demonstrated in Coventry. They threatened to call a national strike if the Government did not concede their demands by December 21st. Intimidated or convinced, the Government quickly dispatched more food to Coventry and succeeded in buying off the more general demands of the workers.[1]

Meanwhile the central issue of shop stewards' recognition had reached and passed its climax. During September there were isolated disputes over recognition, the largest of which was a strike of 700 toolmakers at White & Poppe, one of the largest works in Coventry.[1] Fearing a recrudescence of the unofficial movement at White & Poppe, the CEJC, late in October, put themselves at the head of the agitation for recognition, responding to a renewed rebuff from the Employers' Association by launching a firm-by firm battle for recognition. This strategy met with considerable success. On November 24th the White & Poppe management, acting on the instructions of the Employers'

[1] *Mun.* 2. 28, 29 September, 13 October, 17 November 1917; *Mun.* 1. 2, 19 October 1917; *Midland Daily Telegraph*, 23, 30 April, 16, 17, 23 November 1917; *MM* VI, 2, p. 26; *Mun.* 1.3, 29 December 1917.

[2] *Mun.* 2. 28, 8, 22, 29 September, 13 October, 10 November 1917. White & Poppe employed 11,000 workers in March 1918: *Mun.* 2. 15, 30 March 1918.

Association, offered to compromise: the shop stewards would be recognized *de facto* pending national negotiations at the Central Conference due to be held on 14 December.[1]

It is surprising, and significant, that this very favourable offer was turned down by the CEJC. They refused to accept that 'the local matter' should be taken to York 'to be considered by employers from other parts of the country on the one hand and trade union officials, permanently resident in London, on the other'.[2] Behind this was the knowledge that the shop steward system in Coventry was unique, and that the national trade union officials did not understand its significance and could not therefore be trusted to negotiate it with the employers. The only safe way to fight it out therefore was as a purely local matter. They wanted twelve months in which to try out the shop steward rules under local review and control.[3] Afterwards it could be launched on the nation. On Saturday evening, November 24th, the CEJC met the workshop representatives and decided, unanimously, to strike for outright recognition. The strike was called for Monday the 26th and it lasted a week. It was completely solid and the officials were firmly in command, holding all meetings behind locked doors: 'to keep the men off the streets as much as possible, to avoid demonstrations and to keep the city as peaceful as we can'. A fund was organized, and lavishly subscribed by the strikers, for young women in lodgings, who were put out of work by the strike. Not only were the women thus cemented to the strike, even the clerks came out in sympathy – with the unfortunate result that the men could not be paid wages owing for lack of wage clerks.[4]

This impressive show of disciplined force went some way to achieving the CEJC's objectives. They did not win their claim for complete recognition of the shop steward rules, nor, when they agreed to call off the strike on December 3rd, had they any better guarantee that their original demand for a local settlement would be fulfilled than a promise of a renewed meeting with the local Employers' Association. Moreover, when the local employers refused to make any concessions at this meeting, the CEJC, at a

1 *Midland Daily Telegraph*, 30 November, 29 December 1917; *Mun.* 2. 28, 17, 24 November 1917; *MM* VI, 2, p. 30.

2 *Midland Daily Telegraph*, 29 November 1917.

3 *Cab*. 24. 34, GT 2840.

4 *Midland Daily Telegraph*, 28–30 November 1917. The National Union of Clerks was very strong in Coventry: *ibid.*, 24, 26 April 1917.

meeting with workshop representatives, was prepared to 'defer any action until the decision of the national conference'.[1] But they had won a promise from the Government 'to urge upon the Employers' Federation and the Trade Union Executives the necessity for an immediate settlement [of], among other general questions affecting the relationship between employers and trade unions, . . . the postion of shop stewards in relation to both'.[2] The CEJC leaders correctly understood that the Government was in favour of their demands. The whole movement in Coventry, as the employers bitterly complained, owed a good deal to the encouragement of the Ministry of Munitions.[3] Nevertheless their trust was misplaced: the Ministry did not have sufficient influence over the employers to carry through its policy.

On December 20th an agreement was signed by all the major unions in engineering, craft and unskilled, except the ASE. There was some advance on the revised Terms of 1914, when the only people the employers agreed to meet at workshop level were 'the workmen directly concerned' with the grievance in question. The new agreement allowed for the election of shop stewards and their ratification by their own trade union; recognition of the steward's right to leave his bench in order to investigate grievances; and negotiation with the 'appropriate shop steward and one of the men directly concerned', or 'in the event of a case arising which affects more than one branch of the trade, or more than one department of the works,' negotiations with all the shop stewards concerned or a deputation of seven appointed by them. The main omission was that no permanent shop steward committee or convener was recognized or given any further facilities – only the stewards of individual unions.[4]

This was considerably less than the CEJC had hoped for, but it appears to have satisfied most of its members. There was no

[1] *Midland Daily Telegraph*, 7, 8 December 1917; *MM* vi, 2, pp. 30–1.
[2] *Cab.* 24. 34, GT 2840.
[3] Cf. *Mun.* 2. 28, 24 November 1917.
[4] Engineering Employers' Federation, *Thirty Years of Industrial Concilia-tion* (1928); W. Hannington, *Industrial History in Wartime* (1940), pp. 107–10. Later Murphy wrote: 'It was found that although a committee could be formed, apparently representing all the workshop, yet it represented them not as a unified body, but as antagonistic elements. Although skilled, semi-skilled, unskilled and women workers came on the same committee every question was approached from the point of view of a particular organisation or element in the shop.' *The Socialist*, 18 May 1919.

H

further general strike threatened over the issue of shop steward recognition, though negotiations dragged on.[1] The more militant workers were not yet prepared to accept defeat. During January 1918 unofficial attempts were made to go beyond the terms of the agreement at White & Poppe and at Hotchkiss et Cie, possibly with some success at the latter.[2] But the Hotchkiss management had no intention of making permanent concessions. When the German offensive of the spring temporarily paralysed militancy all over the country, they began to sack the militants. The shop stewards' committee fought back with an overtime ban and several small strikes. The management, 'by way of asserting their authority', sacked a further ten men. The local ASE threatened trouble. But by the end of March fifty-six men had been sacked including several shop stewards and the leader of the unofficial movement in Coventry, Tom Dingley.[3]

Birmingham, like Coventry, was a centre of the new engineering technology of motor car and aircraft production. As in Coventry the Workers' Union, based upon the semi-skilled workers of the engineering factories, was extremely powerful, with twice as many members as the local ASE by 1914,[4] and as in Coventry attempts to establish a Workers' Committee were successfully held in check by a Joint Engineering Trades Committee representative of the District Committees of the local unions. Workshop organization had developed little by 1918. The officials had successfully opposed strike action in May 1917; and they made up for a brief deviation over the food question in December 1917 by passing the mildest recorded resolution in the whole country during the Man Power crisis of January 1918.[5]

[1] Eventually in July 1918 all the unions who had signed the December 1917 agreement formally accepted that this was as much as the employers would grant: Engineering Employers' Federation, *Decisions of Central Conference, 1898–1925* (1926).

[2] *Mun.* 1. 5, 29 January 1918; *Mun.* 5. 80, 1 February 1918; *Mun.* 2. 14, 19 January 1918.

[3] *Mun.* 1. 7, 23 March 1918; *Mun.* 2. 15, 30 March 1918; *Solidarity*, April 1918; *Workers' Dreadnought*, 13 April 1918.

[4] Hyman, 'The Workers' Union', p. 181, and also pp. 54, 174–81.

[5] J. B. Jefferys, *The Story of the Engineers* (London 1946), p. 191; J. Corbett, *The Birmingham Trades Council*, pp. 108, 113. It is possible that William Paul, a leading member of the SLP, had attempted to set up a Workers' Committee in Birmingham earlier in the war; *Mun.* 5. 54, 'Notes on the Shop Stewards' Movement', 29 May 1917. The SLP had a branch in Birmingham at this time: D. M. Chewter, 'The History of the Socialist Labour Party of Great Britain from 1902 to 1921' (Oxford B. Litt., 1964), Appendix B.

One giant factory dominated the engineering industry in Birmingham, the Austin works at Longbridge which employed 20,000 workers by 1918, and it was from Longbridge that the major challenge to the local officials emerged. By December 1917 an Austin Works Committee, representing predominantly the skilled engineers in the plant, had been established. At the beginning of January 1918 the men threatened to strike over a wage issue, but were persuaded by the chairman of the Works Committee, a pacific individual named Peacock, not to resort to 'unconstitutional methods'. Within a week, however, Peacock was notified that, as a War Munitions Volunteer, he was to be transferred to Lincoln. The men smelled victimization, particularly as the firm was refusing to recognize the Works Committee, and 12,000 workers came out on the 16th, demanding the withdrawal of Peacock's transfer.[1]

Two days before the strike broke out at Longbridge, a joint conference of Shop Stewards' and Workers' Committees had been convened in Birmingham at which it was decided to 'fall into line with the North, and appoint a Workers' Committee', linked up with the NAC.[2] Twenty-six factories in south Birmingham were represented. Immediately the Committee involved itself in the Austin dispute, calling a mass meeting on the 16th at which a deputation was appointed to assist the Austin Works Committee in interviewing the management and to arrange with the local officials to call a mass meeting in solidarity on Sunday, January 20th. The success of these tactics was remarkable. The Workers' Committee fully established its point that the Longbridge 'victimization', and the implicit issue of recognition, was properly the concern of the local workers as a whole. Its secretary and other delegates were admitted to the negotiations with Sir Herbert Austin and the Ministry of Munitions. As a result of these negotiations, Peacock's transfer was withdrawn, pending a Ministry enquiry, and the men returned to work the next day.[3]

Following this victory the basis of the Longbridge Works Committee was extended among less skilled workers and women. During April Tom Dingley, the 'notorious agitator' from Coventry, got a job in the Austin gun shop under a false name.

[1] *Solidarity*, July 1918; *Birmingham Gazette*, 12, 14, 17, 18, 21 January 1918. *Mun.* 1. 5, 11 and 17 January 1918; *Mun.* 2. 14, 19 January 1918.

[2] *The Herald*, 9 February 1918.

[3] *Birmingham Gazette*, 14, 17, 18, 21 January 1918; *Mun.* 1. 5, 19 January 1918.

He did not have to wait long for an opportunity to 'revolutionize the Works Committee' and 'put it on a fighting basis'. At the beginning of May the firm cut the gun workers' bonus by 25 %, without any consultation, on the grounds that they had been paying a specially high rate to compensate the men for a temporary shortage of handling equipment. In the ensuing negotiations Dingley was sacked for 'gross insolence' to the shop superintendent. Within ten days over 4,000 workers were on strike, as much in protest against the cut bonus as against Dingley's discharge. They went back on the 24th after the bonus had been restored pending arbitration. But Dingley stayed outside the gate.[1]

The issue of recognition remained. As in January the Birmingham Workers' Committee did its best to generalize the Austin problem, organizing for a general one-day strike throughout the city 'with the object of concentrating attention of those concerned on the question of properly organized works committees and shop stewards'.[2] The strike never materialized. The general campaign to develop workshop organization in Birmingham hung upon the battle for the recognition of the Longbridge Works Committee. Following the resumption in May the gun shop maintained a go-slow to prevent delay in the arbitration on the bonus question. At a mass meeting on June 22nd they decided to wait no longer, threatening strike action from the 26th if the full bonus were not confirmed. To this threat was attached the issue of recognition, now focussed on the workers' dissatisfaction with the quality of management at Longbridge as a whole and in particular with the quality of Sir Herbert Austin. The Ministry of Munitions intervened in force, persuading the trade union officials to recognize the shop stewards, and the shop stewards (including those in the ASE) to accept recognition from the management under the terms of the national agreement of December 1917. In exchange they undertook to investigate the alleged inadequacies of the management. 'In effect', commented the Labour Department of the Ministry of Munitions, 'from the point of view of the employers and the Trade Union officials, the constitutional position has been restored.'[3]

[1] *Birmingham Gazette*, 21 January 1918; *Solidarity*, July 1918; *Mun.* 2. 15, 18 May 1918; *Mun.* 2. 16, 20 July 1918; *Mun.* 1. 9, 10, 11, 13, 14, 20 May, 1918.

[2] *Mun.* 1. 9, 31 May 1918.

[3] *Mun.* 1. 11 (MC), 10 July 1918; *Mun.* 1. 10 21, 22, 26 June 1916; *Mun.* 1. 11, 1 July 1918.

The chief stronghold of the Birmingham Workers' Committee had been, successfully, 'officialized', and though the Works' Committee soon discovered that the agreement did not guarantee its own recognition as such, it was unable to do anything about it. On July 18th the workers struck, demanding that Sir Herbert Austin should meet them within twenty-four hours. But the local officials had seized the initiative in a campaign for direct Government intervention in the management of the firm. The men returned to work and an Advisory Committee on Labour was dispatched from Whitehall to deal with the men's various grievances. So far as the records show this effectively headed off the demand for full recognition of the Works Committee.[1]

In accepting the national agreement of December 1917, the Coventry Engineering Joint Committee had failed in its object of establishing a framework of shop steward recognition within which the new forces of workshop organization could be fully developed under trade union control. This was demonstrated both by the defeats sustained by the workers at the more militant Coventry factories during the spring of 1918, and by the outcome of the struggle at Longbridge. In Coventry and Birmingham the local officials had succeeded in 'containing' workshop organization only at the price of truncating its development. The unity and discipline with which the Joint Committee had led the strike of November 1917 might have been thought to provide some compensation for the failure of a Workers' Committee based in fully-fledged workshop organization to develop in Coventry. The performance of the CEJC in the renewed unrest of the summer of 1918 was to disappoint any such hopes. The militancy of the craft workers over the 'embargoes' imposed by the Government on the employment of new skilled labour at a number of large factories in Coventry and elsewhere was not shared by semi-skilled workers whose mobility remained unrestricted. In the resulting conflict between the Workers' Union and the skilled unions the CEJC disintegrated, Coventry's experiment in 'containment' collapsed, and the leadership of militancy reverted to the District Committees of the individual unions.

Within days of the imposition of embargoes at four Coventry factories on July 1st the workers immediately concerned had threatened strike action if the embargoes were not removed. On July 12th the CEJC met and resolved on a general local strike if the Government had not removed the embargoes within ten

[1] *Mun.* 2. 16, 13, 20 July 1918; *Mun.* 1. 11 (MC), 31 July 1918.

days. The CEJC was, at first quite firm in its decision, demanding that if skilled labour had to be rationed, a scheme should be worked out in consultation with the unions putting control of the details of policy in the hands of local joint committees of employers and unions.[1] The Government took a hard line speaking of 'an attempt to overthrow the policy of the State in time of National danger', and hinting that it would not be reluctant to conscript any skilled men who struck. This pressure, together with a flood of remonstrance from the various union executives, intimidated the CEJC. On Sunday, July 21st, they offered to withdraw the strike notices if the Government would at least negotiate on the possibility of administering the scheme locally. But Churchill, the Minister of Munitions, was 'in one of his Napoleonic moods . . . hot foot against the strikers',[2] and refused to hold any negotiations whatsoever on the subject of the embargoes.[3]

A strike seemed inevitable. The men were due to come out at 5.00 p.m. on Monday the 22nd. But the majority on the CEJC were now set on avoiding action or at least postponing it, and they had one last pretext. Over the weekend delegates had been sent to various other munitions centres to persuade them to come out in sympathy. Reactions were mixed. Barrow, the Clyde and the Tyne showed 'no indication of sympathy with Coventry'. In Sheffield a mass meeting was called on the Sunday, but no strike was suggested or threatened. Only in Birmingham and Manchester was there any firm commitment to strike. In Birmingham a mass meeting called by the JETC threatened strike action on Wednesday, July 24th. In Manchester, where the shop stewards had been agitating for strike action since the embargoes were placed on July 1st, workers in many firms intended to come out on the Monday whatever happened in Coventry, but at the last moment they decided to postpone action for a further seven days. The National Administrative Council of the shop stewards' movement added its voice to the pressure for a postponement of strike action pending a national conference.[4]

---

[1] 'The principles we are fighting for', said one of the trade union officials, 'is freedom of contract as against bureaucracy.' *Midland Daily Telegraph*, 25 July 1918; *Mun.* 1. 11, 17 July 1918; *Mun.* 2. 16, 13 July 1918.

[2] K. Middlemass (ed.), *T. Jones: Whitehall Diary* (1964), vol. I, p. 66; C. Addison, *Four and a Half Years* (1934), vol. II, p. 557.

[3] *MM*, VI, 2, pp. 65–6; *Midland Daily Telegraph*, 19, 22 July 1918.

[4] *Mun.* 1. 11, 20, 22 July 1918; Mun. 1.11 (MC), 17, 20 July 1918; *Mun.* 2. 16, 13 July 1918; *Midland Daily Telegraph*, 22, 23 July 1918.

The CEJC majority jumped at the opportunity presented by the varied response in other centres and the negative reaction of the NAC, deciding, a few hours before the strike was due to start, that: 'as a result of our negotiations with other centres . . . it would be better to defer our action with a view to obtaining the support of the whole of the engineering centres'. A national conference of Joint Engineering Committees was called for the following Thursday, July 25th.[1] Behind this decision stood the Workers' Union, whose members were not directly affected by the embargoes.[2] The officials of the leading skilled unions, on the other hand, were doubtful whether they could hold their members back at such short notice, and voted against the decision. At the appointed time the members of the ASE and the AST struck, splitting the CEJC. While the chairman of the joint body appealed for loyalty from 'those workers who are out for organization', the leading craft officials backed into sectionalism: 'Anything that emanates from the Engineering Joint Committee is quite unofficial.'[3] The CEJC's decision also, caused bitterness in Birmingham, where 'the opinion was strongly expressed that Coventry had "sold the pass". Birmingham very sore.' As in Coventry, 'the rank and file had the acknowledged leaders stampeded, and they, in turn, attempted to stampede the sober elements into striking, with the obvious intention of self-preservation as trade union officials.'[4] The Birmingham officials invited direct representatives of the workshop committees to participate in their Emergency Committee and after a similar offer of compromise to that made in Coventry at the weekend had been similarly rejected by the Government, the men started to come out on the evening of the 24th. During the next twenty-four hours, while the officials wobbled between compromise and militancy, 15,000 men joined the strike. The officials rode the strike – 'In Birmingham, especially, it was pitiful to observe the attempts made by certain of the leading officials to save their faces in this respect.'[5]

[1] *Midland Daily Telegraph*, 22 July 1918. This was a development of contacts established during the latter stages of the Man Power dispute. See below, pp. 265–67.
[2] Though not members of the CEJC, the Workers' Union were the first to declare themselves independently against the strike: *Mun.* 1. 11, 24 July 1918.
[3] *Midland Daily Telegraph*, 23, 26 July 1918; *Mun.* 1. 11, 26 July 1918.
[4] *Mun.* 1. 11, 23 July 1918; *Mun.* 2. 16, 3 August 1918.
[5] *Mun.* 1. 11, 22, 25, 26 July 1918; *Birmingham Gazette*, 24 July 1918; *Midland Daily Telegraph*, 24 July 1918; *Mun.* 2. 16, 3 August 1918.

The CEJC majority had argued that even the *threat* of co-ordinated national action would be more effective than an isolated local strike in forcing the Government to climb down, and in this they were not unrealistic.[1] The call for a national conference met with considerable success. At Barrow the Allied Trades, who had turned a deaf ear to the Coventry delegates a few days earlier, supported the conference, convened a mass meeting, and sent delegates to Leeds briefed to support strike action. In Sheffield the Allied Trades also sent delegates, and when the Leeds conference called for a national strike from Tuesday, July 30th, they put this to a local ballot. The SWC, making no attempt to bring the men out earlier in support of the Coventry strikers, agreed to abide by the Leeds decision. In London the District Committee accepted the strike call, and mass meetings were called to arrange for action on the 30th. In three other important centres, where the local officials remained hostile to strike action – Clydeside, Tyneside and Manchester – the local militants rejected the NAC policy and did their best to get the men out. They had little success in the two former centres, but in Manchester the workers in forty-five firms gave notice of strike action from Monday, July 29th.[2]

These threats, together with the actual strikes in the Midlands, forced the Government to abandon its tough line, though the climb down was heavily disguised. On Saturday, July 27th, Lloyd George threatened to withdraw protection certificates from 'all men willfully absent from their work on or after Monday, July 29th'. The Ministry of Munitions had already prepared the way for conciliation by ascribing the Coventry strike, quite fancifully, to the rather too frank description of the character of the embargoes issued by the Hotchkiss management, and over the weekend a settlement was reached. A Committee of Enquiry into the embargo scheme was to be set up containing representatives of the ASE, AST, and SEM. This Committee effectively ended the embargo scheme. At a mass meeting in Birmingham on Sunday, July 28th, a majority of the strikers voted to reject the settlement, but the officials plucked up the courage to rule that the requisite two-thirds majority had not been attained. The resumption was general on the Monday morning. In Coventry,

---

1 *Midland Daily Telegraph*, 22 July 1918; *MM* VI, 2, p. 67.
2 *Solidarity*, August 1918; *Woolwich Pioneer*, 2 August 1918; *Mun*. 1. 11, 24, 27, 29 July 1918.

the men, thoroughly intimidated by the call-up threat, scuttled back to work in large numbers even before a mass meeting had accepted the settlement.[1]

The adaptation of the structure of trade unionism to enable it to contain workshop organization was potentially a two-edged process. When J. T. Murphy wrote *The Workers' Committee* in the autumn of 1917 he could see no reason why the workshop committees could not be 'part of the official trade union movement'. What mattered was that the control of policy and action should be vested in the workshops, not in the branches or a District Committee elected in the branches. 'It is immaterial whether the first move is made through the local trade union committees, or in the workshops . . .'[2] Of course the local officials in Coventry made no secret of their intention of maintaining the District Committees' authority over the shop stewards. 'The shop steward movement', wrote the Organising District Delegate, 'when once established *under trade union control* will be one of the greatest movements for the good that has ever been brought into existence by the workers of Coventry.'[3] But they themselves were drawn into encouraging militancy, both because of employer resistance to their plans for shop steward recognition, and because they were constantly aware of the need to outbid the unofficial movement. During 1917–18 Coventry had by far the highest strike figures[4] of any munitions centre, and the largest strikes occurred with the sanction of and under the leadership of moderate local officials. It is not to be wondered that the employers found it difficult to distinguish between these officials and the revolutionary shop stewards they claimed to be containing. Nor is it surprising that the ASE Executive, which opposed every wartime strike, should feel as hostile towards the Coventry local officials as it did towards the Workers' Committee of Glasgow or Sheffield. Even the Government officials who most clearly understood the value of the CEJC as a counter to

---

[1] *Midland Daily Telegraph*, 24, 25, 27, 29 July 1918; *Birmingham Gazette*, 29 July 1918; *Mun.* 1. 11, 29 July 1918. In Manchester the District Committee of the ASE, in defiance of its own secretary and the Organizing District Delegate, resisted further dilution until the Committee of Enquiry had reported late in September. This was effective in 'most of the largest firms'. *Mun.* 2. 16, 10, 17 August, 7 September, 5 October 1918.

[2] J. T. Murphy, *The Workers' Committee* (Sheffield, 1917), p. 9.

[3] *Midland Daily Telegraph*, 29 November 1917 (present writer's italics).

[4] I.e. of days lost per worker: Ministry of Labour, *Labour Gazette, passim.*

the unofficial movement tended to lose their nerve when support for containment led them into tacit support for strike action.[1]

Nevertheless the Ministry officials who supported the CEJC against both employers and trade union executives were largely vindicated. The Joint Committee was not a Workers' Committee in disguise; not, as Murphy prescribed, 'an alliance between official and unofficial activities [based on] official recognition of rank and file control'.[2] The shop stewards may have shared in the vital decisions on strike action, but the District Committees led, and determined the goals of this action. The central achievement of the Committee was effectively to circumscribe the shop stewards' power in the workshop, to prevent that full articulation of workshop organization on which alone 'rank and file control' could have been based. Nor did the Joint Committee provide too dangerous a leadership for militant action, as became clear in the summer of 1918. 'Fortunately', wrote a local Munitions officer of the leaders of the embargo strike, 'they handled it very badly, and had the Sheffield shop stewards who managed the 1917 engineering strike been behind it, I am afraid the situation would have proved even more serious.'[3] Above all else, containment succeeded in its primary objective. The revolutionaries of the Coventry Workers' Committee were effectively isolated from the mass of Coventry engineering workers. Measured in terms of working days lost through strike action, the Coventry engineers may have been more militant than their brothers in Glasgow or Sheffield. But they were less political.

The Ministry officials and their local trade union allies cannot, however, be allowed all the credit for the containment of militancy in Coventry. It seems probable that their success was itself rather more the result than the cause of the failure of the mass of engineering craftsmen to respond to the leadership proferred by the revolutionaries. It has been argued that the advanced technology of the Midlands engineering industry provided the essential condition of containment, by undermining the social basis of the Workers' Committee movement. By 1914 the traditional aristocracy, whose wartime trauma underlay the emergence of the movement in the engineering centres of the north, hardly existed in Coventry or in Birmingham. It is to this traditional labour aristocracy that we must return to examine the final phase of the development of the shop steward's movement.

[1] *Mun.* 5. 56, 11 December 1917.
[2] *The Workers' Committee*, p. 9.   [3] *Mun.* 2. 16, 3 August 1918.

Chapter 9

Towards a Revolutionary Shop Stewards' Movement

As the largest strike of the war, May 1917 has often been seen as the climax of the shop stewards' movement.[1] Had this been the case there could be little question about the dismissive picture of the movement as a mere reaction of craftsmen to the wartime threats to their traditional privileges. The history of the movement would hold no more political interest than that of the vain efforts of a handful of revolutionaries to reconcile their universal aims with the merely sectional goals spontaneously generated by the movement they happened to be leading. The May strikes clearly revealed the craft character of the movement, and occurring so soon after the March Revolution in Russia brought home to many socialists quite how remote from revolutionary politics the engineers yet were: 'The strike is now a huge political weapon, though the workers fail to grasp that fact . . . Why are they bothering with trade card schemes when their Russian comrades have accomplished revolution?'[2]

May 1917 was not, however, the climax; and in the months that followed the movement recovered from its lapse into mere craft concerns, expanded its base, developed a national leadership, and by January 1918 had moved into the forefront of militant anti-war politics. The call made at that time for a national strike to force the Government to open peace negotiations was unsuccessful, and this final phase of the movement was rewarded

[1] See, for example, W. Kendall, *The Revolutionary Movement in Britain, 1900–21* (1969), pp. 142, 372.

[2] *The Call*, 24 May 1917. See also the remarks of William McLaine, leader of the Manchester shop stewards, in the issue of 17 May.

for its failure not only by immediate decline but also by the neglect lavished by historians on movements which (apparently) come to nothing. Yet, momentarily, the shop stewards' movement had achieved a significant revolutionary presence. The development of the labour movement during the crucial years of the post-war unrest cannot be understood without allowing full weight both to the disappointments of January 1918, and to the possibilities revealed by the shop stewards' movement in this last period of its growth.

The strike call of January 1918 occurred in the context of deepening war weariness and the emergence of the international revolutionary crisis in which the war was eventually to end. The Western Front had remained in deadlock since the winter of 1915, hungrily consuming men and munitions to no apparent purpose:

'It is no longer a question of aiming at breaking through the enemy's front and aiming at distant objectives. It is now a question of wearing down and exhausting the enemy's resistance, and if and when this is achieved, to exploit it to the fullest extent possible. In order to wear him down we are agreed that it is absolutely necessary to fight with all our available forces with the object of destroying the enemy's divisions.'[1]

The horrors of attrition plumbed new depths in the spring of 1917 when over a quarter of a million men died at Passchendaele for a few insignificant yards of swamp. At home profiteering, rising food prices, overcrowding – especially acute in those munitions centres which had suffered a very heavy influx of labour since the outbreak of war – were identified by the reports of the Commission of Enquiry into Industrial Unrest in July 1917 as basic causes of discontent.

The most acute danger to civilian morale arose from the shortage of food. By the autumn of 1917 the perfection of the convoy system had effectively defeated the German submarine blockade, but this came too late to prevent acute shortages during the winter. 'The situation', wrote Clynes, parliamentary secretary to the Ministry of Food, 'was such that, had details of it been generally known, riots would certainly have occurred.'[2] The

1 General Robertson, 4 May 1917; quoted in P. Guinn, *British Strategy and Politics, 1914 to 1918* (Oxford, 1965), p. 230.

2 J. R. Clynes, *Memoirs*, vol. I, p. 235. 'Without rationing, we're done', Lord Rhondda told his parliamentary secretary: 'It might well be, Clynes, that you and I, at this moment, are all that stand between this country and revolution.' *Ibid.*, p. 234.

queue – a new word in the English language – had been in evidence since the spring. Worst of all was the meat shortage of January 1918 when half a million Londoners were counted standing in queues (by anxious policemen) each week. Unrest was reported from the trenches, where the soldiers wanted 'to return and take their share of queuing'.[1] Food prices and the queues also became a leading issue for the shop stewards.

When the Barrow Workers' Committee discussed whether their delegates to the national shop stewards' conference in August 1917 should support strike action over skilled wages, it was urged, and agreed, that 'they should attack the food prices and leave the question of the advance, as it might seem too selfish . . . The food prices touched every one, and therefore it would be a popular cry.'[2] In Manchester the shop stewards made food prices the main issue of their campaigning.[3] On the Clyde during September, preparations were being made in the ASE for a strike over food prices. There was talk of strike action in Woolwich. In Coventry, a weekend strike and demonstration was successfully held in November, and even Birmingham, not renowned for its militancy, rose to a Trades Council resolution threatening a general local strike in December. During December the Sheffield Workers' Committee had also become closely involved, with the Trades Council, in an agitation against food queues. Both in Coventry and Sheffield munitions workers were reported to have left work to relieve their wives in the queues.[4]

At the beginning of January 1918, the National Administrative Council of the shop stewards' movement was 'anxious to bring about a sufficiently large stoppage of work on munitions

[1] W. Beveridge, *British Food Control* (Oxford, 1928), pp. 204–7; A. Marwick, *The Deluge* (Penguin, 1965), pp. 205–6.
[2] *Mun.* 2.28, 1 September 1917. The Barrow shop stewards devoted much energy to this issue: *Mun.* 2.28, 3 November 1917.
[3] *Mun.* 2.28, 7 July 1917. This may have had some connection with the revolutionary declaration of the Lancashire and Cheshire Federation of Labour Parties in September 1917: 'Unless early and substantial relief is given in the matter of food prices, a general strike will be called with a view to overthrowing the Government and instituting a Labour Government.' *Mun.* 2.28, 22 September, 1917.
[4] ASE, *Coatbridge Branch Minutes*, 20 August 1917; *Mun.* 2.28, 10 November 1917; *Woolwich Pioneer*, 25 January 1918; J. Corbett, *The Birmingham Trades Council* (1966), p. 108; J. Mendelson and S. Pollard, *Sheffield Trades and Labour Council, 1858–1958* (Sheffield, 1958), p. 69; Sheffield Trades Council, *Minutes*, 4, 18, 28 December 1918; Beveridge, *British Food Control*, p. 196.

of war to force the Government to take immediate and drastic steps to ensure the equal distribution of food and to regulate prices'.[1] The shop stewards put their weight behind the National Vigilance Committee which at a conference in London on January 12th and 13th threatened to call a national strike and to seize food supplies and distribute them through Workers' Committees.[2] Although this resolution was echoed by the Liverpool boiler-makers, and strikes against the queues occurred in Manchester, Luton and Erith,[3] there was more bravado than good judgement in the national strike call. In the event the unrest was successfully contained by the introduction of rationing schemes, and by the policy of using the munitions factories as food distribution centres, thus giving preferential treatment to the most dangerous sections of the civilian population.[4] Winston Churchill was right to see the danger of action over food as secondary to the simultaneous 'trial of strength with the engineers' over conscription and peace.[5] Nevertheless, the existence of such widespread unrest over so fundamental an issue as food supplies helped to give revolutionary potential to the other conflicts which came to a head in January 1918.

Before the Russian Revolution of March 1917, opposition to the war, though considerable, was diffuse and unco-ordinated. The Union of Democratic Control countered jingo assumptions on German war guilt and conducted a propaganda campaign against any return to 'international anarchy'. The No-Conscription Fellowship fought conscription with conscientious objection. Both the Independent Labour Party and, after the defeat of the Hyndmanite 'Old Guard' in the spring of 1916, the British Socialist Party opposed the war – but also opposed revolutionary action to bring it to a halt. John Maclean's agitation in the west of Scotland was the only clearly revolutionary campaign against the war, and this, though vigorous, remained on the fringes of the working-class movement. The March Revolution did little to enhance the influence of revolutionary defeatism, but it did serve to release some of the pent up energies of anti-war socialists

[1] *Mun.* 2.14, 12 January 1918.

[2] *The Herald*, 26 January 1918; T. Bell, *Pioneering Days* (1941), p. 305. See also *Workers' Dreadnought*, 12 January 1918.

[3] *Mun.* 1.5, 15, 16 January 1918; *Mun.* 2.14, 2 February 1918; *The Call*, 31 January 1918.

[4] *Mun.* 1.5 (MC), 30, 31 January 1918; *Mun.* 2.14, 12 January 1918; *Mun.* 2.15, 9 March 1918; Beveridge, *British Food Control*, ch. 10 *passim*.

[5] *Cab.* 23.5, 5 February 1918.

in Britain. At last it seemed possible for the masses to make some impression on the European war machine. In a campaign of great enthusiasm the United Socialist Council[1] and George Lansbury's Herald League organized a national rank-and-file convention at Leeds for Sunday, 3 June 1917 to launch a movement for a variety of immediate reforms and 'for a peace made by the peoples of the various countries and for the complete political and economic emancipation of international labour'. The campaign was to take the form of at once establishing 'in every town, urban district and rural district, Councils of Workers' and Soldiers' delegates for initiating and co-ordinating working class activity. . . .'[2]

The convention itself was a 'distinct success from the point of view of its promoters. It was a large and orderly gathering, and its composition . . . could not but impress uncritical opinion as representative . . . It would be a mistake to dismiss it from consideration as negligible.'[3] Subsequently, however, it came to very little, and the attempts to set up local Workers' and Soldiers' Councils failed. In part this was due to the half-heartedness of most of its leaders – the ILP section – who saw the conference as an end in itself, a national demonstration of opinion in favour of an early democratic peace. They indulged themselves in much wild talk about the imminence of revolution and the dictatorship of the proletariat, but, as Lloyd George later pointed out: 'The leaders were mostly men of the type which think something is actually done when you assert vociferously that it must be done.'[4] There was however a serious revolutionary element involved, headed by Tom Quelch, a BSP member and secretary of the national committee set up at Leeds. Quelch was one of the few leaders of the BSP who distinguished firmly between a pacifist and a revolutionary peace movement, seeing as the hallmark of the latter the attempt 'to organize the masses for a definite

[1] The USC was first projected in 1913 as an alliance of the Fabian Society, the ILP and BSP: G. D. H. Cole, *History of the Labour Party from 1914* (1948), pp. 14–15. When the war broke out it lapsed, but was revived as an ILP–BSP anti-war front in November 1916: *The Call*, 2 November 1916, 11, 18 January 1917.

[2] *The Call*, 24, 31 May 1917; *What happened at Leeds* (1917); R. Postgate, *The Life of George Lansbury* (1951), pp. 168–170.

[3] *Cab.* 24.16, GT 1008.

[4] D. Lloyd George, *War Memoirs* (1938), p. 1154; Lord Elton, *The Life o, James Ramsey MacDonald* (1939) p. 312. See also Bell, *Pioneering Days*, p. 148.

resistance to the war on the basis of a general strike in munitions factories and kindred industries'.[1] In his attempts to launch the Workers' and Soldiers' Councils in the localities Quelch was aware of the primary importance of linking up anti-war activity with the shop stewards' movement. Many of the leaders of the shop stewards' movement shared this concern. The Clyde delegates at Leeds, Gallacher, MacManus and Tom Bell, wanted the Councils linked with the Workers' Committees, and at the NAC in August, MacManus spoke of the May strikes as the beginning of revolutionary developments in Britain and called on the delegates to build up the Workers' and Soldiers' Councils in their own localities.[2]

The attempts met with the sternest resistance from the authorities. Prior to the Leeds conference the Cabinet had refrained from repressive action on the grounds that it had been 'too widely publicized'.[3] After the conference, however, the Government intervened to prohibit meetings, conscripted Quelch, the most active leader of the movement, turned a blind eye to the activities of mobs of soldiers in violently breaking up meetings, and was suspected of putting pressure on various people to prevent the hiring of halls, leasing of offices, and so on.[4] Attempts were made to set up local committees in at least eight areas, including London, Tyneside, Glasgow and Sheffield.[5] In London a very representative delegate meeting held on July 29th was broken up by a mob of 'public house loafers' led by colonial soldiers in uniform, and incited by press headlines such as: 'We shoot Huns at the front. Why are we more tender with the treacherous pro-Germans at home?'[6] In Newcastle, where the local labour movement was predominantly 'loyal', only the ASE District

---

[1] This was Theodore Rothstein's (alias John Bryan) formulation: *The Call*, 3 August 1916. Following the defeat of the old guard, Rothstein and Quelch had campaigned during the late summer of 1916 against the 'pacifist' tendency revealed in the BSP in its rapprochement with the ILP.

[2] *The Call*, 19 July 1917; *Cab.* 24.16, GT 1049; T. Bell, *Short History of the Communist Party* (1937), p. 36; J. T. Murphy, *Preparing for Power* (1934), p. 145; J. T. Murphy, *New Horizons* (1942), p. 61.

[3] *Cab.* 23.2, 25 May 1917. The reason was not, as Lloyd George later claimed, because they did not take it seriously; *War Memoirs*, p. 1153.

[4] HC Debates, 5s., vol. 96, cols. 1786ff.; Glasgow Trades Council, *Minutes*, 6 June, 28 August 1917; Sheffield Trades Council, *Minutes*, 28 August 1917; *The Call*, 7 June, 9 August, 13, 20 September, 4, 11 October 1917.

[5] *Mun.* 5.56, Reports on the Industrial Situation as viewed by Labour, June 1917. The other areas were Norwich, Leicester, Bristol and Swansea.

[6] *Daily Sketch*, 26 July 1917; HC Debates, 5s., vol. 96, col. 1785.

Committee supported the meeting, and it was similarly dealt with by 'the violence of an indignant crowd'.[1] 'The people have given their answer!' cried the *Sketch*. On the Clyde, where the *Daily Sketch's* 'people' were silenced by the overwhelming support of all sections of organized labour for the Workers' and Soldiers' Council, the authorities banned the meeting called for August 11th. A protest demonstration was held instead, protected against hostile elements or police by a cordon of shop stewards. In Sheffield the Trades Council was late in deciding to set up a local Council, though virtually unanimous when it got round to it. However, nothing was done, and in September a meeting held in camera decided 'to hold in abeyance the resolution re formation of a local W & S C until a more opportune time arises'.[2]

By October the movement initiated at Leeds was admitted by its leaders to have failed. Though repression partially explains its failure, the underlying reason was the indifference of the shop stewards' movement. The shop stewards at best, might throw a cordon round the anti-war movement, to protect it from the jingo mob, but they were as yet more concerned with sectional wage claims than with peace. In August the national conference cf the shop stewards' movement decided to press for an increase to skilled time workers.

Leeds was premature for the political development of the rank-and-file movement, but for the non-revolutionary forces it was very timely, marking as it did the effective beginning of the reunion of pro-war and anti-war elements in the Labour Party, that made possible the 1918 constitution and the launching of the party as a fully-fledged parliamentary opposition. MacDonald's demonstration of the strength of the demand for peace at Leeds was shortly followed by the Stockholm crisis and Henderson's resignation from the War Cabinet. During the summer and autumn of 1917 Henderson and MacDonald worked together to produce a new constitution for the Labour Party incorporating the socialist Clause Four and, more immediately important, the Party's Declaration of Peace Aims finally accepted on December 28th. Leeds, ostensibly an attempt to reconstruct the labour movement on a revolutionary basis, was in fact the preface to the reconstruction of the Labour Party on a non-revolutionary basis. By the crisis of January 1918 the rank-and-file movement was

[1] *Mun.* 2.28, 21 July, 4 August 1917; *Daily Sketch,* 30 July 1917.
[2] Sheffield Trades Council, *Minutes,* 28 August, 2 October 1917. Glasgow Trades Council, *Minutes,* 1, 6, 13 August 1917; *The Call,* 16 August 1917.

more prepared to capitalize on its political opportunities than it had been in June, and, for a time, its chances of success seemed high both to the revolutionaries and to many of their enemies.

Since the autumn of 1916 Arthur MacManus had been leading the attempt to establish some kind of national organization for the shop stewards' movement. Finally, following the May strikes, his persistence was rewarded. On August 18th and 19th the first broadly representative conference of shop stewards' organizations assembled in Manchester and elected a National Administrative Council. MacManus became chairman, George Peet (Manchester), secretary and Jack Murphy (Sheffield), assistant secretary. The London Workers' Committee was represented by Sam Bradley, Coventry by Tom Dingley and H. King. The two major northern centres where, for the time being, no Workers' Committees existed were represented on the National Committee by William Gallacher (Clyde) and T. Hurst (Tyne).[1]

Outside Glasgow, Sheffield and, for a short period, Manchester,[2] fully-fledged Workers' Committees representative of workshop organization and capable of leading mass strike action in defiance of the trade union officials were never to emerge. Murphy recognized this in September 1919:

'We ask for the affiliation [to the NAC] of all shop stewards' committees, irrespective of their degree of development towards the class organization. This means we have to manifest a degree of tolerance both locally and nationally for the sake of getting unity of action wherever possible.'[3]

It is indicative of the 'immaturity' of the shop stewards' movement in most localities that in the elections for the National Administrative Council in the summer of 1918 proper workshop ballots were held in only three districts. The great majority of affiliated bodies, being incapable of conducting a meaningful ballot in the workshops, had contented themselves with a simple vote at their regular meetings.[4]

[1] Murphy, *Preparing for Power*, p. 136; Murphy, *New Horizons*, p. 59; *Mun.* 5.54, Notes on Recent Rank and File Developments (n.d.).

[2] West London possibly provides a further example during the first half of 1918. Success here however came so late in the war that it is difficult to evaluate the potential of the local movement. See J. Hinton, 'Rank and File Militancy in the British Engineering Industry, 1914–18' (London Ph.D., 1969) pp. 390–95.

[3] *Solidarity*, September 1919.

[4] *Workers' Dreadnought*, 21 September 1918.

Nevertheless, in estimating the potentialities of the shop stewards' movement, full account must be taken of the links provided by the NAC and the national conferences, between groups of militant trade unionists throughout the country who identified with the aims and tactics of the Workers' Committees. The strike movement of May 1917 had involved forty-eight different towns, and thirty-four districts were represented at the Walworth conference. The six national conferences of the movement held between August 1917 and the end of the war were attended by delegates representing affiliated organizations in at least thirty-three different localities.[1]

At the national conference of August 1917 many of the delegates had called for an immediate strike over the narrowing differentials of the skilled timeworkers. The conference decided to postpone action until October, threatening action then unless 'a substantial increase had been made in the skilled men's wages'.[2] Well aware of the severity of this grievance, and greatly disturbed at the prospect of a massive migration of skilled timeworkers on to better paid, but less skilled, piecework when the leaving certificate was abolished in October 1917, the Cabinet decided that some special award was essential.[3] Against the advice of the most experienced labour conciliators the Cabinet decided on a flat-rate $12\frac{1}{2}\%$ increase to all skilled timeworkers.[4]

[1] Murphy estimated 30 towns in *The Socialist*, 8 May 1919. Districts represented at five of the six national conferences are listed, respectively, in Murphy, *Preparing for Power*, p. 147; *Solidarity*, January 1918; Bell, *Pioneering Days*, p. 303; *Worker's Dreadnought*, 20 April, 21 September 1918. The districts listed are: Barrow, Birkenhead, Birmingham, Bolton, Bradford, Bristol, Chatham, Clyde, Coventry, Crayford, Crewe, Dartford, Halifax, Invergordon, Isle of Wight, Leeds, Leicester, Leigh, Lincoln, Liverpool, London, London West, Luton, Manchester, Newcastle, Newton-le-Willows, Salford, Sheffield, Southport, Stockport, Stoke on Trent, Warrington. In addition to these areas there is evidence of links with the shop stewards' movement in wartime in Edinburgh, Erith and Portsmouth.

[2] *Mun.* 2.28, 25 August 1917.

[3] *MM* VI, 11, p. 27; *Cab.* 24.22, GT 1684. The Commission on Industrial Unrest had been unanimous in finding the disparity between the earnings of skilled timeworkers and those of semi-skilled pieceworkers to be a major grievance.

[4] Thus Askwith: 'The principle of removing the disproportion of pay grievance by a uniform percentage bonus is dangerous, and possibly unfair, for there may be many varieties and grades in different trades, or in different establishments in the same trade, of this disproportion between skilled and unskilled remuneration.' G. Askwith, *Industrial Problems and Disputes* (1920), p. 432. See also *Cab.* 23.4, 12 October 1917.

The award was issued on October 13th. Within days the Engineering Employers Federation was demanding the 'suspension of the Order for fear of a general strike'.[1] Every excluded group of workers wanted to be in on the act. One of the leading purposes of the award had been explained to the Cabinet by Sir Auckland Geddes on October 12th:

'there was observable a tendency among the skilled class of instructors and others to regard themselves as the aristocracy of the engineering trade, and split off in the manner of a profession. From the recruiting standpoint this tendency to keep separate from the rank and file was to be welcomed, and if it were encouraged would be helpful.'[2]

As a bribe to the labour aristocracy, the award was worse than useless. Not only did it arouse such resentment among the excluded grades that within four months it had to be extended generally, it also opened the way for an unprecedented display of solidarity between the skilled craftsmen and the less skilled workers. Nowhere was this more apparent than in Sheffield.

The SWC made no attempt to retain the leading position in the local movement that it had seized in the last days of the May strikes, reverting at once to the policy of working as far as possible through the official trade union structures. The militants thought it worthwhile fighting an obdurate battle with the ASE Executive over the suspension of the District Committee, the old Committee refusing to dissolve and resisting re-election.[3] Subsequently efforts were made to work through the local Joint Board of engineering unions in co-ordinating the activity of shop stewards in different unions. Though Murphy later condemned this excursion into 'officialism', it was consistent with the policy expounded by him at the time of shop stewards being elected according to union membership and doing their best to gain official endorsement.[4] In any case rank-and-file control of the officials was ensured by the existence of a broadly based Workers' Committee, 'untrammelled by obsolete rule or law', which would naturally be the leading force in any crisis situation.

---

1 *Mun.* 1.2, 24 October 1917.
2 *Cab.* 23.4, 12 October 1917.
3 ASE, *Executive Minutes*, vol. 198, 7, 13, 19 June, 10 July 1917.
4 J. T. Murphy, *The Workers' Committee* (1917), p. 8; *Firth Worker*, no. 8 (n.d.); *Mun.* 5.56, Reports on the Industrial Situation as viewed by Labour, December 1917.

Certainly the SWC showed no signs of losing its independence, and this was in fact greatly strengthened by the production of a newspaper. At the end of June 1917 the shop committee at Firth decided to produce a works newspaper to counter the influence of a house journal put out by the management. Issued roughly twice a month, the *Firth Worker* was used by the SWC for propagandist and organizational purposes.[1] Later they decided to produce their own paper, the *Sheffield Worker*, and the first issue appeared in December 1917. 'The object of the paper was to keep in touch with the various shop committees that were already in existence, and be a means of educating the rank and file to take a much wider outlook on industrial matters than the four walls of the firm at which they were employed.' It was promptly suppressed by the Government, and subsequently the SWC turned all their energies into promoting the *Firth Worker*, which is said to have reached a circulation of 10,000.[2]

From the autumn of 1917, and especially after the $12\frac{1}{2}\%$ award, militancy revived in Sheffield and the SWC was in the lead as never before. Since the inaugural meeting in January 1917 the SWC had been doing its best to extend workshop organization and with it militant action to all grades and to women. Held back by the May strikes, this effort was greatly advanced by the granting of the $12\frac{1}{2}\%$ bonus on 13 October 1917. Within a month a mass meeting was called by the Joint Committee of Engineering and Allied Trades to discuss means of extending the bonus to the less skilled timeworkers. Ted Lismer, president of the Joint Trades and a leading figure in the SWC, chaired the meeting. It was decided to ballot all timeworkers in the industry: 'Are you in favour of united action with all sections of the engineering industry to adopt a down tools policy in order to extend the award of $12\frac{1}{2}\%$ to the unskilled workers'. The ballot

[1] Leaflet, headed 'Gagged' (n.d.) in *Moore Collection*. There are three copies in the *Moore Collection*, no. 8 (early November 1917), no. 14 (March 1918), and no. 16 (May 1918).

[2] 'Gagged', *loc. cit.*; *Sheffield Worker*, November 1919. No copy of the first issue of the *Sheffield Worker* exists to my knowledge. The suppression was not taken lying down. The SWC set up its secret press. 'In 1918 when I was at Hadfields, two fellows came to my house. The wife called me up and they told me we must dismantle the press as the police were after it. We fetched the press away on a horse and dray up Frederick Street past the police station, up High Street and finished in a back room past the Royal Hospital and installed it there.' W. Moore, *Verbatim Report of a Discussion between Veteran Engineers in Sheffield* (1953), p. 8. But it was not until 1919 that the SWC managed to get the *Sheffield Worker* going again.

went in favour of strike action by a majority of 35 to 1. Throughout, the SWC was operating in close co-operation with the Joint Committee. This was the propaganda of all-grades unionism in concrete form.[1] In other areas the less skilled workers were also agitating for inclusion in the bonus. In response to this pressure, and to demands from the Executives of the general unions, the War Cabinet capitulated. The Sheffield strike was averted at the last minute by the arrival of a telegram: 'Chairman, Mass Meeting, Victoria Hall, Sheffield – $12\frac{1}{2}\%$ granted to timeworkers in all sections of engineering and foundry trades – War Cabinet.'[2]

During the next six weeks both the iron and steel workers and those in the light trades – almost all the remaining industrial workers in Sheffield – were drawn into the orbit of militancy. The iron and steel workers and the light trades won advances from their employers to compensate for the $12\frac{1}{2}\%$ paid in engineering only to find the payment of those advances blocked by the Government. Resentment ran high, and the demand for inclusion in the $12\frac{1}{2}\%$ bonus grew insistent.[3] On Christmas Day a mass meeting called by the Iron and Steel Trades Confederation threatened not to return to work after the Christmas holiday unless the $12\frac{1}{2}\%$ was paid. There had been no substantial strikes of iron and steel workers in Sheffield since the outbreak of war, and the meeting declared its opposition to strikes in wartime in general, but added: 'Other unions had only been successful in moving the Government to concede war bonuses by drastic action.' Militancy spread because militancy paid. When the holiday ended the officials tried to draw back from the brink, and for a few days confused reports of strikes and resumptions in individual firms reached the Ministry of Munitions. On Sunday, December 30th, however, the NAUL and the WU decided to call out their members in the heavy trades in sympathy.[4] After this

[1] A. Gleason, *What the Workers Want* (New York, 1920), p. 190; *Sheffield Daily Telegraph*, 12, 15 November 1917; *Mun.* 5.56, Reports on the Industrial Situation as Viewed by Labour, 7 January 1918; Mendelson and Pollard, *Sheffield Trades and Labour Council*, p. 74.

[2] *Sheffield Independent*, 22 November 1917; *Mun.* 2.28, 3, 10 November 1917; *Mun.* 1.3 (MC), 9, 12, 15 November 1917; *Sheffield Daily Telegraph*, 19 November 1917; *Cab.* 23.5, 21 November 1917.

[3] Iron and Steel: *Sheffield Daily Telegraph*, 27, 31 December 1917; *Sheffield Independent*, 4 January 1918; *Mun.* 1.4, 21, 22 December 1917. Light Trades: *Sheffield Daily Telegraph*, 31 December 1917; *Sheffield Independent*, 12 November 1917.

[4] *Mun.* 1.4, 29 December 1917; *Mun.* 1.5, 1 January 1918; *Sheffield Daily*

the Confederation officials could not hold their men in, and by the beginning of January the strike was general in the iron and steel trades. The half-heartedness of the officials facilitated the intervention of the SWC in close alliance with the most militant of the general unions, the Workers' Union. On Wednesday, January 2nd the WU called a mass meeting for all less skilled workers in the industry, which empowered the leaders to form a general strike committee to which the skilled trades were to be invited to send representatives.[1] 'The shop stewards', wrote the local Ministry of Munitions official, 'are at the back of the movement', attempting to organize a general strike in the Sheffield munitions works. Many skilled engineers, who were already receiving the $12\frac{1}{2}\%$ award, came out in sympathy. On the 3rd large sections of the workers in the light trades joined the strike against the advice of their officials.[2]

Meanwhile, in London a compromise agreement had been reached between unions representing iron and steel workers throughout the country[3] and the Government. Acceptance of this agreement was delayed in Sheffield, because the officials had temporarily lost control to the strike committee of the WU and SWC. On Sunday the 6th battle was joined between the officials and the strike committee. At two mass meetings called by the officials of the Iron and Steel Trades Confederation and those of the less skilled unions, there were large majorities for a resumption, though at the meeting of the general unions there was 'a fair amount of interruption from the political section of the audience'. Later the WU held a separate meeting which condemned its delegates at the earlier meeting for speaking in favour of the resolution. The SWC did its best to stem the tide of resumption and 'to bring about common action to secure $12\frac{1}{2}\%$ in all trades'. Although it had only very limited success in this – almost all the strikers had returned to work by the 11th – the Workers' Committee's role in the $12\frac{1}{2}\%$ strike movement had established its credibility as the direct representative of the

Telegraph, 27, 31 December 1917, 2, 3, 14 January 1918; Sheffield Independent, 3 January 1918. The NUGW refused to call their men out.

[1] Sheffield Daily Telegraph, 2, 3 January 1918. Sheffield provided 'the most notable wartime example of unofficial strike action' in the Workers' Union: R. Hyman, 'The Workers' Union, 1898–1929' (Oxford D.Phil., 1968), p. 108.

[2] Mun. 1.5, 2–4 January 1918; Sheffield Daily Telegraph, 31 December 1917, 3, 5, 12 January 1918.

[3] Mun. 1.5, 4 January 1918. In Leeds and the north-east coast the iron and steel workers were on the point of striking: Mun. 1.5, 1, 3 January, 1918.

feeling of the rank and file in the workshops.[1] When, for example, the Trades Council wanted to estimate local feeling on the food question, it was to the SWC, not the Allied Trades or their own delegates, that they turned to conduct a workshop ballot.[2]

The reconstruction of the Clyde Workers' Committee during the autumn of 1917 lent further strength to the movement. Following the deportations in 1916 the Committee had not entirely disappeared, but was kept alive, chiefly as a fund raising machine for the deportees, by 'the little band who braved the storm' – Jock McBain, A. Smith and others.[3] Inside the factories, however, the workshop movement was split by defeat. On the one hand the diehard dual unionists, now disowned by the SLP and led by the WIIU[4] under T. L. Smith, greatly increased their hold in the factories, paralysing the organization. In their remote vision of a highly educated class-conscious working class which would 'take and hold' the means of production in a general stay-in-strike, there was no role for immediate militant action, for the 'wild adventures' and the 'policy of perpetual strikes' associated with Gallacher and the old CWC. Consequently the workers became apathetic and disinterested in workshop organization. At the same time many of the officially recognized shop stewards had deserted the workshop committees, falling back on their rule-book functions of dues collection and recruitment.[5]

Soon after his release from jail in February 1917 Gallacher, finding himself isolated in a sectarian wilderness, decided to use his position on the Allied Trades to revive the demand for workers' control on the Clyde. In response to a Government

[1] *Sheffield Independent*, 7 January 1918; *Sheffield Daily Telegraph*, 5, 12 January 1918; *Mun.* 1.5, 7 January 1918. Over the next week or so there were sporadic strikes and threats of strikes in several works, including a successful two-day strike of 2,000 women shell workers at Firths supported by the SWC: *Mun.* 1.5, 21 January 1918; *Mun.* 2.14, 26 January 1918; Mendelson and Pollard, *Sheffield Trades and Labour Council*, p. 74.

[2] *Ibid.*, p. 69. Sheffield Trades Council, *Minutes*, 3, 5 February 1918. J. T. Murphy had written: '. . . the trades council is only indirectly related to the workshops, whereas the Workers' Committee is directly related. The former has no power, the latter has the driving power of the directly connected workers in the workshops.' *The Workers' Committee*, p. 12.

[3] Leaflet, 'Clyde Workers Defence and Maintenance Fund' (n.d.), signed John Wheatley, in *Highton Collection;* see also *Forward*, 16 December 1916; Glasgow Trades Council, *Minutes*, 14 February 1917.

[4] The IWGB had become the WIIU in 1915.

[5] W. Gallacher, *Revolt on the Clyde* (1936), pp. 132, 135, 138–40, 143, 148; D. M. Chewter, 'The History of the Socialist Labour Party of Great Britain from 1902 to 1921' (Oxford B. Litt., 1964), pp. 159, 162–4.

drive for increased output, and piecework, in the shipyards, the Allied Trades were persuaded to insist on the control of the details of production by specially elected shop committees before they would permit output to be increased. No mention was made of public ownership and the Government's Shipyard Commissioners (who included Lynden Macassey) appear to have come close to accepting the demand. Although Gallacher claims that this scheme aroused 'the greatest interest and discussion in the factories', it did little to revive the shop stewards' movement. Indeed its main effect was further to convince the WIIU stewards that the 'workers' control' of the old CWC leaders was indistinguishable from that of the Whitley Report.[1]

During May the workshop movement was put to the test by the strike movement in England. Initially the Glasgow district officials were ready to come out, believing the strike to be official. On April 29th and May 6th mass meetings of the Glasgow ASE condemned the withdrawal of the Trade Card scheme and threatened 'drastic action'. When the local officials were assured by the Executive that the strike was not official, the responsibility for organizing 'drastic action' devolved upon the shop stewards.[2] Lacking any central co-ordination they did not meet until May 13th, and when they did meet they were ill-informed as to the extent of the strike in England. Gallacher was deputed to tour the strike centres, and he reported back on the 16th that 'the strike would be over before we could get anything moving on the Clyde'. Dave Ramsay and W. F. Watson arrived hot on the heels of Gallacher with instructions from Walworth to get the Clyde out, but they had no success. The shop stewards had missed the boat: the critical moment on the Clyde had already passed when, on May 9th, a man had been called up and, on producing his trade card, had been told that it was obsolete.[3]

In June the deportees were allowed to return, and Gallacher and Muir were strengthened by the return of Messer, Clark and MacManus.[4] During the next two or three months the leaders'

[1] Gallacher, *Revolt on the Clyde*, pp. 142–3; *The Herald*, 14, 21, 28 April, 12 May 1917; *Labour Leader*, 28 April 1917; *The Worker*, 6 October 1919.

[2] *The Herald*, 5, 12 May 1917; ASE, *Monthly Journal and Report*, June 1917; ASE, *Executive Minutes*, vol. 197, 10, 12 May 1917.

[3] Gallacher, *Revolt on the Clyde*, pp. 144–7; *Mun.* 2.28, 19 May 1917; Kendall, *The Revolutionary Movement in Britain*, pp. 158, 371–2; *MM* VI, 1, p. 111.

[4] Gallacher, *Revolt on the Clyde*, pp. 151, 153; *Forward*, 20 June 1917; Glasgow Trades Council, *Minutes*, 30 May 1917. Gallacher says that Muir had

time was fully occupied with campaigns for the release of John Maclain (finally achieved at the end of June), for the re-employment of the deportees, and to set up a Workers' and Soldiers' Council on the Clyde.[1] Meanwhile factory activity revived, and on 9 September 1917 the remains of the old CWC, a newly formed Provisional Workers' Committee (probably consisting of the old CWC leadership), and the WIIU met with a view to the fusion of the three movements.[2] The WIIU was more hostile to Gallacher and his associates than ever. Shortly before the meeting Gallacher and Paton had published 'Towards Industrial Democracy', announcing that at least one of the old CWC leaders had fallen under the influence of the Guild Socialist 'coterie of so-called intellectuals'.[3] Consequently they insisted that if any fusion was to take place they should be the controlling organization. When this was defeated by a narrow majority the leaders of the WIIU walked out of the meeting 'very sore at their repulse'. The CWC and the Provisional Committee then amalgamated under the former title, and by the end of September had formally reconstituted themselves with Gallacher as chairman and Messer as secretary.[4]

By January 1918 the Clyde was back in the vanguard of the national movement. In contrast to the 1915–16 period its leadership was based on an alliance of workers in all sections of the Glasgow metal industries, though, unlike Sheffield, the relative

been, since his release from jail in February, 'just a shadow of what he had been' and totally dependent on Wheatley: *op. cit.*, p. 141. Kirkwood also returned in June, but 'settled down' happily as a foreman in one of Beardmore's shell factories: *Mun.* 5.56, Reports on the Industrial Situation as viewed by Labour, October 1917.

[1] Gallacher, *Revolt on the Clyde*, p. 155; ASE, *Monthly Journal and Report*, July, September 1917; Glasgow Trades Council, *Minutes*, 29 August 1917; ASE, *Executive Minutes*, vol. 198, 31 July 1917; *Mun.* 2.28, 2, 9 June, 11 August 1917.

[2] *Mun.* 5.54, Notes on Recent Rank and File Developments (n.d.). During the summer an Engineering Shop Stewards' Committee seems to have been formed in rivalry with the WIIU. But this had disappeared by September: *Cab.* 24.16, GT 1008; Glasgow Trades Council, *Minutes*, 13 August 1917.

[3] *Glasgow Herald*, 9 October 1917. Kirkwood was also preaching the Guild Socialist doctrine: *Forward* 9 December 1917.

[4] Gallacher, *Revolt on the Clyde*, pp., 169–70; *Cab* 24.16, GT 1008; *Mun.* 5.56, Reports on the Industrial Situation as viewed by Labour, October 1917. Leaflet, 'To All Clyde Workers' (n.d.), in *Highton Collection*. After the new CWC was formed there was a short period of bitter competition between the rival tendencies, but from November relations became 'less strained': *Mun.* 5.56, *op. cit.*, November, December 1917.

neglect of organization among the less skilled workers continued. The c w c's leadership was powerfully reinforced by the emergence of an allied independent rank-and-file movement among foundry workers. During 1917 Jock McBain, the Parkhead moulder who had held the c w c together after the deportations, Tom Bell, Jim Gardner and others had been leading a movement for workshop organization in the Scottish foundries. In August 1917 they called a mass meeting to discuss action against an unsatisfactory wage award. An unofficial Emergency Committee was set up, and from September 13th foundry workers all over Scotland came out on strike for three weeks. The strike was not directly successful (though it probably played a part in the Government's decision to award the $12\frac{1}{2}$%), but it was called off in good order and the Emergency Committee remained in being, leading rank-and-file activities among the foundry workers over the next two years and working closely with the c w c.[1]

The first effective intervention of the reconstructed Committee occurred in relation to a strike of women workers at the Parkhead factory. Following a go-slow in November 1917, four girls were victimized at Beardmore's East Hope Street shell factory, and the bulk of the women came out on strike for their reinstatement. Although the n f w w formally disowned the strike, the Glasgow a s e instructed its members to refuse to set up tools for the women who had not struck. The c w c provided the strikers with funds, and on November 25th organized a mass meeting on Glasgow Green in solidarity with the women. Eventually Beardmore offered to reinstate the women pending arbitration and by the beginning of December work was resumed. This was not the end of the matter. Fearing that the victimizations would be renewed by the management as soon as the agitation died down, shop stewards from all the Beardmore works met to discuss joint action, and on December 30th the c w c called a 'general meeting of convenors, shop stewards and representatives of all classes of workers in the Clyde area' to demand the reinstatement of the women. Failing this they threatened to organize a general strike throughout Scotland, and if possible England. 'The situation is looking serious', commented a report to the Ministry of Munitions, 'as the men who attended the meeting in question are those who practically have the Clyde at their backs.' In the

1 Gallacher, *Revolt on the Clyde*, pp. 172–3; Bell, *Pioneering Days*, pp. 130–7, 299–300; H. J. Fyrth and H. Collins, *The Foundry Workers*, pp. 144–7; *Mun.* 2.28, 3 November 1917; *Forward*, 10 February 1917.

second week of January the Moulders' Emergency Committee declared that 'the Beardmore Combine has thrown down the gauntlet to all the Clyde Workers' and urged them 'to accept the challenge'. However the intervention of Sir George Askwith as arbitrator appears to have settled the issue and satisfied the workers.[1]

At the end of September 1917 the local official of the Ministry of Munitions on the Clyde reported: 'All bodies in the engineering trades are likely to join in the demand for a higher rate of wage at the next revision . . . everything points to a big movement in October.' The 12½ % bonus did little to buy off unrest, and by the beginning of November agitation arising out of the bonus was worse on the Clyde than anywhere else in the country, aggravated by the inclusion of the moulders. The inequalities which the bonus were intended to remedy were those arising out of dilution: but the moulders had vigorously and often successfully resisted dilution. Their inclusion in the award therefore could only be explained – ran the 'sinister suggestion' – by the recent strike. In several firms where the timeworkers were paid output bonuses above the district rate the employers tried to absorb the new bonus into the old, arousing the ire of the ASE. More important however were the grievances of the pieceworkers excluded from the bonus. Many of them 'don't make 12½ % over their timerates even when they are doing their utmost, so there is bound to be discontent', commented the ASE district organizer in December. 'If things don't quieten down I am afraid those belligerents will have the societies officials as daft as themselves before long.'[2] Those on the Premium Bonus system had a special grievance, believing that the system was in fact a form of timework, and that they were therefore automatically entitled to the award. After threatening strike action the workers on Premium Bonus at Parkhead and at David Rowan were paid the 12½ % despite Government orders to the contrary. Workers in other firms demanded similar treatment, and during December with sporadic strike action and a general go-slow. Faced with a 25–40 % reduction in output the local Engineering Employers' Federation defied the Government and offered a 12½ % rise to all pieceworkers.

[1] *Mun.* 2.28, 17, 24 November 1917, 1 February 1918; *Mun.* 5.56, Reports *cit.*, November, December 1917; *Mun.* 1.4, 18 December 1917; *Mun.* 2.14, 5, 12 January 1918.

[2] ASE, *Monthly Journal and Report*, December 1917, January 1918; *Mun.* 2.28, 29 September, 3 November 1917.

The men accepted this only to find it promptly withdrawn on Government instructions. From January 8th engineering and shipbuilding workers on piecework started to come out throughout Glasgow. By the 19th 10,000 shipyard workers were out, and many workers in the engineering shops had struck.[1] After the promise of a decision on the extension of the award to pieceworkers within two weeks on January 20th most of the shipyard workers went back. Against the Ministry of Munitions' advice – they were attempting to remove the inequalities by adjusting piece rates at shop level – the War Cabinet subsequently gave a compensatory $7\frac{1}{2}\%$ award to the pieceworkers.[2] Not only the engineering and shipbuilding workers were affected by the $12\frac{1}{2}\%$ 'delirium'.[3] On December 17th bricklayers in the engineering works, shipyards and iron and steel had threatened strike action, and ten days later the Parkhead bricklayers brought the Howitzer shop to a halt.[4] It was also at Parkhead that the discontents of the iron and steel workers were focussed. Here it was the Emergency Committee of the moulders which took the lead – though the moulders already had the bonus. During December they demanded the extension of the $12\frac{1}{2}\%$ to all workers in the plant. threatening an overtime ban from the 22nd to enforce this. By the 29th 300 steel workers in the Howitzer shop had struck, and nearly 5,000 others were banning overtime and weekend work. Meanwhile, in other parts of the country, as we have seen, there were general strikes of iron and steel workers, and on January 6th the bonus was extended to cover them. However, because this award was to merge with existing bonuses, the Parkhead

[1] *Mun.* 2.28, 8 December 1917; *Mun.* 1.4, 28 December 1917; *Mun.* 1.5, 8, 15 January 1918; *Mun.* 2.14, 12, 19 January 1918; *Glasgow Herald*, 19 January 1918.

[2] *Glasgow Herald*, 19 January 1918; *Mun.* 2.14, 19 January 1918; *Mun.* 1.2, 22 January 1918; *Cab* 24.40, GT 3417; Cole, *History of the Labour Party from 1914*, p. 172; *MM* VI, 2, pp. 28–9.

[3] ASE, *Monthly Journal and Report*, December 1917. The unskilled workers do not appear to have been particularly vocal, as one would expect in an area where they were weakly organized. Early in January 1918 the Workers' Union was reported to have threatened strike action over the $12\frac{1}{2}\%$ bonus; *Mun.* 1.5, 7 January 1918.

[4] *Mun.* 1.4, 17, 28 December 1917. The Howitzer shop had a very militant record and a strong 'rebel element': *Mun.* 2.28, 14 April 1917. Among the rebel shop stewards were Harry McShane and Tommy Linden. In November 1917 McShane, a toolsetter, was victimized for presiding over a works meeting. The men forced his reinstatement with a stay-in strike, and proceeded to claim payment for time lost. Interview with Mr McShane; *Mun.* 2.28, 10 November 1917; ASE, *Monthly Journal and Report*, December 1917.

workers only received $6\frac{1}{4}$%. Under the leadership of the Emergency Committee 1,500 steel workers left the British Steel and Smelters Union and formed their own 'dual' union threatening to restart the overtime and weekend work ban unless the full $12\frac{1}{2}$% were paid. The management took a strong line, and with the approval of the union officials, attempted to stamp out the new union. On 2 February 1918 its 1,500 members were locked out. The Emergency Committee struck with their protégé, and by the 8th 4,000 moulders were out in sympathy, and a general strike throughout the Clyde was feared. The firm climbed down and the men returned victorious on February 11th.[1]

The winter of 1917–18 saw a great extension of the basis of militancy, radiating out from the engineering vanguard. The isolation of the militant vanguard on the Clyde was at last broken. In Sheffield the rank-and-file movement now embraced almost all the local factory workers, and in the country as a whole the effect of the $12\frac{1}{2}$% bonus had been to break down the divisions between skilled and less skilled workers. The potential of the movement had been further advanced by the establishment of a national leadership, and the extension of its influence into a large number of centres. In the middle of December 1917 the Ministry of Munitions anticipated that 'the early months of 1918 may reveal industrial action with a view to the achievement of political ends in the termination of war conditions'.[2] In conditions of profound unrest caused by food shortage, and general war weariness throughout the community, relatively little would be needed to precipitate the movement into the revolutionary alliance with the peace movement that it had declined in the summer of 1917.

[1] Glasgow Trades Council, *Minutes*, 6, 13 February, 26 March, 9 April 1918; *Mun.* 1.6, 4, 7, 8, 9, 11 February 1918; *Mun.* 5.56, Reports on the Industrial Situation as viewed by Labour, December 1917; *Mun.* 2.28, 29 December 1917.

[2] *Mun.* 2.28, 15 December 1917.

Chapter 10

Climax and Defeat

Towards the end of 1917 the Cabinet became convinced of the need to take more skilled young men from the munitions works for the army and, to make this possible, to overide the guarantees contained in the Schedule of Protected Occupations. Aware of the unrest this was likely to cause the Cabinet prepared the ground thoroughly. It decided on a two-pronged strategy. On the one hand the ASE was to be isolated by a refusal to grant separate negotiations due to it both as the major union affected by the new Man Power proposals, and as the union with which the Schedule had been originally negotiated in April and May 1917. The protests of the ASE could be met with insinuations that its members desired preferential treatment, with encouragement of the hostility felt towards it by the other skilled engineering unions and the general unions.[1] On the other hand the danger of fusion between industrial unrest provoked by the Man Power proposals and the anti-war movement was met by an attempt to help the Labour Party to contain the latter. On January 5th Lloyd George stated Britain's war aims publicly for the first time, and stated them to a conference of trade union Executives summoned to consider the Man Power proposals. The terms of his statement, though vague, were close to those adopted by the Labour Party on December 28th.[2] Having prepared its ground the Cabinet had no qualms about fighting.

On January 14th, the day the new parliamentary session opened, Sir Auckland Geddes, Minister of National Service,

---

[1] C.f. *The Herald*, 12 January 1918.
[2] *The Times*, 7 January 1918. See *The Herald*, 19 January 1918, for the major differences.

introduced the Military Service Bill. He was adamant on the intention of the Government to proceed without the ASE so long as the ASE insisted on separate negotiations. He issued a stern warning to the rank-and-file movement: 'Efforts are now being made by pacifists to stir up strikes in the munitions factories . . . [Maintaining a privileged position for young engineering workers] is their claim, and they are going to take direct action to enforce it. We shall see.' The Cabinet had chosen confrontation.[1]

The Military Service Bill succeeded where the Leeds Conference had failed: it united industrial unrest with the anti-war agitation. Inspired by the example of the Bolshevik Revolution, and in particular by the Bolshevik peace terms and Trotsky's call for peace, the leaders of the rank-and-file movement were poised for revolutionary action against the war. On January 5th and 6th the shop stewards' movement met in national conference at Manchester to discuss two major questions, food and manpower. Agitation over the former, as we have seen, continued throughout the crisis month. About forty delegates attended, and 'reports were given as to the feeling which exists in the . . . large industrial centres . . . The essence of all the reports submitted was to resist any further taking away of men to the army.' The conference recommended national strike action to prevent the passing of the Military Service Bill. At the same time it decisively rejected any narrow defence of the craftsmen's privileged exemption, advising the movement to 'demand that the Government shall at once accept the invitation of the Russian Government to consider peace terms'. No strike was called, but delegates were instructed to 'ascertain from the workers in the districts, what form this action should take, and to at once acquaint the National Administrative Council'.[2]

The Clyde took the lead. The CWC and the Emergency Com-

---

[1] HC Debates, 5s., vol. 101, cols. 68–70. Tom Jones, assistant secretary to Lloyd George's cabinet, was already so worried that he was pressing for the replacement of Milner, Curzon and Carson by Henderson, Thomas and Smillie in the War Cabinet in order to prevent unrest taking on revolutionary dimensions: K. Middlemass (ed.), *Thomas Jones, Whitehall Diaries*, vol. I, 1916–25 (1969), pp. 43–4.

[2] T. Bell, *Pioneering Days* (1941), pp. 303–4; *Solidarity*, February 1918; *Mun.* 2. 14, 12 January 1918; *Mun.* 1. 5, 14 January 1918; *Mun.* 1.5 (MC), 28 January 1918; *Mun.* 1.6 (MC), 2 February 1918. The conference also passed a resolution demanding the 'conscription of wealth', but little more was heard of this during the crisis that followed.

mittee were fresh from their victory in the Beardmore victimization case. Many thousands of shipyard pieceworkers were on strike for the $12\frac{1}{2}$ % bonus. There was widespread unrest over the food question. Politically temperatures had been rising with a battle against censorship of anti-war propaganda led by the rapidly growing Women's Peace Crusade – 'If you have the women with you. there are no heights to which you cannot rise' – and the organization for a demonstration in support of the Bolshevik Revolution, supported by the Glasgow Trades Council and banned by the police.[1] Into this turmoil Geddes threw the Man Power proposals. The District Committee of the Federation of Engineering and Shipbuilding Trades was quick to take up the challenge. On Sunday, January 13th they passed a resolution: 'That if the Government do not withdraw the new man power bill before the end of January we advise our members in the Clyde district to down tools, and, further, that we ask the Government to call an international conference to discuss the terms of peace.' Immediately the shop stewards carried the agitation for a strike into the workshops, and the CWC arranged a ballot on the resolution which gave a majority in favour of strike action.[2]

Two days later Sheffield came into line, the Trades Council protesting 'against any further comb out or compulsory service unless the Government gives guarantees that they will not prolong the war longer than is necessary to carry out the policy of no annexations or penal indemnities as laid down by our brother democrats in Russia, and that a ballot be taken of all workers skilled and unskilled in order that the rank and file may have the opportunity to accept or refuse these proposals'. The particular importance of this resolution lay in the fact that it was moved by the Workers' Union, thus emphasizing the solidarity of skilled and unskilled workers in the demand for a democratic peace. Two delegates were appointed to attend the SWC meeting, and, presumably, to arrange with the Workers' Committee for the balloting.[3]

[1] *Cab.* 24. 40, GT 3424; *Mun.* 2. 14, 19 January 1918; *District Record* (Glasgow), 19, 28 January 1918; *Glasgow Herald*, 28 January 1918; W. Gallacher, *Revolt on the Clyde* (1936), pp. 177–8; Glasgow Trades Council, *Minutes*, 19 December 1917, 16 January, 27 February 1918.

[2] *Glasgow Herald*, 19 January 1918; *Mun.* 2. 14, 26 January 1918. On the same day a mass meeting of the Moulders' Emergency Committee passed a similar resolution, though it contained no specific strike threat: Glasgow Trades Council, *Minutes*, 16 January 1918.

[3] Sheffield Trades Council, *Minutes*, 15 January 1918; *ibid.*, *Executive*

I

By the weekend of January 19–20th similar resolutions, threatening direct action, had come from ASE committees in many other areas, including Barrow, Coventry, Erith, London and Woolwich. Additional demands, made by the national conference on the 6th, for the conscription of wealth and adequate provisions for wounded soldiers were frequently appended. On the 20th a national conference of the Local Allied Trades Committees met in Leeds and added its voice to the swelling demand for peace negotiations to be started before any further consideration could be given to the Man Power proposals.[1] All these resolutions repudiated the sectionalism on which Geddes was relying to force through his man power policy, protesting, as *The Herald* pointed out on the 19th: 'not against the combing out of this trade or that, but against the continuance of the war. That is the fact to which the Government is vainly trying to turn a blind eye. The game of "divide and conquer" has been played once too often . . .' If one leg of the Government's strategy, the isolation of the ASE was being undermined, how was the other, the attempt to contain the peace movement, faring?

The Labour leaders had welcomed Lloyd George's declaration of war aims with great enthusiasm, as *The Times* noted with satisfaction:

'The Prime Minister's war aims speech dominates everything else. There has been no political event at all comparable with it since the war began. It has provided a fresh rallying-point, and the unanimity of the response is a remarkable tribute to the essential unity of the nation after three and half years of war.'[2]

That was on January 8th. Two weeks later the Labour leaders were 'distinctly uneasy about the spirit of revolt among the rank and file, which openly declares its sympathy with the lurid doings in Petrograd . . . They believe that there may be an epidemic of "down-tools" . . .'[3] In the face of this threat Lloyd George's war

Minutes, 8 January 1918. The patriotic leadership of the Workers' Union was seriously alarmed by such manifestations of revolutionary solidarity. C.f. R. Hyman, 'The Workers' Union, 1898–1929' (Oxford D.Phil., 1968), p. 237.

[1] *The Herald*, 12, 26 January, 1918; *Woolwich Pioneer*, 25 January 1918; *MM* VI, 11, p. 44.

[2] *The Times*, 8 January 1918. For the attitude of the labour leaders see *The Times*, 7 January 1918.

[3] M. Cole (ed.), *Beatrice Webbs' Diaries, 1912–24* (1952), p. 107. See also Sidney Webb's letter to Tom Jones on 20 January 1918, in Middlemass, *Thomas Jones, Whitehall Diaries*, p. 48.

aims declaration had to be made to fulfil its function as a device
to contain the peace movement, to prevent the effective alliance
of industrial unrest with anti-war politics. It succeeded in so far
as right and left were successfully united against the revolutionary
movement at the Labour Party Conference when it opened in
Nottingham on January 23rd. The general opinion of the Conference was accurately expressed by W. C. Anderson, the left-
wing Sheffield MP who had been one of the organizers of the
Leeds conference. 'A terrific industrial upheaval at the present
moment might be dangerous from the standpoint of a democratic
People's Peace. There was need for restraint . . .'. With the war
aims speech, by which the Government accepted 'in essentials'
the policy of the Labour Party, democratic diplomacy had begun.
Of course, Henderson explained, there was a danger that whatever was said in public Britain's war aims would be perverted by
'sinister imperialistic ambitions'. All the more reason, therefore,
for the Labour Party to concentrate on holding the Government
to its declared aims and to avoid hasty adventures. The demand
for an immediate armistice and peace negotiations, and the threat
of strike action to enforce it, were potentially fatal to the prospects
for peace and to the prospects for the labour movement alike.[1]

Lloyd George's war aims speech made it possible for the
labour leadership to condemn the revolutionary movement in
the name of democratic diplomacy. Nevertheless the Labour
Party Conference failed to contain the revolutionary tide. The
largest mass meeting of the crisis took place two days after the
Labour Party Conference finished on Sunday, January 27th.
10,000 skilled engineers, from several unions, rallied in the Albert
Hall and, pledging themselves to resist the Man Power proposals,
demanded the opening of peace negotiations. The meeting made
it clear, commented *The Herald*, 'that the struggle really centres
far more round the Government's war policy and the possibility
of a democratic peace than round any question of preferential
treatment'.[2] The next day Geddes, who had already been hounded
by the Liverpool engineers, faced a meeting of 3,000 accredited
shop stewards of Federated societies on the Clyde. The CWC had
laid their plans and were well represented. Geddes was greeted with

---

[1] Labour Party, *Report of the Annual Conference*, Nottingham, 1918,
p. 129. For Henderson's attitude at this time see his statements published in
The Times, on 7 January and 1 February 1918; and Cole, *Beatrice Webb's
Diaries*, p. 107.
[2] *The Herald*, 2 February 1918.

'The Red Flag', and could only make himself heard after Gallacher's intervention. After his speech MacManus moved a resolution decided on by the CWC the night before, and Maxton seconded it. The resolution, passed almost unanimously, read:

'(1) That having heard the case for the Government, as stated by Sir Auckland Geddes, this meeting pledges itself to oppose the Government to the very utmost in its call for more men.

(2) that we insist on, and we bind ourselves to take action to enforce the declaration of an immediate armistice on all fronts.

(3) And that the expressed opinion of the workers of Glasgow, from now on, so far as this business is concerned, is that our attitude should be to do nothing, all the time and every time, in support of carrying on the war, but to bring the war to a conclusion.'[1]

Next day the *Glasgow Herald* spoke of British Soviet and demanded 'strong courageous and immediate action' against the political activists who were exploiting the economic grievances of the rank and file. 'The industrial situation on the Clyde is grave', reported the Ministry official, 'and a stoppage of work on a large scale seems extremely probable . . .' The apparent fusion of industrial militancy and anti-war politics swept the revolutionaries up on a great wave of enthusiasm. *Solidarity* – headlined 'The Great Revolt. Awakening of the Engineers. Strike Movement to Stop the War.' – expressed what many revolutionaries must have been feeling at the end of January 1918.

'This final turn of the screw [the Man Power Bill] has broken the thread at last, and as we go to press, news comes pouring in from every side of immense mass meetings . . . protesting in the name of the workers, the soldiers, and of our common humanity against any further continuance of the barbarous and bloody war to which the people's rulers condemned them three and a half years ago. The uprising of skilled and unskilled labour in this country is but part of the revolutionary movement of the people all over Europe . . . In England the engineers lead the way, and it will not be long before they are followed by the whole body of organized labour. Perhaps it will be necessary to

[1] Gallacher, *Revolt on the Clyde*, pp. 179–84; *Glasgow Herald*, 28, 29 January 1918; *Mun.* 2. 14, 2 February 1918.

start this Class War in every belligerent country before we shall be able to stop the other War.'[1]

If the revolutionaries exaggerated, so did many of their opponents. By the end of January the fear of 'an epidemic of "down tools" ' had become general. Criticism of the Government's handling of the crisis concentrated on its refusal to grant separate negotiations to the ASE: 'There was . . . widespread feeling in the country that the Government was standing aloof solely on a point of form.'[2] Not only was it thereby forfeiting the national leaders of the ASE as allies against the rank-and-file movement, but it also appeared to be neglecting the danger of an escalation of strike action over the specific Man Power issue into a political strike against the war.[3] Henderson summed up the general feeling on January 31st:

'From evidence and information in my possession I am afraid that at no period during the war had the industrial situation been so grave and so pregnant with disastrous possibilities as it is today. The unfortunate and avoidable impasse between the Government and the ASE threatens to develop into a crisis of the first magnitude. The temper of the workmen is dangerous and the unyielding attitude of the Government is bringing the country to the verge of industrial revolution . . .'[4]

In the event the Government did not climb down and the revolution did not occur. The Cabinet was confident throughout that firmness would succeed, and conscious that 'any sign of wavering would give an opportunity for the Opposition to pull together'.[5] A closer look at the continuing internal weaknesses of the rank-and-file movement reveals the justification for the Government's attitude.

On January 25th the NAC reassembled to consider the results of its appeal to the localities. The delegates could hardly have

[1] *Glasgow Herald,* 29 January 1918; *Mun.*2. 14, 2 February 1918; *Solidarity* February 1918.
[2] *Cab* 23. 5, 1 February 1918.
[3] *The Times*, 31 January 1918. C.f. telegram from the Engineering Employers' Federation on 29 January 1918, stressing 'the extraordinary difficulty of arriving at a satisfactory settlement of strikes at a time like the present when the minds of men are rather disturbed by so many considerations . . .' *Cab.* 24. 40, GT 3486.
[4] *The Times*, 1 February 1918.
[5] *Cab.* 23. 5, 17 January 1918.

been unaware that their decision would largely determine whether or not the strike threats of the past two weeks would materialize. The Council was well aware of the need for co-ordinated national action and knew that it was up to them to issue a definite call for a strike action.[1] The delegates from London and the Clyde were keen for strike action, W. F. Watson telling the conference that '100,000 workers in London were ready to strike against the war'. Questioned by the other delegates, Watson had to admit that no attempt had been made to hold a workshop ballot on the question. Nor had the CWC held a ballot, and an ASE ballot held on the Clyde had shown an almost equal division of opinion on the narrow question of whether or not to strike against the removal of the craftsmen's exemption. But the decisive reports came from Manchester and Sheffield, where the views of the rank and file had been tested in workshop meetings: 'They were opposed to strike action against the war.'[2]

The movement in Sheffield had collapsed. The Trades Council meeting on the 15th demonstrated the solidarity of unskilled and skilled on the issue of a democratic peace. During the same week, however, the ASE District Committee held an aggregate meeting attended by about 3,000 workers. The official report of the meeting is, in the circumstances, surprising:

'The meeting was one of the best I have ever attended, and the whole position was discussed from all points and with a full responsibility of the situation [sic], without any excitement *or attempt to introduce any other matter apart from the refusal of the Government to discuss the breaking of their agreement with the ASE.*'[3]

Not only had the skilled men entirely neglected the political aspect of the Man Power proposals: more important, their unofficial leaders had made no attempt to enlighten them. When the SWC met on January 19th it took its cue, not from the anti-war resolution passed at the Trades Council, but from the aggregate meeting, threatening 'drastic action unless all men who have started in munitions factories since the commencement of the

[1] After the strike in November 1917, for example, the NAC had urged the Coventry workers to 'defer any further down tools action until the move can be made national': *Solidarity*, January 1918.

[2] J. T. Murphy, *Preparing for Power* (1934), p. 155. Judging from reports received by the Ministry of Munitions by the end of the month it is likely that the NAC received similarly discouraging reports from other centres.

[3] ASE, *Monthly Journal and Reports*, February 1918 (authors' italics).

war are taken first, irrespective of their trade unions, and that less ASE apprentices are to be taken thereafter in proportion to others'.[1]

The collapse of the Sheffield Workers' Committee is surprising. The close association of the Workers' Union and the ASE militants during the movement for the extention of the $12\frac{1}{2}\%$ award had been reaffirmed over the Man Power issue at the Trades Council on January 15th. The Trades Council had recognized the leading role of the SWC both in the food question and over Man Power. Nevertheless the workshop meetings seem to have gone against strike action to end the war, and the Workers' Committee retreated into the mere defence of craft privilege. Once again the unreliability of the craftsmen as a militant vanguard was demonstrated: faced with the prospect of leading an all-out struggle against the war itself, their confidence crumbled at the eleventh hour.

These reports presented the National Administrative Council with a cruel dilemma. Despite the great widening of the movement's basis, despite the wave of revolutionary resolutions, militancy still, as in May 1917, posed itself as an alternative to class politics. A strike called to force the Government to open peace negotiations would, it seemed, be easily sidetracked into a struggle by the skilled men in defence of their privileges in relation to conscription. To call a strike solely on the narrow issue would have been to invite the hostility of other sections of organized labour, to capitulate entirely to the craft orientation of the rank and file. Against the protests of an unrepentant Watson, the Council decided to solve their dilemma by abdication, resolving 'that they were not the body to deal with technical grievances arising out of the cancellation of occupational exemptions, but that such grievances should be dealt with by union executives'.[2] In the days following January 25th leadership reverted to the Clyde, but the Clyde also had its troubles. Already on the 26th the local Ministry official had reported 'a feeling of

[2] *MM* vi, 11, p. 44. Watson continued to protest: '. . . everything pointed at that time to an international peace offensive, and I am absolutely certain that had . . . those who claim to be guiding the destinies of the rank and file movement possessed a little more courage and imagination, we should have developed such a movement as would have compelled the powers that be to open up peace negotiations and declare an armistice. That the rank and file would have responded I am certain.' *Workers' Dreadnought*, 6 April 1918.

[1] *Mun.* 2. 14, 26 January 1918; Sheffield Trades Council, *Minutes*, 15 January 1918.

resentment at the attempt of the engineers to obtain specially favourable treatment'. The Geddes meeting on the 28th provoked a stream of 'loyal' resolutions from workshops and shipyards throughout the Clyde, organized by a body calling itself the War Aims Committee. Such open resistance to the militants, political or industrial, was unprecedented on the Clyde – 'gratifying if somewhat astonishing'. It was not, of course, a spontaneous working-class organization, and it worked closely with the employers, the Ministry and the police. Nevertheless, as Churchill was well aware, it had an important propagandist use and 'a marked effect on the disaffected elements'.[1]

On January 30th the Clyde District Committee of the Federation met to consider the results of its challenge two weeks earlier. Then it had threatened strike action unless the Man Power proposals were withdrawn by the end of January. Now it put the date forward to February 6th, and, more significantly changed its demand to one that the Government 'should give satisfactory guarantees that they will open up negotiations'.[2] This vague formulation gave notice to the ASE that if they wanted to fight over the Man Power issue, they would fight alone, and the 'loyal' resolutions from the shops reinforced the message. Nationally this resolution 'had the effect of postponing the actual crisis, and thus giving the Government time to find a way out of their difficulty . . .'[3] On February 5th a meeting of the London shop

1 *Mun.* 2. 14, 26 January, 2, 9, 16 February 1918; Bell, *Pioneering Days*, p. 297; *Glasgow Herald*, 30 January, 6 February 1918; *Cab.* 23. 5, 5 February 1918. Churchill thought: 'It should be possible to obtain from the great munitions areas a stream of resolutions in favour of the vigorous prosecution of the war. Such resolutions should appear in increasing numbers day by day in the newspapers for at least a fortnight.' *The Herald* had something to say about how these resolutions were obtained: 'there had been an influx of war-aim experts into factories and workshops to explain to the workers why peace without further loss of life would be akin to defeat. Every facility had been given by the profiteers for their employees to attend these meetings inside the bosses' fence – and after the orations have proved that peace and treason are twins, a motion pledging those present to continue their support of the war is moved and carried "unanimously". The boss usually presides at these meetings.' *The Herald*, 9 February 1918. For contact of War Aims Committee with Scotland Yard, see *Cab.* 24. 34, GT 2809, and Lord Riddle, *War Diary* (1933), p. 292.

2 *Glasgow Herald*, 31 January 1918.

3 *The Herald*, 23 February 1918; *The Call*, 14 February 1918. It was felt by some in the rank-and-file movement that the Clyde was chiefly responsible for the failure: 'the whole of the movement looked to the Clyde for that 'drastic action' which they so emphatically promised us'. *Solidarity*, May 1918.

stewards passed a similar motion and refused to set any date at all for strike action. Subsequently, both in London and on the Clyde the engineers decided to postpone any further action until after the Allied Socialist Conference – hardly a revolutionary international – had met in London on February 20th. In Manchester the ASE was completely isolated by the beginning of February.[1] In Coventry, when the Joint Committee submitted the Leeds resolution to mass meetings of constituent unions on January 27th, the Workers' Union rejected outright any strike action over the Man Power proposals. Subsequently a workshop ballot showed 'in an unmistakeable manner' that there was little support for drastic action even among the skilled workers. By the middle of February it was clear in Sheffield that the engineers stood alone in their opposition to the Man Power proposals.[2]

Deprived of leadership from the NAC, the unofficial elements in the ASE were slow to organize. Nevertheless the danger of sectional strikes remained, especially when skilled men were taken from the workshops before dilutees. On February 12th the results of the official ASE postal ballot were known. Nearly half of the unions members had voted – a record proportion – the overwhelming majority of them in favour of strike action. Two weeks later the Government agreed to meet the ASE Executive separately to discuss the question, but it made no other concessions. On March 5th the Cabinet still thought that a local strike was likely: 'e.g. if one or two shop stewards were called up on the Clyde or at Sheffield', and feared that 'a strike once begun in one area may spread to others and become general. If the ASE were to strike the ETU, the Moulders and some other Unions would be likely to follow.'[3] Eventually, on March 21st, the ASE militants succeeded in getting together an unofficial national

---

[1] *Workers' Dreadnought*, 6 April 1918; *The Call*, 9 February 1918; *Mun.* 2. 14, 2 February 1918. The mutual bitterness continued. In April it was reported that 'a good deal of general ill-will [is] shown by other trade unions towards the A.S.E.' in Manchester. The ASE itself had taken up a very sectional position, claiming that the introduction of members of the United Machine Workers on to skilled jobs constituted dilution: *Mun.* 2. 15, 13 April 1918.

[2] *MM* VI, 11, p. 47; *Midland Daily Telegraph*, 28, 29 January, 4 February 1918; *Mun.* 2. 14, 16 February 1918.

[3] *Mun.* 2. 14, 2, 16 February 1918; ASE, *Monthly Journal and Report*, March 1918; *MM* VI, 11, p. 47; *Cab.* 24. 44, GT 3814. The Government was sufficiently worried discreetly to suspend further pressure for dilution for the time being: *Mun.* 5. 72, Dilution Section Minutes, no. 105, 15 February 1918.

conference of District Committee representatives to plan how to implement the members' strike decision.[1]

On the day the conference assembled the Germans launched their last great offensive of the war, and the belated unofficial efforts came to nothing.[2] Strikes and threats of strikes evaporated overnight, militancy was temporarily paralysed by the sudden awareness of military danger. During April 1918 only 3,900 working days were lost through strike action in the engineering and shipbuilding industries, one of the lowest figures of the war.[3] 'This ghastly offensive, with its fearful toll of human life, has apparently reduced the people to a state of coma from which it is for the moment well nigh impossible to rouse them.' The employers took the opportunity to launch a campaign of victimization which forced the shop stewards thoroughly on to the defensive.[4]

---

[1] *MM* VI, 11, p. 47; *Mun.* 2. 15, 30 March 1918; *Glasgow Herald*, 25 March 1918. The shop stewards at Elswick had instructed ASE members to refuse to submit to medical examinations: 'This is in conformity with the policy adopted in other parts of the country.' *Mun.* 2. 15, 9 March 1918.

[2] The agitation continued for a few days longer on the Clyde: *Glasgow Herald*, 25 March 1918. When the offensive was over there was some 're-crudesence of the movement . . . subterranean efforts are being made to inspire apprentices with opposition to recruiting'. *Mun.* 2. 15, 1 June 1918.

[3] Ministry of Labour, *Labour Gazette*, May 1918; *Mun.* 2. 155, 30 March, 6, 13, 20 April 1918. The miners had also been mobilizing against the Man Power Bill, and on April 6th *The Herald* commented: 'It is quite clear that, but for the offensive we should have been by now in the middle of the biggest strike of the war – a strike which would have included miners as well as munitions workers.' This is possible, but unlikely. As we have seen the most potentially effective leaders of engineering militancy had already retreated, long before the German offensive.

[4] *Workers' Dreadnought*, 4 May, 13 April 1918. The first large-scale wave of victimizations of militant shop stewards took place at this time (though it seems to have started some time before the German offensive of 21 March 1918). It was a small foretaste of what would happen after the war. For victimizations in Coventry and Birmingham, see above, pp. 226, 228 in London see J. Hinton, 'Rank and File Militancy in the British Engineering Industry, 1914–1918' (London Ph.D., 1969), pp. 391–2; in Manchester see *The Call*, 30 May 1918. J. T. Murphy was sacked from the Vulcan works at Southport, where he had taken a job in mid-February 1918, having voluntarily left Vickers and Sheffield. According to his autobiography he did this in order to further his knowledge of the craft. He was sacked on March 7th, and reinstated after a two-week strike by the 1,000 workers at the factory, and threats of strike action from several Manchester firms and many other parts of the country, including Barrow and Sheffield. Shortly after this he returned to Sheffield 'because my political and trade union work could not be carried on from such a distance'. J. T. Murphy, *New Horizons* (1942), p. 65; *Firth*

The national leadership of the shop stewards' movement may well have had no option but to abdicate responsibility for the mass movement on 25 January 1918. Nevertheless that decision proved a fatal blow from which the movement was never fully to recover. The magnitude of the opportunity missed soon became clear to some of the movement's leaders and sympathizers.

Writing at the end of March, George Lansbury indicated what had been lost:

'Unfortunately no effective action was taken to enforce the demands put forward [by the mass meetings]. In fact, the golden moment for action passed when British and French labour allowed Trotsky's appeal to pass almost unheeded and the Austrian and German strikes to remain isolated national incidents instead of becoming international action.'[1]

The opportunity to initiate revolutionary action against the war was not to recur. Moreover, by backing down – however justifiably – at the height of the struggle the National Administrative Council sacrificed its claims to lead militancy in the future. Although the local official bodies which met on March 21st failed to organize strike action against the Government's attack on craft exemptions, it was to these elements that the leadership of militancy passed when militancy revived again during the summer of 1918. Not Glasgow and Sheffield, but Coventry and Birmingham led the national movement against the Embargo system in July. Under the leadership of these centres the local officials up and down the country regained the initiative, while the revolutionary shop stewards, and in particular the NAC, remained absorbed in licking the wounds inflicted six months earlier.

Forced to abdicate the leadership of craft militancy the National Administrative Council turned initially to grandiose schemes

Worker, no. 14 (March 1918); *Mun.* 1.7, 15–17, 19 March 1918. The Vulcan works had a militant record: see *Mun.* 1.4 (MC), 1 December 1917.

1 *The Herald*, 30 March 1918. The response of certain sections of the press at the end of January throws an interesting light on this 'missed opportunity'. On January 31st, *The Times* leader floated the idea that the German strikes were being 'encouraged and tolerated' from above, in order to encourage British and French workers to take similar action in the name of internationalism, and thereby bring defeat to the Allies. The *Glasgow Herald*, on the same day, took this idea further, urging that the strikes had actually been engineered by the German militarists in order to spread the Bolshevist germ to England: 'The German workmen is merely an accomplice of his government in a gigantic conspiracy to befool the British working class.'

of political agitation. Early in March 1918 the Council was reported to be 'circularizing all Trades Councils, trade unions, allied trade boards, and Workers' Committees with a view to convening of an "industrial parliament" which should express the views of the rank and file of labour on the war'. Apparently the scheme involved not only the calling of district and national conferences of 'all trade union bodies', but also a plan for a referendum on the question of an immediate armistice with no indemnities or annexations intended, hopefully, to force a general election. A national conference of the movement assembled at Sheffield on 9 and 10 March 1918, but, apart from drawing a sharp line between their activity and that of the craft-inspired militant movement in the ASE, this conference took no decisions and referred the whole question back to the districts.[1] When the delegates reassembled in Manchester a month later they reported that the workers were not ready to support a general peace movement. The delegates from Leicester and London disagreed, and W. F. Watson, who was bitterly critical of the NAC for failing to call the strike in January, and who had ambitions to capture the leadership of the shop stewards,[2] pressed the conference to 'declare clearly in favour of peace'. J. T. Murphy countered:

'When the programme was drafted there was a possible chance that it might succeed, but the great offensive had changed the temper of the people. Events were moving very rapidly and before long there might be a better chance for an advanced programme. In the meantime, we should discuss workshop organization.'

Murphy was supported by George Peet of the BSP, and the conference endorsed this line. As a result no decisions of any importance were taken and the NAC was left to arrange the next national conference when it saw fit.[3]

The bankruptcy of the shop stewards' movement became quite clear in the course of the Embargo strike. When the Government

[1] *Mun.* 2.15, 9 March 1918; *Firth Worker*, no.14 (? March 1918); *Workers' Dreadnought*, 30 March, 20 April, 4 May 1918; *The Herald*, 6 April 1918.

[2] *Workers' Dreadnought*, 9 March 1918: 'It is our intention to make the *Dreadnought* the medium for nationally co-ordinating the movement.' From early in 1918 W. F. Watson was working closely with Sylvia Pankhurst, and contributing regular articles to the *Dreadnought*.

[3] *Workers' Dreadnought*, 20 April 1918. See also what is probably a report of this conference in Bell, *Pioneering Days*, p. 300.

first put its proposals for compelling men to join the War Munitions Volunteers before the trade unions, *The Herald* had predicted the 'reawakening of a large scale of the shop stewards' movement'.[1] Instead of trying to spread the strike, however, the NAC's intervention was limited to a telegram from Peet to the Coventry Engineering Joint Committee proposing the suspension of the Coventry strike notices pending a national conference in Sheffield. The CEJC, who had no desire to become entangled with the unofficial movement, did not reply; but they convened their own national conference of local officials in Leeds, to which the shop stewards were not invited. Peevishly, the NAC decided to 'oppose sectional disputes . . . by standing aloof'. 'The unofficial stewards movement', wrote Murphy, 'had nothing to do with the business throughout.'[2] William McLaine, the Manchester shop stewards' leader, drew the moral: 'The Coventry strike would have succeeded if the shop stewards' movement had been ready to take charge of it. They were not ready. It passed into other hands and collapsed.'[3]

The final wartime conference of the movement – it was, in fact, to be the last conference before January 1920 – assembled in Birmingham on September 7th and 8th. Attended by about fifty delegates from twenty-three different localities, the conference was, according to W. F. Watson, 'as encouraging and inspiring as the April conference was discouraging and depressing'. A resolution 'requesting' the Government to withdraw Allied troops from Russia was carried by 33 votes to 13. The shop stewards, however, were still a long way from committing themselves to action against the war, and the trauma of January was still in evidence in the decision of the thirteen delegates to vote against the resolution on Russia on grounds of 'expediency'.[4] Apart from this, the conference devoted itself to debating the movement's relationship to official trade unionism. That debate will be dealt with in the next chapter. It is evidence of the continuing defeatism of the revolutionary shop stewards that this was the one occasion in the movement's history where they came near to the sectarian 'dual unionist' position the rejection of which had been central to the achievements of the wartime movement.

The rank-and-file movement did not recover after the war.

1 *The Herald*, 22 June 1918. 2 *Solidarity*, September 1918.
3 *The Call*, 8 August 1918.
4 *Workers' Dreadnought*, 21 September 1918.

During January and February 1919 three times as many working days were lost in the industry from strike action as in May 1917, largely, of course, due to the forty hours strike in the west of Scotland and in Belfast.[1] While this strike represented the high point of the Clyde Workers' Committee's local influence it met with little response in England and was a fiasco so far as the NAC was concerned.[2] Of the areas where the rank-and-file movement was established only London showed any fight. Even here, however, the militants hesitated too long and achieved nothing better than the suspension of the ASE District Committee.[3] During the remainder of 1919 considerable organizational advances were made. Tom Dingley, victimized in Coventry and in Birmingham, had been made a full-time organizer for the movement in the autumn of 1918, and during 1919 further full-timers were appointed. Workers' Committees were established or re-established in several Scottish towns, in London and in Liverpool, and new advances were made towards linking up the Workers' Committees with unofficial tendencies in other industries particularly the miners' Reform Committees. Much was achieved on paper, little in practice.[4]

After the forty hours strike the level of militant activity remained for three years at a lower level than it had been during 1917–18, when most strikes were illegal.[5] In that period no local

[1]

	Working days lost in engineering and shipbuilding	
May 1917		1,355,000
Jan.–Feb. 1919		3,788,000

Ministry of Labour, *Labour Gazette, passim*.

[2] For an account of the strike see W. Kendall, *The Revolutionary Movement in Britain, 1900–21* (1969), pp. 136–40.

[3] *Solidarity*, February, March 1918; J. B. Jefferys, *The Story of the Engineers* (London, 1946), pp. 187–8.

[4] *Mun.* 2. 17, 21 September 1918; *Solidarity, passim;* B. Pribicevic, *The Shop Stewards' Movement and Workers' Control* (1959), pp. 103, 105; Kendall, *The Revolutionary Movement in Britain*, p. 263.

[5]

	Working days lost in engineering and shipbuilding, monthly average
March 1917–March 1918 (excl. May 1917)	145,000
March–Aug. 1919	102,000
Feb. 1920–Oct. 1921	118,000

The figures for September 1919 to January 1920 are much higher, but this is due to the long-drawn-out moulders' strike and not to strikes of engineering workers.

Workers' Committee led a strike movement of any significance.[1] By 1922, when the AEU faced a national lockout, large-scale unemployment had entirely destroyed the rank-and-file movement's workshop base – though as organizers of the National Unemployed Workers' Committee Movement the ex-shop stewards played an important part in organizing the locked out workers: 'It was these organizations which conducted the fight', claimed Murphy, 'and rarely those who were actually locked out workers from the factories.'[2] Within weeks of the armistice the abnormal wartime demand for labour had eased off sufficiently for the employers to weed out key men in the shop stewards' movement, and wreck the organization.[3] As soon as the forty hours strike was over on the Clyde the employers launched a campaign of 'systematic victimization' aimed to 'stamp out the unofficial movement', and similar campaigns were waged in other centres. 'Since the armistice', wrote Murphy, at the beginning of 1920, 'unemployment has decimated the ranks of the unofficial movement.'[4]

Two further national conferences were held after the war, in January 1920 and in March–April 1921. A broadly representative rank-and-file conference was convened in parallel with the Special Trade Union Congress of March 1920. Between conferences the movement hardly existed outside the activities of its NAC and the propaganda of its two papers, *The Worker* in

[1] 'The 40 hours strike was the last occasion on which the shop stewards initiated and played an independent part in a great strike movement.' Murphy, *New Horizons*, pp. 207–8.

[2] *Bulletin of the IVth Congress of the Communist International* (Moscow, 1922).

[3] Unemployment among insured workers in engineering and ironfounding

	%
end of Oct. 1918	0·68
end of Nov. 1918	0·85
end of Dec. 1918	8·62
end of Jan. 1919	13·06
end of Feb. 1919	14·18

Board of Trade, *Labour Gazette, passim.*
The unemployment returns of the metal, engineering and shipbuilding trade unions rose from 0·2% during both 1917 and 1918, to 3·2% during both 1919 and 1920. These figures for 1919–20 were substantially above the national average of trade unionist unemployment. B. Mitchell, and P. Dean, *Abstract of British Historical Statistics* (Cambridge, 1962), pp. 71–2.

[4] *The Worker*, 22 February 1919; *Solidarity*, June – November 1919, January 1920; Pribicevic, *The Shop Stewards' Movement and Workers' Control*, p. 103; *Sheffield Worker*, March 1920.

Scotland and *Solidarity* in England. Finally, in June 1922, more than a year since the last delegate conference, the NAC decided to wind up the movement by merging it into the British Bureau of the Red International of Labour Unions. 'How can you build factory organizations when you have 1,750,000 workers walking the streets? You cannot build factory organizations in empty and depleted workshops'.[1] It was, however, precisely while the forces of the independent rank-and-file movement were being defeated on the ground, that the lessons of its wartime practice were brought home to the revolutionary left, and came to play a decisive part in the emergence of the British Communist Party. Much of the strength, and much of the weakness, of the early Communist Party is to be explained by this fact.

[1] J. T. Murphy, reported in *Bulletin of the IVth Congress of the Communist International*.

Part Three

Interpretation and Significance

Chapter 11

The Theory of Independent Rank-and-File Organization

'Of the eight members of the National Administrative Council elected in August 1917, six [had] joined the Communist Party by the time of the Leeds Unity Convention in January 1921.'[1] Most of these men, and other shop steward leaders who joined the Communist Party after the war, had served their political apprenticeship under the influence of syndicalist thought, some from within the British Socialist Party (Gallacher, Peet),[2] some in the Socialist Labour Party (MacManus, Dingley), some in the Amalgamation Committee movement (Murphy, and also Peet)[3] Clearly the movement stood, ideologically, at a point of transition between syndicalism and communism. What is surprising, at first sight, is how little the movement in wartime departed from many of the syndicalist notions which it inherited. The tenor of the movement's thinking was organizational; its innovations lay

[1] W. Kendall, *The Revolutionary Movement in Britain, 1900–21* (1969), p. 164. Moreover it was the SLP group in the leadership of the shop stewards' movement – MacManus and Murphy (together with Tom Bell and William Paul) – who 'became the dominant figures in the Communist Party during its first four years': L. J. MacFarlane, *The British Communist Party* (1966), p. 28.

[2] Syndicalist ideas gained extensive influence in the BSP before the war: Kendall, *The Revolutionary Movement in Britain*, pp. 38–45, 56–60.

[3] Other organizations were also of importance in spreading syndicalist ideas in the industry, especially the Herald League and the Plebs League. For the sake of simplicity this chapter concentrates on the influence of the SLP and the Amalgamation Committees as representing the two major schools of syndicalist thinking in Britain. The best history of British syndicalism is E. Burdick, 'Syndicalism and Industrial Unionism in England until 1918' (Oxford D. Phil, 1950).

in the field of industrial tactics, not of political strategy as such. Its leaders were practical men whose thinking, so far as it rose above every day concerns, was more concerned to elaborate the tactics than to debate the long-term strategy or ultimate goals of the class struggle. The most intellectually able of them, Jack Murphy, did not, during the war, go beyond tactical thinking, important and often original though that was. 'Humanity', he wrote, is intensely practical', and he quoted with approval: 'No nation ever yet made itself by theories of social contract or by any other explicit theories; the work was done first and the theories came afterwards; the reason was latent in the fact before it was patent in the explanation.'[1] The object of this chapter is to show how 'latent in the fact' of the wartime shop stewards' movement, though never fully grasped or expounded theoretically during the war, was the development from syndicalsim to communism. The next chapter will deal with the post-war period when – paradoxically, in the context of the decline and defeat of the mass movement – this development was made 'patent in the explanation' by Jack Murphy and others.

The syndicalist and communist doctrines are most commonly distinguished by their attitudes towards political action, and more particularly, towards the need for a revolutionary party. Syndicalism is characterized by an exclusive emphasis on social relations at the point of production as the determining factor in the social structure, an emphasis which prevents the syndicalist from appreciating the need for politics, and from grasping the dialectical relationship posited in all communist thinking (with whatever nuances) between the 'spontaneous', economically based organization of the masses and the political vanguard of the class, the revolutionary party. This aspect of the development from syndicalism to communism is *not* dealt with in this study, and for two reasons. First, it is very doubtful whether, by the time of the formation of the Communist Party in 1920–1, any substantial proportion of its members or leaders had grasped the Bolshevik idea of the party or would have approved of it had they done so. In this sense they carried their syndicalism over into the new party. Second, the contribution of the shop stewards' movement to the ideological development of its leaders had nothing to do with the idea of the party, but it did have a great deal to do with a second, and neglected, aspect of the transition

[1] *The Socialist*, September 1917. See also J. R. Campbell, in *The Worker*, 10 January 1920.

from syndicalism to communism. What the shop steward's movement implicitly challenged in the syndicalist doctrine was the idea that the trade unions would constitute both the chief agency of transition to socialism and the basic structure of socialist society thereafter. The characteristic and distinguishing feature of communism in Britain during 1919–21 was not the idea of the revolutionary party, but the idea of soviet power. In the communist model of transition the soviet replaced not only the parliamentary party of the state socialist but also the revolutionary industrial union of the syndicalist. The chief ideological significance of the shop stewards' movement is to be found in its contribution to the growth of the revolutionary left who supplied it with leadership.

The chief sources of the ideology of the shop stewards' movement were the French and American doctrines of revolutionary syndicalism and Industrial Unionism, imported into Britain before the war. From its foundation in 1903 the Socialist Labour Party (SLP) had been preaching Industrial Unionism in Britain. Ferociously sectarian, and its direct industrial influence confined largely to the Clyde, the SLP was nevertheless to make a more important contribution than the much larger British Socialist Party (or any other Marxist grouping) both to the development of the shop stewards' movement and to the subsequent foundation of the Communist Party. The key to this influence, apart from the outstanding ability as leaders of industrial militancy of several of its members, was its pre-war preservation – one might almost say refrigeration – of the clear and systematic De Leonite alternative to state socialism.[1]

The revolutionary syndicalist contribution was a very different one. Tom Mann, who launched a largely French-inspired Industrial Syndicalism in Britain in 1910, was the perfect personification of the movement. Enthusiasm, rhetoric and ceaseless energy; an unsectarian, unsystematic, eclectic thinker capable of an extraordinary range of responses; above all else an agitator, his life a whirlwind tour of trouble spots (an hour-by-hour itinerary of Tom Mann's life would provide an unparalleled map of the

[1] 'Marxism, which the SDF had interpreted as an exclusively political doctrine, was turned by the SLP into a justification for concentration on the industrial scene. In so doing it did a great deal to provide an ideological basis for the industrial militancy and the shop stewards movement which developed both during and before the war.' Kendall, *The Revolutionary Movement in Britain*, p. 76.

growth points of class struggle over half a century), always there on the platform, in the strike committee's rooms, directing, speaking, casting the spell of revolution, bringing 'life and health and sympathy and hope into the most sordid of human lives'. 'Syndicalists',[1] writes Pribicevic,

'were generally much more concerned with the burning questions of the day than with the distant future, much more with the methods and tactics of the class struggle than with its ultimate aims. Everybody who was willing to take part in the class struggle, regardless of his organization or his political views, was welcome in the Syndicalist League. They maintained that it would be idle to insist on theoretical distinctions at a time when the main body of the workers were engaged in practical class struggles.'[2]

Lacking any systematic doctrine, entirely dependent on the momentum of industrial militancy, the syndicalist movement grew with meteoric speed during the great strike movement of 1910–12 – and fell just as fast in the year before the war. After 1914 its influence was diffuse and difficult to trace, though the syndicalist-inspired Amalgamated Committee movement played an important role in the origins of the shop steward movement in England.

The common doctrinal element of Industrial Unionism and revolutionary syndicalism was their rejection of State Socialism, and their vision of a reconstructed industrial unionism as both the chief agency of class struggle in the present, and as the embryonic administrative structure of the Socialist Common-wealth, 'the skeleton structure of that parliament of socialism wherein the government of men . . . gives place to the peaceful administration of industry'.[3] Both rejected the orthodox social democratic notion of a transition to socialism through the conquest of parliamentary power followed by nationalization, but they differed radically in their attitude to parliamentary politics. The syndicalists, reflecting their French inheritance and the disillusion felt by many active militants with the Labour Party's parliamentary antics, neglected politics and the role of

---

1 T. Mann, writing in *Industrial Syndicalist*, September 1910.

2 B. Pribicevic, *The Shop Stewards' Movement and Workers' Control* (Oxford, 1959), p. 17.

3 *The Socialist*, February 1910; cf. *Industrial Syndicalist*, December 1910, p. 45.

the state altogether. Their strategy of transition rested solely upon the intensification of the class struggle in industry to its logical culmination in the revolutionary General Strike, which would paralyse society, fragment the forces of bourgeois repression, and enable the workers to take over the functions of production, distribution and social administration through the machinery of their industrial unions, trade councils, etc.

The SLP, following Marx, believed that it was only in the arena of politics that the working class could clearly establish its own self-awareness; and it identified political with parliamentary action:

'If we accept the definition of working class political action as that which brings the workers as a class into direct conflict with the possessing class AS A CLASS, and keeps them there, then we must realise that NOTHING CAN DO THAT SO READILY AS ACTION AT THE BALLOT BOX.'

The role of political action was exclusively educative, not the battle but 'the echo of the battle'.[1] The growth of Industrial Unionism and the SLP representation in Parliament would go hand in hand until the Party was able to form a government; at which point its job would be done. This approach was elaborated during the war:

'The SLP enters the political field to capture the political STATE – not with the idea of perpetuating it under socialism, but with one object of wrenching from the capitalist class its power over the ARMED FORCES. The SLP enters the political field to enable Labour to accomplish a PEACEFUL REVOLUTION. With the State in the hands of Labour, the workers functioning through their industrial organization will assume control over the means of production. This being accomplished the STATE will function no more: it will, to quote Engles, die out.[2]

From its origin the Workers' Committee movement was committed to the goal of workers' control of production. During the war, however, it made no significant contribution to the discussion of how this was to be achieved.[3] A constant theme in

[1] J. Connolly, *Socialism Made Easy* (1907), p. 24.
[2] *The Socialist*, December 1916.
[3] It was only on Clydeside that any systematic thought was given to problems of workers' control during the war, first in the dilution programme of 1915–16, which was in theory and in practice a complete abortion, secondly

the discussion of workers' control in the shop stewards' movement was the syndicalist assumption that industrial organization of the workers in production, would, by virtue of its own tremendous weight, displace capital much as a ship displaces water and thereby usher in the Socialist Commonwealth. 'The *ultimate aim* of the Clyde Workers' Committee', Gallacher had written in January 1916, 'is to mould these unions into one powerful organization that will place the workers in complete control of the industry.' The profound complacency of this formulation derives from its neglect of the role of the state in maintaining the domination of capital.[1] On the question of political action, the shop stewards' movement was no more successful in advancing beyond its pre-war sources. The dispute over parliamentary action continued within its ranks, eventually coming into the open in the spring of 1918 as a split between the CWC (where SLP influence was strongest), and the English movement, especially as represented by *Solidarity*, where revolutionary syndicalism held sway.[2] It was in its attitude towards the existing trade unions that the wartime movement departed fundamentally from both revolutionary syndicalism and the Industrial Unionism of the SLP.

Both pre-war tendencies saw the existing trade unions as inadequate agencies of revolutionary transition, because of their sectionalism and because of their generally oligarchic and collaborationist character. They disagreed fundamentally on the tactics of reconstruction. The revolutionary syndicalists sought amalgamation of the existing unions on an industrial basis, and believed that the character and goals of the unions could be transformed from within: 'The Trade Unions are truly representa-

by Gallacher and J. Paton in their pamphlet, *Towards Industrial Democracy* (1917). This is remembered chiefly for its 'unrivalled lack of realism'; Pribicevic, *The Shop Stewards' Movement and Workers' Control*, p. 153. It is the inadequacy of these programmes that vitiates Pribicevic's attempt to discuss the movement primarily in terms of the articulation of the demand for workers' control.

[1] *The Worker*, 29 January 1916; see also Pribicevic, *The Shop Stewards' Movement and Workers' Control*, pp. 129–30. As the post-war communist critics of syndicalism were to delight in pointing out, encroaching control, 'the wringing of step by step concessions from the capitalists' in the workshops would, as it approached success, inevitably come up against the armed might of the state. W. Gallacher and J. R. Campbell, *Direct Action* (Glasgow, 1919), p. 27.

[2] Pribicevic, *The Shop Stewards' Movement and Workers' Control*, p. 92. See also *Workers' Dreadnought*, 9 March, 20 April 1918; *Solidarity*, May 1918.

tive of the men, and can be moulded by the men into exactly what the men desire.'[1] The Industrial Unionists saw no alternative to root-and-branch opposition to the existing unions – bulwarks of capitalism – and the construction of new revolutionary unions. In British conditions 'dual' unionism was a non-starter. A relatively high level of trade union organization, and the existence of general unions willing and able, when conditions were ripe, to recruit previously unorganized workers on a massive scale, left little room for the development of new revolutionary unions outside and antagonistic to the existing movement on the model of the IWW in America. The only success for SLP Industrial Unionism in Britain, the organization of the Singer's works at Clydebank in 1910–11, arose out of quite exceptional circumstances, and was rapidly suppressed.[2]

While the Industrial Unionists strove in vain to establish an alternative leadership to the existing trade unions, the revolutionary syndicalists concentrated on propaganda and education within them. 'It is too early at present to go beyond the educational stage', Tom Mann told the founding conference of the Industrial Sydicalist Education League in 1910.[3] When in the great battle of 1910–12 masses of workers struck work without the sanction of their trade union officials, the syndicalists were ready to take the lead, as they did most successfully in the Cambrian coal strike of 1910–11 and the Liverpool Transport strike in the summer of 1911. Their main effort, however, was not to construct an alternative leadership to that of the unions, but rather to canalize this militancy into the restructuring of the unions. The lesson drawn by the South Wales syndicalists from the situation of dual power between the unofficial strike committees (which they themselves had manned) and the South Wales Miners Federation Executive during the Cambrian strike, was not that this independent rank-and-file organization provided an important counter to the passivity of the Executive, but that such a dualism divided and weakened the fighting strength of the union. In future the need for independent rank-and-file organization must be eliminated by the reconstruction of the union on a more democratic basis.[4] When members of the various railway

---

[1] T. Mann, in *Industrialist Syndicalist*, November 1910.

[2] *The Socialist*, October 1910, April–July, December 1911; *Forward*, 10 February 1917.

[3] *Industrial Syndicalist*, September 1910.

[4] *The Miners' Next Step* (Tonypandy, 1912), pp. 10–11.

unions, together with non-unionists, precipitated the conflict of 1911 by striking unofficially on a very large scale, the syndicalists did not seek to use this rank-and-file revolt against sectionalism and collaboration in order to construct a new industrial union from the bottom up. Instead they devoted themselves to making propaganda for the amalgamation of the existing railway unions.

Amalgamations and greater unity would certainly be essential if the existing trade union movement was to become capable of mounting a revolutionary general strike and of taking control of the means of production. They were also, however, necessary for quite different purposes. The leaders of the railway unions agreed to amalgamate in 1912 because they had, in the strikes of the previous summer, learned that unless the Executives could unite they were likely to be supplanted from below.[1] To many of its founders the Triple Alliance was valued, not as a means of promoting and extending sympathetic strike action, but as a means of preventing spontaneous outbreaks, of controlling and disciplining militancy. James Connolly's characterization of the Triple Alliance contains an important element of truth:[2]

'The frequent rebellion against stupid and spiritless leadership and the call of the rank and file for true industrial unity seems to have spurred the leaders on, not to respond to new spirit but to evolve a method whereby under the forms of unity [it] could be trammelled and fettered . . . a scheme to *prevent* united action rather than facilitate it.

No one was more aware than the syndicalists of the dangers of oligarchy, of 'the bad side of leadership', but, eloquent exhortation apart, they could find no satisfactory solution to the perennial problem of combining participatory democracy with large-scale and efficient trade union organization.[3]

In March 1921 Jack Murphy, by then a communist, distinguished two phases 'of our development as revolutionary' agitators in the trade union movement:[4]

'The first phase [pre-war] was that of propagandists of industrial unionism, amalgamation of the unions, ginger groups within

[1] P. S. Bagwell, *The Railwaymen* (1963), pp. 289–91, 325–7.
[2] *Workers' Republic*, 12 February 1916; quoted in B. Pearce, *Some Past Rank and File Movements* (1959), p. 38.
[3] *The Miners' Next Step*, pp. 13–15. For further analysis of the pamphlet's attitude to the question of leadership see below, pp. 311–12.
[4] *The Worker*, 19 March 1921; cf. J. R. Campbell, in *The Worker*, 10 January 1920.

the various organizations. The second [wartime phase] was characteristically the period of action, the attempt to adapt industrial-unionism principles to the immediate struggle, and to take on the direct responsibility for the conduct of the fight against the bosses and the State.'

The wartime shop stewards' movement carried Industrial Unionism and revolutionary syndicalism from propaganda to action, from the branch to the workshop. In so doing – though this was not fully grasped at the time – the movement laid the basis in practice for a theoretical solution to the problems of oligarchy and leadership in trade unionism that had eluded the pre-war syndicalists.

The urgency of the problems raised by the impact of war on the workshops, and the failure of the trade union leadership to advance any realistic policy, forced revolutionary engineers to concentrate their attention on throwing up organs of rank-and-file self-defence, capable of immediate and effective action. The long-term goal of industrial unionism – approached by whatever path – could not answer the needs of the moment. Confronted with the spontaneous growth of workshop organization and the fact of its own leadership of rank-and-file militancy on the Clyde, the SLP abandoned dual unionism. 'This is no time for intolerant doctrinaires, this is no place for bigoted critics', wrote the editor of *The Socialist* in July 1917, urging that the propaganda of Industrial Unionism could now be translated into concrete form, not in antagonism to the trade unions but by building all-grades organizations in the workshops. The Industrial Unions of the future would grow, were growing spontaneously, out of the existing trade unions, not alongside them. 'Our policy', declared Murphy, newly admitted to the SLP, 'must be a natural development from within the trade union movement'.[1]

The Amalgamation Committee movement had collapsed after the outbreak of war, but from the beginning of 1916 it revived and became increasingly closely linked up with the growing

---

[1] *The Socialist*, September 1917. Pribicevic, *The Shop Stewards' Movement and Workers' Control*, p. 86, is very misleading about the SLP attitude, quoting an article of June 1917, but not that of July which marked a decisive shift in the Party's position. The SLP had never opposed working within the existing unions at a grass roots level, but members were forbidden to stand for trade union office on the grounds that the existing unions were bulwarks of capitalism and must eventually be destroyed rather than taken over by the left. T. Bell, *Pioneering Days* (1942), p. 42.

power of the English shop stewards.[1] In November 1916, infuriated by the dilatory attitude of the trade union Executives towards amalgamation, and encouraged by the growing power of the shop stewards, the movement presented the Executives with a three month ultimatum to amalgamate, failing which a new 'dual' union would be formed. Thus, paradoxically, just as the SLP was abandoning dual unionism owing to its members' experience in the shop stewards' movement, the revolutionary syndicalists were pointing to the power of the shop stewards as their justification for swinging towards dual unionism. When the ultimatum ran out in March 1917 W. F. Watson, since 1910 the leader of the movement, wanted to press ahead with the formation of the new union. The shop stewards', arguing that the time was not ripe for a head on collision with the trade union Executives, opposed Watson:

'Remember it is not only the amalgamation of unions you require, but the amalgamation of the workers in the workshops . . . Let your propaganda take concrete form by transforming the Amalgamation Committee into the Workers' Committee. Make the amalgamation of unions incidental, the amalgamation of the workers fundamental.'[2]

The March conference compromised, agreeing to defer, but not abandon, Watson's ultimatum, and, in the meantime, to concentrate effort on forming Workshop and Workers' Committees.[3]

When the deferred deadline passed without visible response from the major union Executives, pressure for the immediate formation of a new union again mounted in the Amalgamation Committee movement. Watson initiated a workshop ballot on amalgamation in August and declared that if the result were favourable the new union would be formed without further delay.[4] For a short while *Solidarity*, closely linked with the English shop stewards, went over to Watsons' dual unionist position, declaring in a front page editorial in September 1917: 'Every penny paid into a Craft Union now is a penny given to

[1] The Amalgamation Committees themselves were purely propagandist organizations with no foothold in the workshops.

[2] J. T. Murphy, in *Solidarity*, March 1917.

[3] *Solidarity*, April 1917; *The Herald*, 31 March 1917; Pribicevic, *The Shop Stewards' Movement and Workers' Control*, pp. 74–7.

[4] *Fusion of Forces, Report of the Fifth National Rank and File Conference*, Newcastle-on-Tyne, 13–14 October 1917, *passim*.

subsidize and reinforce the power of Capitalism.'[1] When the issue was debated at the Newcastle conference of the Amalgamation Committee movement in October the shop stewards – who appear to have ensured the failure of Watsons' ballot by the simple expedient of not conducting it – consolidated their victory of the previous March. A resolution from the Sheffield and Manchester Workers' Committees for the fusion of the two movements was carried by 78 votes to 24: 'That the members of the Amalgamation Committee unite with the Shop Steward and Workers' Committees with a view to concentrating activity on the point of production.'[2] The merger finally took place in January 1918.[3] *Solidarity* now gave its whole-hearted support to the shop steward position. The industrial union, when it came, must be a growth from below and not an imposition from above:

'The very healthy suspicion is abroad, even among the stalwarts of workshop organization, that any sort of Industrial Union that was set up in the Engineering trade at this moment would not be the real article, such as we hope to develop when education and propaganda have done their work, but only another overlapping and time-serving organization which would crab the genuine and solid achievements of the Workers Committees.'[4]

In building up the Workers' Committees for practical and immediate purposes the leadership of the shop stewards' movement had registered – though with no sophisticated theoretical

1 *Solidarity* had been founded by the leading central group of revolutionary syndicalism, Tom Mann, Will Hay, W. F. Watson, J. V. Willis, in 1913, after their original paper, *The Syndicalist and Amalgamation Committee News*, had been taken over by the anarcho-communists. The paper collapsed on the outbreak of war, but in December 1916 it was revived by a group of London Industrial Unionists allied to the Chicago (anti-political) IWW rather than the Detroit (De Leonist) section. Despite intimate relations with the shop stewards, on whom the paper rapidly became dependent for its workshop sales, E. C. Pratt and S. A. Wakeling, the editor and manager, remained unrepentant dual unionists. Ultimately they were forced to resign, and in the summer of 1918 were replaced by Jack Tanner, leader of the west London engineers who was much closer in outlook to the dominant sections of the shop stewards' movement. After the war *Solidarity* was formally adopted as the organ of the English shop stewards' movement. In May 1921, when the shop stewards decided to concentrate their resources on the Scottish *Worker*, the editorial team of *Solidarity* announced their intention of continuing the paper under the new name *The Liberator*.

2 *Fusion of Forces*, pp. 19–21.
3 Bell, *Pioneering Days*, pp. 302–3.
4 *Solidarity*, January 1918.

explanations – their refusal to accept the assumption that a principled choice must be made between amalgamation and dual unionism. They did not abandon the long term aim of constructing a revolutionary industrial union. In *The Workers' Committee* Murphy outlined a structure of national industrial unions based on workshop committees integrated with a class unionism based in local Workers' Committees representative of all industries. But in advocating industrial unionism neither Murphy nor the movement as a whole saw any need to plump for one tactic or the other. In 1917 Murphy left it an open question how far in the ultimate process of merging into the 'larger and more powerful structure' of industrial unionism the existing trade unions would be amalgamated or 'thrown off'.[1] Two years later he repeated the same point,[2] as did Gallacher and J. R. Campbell[3] in the pamphlet they wrote for the Scottish Workers' Committees in the autumn of 1919:[4]

'The bringing together of the rank and file of all trades will create a class outlook amongst the workers that will compel the official organizations to weld themselves together as a compact industrial force, and to remould their internal structure and accept the workshop as the basis of the organization. Either that or they will find themselves ignored in the industrial struggles of the future, functioning merely as sick benefit societies and leaving the actual industrial fighting to be done by the Workers' Committees.'

It is in the light of this rejection of the terms of the pre-war syndicalist argument – dual unionism *or* amalgamation – that the

[1] J. T. Murphy, *The Workers' Committee* (Sheffield, 1917), p. 14.

[2] A. Gleason, *What the Workers Want* (New York, 1920), p. 199.

[3] J. R. Campbell (b. 1894). Shop assistant and member of BSP. Volunteered for service in war. Organizer for Scottish Workers' Committees, 1919–21. Founder member of Communist Party and editor of *The Worker* from 1922.

[4] *Direct Action*, pp. 20–1. Pribicevic, *The Shop Stewards Movement and Workers' Control*, p. 90, draws a contrast between *The Workers' Committee* and *Direct Action*, arguing that while the former assumed that the growth of the rank-and-file movement would ultimately be bound to disrupt rather than amalgamate the existing unions, Gallacher and Campbell laid exclusive emphasis on the task of remoulding the existing unions. This constitutes a misreading of both pamphlets; throughout it remained an open question how far trade unionism would be superseded or remoulded. In so far as there was a change in emphasis between 1917 and 1919, however, it was in the reverse direction to that suggested by Pribicevic.

attitude of the shop stewards both towards their own organization and towards the existing trade unions can be best understood.

The rejection of Watson's dual unionism necessarily entailed a reluctance to develop any powerful national leadership for the movement. When, in August 1917, a national leadership was eventually established for the movement, the delay and hesitation involved in its evolution was confirmed in its constitution. The National Administrative Council, as its name implied, held no executive power and was intended to function as 'little more than a reporting centre for the local committees'.[1] 'No committee shall have executive power, all questions of policy and action being referred back to the rank and file', was a principle accepted throughout the movement.[2] This weakness of the national leadership has, following the subsequent self-criticisms of the leaders of the shop stewards movement, been attributed to anti-leadership prejudices inherited from pre-war syndicalism. 'Thus', wrote Murphy in 1934, 'the first national committee was formed, but held theories which prevented it giving the leadership which the movement needed more than at any time since its foundation.'[3] At the time, however, Murphy justified the weakness of the national leadership not in the language of a doctrinaire blind to the lesson of events, but in terms of immediate practicalities. Any powerful national co-ordination of the Shop Stewards' and Workers Committees would be indistinguishable from the establishment of a new 'dual' union: 'It must be clearly understood that the National Committee is not to usurp the functions of the executives of the trade unions. Power to decide action is vested in the workshops . . .'[4]

In examining the history of the movement there is nothing to show that its failure to develop an Executive leadership neutralized its potential for action.[5] In the localities the shop stewards

[1] J. T. Murphy, *New Horizons* (1941), p. 61.

[2] *Solidarity*, February 1919. Cf. Murphy, *The Workers' Committee*, pp. 4–5: 'The functions of an Elected Committee, therefore, should be such that instead of arriving at decisions *for* the rank and file they would provide the means whereby full information relative to any question of policy should receive the attention and consideration *of* the rank and file, the results to be expressed by ballot.'

[3] J. T. Murphy, *Preparing for Power* (1934), p. 152, also pp. 97, 146, 159; W. Gallacher, *Revolt on the Clyde* (1936), pp. 220–1; Pribicevic, *The Shop Stewards' Movement and Workers' Control*, p. 99; Kendall, *The Revolutionary Movement in Britain*, pp. 142, 165.

[4] Murphy, *The Workers' Committee*, p. 14.

[5] As Kendall argues in *The Revolutionary Movement in Britain*, p. 142.

seem to have had little reservation about grasping the lead from the officials whenever the opportunity presented itself. On the Clyde 'the most trusted men of the labour movement'[1] had lain in wait for a situation where they could wrest the initiative from the local officials, and had successfully done so late in 1915. The Joint Engineering Shop Stewards' Committee in Manchester did not hestitate to seize the lead from the trade union officials and initiate the national strike movement of May 1917. Nor can the two major fiascos of the movement, the collapse of the May 1917 strike movement, and the failure of the strike call of January 1918, be attributed to any marked degree to a failure of leadership. Of May 1917 Kendall, following Murphy, has argued that:

'The wave of arrests created a crisis, posing an immediate question: what action did the strike committee propose to take in reply? The leadership, feeling themselves responsible to a "rank and file" whose views were unknown, hesitated and proved quite unable to respond with an initiative of its own. In such a situation retreat followed inevitably.'[2]

The analysis is misleading: the views of the rank and file were far from unknown. The arrests took place precisely because the Government knew that in several key centres the strike had already collapsed. Where the possibility existed, as in Sheffield, the shop steward leaders were quite ready and able to make the urgent assertion of leadership necessary to keep the men out after the arrests. The collapse of the strike was due to factors largely independent of a failure of leadership. Similarly, it was the rank and file, not the leadership, which failed in January 1918.[3]

Murphy's contemporary judgement was more realistic than his later reflection. To have attempted a premature assertion of Executive leadership would not have enhanced the potential of the movement: it would merely have isolated the leaders. The shop stewards' decision to establish a National *Administrative* Council and the subsequent practice of that Council undoubtedly

[1] *Vanguard*, October 1915.

[2] Kendall, *The Revolutionary Movement in Britain*, pp. 160–1; cf. Murphy, *Preparing for Power*, p. 141.

[3] Both Kendall (p. 166) and Pribicevic (p. 102) assume that the NAC's decision to ballot the workshops early in January 1918 was responsible for a delay in the call for strike action which prevented any decision being made until the German spring offensive had been launched. This is, of course, quite untrue. The threat of strike action against the war had collapsed long before the German offensive.

reflected inherited ideology. The leaders were deeply conscious of what *The Miners' Next Step* had called the 'bad side of leadership':

'This power of initiative, this sense of responsibility, the self respect which comes from expressed manhood, is taken from the men, and consolidated in the leader. The sum of *their* initiative, *their* reponsibility, *their* self respect become his. . . The order and system he maintains, is based upon the suppression of the men, from being independent thinkers into being "the men" or "the mob"... Sheep cannot be said to have solidarity. In obedience to a shepherd they will go up or down, backwards or forwards as they are driven by him and his dogs. But they have no solidarity, for that means unity and loyalty. Unity and loyalty, not to an individual, but to an interest and a policy which is understood and worked for by all.[1]

Convinced of the need to wrench the rank and file from unthinking loyalty to old established institutions, the leaders set out to build a movement which substituted 'organized expression on the part of the mass', for the deeply ingrained principle of reliance on representatives.[2] 'Whereas we used to be plagued with the collectivists, who gloried in the production of a special class of officials to regulate the workers and do things for them, nowadays we take pleasure in the growth of the capacity in the rank and file to do things for themselves.'[3]

These attitudes stemmed not only from the leaders' ideological inheritance[4] but equally from their assessment of the character of the movement they were leading. Syndicalist concerns merged naturally with craft traditions of local autonomy and democratic control. Moreover, as Pribicevic has observed:

[1] *The Miners' Next Step*, pp. 13–14. This pamphlet was very influential among the shop steward leadership: Murphy, *Preparing for Power*, p. 152. There is an article by J. R. Campbell in *The Worker*, 1 January 1920, which repeats the above quotation almost word for word without acknowledgement.

[2] *Solidarity*, July 1917.

[3] J. T. Murphy, in *The Socialist*, 26 June 1919.

[4] This would be a difficult thesis to sustain in any case since the syndicalist tradition was far from singleminded on the question of leadership. One would still have to explain why the shop stewards chose to emphasize the 'bad side of leadership', rather than the equally 'syndicalist' insistence on the need for centralized, executive authority. See, for example, W. F. Hay's important statement of this characteristic of syndicalism in *Solidarity*, September 1913.

K

'The power of the movement did not depend on the number of members, on contributions, or on solid organization – all of which were decisive in the case of trade unions – but rather on the capacity of the local leaders to interpret the desires, demands and grievances of the main body of the workers. To ascertain when this main body of workers wanted action on any particular issue and then to place themselves at the head was the correct policy for a movement of this kind.'[1]

A movement springing up so rapidly did not possess the institutional inertia that makes it so difficult to decide in the case of an old-established organization how far, in any particular action, the rank and file is pursuing its own conscious purpose or how far it is responding loyally but blindly to the instructions of respected leaders operating with a legitimacy sanctioned by tradition. The leadership of the shop stewards' movement, almost all young men unknown before the war, whose names carried no charisma, could only lead the rank and file where it positively wanted to go.

While rejecting dual unionism the shop stewards' movement equally refused to 'centre its activity' on capturing the existing trade unions.[2] The need for independent rank-and-file organization was argued (as indeed it was felt) from the structural inadequacies of engineering trade unionism. As dilution advanced and the interdependence of all crafts and grades in production became a matter of daily experience, the multiplicity of sectional societies stood in growing contradiction to the needs of the workshop community. Sectional trade unions appeared positively anti-social, 'maintaining distinctions which the social processes are rapidly making artificial', and tending to split up the spontaneous unity of the workers in modern socially organized production.[3] In this situation it was folly to expect that 'by the capturing of official positions we can change the nature of the organization . . . A craft organization conserves a craft psychology or outlook and everything is determined in similar terms'.[4] At the same time, as the extent and power of organization at the workplace increased, the inadequacy of a trade unionism based in residential branches

---

[1] Pribicevic, *The Shop Stewards' Movement and Workers' Control*, p. 99.
[2] *Solidarity*, June 1918.
[3] J. T. Murphy, in *The Socialist*, 8 May 1919. See also *The Workers' Committee*, pp. 5–6.
[4] J. T. Murphy, in *Solidarity*, September 1918.

became ever more apparent. 'In a large industrial centre half of the men in the branch will work outside the neighbourhood from which the branch draws its members, and the other half are scattered amongst a number of shops in the neighbourhood.'[1] The inability of the branches to deal with the immediate problems of the workshop; the low level of attendance at branch meetings and the absorption of the branches in the routine administration of friendly benefits, made them unfit organs on which to base a militant organization.[2]

'In so far as the branch of any organization corresponds to the grouping of the workers in their industrial activity, so far can it reflect directly the wishes of the members as a whole, check oligarchical tendencies, and act organically. In so far as the branch deviates from this primary principle it ceases to reflect the membership efficiently, develops caucus rule, and becomes involved and cumbersome in action.'[3]

In the absence of fundamental structural reform which replaced branch by workshop as the formal basis of the union, or, failing this, of a strong and independent rank-and-file movement based in the workshops, any full time official, whatever his original opinions, would in this situation find it difficult to resist the pressures of bureaucratic rationality, and collaboration.

Given such a critique, which owed little to syndicalist doctrine and much to immediate wartime experience, the value of participation in the official union machinery necessarily appeared

---

[1] *Consolidation and Control* (1921), published in *The Worker*, 27 August 1921.

[2] The level of attendance at branch meetings can be judged from the percentage of members voting in the major wartime national ballots:

	Membership voting %
Treasury Agreement 1915	11·5
Election of general secretary, 1916	15·6
Munitions Bill, 1917	21·7
Secession from Federation, 1918	13·0
Amalgamation scheme, 1918	10·0

ASE, *Monthly Journal and Report, passim.*
Significantly, in the only postal ballot of the period which did not require members to make the effort to attend a branch meeting – the vote on the Man Power proposals early in 1918 – over 50% of the membership took part.

[3] J. T. Murphy, in *The Socialist*, 10 April 1919; *The Workers' Committee*, p. 5. Murphy, quoted in K. Coates and T. Topham, *Industrial Democracy in Great Britain* (1967), pp. 84–5.

limited. No organized effort was made to capture full-time trade union office, though this was never ruled out in principle by the movement. Sam Bradley, the secretary of the first national conference of Workers' Committees, became full-time district secretary of the London ASE in 1917. George Peet, leader of the Manchester shop stewards and secretary of the movement from August 1917, had stood unsuccessfully for full-time office in the ASE early in 1917.[1] The shop stewards believed that the growth of all-grades workshop organization and of Workers' Committees, might force the existing officials 'to remould their internal structure and accept the workshop as the basis of the organization', but they did not intend to encourage this process by capturing official positions and fighting for such a reconstruction of trade unionism from above as well as from below. They were content to rely on putting pressure on the trade union officials from the strongholds of independent rank-and-file organization, confident that if the officials failed to respond to this pressure the existing unions would eventually be 'thrown off' and replaced in all their essential functions by the Shop Stewards' and Workers' Committees. 'We did not conduct the fight so much against the officials, but rather ignored them and fought the employing class directly.'[2] This refusal to campaign directly for full-time union office has been widely attributed, following Jack Murphy's later comment, to an irrational, childish 'rank and file-ist' prejudice on the part of the movement's leaders.[3] There is some truth in this criticism, but its significance should not be exaggerated.

In so far as the task of capturing the existing trade unions presented itself as an alternative to the construction of independent rank-and-file organization (as would tend to be the case in any movement lacking an unlimited supply of able militants) it would be rightly rejected, *firstly* as not answering to the urgent

[1] *Solidarity*, January 1917; ASE, *Quarterly Report*, March 1917, election addresses. Both Pribicevic (p. 91) and Kendall (p. 167) give exaggerated prominence to the movements reaction against 'officialization' in the summer and autumn of 1918. As we shall see, this represented only a partial and temporary deviation from the more flexible position which characterized the movement.

[2] J. T. Murphy, in *The Worker*, 10 January 1920; 'The official unions will have to come together and democratize their government or leave the actual fighting to be done by the Workers' Committees.'

[3] Murphy, *New Horizons*, p. 81; Pribicevic, *The Shop Stewards' Movement and Workers' Control*, pp. 91–2; Kendall, *The Revolutionary Movement in Britain*, p. 167.

immediate needs of the workers, *secondly* as worthless by itself. Only on the basis of an independent rank-and-file movement in the workshops could even a sympathetic trade union official hope to build the revolutionary Industrial Union. Moreover, despite Murphy's later optimism on this score, it is far from certain that the revolutionary shop stewards could have made any very substantial inroads into trade union officialdom had they tried.[1] In most areas the appeal of their distinctive policies was limited to a small minority of the more militant workers. Only in situations of extreme and temporary crisis, if at all, did they gain general support. Trade union elections cannot be expected to occur only, or even predominantly, at such moments. Given this minority position as leaders of an advance guard of the movement, it would always seem more important to the shop stewards to concentrate their energies on enlarging the effective size of this vanguard (which could only be done in the workshops), than to build an electoral machine which, because of its branch base, would be valueless for fighting purposes.

While the movement may be criticized for its failure seriously to contest full-time trade union office, it is quite wrong to suggest that it refused to participate in the official trade union machinery at a local level.[2] In Glasgow, where in 1915–16 the Workers' Committee represented only a minority of the engineering workers and consequently could not control the local District Committees, the rank-and-file movement tended to stand outside and in antagonism to the official structures of trade unionism. In Sheffield, on the other hand, the Workers' Committee, representing the great majority of local engineering workers, worked closely with the ASE District Committee, the two structures acting as 'legal' and 'illegal' wings of a single organization. One of the most prominent members of the Sheffield Committee, Ted Lismer, was also a local official of his union, the Steam Engine Makers. Murphy, in *The Workers' Committee*, which draws heavily on the Sheffield experience, naturally stresses the possibilities of working within the unions, proposing shop steward rules for adoption by the District Committees which would make it possible for the workshop committees to operate as 'part of the official movement... The means are then assured of an alliance between official

---

[1] Murphy, *New Horizons*, p. 81.
[2] Contrast Kendall, *The Revolutionary Movement in Britain*, p. 294: 'The shop stewards ... refused to participate in official union machinery beyond shop floor level.'

and unofficial activities by the official recognition of rank and file control.'[1] In January 1918 the movement adopted Murphy's pamphlet as its official statement of policy.'[2] Branch and workshop activity has always been our rule', wrote Campbell in 1922. 'The emphasis we place on either line of action depends on conditions.'[3]

During the late summer of 1918, in the aftermath of January and the context of defeat and inactivity, there was a temporary hardening of attitudes towards the existing trade unions. When the national conference assembled in Birmingham in September 1918 delegates from Liverpool, which had a long record of official activity to 'counteract the non-official anti-trade union movement', advanced a scheme of organization which had been formulated locally following a militant wage movement in July. They argued that local General Councils, representative of the District Committees as well as the workshops, and closely analogous to the organization of the Coventry Engineering Joint Committee, should be established as the new 'basis of the movement'.[4] This motion provided the occasion for a vigorous attack upon the 'officialization' of the movement. Unrepentant dual unionists reasserted their position.[5] More important, J. T. Murphy now took his own pamphlet, *The Workers' Committee*, to task for having exaggerated the possibilities of working in the unofficial movement: 'We must be prepared to profit by experience and realise the impossibility of the Workers' Committees working with the unions.' The experience he had in mind was that of Coventry. This had shown that attempts to reconcile all-grades workshop organization with the existing trade union structure by the construction of local Joint Boards of union District Committees to which the shop stewards were responsible led only to the preservation of sectionalism.

The continued existence of the separate unions in the joint body provided 'centres round which can gather elements of discontent, which can easily break away . . . ', as occurred in

[1] *The Workers' Committee*, pp. 8–9. The West London Workers' Committee in 1918 adopted a similar position, allowing branch delegates to attend its meetings in a non-voting capacity: *Solidarity*, May 1918.

[2] *Solidarity*, February, May 1918.

[3] *The Worker*, 4 February 1922.

[4] *Mun.* 2. 28, 20 October 1917; *Mun.* 2. 16, 13 July 1918; *Solidarity*, October 1918, March 1919. The motion was seconded by H. King, the National Council member for Coventry.

[5] Cf. *Solidarity*, June 1918, 'Should we Capture the Trade Unions'.

Coventry during the Embargo strike.[1] Most of the delegates agreed with Murphy and the Liverpool scheme, identified as being 'better suited for adoption by an Allied Trades Conference, was rejected by 40 votes to 9. 'The feeling of the conference was against trying to square with the official movement.' The retreat into dual unionism was, however, neither complete nor permanent. While the conference repudiated the Liverpool scheme, and with it any attempt as in Coventry to *fuse* the shop stewards' movement with the local official structures, it did not close the door on the policy of *alliances* with the local officials from an independent, 'unofficial' basis. Arthur MacManus, in the chair, was careful to block any attempt to formally commit the movement to a dual unionist position. Steering the delegates away from any 'specific resolution' of their attitude to the unions, he re-emphasized that the primary object of the movement was neither amalgamation nor Industrial Unionism: 'The crucial point had been missed. The discussion had concentrated around organization outside the shop, whereas we should be discussing shop organization.'[2] This left the way open for the explicit reassertion of the movement's flexible attitude towards the local official structures of trade unionism during 1919.[3] Like *Solidarity*

[1] *Workers' Dreadnought*, 21 September 1918; *Solidarity*, September 1918. The dual unionist implications of these remarks were, for Murphy, only a temporary deviation. In 1919 he was again reiterating the orthodox shop steward formula: 'We must be in the unions, of the unions, but not determined by their limitations.' *The Socialist*, 18 December 1919. See also Pribicevic, *The Shop Stewards' Movement and Workers' Control*, p. 91. There was, however, one permanent change, both for Murphy and for the movement as a whole. The disastrous effects of the December 1917 shop stewards' agreement, which recognized the stewards only of individual unions, led Murphy to abandon his previous careful insistence that the separate representations of each grade on the shop stewards' committee was necessary if the interests of the less skilled were not be be subordinated to those of the craftsmen. The danger of craft domination now seemed less than the danger of sectionalism and disintegration. The earlier position is expounded in *The Workers' Committee*, p. 8; *Firth Worker*, May 1918; the later attitude in *Solidarity*, August 1918; *The Socialist*, 18th May, 1919; and the 1919 rules of the shop stewards' movement.

[2] *Solidarity*, October 1918; *Workers' Dreadnought*, 21 September 1918.

[3] At the national conference of January 1920: 'D. Ramsey, on behalf of the NAC explained at length the position of the shop stewards' movement in relation to the official Unions. So far as that was concerned, there was no need to change the policy of the movement.' *The Worker*, 14 February 1920. According to Jane Degras, the *Communist International, 1919–1943, Documents*, vol. I, 1919–1922 (1955), p. 145, Gallacher put a dual unionist position at the second congress of the Communist International in August 1920. This

earlier in the year MacManus had successfully invoked the 'solid and genuine achievements of the Workers' Committees' against any precipitate rush to dual unionism.

At the height of its power the rank-and-file movement co-ordinated and led militancy through a local Workers' Committee representative of the organization in the workshops. Because of their delegatory character these committees were capable of initiating and carrying through strike action independently of the trade union officials. It is this independence that primarily defines the rank-and-file movement:

'We will support the officials just so long as they rightly represent the workers, but we will act independently immediately they misrepresent them. Being composed of delegates from every shop and untrammelled by obsolete rule or law, we claim to represent the true feeling of the workers. We can act immediately according to the merits of the case and the desire of the rank and file.'[1]

The movement did not seek, for the time being, to replace the existing structures of trade unionism, but to co-exist with them while working (with more or less energy) for constitutional reform and – most important – to 'erect a structure inside and outside the trade union movement, which will unite the workers on a class basis', and thus to place the workers 'in a position to act independently in case of faulty leadership'.[2] Not the suppression of sectional and collaborationist trade unionism, but the establishment of a situation of 'dual power' between trade union officialdom and independently organized militant sections of the rank and file – this was the essence of the wartime practice of the shop stewards' movement.

The shop stewards' movement pursued neither dual unionism nor amalgamation, but attempted to straddle and go beyond the two tactics. Inevitably such a movement laid itself open to criticism for the incompleteness of its attention to either or both of the tactical legs upon which it stood, and much criticism

is a misreading of his position. Cf. J. Klugmann, *History of the Communist Party of Great Britain*, vol. I (London, 1968), p. 52. This misunderstanding occurred also in Moscow. See J. T. Murphy's complaint in *The Reds in Congress* (London, ? 1921), pp. 19–20; and contrast RILU, *Labour's New Charter* (Glasgow, 1922), p. 37.

[1] *Bev*. iii, p. 96, 'Fellow-workers', the CWC's first leaflet (? November 1915).
[2] J. T. Murphy, in *Solidarity*, April 1917, November 1919.

of this nature has been levelled against it. It is true that the movement 'failed to capture any major trade union': it is also true that the shop stewards failed to create any overall alternative organization to the existing trade unions.[1] Because, during the war, the movement achieved no theoretical elaboration of its practice, it was easy to see it merely as an evasion of those ultimate problems about the role of trade unionism in the transition to socialism which had exerised the imagination of Industrial Unionists and revolutionary syndicalists before the war. It was not until 1919 that the movement's leadership was able to draw out the full implications for the theory of socialist revolution of the wartime practice of 'dual power' between trade unionism and independent rank and-file organisation. Only in the light of this later theoretical development can the 'failure' of the wartime movement to adopt a 'consistent' position of dual unionism or amalgamationism be fully evaluated.

[1] Pribicevic, *The Shop Stewards' Movement and Workers' Control*, p. 91; Kendall, *The Revolutionary Movement in Britain*, p. 169.

Chapter 12

The Soviet Idea

The wartime practice of the shop stewards' movement was an important source of that ideological development in the British revolutionary movement that made possible the foundation of a united Communist Party. Historians of the Communist Party have paid scant attention to the distinctive ideas – ideas about the nature of socialism and the character of the transition to socialism – around which revolutionary unity was achieved during 1919–21. Disputes over tactics – whether the new party should work in Parliament, and if so, whether it should work within the Labour Party – have been allowed to obscure the more fundamental unity of principle on which the negotiations were based. The Communist Party was founded on the rejection of any parliamentary road to socialism, commitment to the dictatorship of the proletariat and to the struggle for soviet power. The importance of the direct influence of the Russian example in this is not in dispute, but the impact of that foreign revolutionary experience was mediated and enhanced by wartime developments in the British movement, and, in particular, by the lessons being drawn for revolutionary theory from the wartime practice of the shop stewards' movement.

The first major step towards the formation of the British Communist Party occurred at Easter 1918 when the annual conference of the British Socialist Party resolved: 'That the time has arrived for the co-operation of all active Socialist forces, with a view to formulating a common working basis . . .'[1] The fight for peace, the need to rally in defence of the Russian Revolution, and the intensification of Government repression

[1] BSP, *Report of the Annual Conference*, 1918, p. 34.

against socialists were the reasons advanced for this new effort
for socialist unity. The resolution was carried by 89 votes to 2.
Behind the apparent unity, however, lay an important division
of opinion in the BSP.[1] For E. C. Fairchild, Jo Fineberg, George
Roberts and others the most important condition of closer unity
with other socialist groupings was affiliation to the Labour
Party. In 1916, as a result of a decision made two years earlier,
the BSP affiliated to the Labour Party. At the same time the
repudiation of the pro-war Old Guard of the party made possible
a rapprochment with the ILP and the path seemed open for
the effective entry of the party into the Labour Party.[2]
However a further process of leftward differentiation was occurring within the party. The majority, led by Fairchild, held to the
centrist view that working-class action against the war must wait
upon the reconstruction of the International. The revolutionary
defeatist position, represented above all by John Maclean in
Scotland, still appealed to only a minority of party members.
The growth point of the revolutionary movement, however, lay
not in the conflict between centrism and revolutionary defeatism
in the BSP but in the related area of dialogue between the socialist
parties and industrial militancy. Before the war the failure of the
BSP internationalists to overthrow Hyndman was due largely to
their inability to sustain the alliance with the syndicalist-influenced
sections of the Party.[3] The fusion of anti-war politics and industrial
unrest was similarly crucial to the development of the revolutionary tendency within the BSP after 1916. Maclean recognized
this, but was not himself in any position to deliver the shop
stewards' movement to the BSP. The revolutionaries in the
English BSP also recognized it in their attempts to promote a
fusion of anti-war politics and the shop stewards' movement
after the Leeds convention of June 1917.

The two tendencies emerged clearly in the debate on closer
unity at the 1918 BSP conference. For the mover of the resolution,
George Roberts of Openshaw, and for E. C. Fairchild unity
with the ILP within the Labour Party was at least as attractive
a proposition as the attempt to secure unity with the Socialist
Labour Party on the industrial battlefield. Most other speakers
in the debate, however, saw little possibility of unity with the

1 This is noted by J. Klugmann, *History of the Communist Party of Great
Britain* (London, 1968), p. 29.
2 W. Kendall, *The Revolutionary Movement in Britain* (1969), pp. 181–3.
3 *Ibid.*, p. 59 and *passim*.

ILP. 'The ILP was not a Marxian organization.' 'If we are to co-operate, he preferred it should be with a revolutionary rather than a non-revolutionary body.' William Mclaine, the Manchester shop steward leader, supported unity with the SLP:

'Within the last two or three years he thought the most important factor, so far as Socialist unity was concerned, had been the activity of various SLP and BSP members in industrial districts. In consequence of unity of action on the industrial field, closer unity was now desired in all aspects.'

Mclaine went on to call on the Party to 'study our principles anew', in order to hammer out a common basis with the SLP. The conference had already taken hesitant steps in this direction, moving some way towards the SLP's position on industrial unionism,[1] and welcoming the shop stewards' movement 'as a change in working class organization rendered essential by altered conditions of capitalist production . . .' Mclaine spoke of the shop stewards' movement as 'the only active revolutionary movement in the country' and the chairman of the conference, Fred Shaw, an ASE official from Huddersfield, argued that: 'By this movement, and by it alone, could we get the force we needed behind our demands.' It was left to George Roberts, spokesman for the Fairchild line, to oppose 'committing the organization as such to any definite alliance with the Shop Stewards' movement'.[2]

Following the conference the BSP Executive invited both the SLP and the ILP to a joint conference to discuss unity. When, after various difficulties, representatives of the three parties met in November 1918 they agreed (following the suggestion of the BSP's conference resolution) to issue a joint manifesto on the 'International Crisis'. In addition it was suggested 'that a useful purpose would be served if a statement were prepared, for submission to a later Conference, setting out the tactics to be pursued' in the transition to socialism. These statements would then form the basis of further unity negotiations. The ILP prepared no statement, and following further fruitless negotiations in March, was finally dropped from the project of revolutionary

[1] 'This Conference declares that no form of industrial organisation can be effective unless it is based upon the complete recognition of the class struggle and has Socialism for its objective. The B.S.P. advocates industrial unionism as a class conscious weapon for the workers to fight the capitalist class.' BSP, *Report of the Annual Conference*, 1918, p. 23.
[2] *Ibid.*, pp. 19–21, 36.

unity. The BSP's statement contained no concessions to the SLP's Industrial Unionism or to its rejection of a parliamentary party as the main agency of the transition to socialism[1]

The SLP's contribution was of a very different order. During the weeks following the unity negotiations of November 1918, the SLP negotiators, Tom Bell, the national secretary, and Arthur MacManus, editor of *The Socialist*, together with two other leading figures, Jack Murphy and William Paul, set about reshaping the policy of the party.[2] In 'A Plea for the Reconsideration of Socialist Tactics and Organization', which attacked 'the bias of party . . . and the fetishism of the doctrinaire', they sought to bring traditional SLP theory into harmony with the experience of the Russian Revolution and of the shop stewards' movement in Britain.[3] It is no accident that it was the same four men who became the most powerful figures in the Communist Party during the first few years of its existence – it was just this convergence of De Leonism and the lessons of the shop stewards' movement that stood at the centre of the ideology of the early Communist Party.[4] The essence of their ideological achievement at this point was to substitute the local soviet representative of all industries for De Leon's national Industrial Union as the basic unit of working-class political power. De Leon had envisaged the perfection of the national Industrial Unions enabling the working class to break through the shell of the capitalist

[1] Kendall, *The Revolutionary Movement in Britain*, pp. 198–200; Cf. the Party's election programme in 1918, *The Call*, December 1918.

[2] This is noted by both Kendall (p. 199) and L. J. Macfarlane, *The British Communist Party* (1966) (p. 29). Neither, however, attempts to explain the nature of the new departure in policy. This is particularly strange in the case of Kendall, who devotes considerable attention to allegations of Bolshevik finance behind the Bell-MacManus-Murphy-Paul group (pp. 252–3), without apparently being interested in discovering what it was that all this money (whether real of imagined) was paying for.

[3] *The Socialist*, 2 January 1919. MacManus, Murphy and Paul stood as the three SLP parliamentary candidates in the Coupon election, financed, according to Sylvia Pankhurst, by the Russians (Kendall, *The Revolutionary Movement in Britain*, p. 413). The new policy was first expounded in their joint election address (*The Socialist*, December 1918), and further explored in a major article, 'A Soviet Republic for Britain', published in the first weekly edition of *The Socialist*, 12 December 1918. It is conceivable that this article was written by Theodore Rothstein, who was later to play the leading role in converting the BSP to sovietism.

[4] Cf. Lenin's acknowledgement of the importance of De Leon reported by A. Ransome, *Six Weeks in Russia* (1919), pp. 80–1. See also V. I. Lenin, *Selected Works*, vol. III (Moscow, 1961), pp. 402–3.

political state and usher in the administrative utopia of the Socialist Commonwealth.[1] In contrast, the SLP leaders now found in the local Workers' Committees the embryonic form of a proletarian state power, of the organization of the workers as 'the ruling class'. 'The striking masses have spontaneously created' the Workers' Committees, the basis of a workers' state, declared *The Socialist* at the end of January 1919: 'These committees representing every department in every mine, mill, railway, or plant, contain the elements of an organization which can transform capitalism into a Soviet Republic . . . All Power to the Workers' Committees.'[2] At a specially convened national conference on 11–12 January 1919 the SLP endorsed this programme as the basis of a revised constitution and appointed its authors to submit it to the BSP and ILP as the basis for further negotiations.[3]

The BSP's contribution to the unity discussions in the first months of 1919 was evidence that the process of leftward differentiation in the party which had been proceeding since the ousting of Hyndman in 1916, and which was clearly apparent at the conference of Easter 1918, was not yet complete. It was only after the final triumph of sovietism over parliamentarianism in the party that the unity negotiations could proceed. The foundation of the Third International in March 1919 – an event long awaited by the revolutionary defeatists in the party[4] – helped them to settle accounts with the Fairchild wing at the annual conference of April 1919. 'The time . . . has arrived when we, of the BSP, must make up our minds where we stand', wrote Theodore Rothstein in the pre-conference issue of *The Call*. 'Are we to join the Moscow International or shall we remain in the fold of the Berne one.' The critical choice, he argued, lay between

[1] See for example Daniel De Leon, *The Burning Question of Trades Unionism* (New York, 1964), pp. 34–5. See also J. Connolly, *Socialism Made Easy* (1907), pp. 15–19.

[2] *The Socialist*, 12 December 1918, 30 January 1919. The relation of this change of policy to the SLP's evolution away from dual unionism and to its role in the development of independent rank-and-file organization is further explored below. It may be noted here that the SLP was aware of the inadequacy of councils based in the factories alone, and advocated the establishment of residential committees which would also send representatives to the local 'Peoples' Administrative Committee'.

[3] A. Gleason, *What the Workers Want* (New York, 1920), pp. 203–4; Kendall, *The Revolutionary Movement in Britain*, p. 199.

[4] Kendall, *ibid.*, pp. 245, 406–7. The foundation of the Third International was reported in *The Call* on 3 and 17 April 1919.

the parliamentary road and the struggle for soviet power.[1] At the conference, on an emergency motion introduced by the Executive, an overwhelming majority opposed 'Parliamentarianism and sham democracy' and declared for the 'direct rule of the workers by means of Soviets'. The question of affiliation to the Third International was debated and referred to the branches for decision. Over the summer, E. C. Fairchild and H. Alexander fought a rearguard action against the commitment to sovietism, but they found little support inside the party. In May Fairchild resigned from the editorship of *The Call* (following a dispute over the publication of an article by Rothstein), and in October, when it was reported that the branches had voted 98 to 4 in favour of affiliation to the Third International, he and Alexander resigned from the party. The reason they gave was 'emphatic disagreement . . . with the advocacy of forcible revolution in preference to action through Parliament, municipal bodies and trade unions'.[2]

Underlying the conversion of the BSP rank and file to the theory of soviet rule was their belief in the imminence of proletarian revolution in the West. Fairchild and Alexander denied the imminence of revolution.[3] They also denied that the struggle for soviet power would be relevant in Britain, even in a revolutionary situation. While they were quite prepared to accept that institutions of the soviet type would be the appropriate basis for the administration of the socialist economy,[4] and even talked of the 'abolition of Parliament as we know it', they insisted that such institutions would only come into being after the revolutionary

[1] *The Call*, 17 April 1919.

[2] Walter Kendall's attempt to show that the conversion of the BSP to sovietism and to support for the Third International was the result of alien monies and improper influence is unconvincing. It seems certain, from his account, that Rothstein, who led the fight against Fairchild, was in very close touch with Moscow, and that he had a certain amount of cash at his disposal. No doubt the machinations of the Bolsheviks were a contributory cause of Fairchild's resignation, an added irritant. However there seems no reason to doubt that it was the Party's decisive repudiation of Fairchild's political line that was the basic cause of his resignation. No conspiracy theory can explain why in the summer of 1919 the overwhelming majority of the BSP branches rejected Fairchild's position.

[3] Kendall, *The Revolutionary Movement in Britain*, pp. 245, 406–7, *The Call*, 19 June, 28 August 1919.

[4] But, as Rothstein pointed out in his summing up, it is dubious whether they understood the meaning of this: *The Call*, 11 September 1919. See Fairchild's opposition to the fusion of executive and legislative power in the soviet, *The Call*, 26 June 1919.

conquest of power and by a gradual process of devolution of power from a socialist government resting on a parliamentary majority. The agency of the revolution therefore remained the political party working for a parliamentary majority and backed up by the industrial power of the unions. Only the capture of 'the central, national . . . political power', in essence the power (or supposed power) of parliament to direct the army and the civil service, could effect the transition to socialism. Any attempt to seize power through locally based soviets 'more or less concerted' would only lead to chaos and defeat. Though revolution was not around the corner, the prospects for the Fairchild strategy were, he argued, good: 'By dint of tremendous work the Labour Party pools two and a half million votes for a workers' political party, and at last the idea of the political strike spreads abroad.' Was this the time to go haring off after quite novel forms of organization alien to the traditions of British labour, to 'start afresh as though there had been neither Parliament nor trades unions in British history'?[1]

The BSP majority did not deny the importance of working in Parliament, in the Labour Party and in the trade unions, indeed they insisted upon it, but they rejected the idea that either the trade unions or a socialist party with a parliamentary majority could, separately or together, make the revolution. The soviets, based upon elections 'in the workshops and various Labour organizations', systematic reporting back and the instant re-callability of delegates, could truly represent the corporate will of the workers organized as a class, rather than the conflicting wills of the atomized individual voter in a parliamentary constituency. By combining legislative with executive power the soviets were proof against any abdication of real power by elected representatives to bureaucrats. While Parliament was 'the specific form of the political rule of capitalism', and the trade unions were organizations designed to negotiate with, not to overthrow capitalism, the soviets would constitute the basic organs of working class state power: 'The Revolution will not come about through the instrumentality either of Parliament or the trade unions, but by the direct action, political and economic, of the rank and file through their politico-economical organizations of the soviet type.'[2] Rothstein was at pains to point out that this was not mere constitution mongering (as Fairchild

---

[1] *The Call*, 6 March, 19, 26 June, 28 August 1919.
[2] Rothstein, in *The Call*, 5, 12 June 1919.

alleged) unconnected with the actual experience of class struggle in Britain. The adoption of the theory of soviet power represented precisely the convergence of the internationalist with the 'industrialist' strain within the BSP which had been in the making at least since the abortive Leeds convention, a convergence made possible only by the very concrete (if ultimately disappointing) experience of the shop stewards' movement:

'That the rank and file of the workers, in spite of the long traditions of trade unionism, are gradually becoming aware of the inadequacy of their trade unions in modern class warfare is clear from the rise and spread of the shop stewards' and workers' committees movement. It should be our business to encourage and foster this movement . . . We must propagate the idea of the rank and file organizations . . . because they will prove a fit instrument of the Revolution and because they are, in type, much akin to the Soviets which we are advocating on other grounds.'[1]

While this discussion was going on the columns of *The Call*, the unity negotiations had been carried forward, under pressure from the newly founded International. New unity negotiations were held in June in which the SLP and the BSP were joined by Sylvia Pankhurst's Workers' Socialist Federation[2] and the South Wales Socialist Society. Between these groups there were important tactical differences. The negotiations went a long way towards resolving them. The WSF, opposed to participation in Parliament on principle, agreed not to allow this to stand in the way of unity. The BSP's commitment to working within the

[1] *The Call*, 12 June 1919. Fairchild pointed out that the shop steward movement was moribund, and wondered 'why an innocuous proposal to revive the . . . movement and to establish highly unstable Workers Committee needs so elaborate a political philosophy': 26 June 1919.

[2] The importance of the WSF in the formation of the Communist Party is stressed by L. J. MacFarlane, *The British Communist Party*, pp. 30–2. The *Workers' Dreadnought*, Pankhurst's paper, was the first British revolutionary organ to grasp fully the sovietist implications of the Russian Revolution – see the issues of 17 November 1917 and 26 January 1918. In addition to its connections among the South Wales miners and East End women, the Federation established close relations with the shop stewards' movement in London from the beginning of 1918. In May 1918 a new constitution was adopted which committed the Federation to the abolition of the capitalist system – the workers to organize on an industrial basis and build up a National Assembly from local Workers Committees. *Workers' Dreadnought*, 1 June 1918.

Labour Party caused greater difficulty, but after considerable debate the negotiators agreed to recommend that 'the question of the affiliation of the new Party to the Labour Party . . . be decided by a referendum of the members three months after the new party is formed'. With this condition, the delegates departed to urge their respective Executives to conduct referenda on the formation of 'a united party having for its objects the establishment of Communism by means of the dictatorship of the working class working through Soviets . . .'[1]

It took more than eighteen months from this point for a united Communist Party to be finally established. The delay is to be explained partly by the victory of the old doctrinaire element in the Socialist Labour Party over the pro-unity 'big Four' – Bell, MacManus, Murphy and Paul – in the Executive elections of the autumn of 1919. Once the SLP disrupted the arrangements for unification set up in June, the two smaller parties also drew back, fearing to be submerged by more 'moderate' BSP members in the new party. The ultra-left Amsterdam meeting of the West European Communist Parties in February 1920, which temporarily eclipsed the guiding hand of Moscow, also had a disruptive effect in British unity negotiations.[2] These delays, however, should not be allowed to obscure the fact that it was the acceptance of the soviet as the only possible agency of the socialist revolution that marked the decisive break with social democratic orthodoxy and constituted the ideological basis for the formation of a united revolutionary party.[3] Despite the decisive part played by the Communist International in resolving the sectarian wranglings of 1919–21, the central ideological development underlying the foundation of the Communist Party was organically linked with the domestic experience of the revolutionary movement. Gallacher's oft-quoted story of the trip to Moscow in which he went as an infantile leftist and, after a

[1] Kendall, *The Revolutionary Movement in Britain*, pp. 204–5; MacFarlane, *The British Communist Party*, p. 48.

[2] Kendall, *The Revolutionary Movement in Britain*, pp. 205ff.

[3] 'It is . . . the struggle for Soviet power . . . which is able to unite and must now unite without fail all sincere, honest revolutionaries from among the workers . . . What if in a given country those who are Communists by conviction and by their readiness to carry on revolutionary work, sincere partisans of Soviet power . . . cannot unite owing to disagreement over participation in Parliament? I should consider each disagreement immaterial at present, since the struggle for Soviet power is the political struggle of the proletariat in its highest, most class conscious, most revolutionary form.' Lenin to Sylvia Pankhurst, written 28 August 1919, published in *The Call*, 22 January 1920.

conversation with Lenin returned a mature revolutionary does
not epitomize the intellectual history of British communism.[1]
The BSP's swing from social democratic parliamentarianism to
sovietism during 1919 cannot be seen merely as the product of
Bolshevik interventions (though these certainly added to the
bitterness of the defeated Fairchild wing): rather it was the culmination of a conflict which had been going on inside the party
since Hyndman's overthrow in 1916. The Socialist Labour
Party's new departure in January 1919 – the repudiation of
which nine months later was to lead to the expulsion of the
Party's most able and experienced members – was quite clearly
the result of the party's experience in the shop stewards' movement
not of any artificial Bolshevik imposition.

Of course the development of the idea of soviet power in the
British revolutionary movement owed a very great deal, including
the word, to the Russian Revolution. But the 'soviet heresy' was
not simply an attempt to graft alien experience on to the British
labour movement. To say, as Eldon Barry has, that 'attempts
to relate soviets to something practicable in Britain often resulted
in equating them with the Shop Stewards' and Workers' Committees', is to risk turning the real development on its head.[2] The
enthusiasm with which sections of the left took up and developed
the soviet idea in Britain is to be explained not only by understandable elation over the Russian Revolution, but also, and
primarily, by the fact that this idea answered to a real theoretical
need felt by British revolutionaries as a result of their own
domestic experience. Barry might more appropriately have
written, 'attempts to spell out the potentialities apparent in the
Workers' Committees resulted in equating them with Soviets'. It
was not only within the revolutionary parties that such a theoretical
effort was going on during 1919. Equally important – and, of
course, very closely related – were the attempts of the leaders of
the shop stewards' movement to make theoretical sense of the
wartime practice of independent rank-and-file organization.

The leaders of the shop stewards' movement had been quick to
see a parallel between the Workers' Committees and the Russian
soviets. If, at first, 'we knew next to nothing about how the
Workers' and Soldiers Committees were constructed, and had
the vaguest ideas as to the conditions in which they could and

[1] W. Gallacher, *Revolt on the Clyde* (1936), pp. 251–3; Kendall, *The
Revolutionary Movement in Britain*, p. 229.
[2] E. E. Barry, *Nationalisation in British Politics* (London, 1965), p. 225.

should be formed',[1] by the end of the war the experience of the Russian Revolution, relayed through the socialist press (especially *Workers' Dreadnought*), had gone some way to familiarizing the leadership with the idea of soviet power. When the forty hours strike of January and February 1919 momentarily raised expectations of imminent revolutionary confrontation in the movement, *The Worker* drew out the Russian parallel:

> 'The Soviet Government of Russia sprung from the Workers' Committees, from the unofficial rank and file movement of the Russian people. The shop stewards are the first stage in the Soviet development; and when you read of the Workers' Committee in Belfast taking over civil control in the town, you are reading part of the history of the Russian Revolution in your own land.'[2]

The hopes generated by the forty hours strike were soon disappointed, and the focus of the industrial struggle shifted away from engineering workers to the miners and railwaymen. Paradoxically it was while the shop stewards' movement was in decline and divorced from the leadership of mass activity that its leaders, responding to the great struggles in progress between other sections of the workers and the state, were to draw out the revolutionary implications of their own wartime practice of independent rank-and-file organization. Aided by the theoretical developments within the SLP and BSP, which their own practice had helped to promote, the shop stewards, led by Jack Murphy in England and by William Gallacher and J. R. Campbell in Scotland, initiated a new burst of theoretical activity during the autumn of 1919. The immediate upshot of this activity was to be the formal commitment of the movement to the struggle for soviet power at its first post-war conference in January 1920.

During 1919 the national trade union leadership, riding a massive wave of rank-and-file militancy in a number of industries, moved significantly to the left. Faced with the impotence of the Parliamentary Labour Party, and in the aftermath of an apparently fraudulent general election which had returned to power a reactionary government bent on thwarting the aspirations of the masses for genuine peace and reconstruction, many trade union leaders began to talk the language of 'Direct Action', of

[1] J. T. Murphy, *New Horizons* (1941), pp. 61–3; J. T. Murphy, *Preparing for Power* (1934), p. 152.

[2] *The Worker*, 15 February 1919.

the political general strike. If Labour had been cheated out of its proper influence in the political system it was up to the unions to use their unprecedented post-war strength to shatter the political despotism of the coalition and force Parliament to respond to the just demands of the people.[1] In the course of 1919 several unions threatened to take Direct Action to enforce the nationalization of the mines, the ending of conscription, the withdrawal of troops from Russia and Ireland. The Triple Alliance had emerged from its wartime hiberation to co-ordinate the demands and activities of the great industrial unions and, it might seem, to lead the political general strike when this materialized. Towards the end of 1919, following the railway strike of October, the decision was taken to replace the old and ineffective Parliamentary Committee of the TUC by a General Council – potentially the General Staff of the trade union army in its final confrontation with the power of capital.

Here indeed was fertile ground for the re-emergence of syndicalist illusions about the revolutionary potential of trade unionism. Despite Rothstein's clear analysis of the nature of the trade union bureaucracy, there was a strong tendency even within the revolutionary majority of the British Socialist Party to over-estimate the revolutionary potential of the left trade union leadership. Thus John Maclean, in the autumn of 1919, was looking to a broadening of the Triple Alliance to create the 'executive of the class struggle – the central committee of the New Society', and arguing that the recipe for revolution was to replace the 'Labour Fosils with real Revolutionaries', to 'add Mann to Smillie'.[2] Tom Quelch took a very similar line in response to the proposals for a General Council in November 1919.[3]

The revolutionary possibilities of the political strike were not lost on the shop stewards' leaders; but they approached the rhetoric of Direct Action with caution. The steps taken towards greater unity in the movement had not eliminated sectionalism. It was easy for Smillie, Hodges, Robert Williams to talk of Direct Action, but, as the breakdown of the Triple Alliance was to show, very much more difficult to achieve the necessary unity in action. By playing on the different sectional interests of rail-waymen or transport workers the Government was able during

1 Cf. Frank Hodges at the 1919 TUC. TUC, *Report of the Annual Conference*, 1919, pp. 296–7.
2 *Solidarity*, October 1919. See also *The Call*, 25 September 1919.
3 *The Call*, 16 October 1919.

1919–21 to prevent the Triple Alliance from ever deploying its full industrial power. Arthur Gleason, an American observer, clearly saw how the formal unity between the top officials of the trade union movement disguised more disunity than it abolished:

'By direct action the British workers mean first of all a consultation by every trade union of its rank and file. This is a process requiring many weeks. They mean consultations between the committees of the Labour Party and the TUC. They mean a thrashing out of the matter on the floor of the congress at Glasgow on September 8th. . . . They mean Clause 8 of the constitution of the Triple Alliance, which reads: " Joint action can only be taken when the question at issue has been before the members of the three organizations and decided by such methods as the constitution of each organization provides." '[1]

It is difficult to trace the progress of the demands for direct action during 1919 without losing them in the veritable orgy of consultation, and buck-passing, that occurred among the various leading organs of the labour movement.

This continuing sectionalism was not merely a result of insufficient unity at the top: rather it was a symptom of the inadequacy of any attempt to achieve united political action by the trade union movement by agreement between the top leadership. We have seen how the Triple Alliance, though formed in response to militant rank-and-file demands for greater unity in action, was dominated from its foundation by the bureaucrats' desire to prevent spontaneous sympathetic actions, to contain rather than to lead militancy. At the core of the drive for greater unity in the movement was the articulation of the trade union bureaucracy as a separate social stratum. At the end of 1919 Murphy was warning clearly against the illusion that the formation of a General Council for the TUC could succeed where the Triple Alliance had already (in relation to the Railway strike) manifestly failed:[2]

'One of the most dangerous developments in the industrial organizations of the working class . . . is the growth of an official class with its own vested interests and an excessive control over all the movements of the workers . . .
'The call comes for a General Staff for the labour hosts [the

---

[1] Gleason, *What the Workers Want*, pp. 105–6.
[2] *The Socialist*, 18 December 1919; *Solidarity*, December 1919.

General Council], and again the principle thought impressed is conservative and reactionary. The General Staff of officialdom is to be a dam to the surging tide of independent working class aspirations and not a directing agency towards the overthrow of capitalism . . .

'The unity we have appealed for becomes a unity to stop action by the mass rather than unity which shall lead them to victory.'

The clarity of the shop stewards' identification of the limitations of unity from above rested upon their understanding of the inevitable ambivalence of the trade union bureaucracy. Before the war the syndicalists had acknowledged this ambivalence, but, in urging the possibility of reconstructing the unions within capitalism as the chief agencies of a socialist revolution, they had failed to grasp the true nature of the bureaucracy. One of the basic sources of syndicalist support before the war had been the frustrations occasioned by the operation of the emergent machinery of national collective bargaining in conditions of falling real wages, on the one hand, and enhanced industrial power caused by relatively full employment, on the other. Opposition to conciliation and procedural agreements which prevented the full and immediate use of industrial power when militancy was at its peak and the employer unprepared, appealed equally to miners, railwaymen and engineers angered by the delays and compromises involved in orderly collective bargaining:

'All the procedure mentioned in the Terms [of Agreement] can be gone through if circumstances suggest that such a procedure is good policy, but we must keep ourselves free to adopt strong measures when required . . . The non-unionist question, e.g., will not be solved by talking and to be bound to go through a certain procedure before drastic action can be taken is ridiculous in the extreme . . . We want swift and powerful action, a want which cannot be gratified if we are forever flying the flag of truce.'[1]

Similarly *The Miners' Next Step* proposed an 'organization constructed to fight rather than to negotiate. It is based on the principle that we can only get what we are strong enough to win and retain'.[2]

[1] J. T. Murphy, in *Sheffield Guardian*, 7 August 1914.
[2] *Loc. cit.*, p. 20. See also, for the railwaymen, P. Bagwell, *The Railwaymen* (1963), p. 304.

The syndicalists understood that there was a connection between centralized collective bargaining and the tendency to oligarchy in trade union government. For the authors of *The Miners' Next Step* it was 'the policy of conciliation [that] gives the real power of the men into the hands of a few leaders . . . What is really blameworthy is the conciliation policy which demands leaders of this [autocratic] description'.[1] If 'conciliation' was to be rejected, however, what was to be put in its place? Few British syndicalists would go so far as the IWW leader, Big Bill Haywood: 'No contracts, no agreements, no compacts; these are unholy alliances, and must be damned as treason when entered into with the capitalist class.'[2] Some engineers wanted unilaterally to abolish the Terms of Agreement with the employers, but the worthlessness of this strategy was revealed in 1913–14.[3] Tom Mann objected to *timed* contracts, but not to agreements as such.[4] *The Miner's Next Step* recognized the necessity of collective bargaining – the only alternative was a return to individual bargaining – but it could suggest no realistic counter to the oligarchic tendency inevitably set up by centralized bargaining. Instead, it fell back on the merest wishful thinking:

'. . . it is being realized, that collective bargaining can be made so wide reaching and all embracing that it includes the whole of the working class. In this form . . . the old school of labour leaders have no love for it . . . because it will degrade their power and influence by necessitating a much more stringent and effective democratic control than at present obtains . . .'[5]

This is the 'necessity' of democratic optimism, not of history.

The wartime practice of independent rank-and-file organization had not been directed to replacing trade unionism and exercising its functions within capitalism. The intention was to create a situation of 'dual power' between the official leadership of the trade unions and the Workers' Committees. So long as the officials 'rightly represented' their interests the workers would follow them; as soon as the officials misrepresented them, they would rally behind the Workers' Committee. Though this practice arose from the immediate necessities of wartime, it contained within it a solution to the theoretical problem that confounded *The Miners' Next Step* – and syndicalism generally.

---

[1] *The Miners' Next Step*, p. 8.   [2] *Industrial Syndicalist*, October 1910.
[3] See above, p. 84.   [4] *Industrial Syndicalist*, September 1910.
[5] *Loc. cit.*, pp. 11–12.

The centralization of trade unionism, whether it be in the Miners' Federation, the Triple Alliance or the putative General Council of the TUC, had proceeded in response to the concentration of the forces of capitalism. But this centralization occurred at the expense of 'much of the early democracy'. Centralized collective bargaining was a necessity for the workers: so long as capitalism existed the workers would need some machinery of negotiation and compromise with the the power of capital. Such bargaining necessarily involved the creation of a 'big specialized official army' which, because in striking bargains they must take on certain disciplinary functions over their members on behalf of the employers, tend to 'run the organization in oligarchical or caucus fashion'.[1] The association between national collective bargaining and the tendency to oligarchy in trade union government, which the syndicalists observed, was therefore a necessary one, not merely a product of immature collective bargaining procedures.

In addition to oligarchic control, collective bargaining tended to produce a leadership incapable of seeing beyond compromise with capitalism: 'When it is remembered that Trade Unions are limited, constitutionally, to narrow channels of activity, and that officialdom is a product of this limited activity, it is only to be expected that the official leaders are essentially conservative in outlook and action.'[2] Whatever his original political intentions the trade union official, by the nature of the activity in which he is engaged, must tend to detach himself from democratic control and, at every crisis, to place the interests of his members within capitalism before the interests of the working class as a whole in abolishing capitalism. Because his whole function was to negotiate, the trade union official had come to see collective bargaining procedures not as a temporary truce but as a permanent peace with capital. National collective bargaining became the object, not a method, of trade unionism. 'The whole machinery of the Trade Unions is constitutionally directed into channels of adaptation . . . to the capitalist system . . .' 'Trade unions . . . are organized bodies for the modification of the existing system, accepting the capitalist idea of society.'[3]

From this argument it follows that the only way finally to

---

[1] J. T. Murphy, in *Solidarity*, December 1919.
[2] J. T. Murphy, in *The Socialist*, 18 December 1919.
[3] *Solidarity*, December 1919; J. T. Murphy, quoted in K. Coates and T. Topham, *Industrial Democracy in Great Britain* (1968), p. 81.

defeat the oligarchic and collaborationist tendency of trade unionism is to overthrow capitalism and wage slavery itself. Of course, in a period of revolutionary upheaval, it might be possible for the workers to replace existing collaborationist leaderships with revolutionaries and to remould the structure of the unions 'on the lines indicated by the Workers' Committees'.[1] Unless the revolution was successfully carried through, however, the same tendency to oligarchy and collaboration would rapidly assert themselves amongst the new leadership. After the war the shop stewards acknowledged that even the achievement of Industrial Unionism and the replacement of the branch by the workshop as the basis of the union could not ensure democratic control of the officials. These conditions were already broadly established in the Miners' Federation, but 'caucus rule' remained and must be countered, as in engineering, by the construction of independent rank-and-file organization based on the pits.[2] Moreover, during 1919 more immediate considerations dictated that independent rank-and-file organization not the reconstruction of trade unionism as a whole should continue to dominate the thinking of the shop stewards: 'Immediately we proceed to consider how [rank and file control of the unions] can be accomplished we are faced with the caucus-ridden bodies in power, many constitutions and long drawn out proceedings for alterations. Meanwhile Rome burns and deeds are demanded.'[3] And if campaigns for amalgamation were inadequate to the situation, so also, as Murphy had told an unrepentant 'Wobbly' in May 1919, was any attempt to construct Industrial Unionism *de novo*: 'Lenin and his comrades have many times repeated that Industrial Unionism is the basic state of the Industrial Commonwealth. True, and I agree. But neither Lenin nor his comrades waited for Industrial Unionism as a means to achieve social revolution.' It seemed likely that the revolutionary crisis would not wait upon the perfection of Industrial Unionist structures: this might well prove to be a post-revolutionary task.[4]

'We live in a revolutionary epoch, and the ferment of revolution moves steadily westward', Murphy had written.[5] During the war

---

[1] Gleason, *What the Workers Want*, p. 199.
[2] Coates and Topham, *Industrial Democracy in Great Britain*, p. 81; *Solidarity*, September, October 1919; *The Worker*, 29 May 1920.
[3] *The Socialist*, 18 December 1919.
[4] *Ibid.*, 26 May 1919. Cf. Lenin, *Selected Works*, vol. III, pp. 400–2.
[5] *The Socialist*, 20 May 1919.

independent rank-and-file organization had been developed primarily as a counter to the oligarchic and collaborationist tendencies characteristic of trade unionism within capitalism, with no immediate revolutionary intent. It was only in the context of the revolutionary optimism of 1919 that the larger implications of wartime practice came to be understood. Increasingly the purpose of the Workers' Committees was seen as independent *revolutionary* action, not the organization of a strike for immediate demands, but the transformation of a strike into the final struggle for power. At the 1919 Labour Party Conference Sexton, the right-wing dockers' leader, had challenged Smillie and Hodges to face up to the revolutionary implications of their doctrine of Direct Action: 'Supposing they destroyed the Government by a national strike, what were they going to put in its place? . . . They had no machinery to replace what they had destroyed. Their only machinery would be revolution.'[1] Hodges, in reply, indignantly denied any partiality for the 'machinery of revolution'. In fact, both he and Smillie remained throughout this period firmly committed to parliamentary socialism.[2]

In the aftermath of the railway strike of October 1919 the shop stewards' movement came to believe, with Sexton and J. H. Thomas, that any large strike would take on the character of a confrontation between the organized workers and the state, a confrontation which could only be resolved either by the complete defeat of the unions, or by the 'machinery of revolution'.[3] In this situation it became possible, and necessary, for the movement to be ready to 'seize on any passing opportunity which may present itself, in order to convert it into a Revolutionary situation'.[4] This required more centralized leadership than had seemed necessary or desirable in the less cataclysmic struggles of wartime, more attention to forging an alliance with revolutionary elements in the mines, railways and other industries, and thus the construction of 'a working-class alliance in every locality that will be far superior to a top-heavy Triple Alliance'.[5] Above all, the function of the Workers' Committees was redefined as involving

[1] Labour Party, *Report of the Annual Conference*, 1919, pp. 119–20.

[2] A. Hatchett, 'Direct Action and the Role of the Daily Herald' (Warwick M.A. Dissertation, 1972), pp. 92–3.

[3] W. Gallacher and J. Campbell, *Direct Action* (Glasgow, 1919), pp. 16, 21.

[4] A. MacManus at the national conference of the shop stewards' movement, reported in *The Worker*, 14 February 1920.

[5] *The Socialist*, 18 December 1919; *Solidarity*, December 1919; *The Worker*, 14 February 1920; Gallacher and Campbell, *Direct Action*, p. 16.

not only the leadership of strike action but also its direct development into a revolutionary seizure of power. By the end of 1919 both Murphy and the Scottish shop stewards' leadership had identified the central task of the shop stewards' movement as that of turning the 'passive' into the 'active' strike.[1]

'The most the rank and file have ever been asked to do is to stand still, to stop work and wait and wait until somebody has done something for them . . . The working class needs more than the grim tenacity of negative pacifism . . . The bravery which can stand aside and see wives and children starve is not the bravery of the man who would be free. It is the bravery of obedience, the bravery of the slave, prepared to endure as a slave, created by sectional unionism and encouraged by caucus control.'[2]

Murphy described how, in his view, soviet institutions capable of replacing bourgeois law and order and exercising a dictatorship of the proletariat would come into being:

'There are masses of workers who want to solve a particular problem, and in the course of development you have a negative action, the stoppage of production. The issue changes, and a general strike committee is formed, not particularly dominated by the trade union outlook, but by the psychology of the situation, and the fact that all are working with one particular object in view. Yet the objective becomes subordinate to the demand to satisfy their immediate wants, as we saw was the case in Limerick and Belfast. What is the demand? First of all probably, for light for hospitals. What happens then? At once the strike committee has to take upon itself positive functions; it sends men back to the electricity stations for the production of electricity, and it may send others to work too. They thus take upon themselves positive functions, and in doing so they immediately step into the arena of the control of industry and of distribution. The longer they are on strike the more insistent becomes the demand for food. We are faced with another problem and have to find the solution to it. Where are the bakers? Are they with us? Can we control them? Can the bakers provide sufficient food for the needs of the people? Again the strike committee had to function, and it becomes

[1] Gallacher and Campbell, *ibid.*, p. 21; see also *The Worker*, 14 February, 12 June 1920.
[2] *The Socialist*, 18 December 1919.

a positive work to control the millers to mill the flour and the bakers to bake the bread, and so right in the centre you have a strike committee as a committee controlling industry in various directions.'[1]

Direct Action similarly concentrated on the problem of the food supply as the crucial moment in the development from strike to revolution:

'Several courses are open to the State. It can, for example, declare the strike illegal, and arrest all the active men. It can attempt to overawe the strikers by a display of armed force. If these measures are not productive of the desired results it can proceed to kick the workers in the stomach. It can interfere with the food supply. In the case of an industry that is highly localized, as is the case with the mining industry, the cotton industry, or the engineering industry, in some place it can blockade the affected districts, preventing food supplies reaching the striking workers. In the case of an industry like the railways where the workers are scattered all over the country, it would endeavour to get at them through the ration cards, so long as a rationing system exists.

'The workers have therefore got to create organization to counter the State organization of Capitalism. Social machinery must be developed to attend to the social needs of the workers when they are in conflict with the employers.'

In such ways, expanding beyond the narrow functions of a strike committee the Workers' Committees would become 'the nucleus of working class political power. As the industrial and social organization grows strong enough it will be forced to fight the Capitalist State. It will fight the Capitalist State not to take possession of it, but to smash it.'[2]

The essential contribution of the shop stewards' movement to the ideological development of the revolutionary left was that, in going beyond the purely propagandist activities of the revolutionary syndicalists within the existing unions, while yet rejecting any attempt to establish rival Industrial Unions to take over the essential functions of trade unionism within capitalism, the movement laid the foundations for the replacement of the syndicalist by the soviet idea of revolution. While syndicalist elements

[1] Coates and Topham, *Industrial Democracy in Great Britain*, pp. 82–3.
[2] Gallacher and Campbell, *Direct Action*, pp. 22–3, 25–6.

on the *Daily Herald* and even within the British Socialist Party continued to exaggerate the revolutionary possibilities of the left trade union bureaucracy, the shop stewards' leaders pointed the way forward. The establishment of the Workers' Committees had made it possible to conceive of an agency of working-class power which was neither the reformist conception of the existing state machine controlled through a parliamentary majority, nor a Congress of Trade – or Industrial – Unions (which, however 'reconstructed', must continue to operate as the machinery of compromise with capital until the revolution is accomplished), but a specific organ of working class dictatorship, the soviet.

Engineering workers played a very important part in the Communist Party during its early years.[1] Only the miners have a claim to have made a greater contribution, and this occurred predominately as a result of the two great lockouts of 1921 and 1926. Probably the engineers were the largest section of workers represented in the unity negotiations of 1919–21. It has been argued that the shop stewards' wartime experience of independent rank-and-file organization enabled them to bring to the revolutionary movement an understanding of the struggle for soviet power more profound and more effectively adapted to British conditions – in particular to the strength and importance of the trade unions – than could have been acquired merely from the contemplation of events in Russia. The account so far, however, is one-sided. Even before the formation of the Communist Party the theory of soviet power on which the unity negotiations were based underwent some strange distortions. It is beyond the scope of this study to discuss the attitudes and experience of the other sections of revolutionary workers and intellectuals involved in the unity negotiations, and the way in which these conditioned the outcome.[2] But the engineers themselves contributed their own share of confusion to the new party, primarily because already in 1919 the shop stewards' movement was undergoing a tremendous defeat, the destruction of its wartime strength and militancy. Not unnaturally this had implications for its ideological as well as its practical contribution to the new party.

From the outset the shop stewards' development of the theory

[1] MacFarlane, *The British Communist Party*, pp. 284–5.
[2] In particular the influence of the traditional attitudes of the miners towards the state in the revolutionary movement at this time would repay investigation.

of soviet power had rested upon an objective contradiction. It was the intensified industrial struggle of 1919–20 which, together with the international revolutionary crisis centred in Russia, inspired the shop stewards and their allies in the Marxist parties to explore theoretically the revolutionary implications of the practice of the Workers' Committees. At the same time, however, the revolutionary optimism on which this exercise rested was being undermined by the collapse of the shop stewards' power within the engineering workshops. Having no equivalent influence among the miners or railwaymen who now led the industrial struggle, the shop stewards' theoretical advances of 1919 appeared not as an organic reflection of the immediate needs of the struggle, but as commentary offered hopefully and a little shrilly from the sidelines.

From the spring of 1919 it was impossible not to acknowledge that the lead had passed out of the hands of the craftsmen, back to the great industrial unions of the Triple Alliance. 'Think of it', Gallacher was writing within five months of the Armistice,

'Think of it, you engineers who used to pride yourselves in being the vanguard of the working class movement. The despised dockers and railwaymen, the miners – because they had the good sense to organize by industry, while you were strutting around bleating about the sanctity of your craft – have now become the pioneers of emancipation from the demoralizing power of capitalism, while you wallow pitifully in the slough of despond.'[1]

It is in this context of defeat that the political development of the rank-and-file movement after the war must be understood. As the Workers' Committees contracted they ceased to be mass organizations capable of initiating direct action and became, more or less consciously, district committees of a future revolutionary political party. No longer were the leaders searching for solutions to the problems of how a politically conscious vanguard could best lead and develop a spontaneous and vigorous mass movement. Rather their efforts were directed to discovering how this vanguard could survive the defeat and disintegration of that movement. So far as the shop stewards were concerned, though they were hardly conscious of this fact, revolutionary socialist unity became, not a forward step on a rising tide of struggle, but a retrenchment, a consolidation of what forces remained.

[1] *The Worker*, 12 April 1919; cf. *Solidarity*, March 1919.

The wartime experience of the Workers' Committees had laid a genuine basis for the development of the soviet theory of revolution. But in the circumstances of 1919–21, much of this experience seemed increasingly irrelevant to the immediate possibilities. Consequently the politics of the revolutionary left tended to become an abstract and cantankerous exercise in which tactical differences between the parties easily became inflated into matters of principle, while the basic uniting commitment to the struggle for soviet power was pushed into a position of secondary importance. In their efforts to promote unity by placing the struggle for soviet power at the centre of the political agenda the shop stewards could not avoid revealing their own isolation from the mass of the workers, and the extent to which the lessons of wartime were becoming irrelevant precisely at the moment when they were being learned. This is revealed most clearly in the confused and curious elaboration of the idea of the soviet that stemmed from the Clyde in the autumn of 1919.

During the autumn of 1919 the Scottish shop stewards launched a campaign for the establishment of Social Committees based upon the organization of the workers residentially, where they lived, rather than industrially, where they worked.[1] Underlying this campaign lay a significant mixture of motives. Two quite contradictory reasons were put forward for the formation of Social Committees. In the first place, in their pamphlet *Direct Action*, Gallacher and Campbell argued that if the positive functions of local government were to be successfully fulfilled by the workers in the forthcoming revolutionary crisis, the Workers' Committees would need to be supplemented by *representative* Social Committees capable of organizing the food supply and of making arrangements for the supplies of raw materials needed to keep local industry operative. The Workers' Committees organizing the workers at the point of production, and the Social Committees organizing the workers where they lived would combine to form 'the nucleus of working class political power'.[2] Since Gallacher and Campbell were at pains to stress that the Social Committees would not represent a different body of people from the Workers' Committees, it is difficult to see what functions these residentially elected bodies

[1] There was no novelty in this idea as such. See Gallacher in *The Call*, December 1917; *The Socialist*, 2 January 1919.
[2] Gallacher and Campbell, *Direct Action*, pp. 25, 22, 24.

could fulfill that could not be undertaken within a single unified Workers' Committee.[1]

The truth of the matter is that the Social Committees, far from springing from any theoretical recognition of the necessity of such bodies as revolutionary instruments, were a symptom of the retreat of the shop stewards' movement from their power base in the workshops. In the aftermath of the forty hours strike on the Clyde it proved impossible, in many cases, to re-establish organization inside the factories, and the CWC had responded by maintaining the local strike committees in existence as a refuge for victimized members no longer able to organize on the job. The committees were granted representation on the Workers' Committee, which thereby formally acknowledged the need for organization outside the factories.[2] The Social Committees which the CWC promoted from the autumn of 1919 were simply an extension of these defunct strike committees, and the success of this campaign can be seen as an index not of the continuing vigour of the movement, but of the degree to which the militant and revolutionary elements on the Clyde had already been driven out of the factories or rendered powerless inside them. *Direct Action* can best be seen, therefore, as an attempt to validate theoretically, with the context of an increasingly unrealistic revolutionary optimism, a form of organization which had already sprung up spontaneously as a response to the weakness of the movement, its defeat in the workshops. When Gallacher and Campbell proposed that the Social Committees undertake elaborate surveys of the problems of local food supply and industrial administration in preparation for their revolutionary roles, what they were really doing was inventing pseudo-revolutionary tasks in an effort to prevent unemployed militants from dropping out of the movement altogether.[3]

But this was only half the story. Writing in *The Worker* in November 1919, J. R. Campbell put forward a quite different theoretical justification for the formation of the Social Committees, and one which came a good deal nearer being a true statement of their nature and potential. In an article entitled

[1] Cf. B. Pribicevic, *The Shop Stewards' Movement and Workers' Control* (Oxford, 1959), pp. 136–8.

[2] *The Worker*, 22 February, 15, 22 March 1919.

[3] This is not to say that such work would not have been of use to a revolutionary administration, but that the very reasons which prompted Gallacher and Campbell to think up these tasks were such as to indicate that there was no immediate prospect of such an administration.

L

'Towards Revolutionary Unity' he argued that all revolutionaries were now agreed on the need for soviets and were being kept apart merely by tactical differences over the use (if any) to be made of Parliament in the meantime. He proposed that the Social Committees undertake not only the commissariat and preparatory economic tasks outlined in *Direct Action*, but also 'the educational work of the movement . . . such as manning education classes, and propagating the general ideas of revolution . . .' All the essential functions of the revolutionary party (as Campbell saw them at this point) were thus to be fulfilled by the Social Committees in which all revolutionaries would work together despite their differences over 'political' activity. Meanwhile, 'those who believe in political action [may] keep in being the present political organizations on the left with a view to being able to take electoral action if they so desire'.[1] Prompted by the difficulties experienced in the negotiations for communist unity since the summer of 1919, Campbell seized on the Social Committees as the means of achieving revolutionary unity from below, dispelling or if necessary bypassing the sectarianism of the Party Executives. In January 1920 the publication of Lenin's letter to Sylvia Pankhurst in which he urged that the disagreement over participation in bourgeois parliaments was 'immaterial at present . . . a partial, secondary question' seemed to lend support to Campbell's argument, and in February 1920 Gallacher was explicitly calling for the construction of 'a Communist Party based on social committees throughout the country'.[2]

Had this line of argument rested explicitly on the repudiation of the earlier view that the Social Committees were potentially mass, representative organizations, organs of the future proletarian state machine, it would have been theoretically unobjectionable. But Gallacher and Campbell wanted it both ways. They wanted the Social Committees to serve *both* as potential soviets *and* as branches of the future revolutionary party. Party and soviet were thus inextricably confused in their theory. By the spring of 1920 this confusion had spread in the English movement. At a rank and file conference called by the NAC of the shop stewards' movement to coincide with the March 1920 TUC in London, two hundred delegates issued a call for 'the formation of Soviets throughout the country, so that when a

---

[1] *The Worker*, 15 November 1919.
[2] *The Call*, 22 January 1920; *Workers' Dreadnought*, 21 February 1920. See also J. R. Campbell in *The Worker*, 21 January, 10, 17 April 1920.

crisis arrived the workers would have the necessary machinery to take advantage of and maintain the revolution'.[1] On the final day of this conference a special meeting assembled to 'consider the best practical and immediate steps for giving effect to the resolution'. After careful discussion this meeting called for the formation of Social Soviets with functions similar to their Scottish counterparts. The central task of these 'Soviets' was clearly spelled out:

'. . . it was further agreed that the tasks to be undertaken by the social bodies would best be fulfilled by a revolutionary Communist party affiliated to the Third International as soon as such a party could be found in Great Britain. The new organizations, those organized socially on the basis of locality, will therefore be transformed into branches of the Communist party as soon as this party is constituted by the fusion of the existing left wing organizations, or will themselves become the Communist party should the desired fusion still be indefinitely postponed.'[2]

In the event no Social Soviets appear to have been established and nothing came of this resolution – though it may have had some effect in hastening the final stages of the unity negotiations.[3] But it does help to explain the confusion of motives which underlay the theoretical confusion both at this conference and in the Scottish movement. In promoting a form of organization described as a soviet as the means of forcing forward the formation of the revolutionary party, the shop stewards were giving expression – in a theoretically very confused way – to the belief that a revolutionary party was needed because of the proximity of a revolutionary crisis. The rank and file conference decided to call the social organizations Soviets in order to emphasize their revolutionary nature and to deter those who did not believe that 'a revolutionary situation is close at hand' from joining.[4] They called it a Soviet, that is to say, in order to ensure that it remained the organization of the politically conscious vanguard (i.e. the party) and did not become a representative mass organization (i.e. the soviet). At the same time, however, the very origin of this form of organization, the Social Committee, in the decline of the mass movement, in the need to allow for unemployed

[1] *Solidarity*, April 1920.   [2] *The Worker*, 27 March 1920.
[3] Cf. J. Klugman, *History of the Communist Party of Great Britain*, p. 36.
[4] *The Worker*, 27 March 1920.

and victimized members, bore witness to the falseness of the revolutionary optimism with which the theorists attempted to invest it. So far as the shop stewards were concerned the real need for a united party lay not in the immediacy of any revolutionary crisis, but in the urgent need to limit their losses, to consolidate their forces on the ebb tide of militancy. If revolutionary optimism was the precondition of the formation of a united party, and a united party was felt to be urgently necessary precisely because of the experience of defeat and demoralization, the political problem facing the stewards was insoluble. Instead of questioning the premise, the necessity of revolutionary optimism, the shop stewards resorted – not of course consciously – to the use of a revolutionary myth to cover their retreat. Hence the opportunistic talk of soviets, and hence the confusion between soviet and party.

Over the summer of 1920 these theoretical confusions were finally ironed out. At the second congress of the Third International, Jack Tanner and Dave Ramsay, representing the English shop stewards, urged that there was no need to establish a Communist Party in Britain since the shop stewards' movement already organized the politically conscious vanguard of the proletariat. Lenin's reply was conciliatory – he could not afford to alienate a movement for which such claims could be made – but the congress overruled Tanner's position.[1] In January 1920 the shop stewards had requested affiliation to the Communist International. This was now refused on the grounds that the shop stewards' movement was not a political party, did not rest upon any test of political commitment, but was open to any bona fide worker.[2] When Tanner and Ramsay reported back in September 1920 the NAC accepted the logic of this decision and agreed to affiliate to the incipient Red International of Labour Unions (RILU) instead. At the same time they undertook to promote the negotiations for a united Communist Party, to encourage members of the movement, *as individuals*, to join whatever united organization was formed, and to affiliate the shop stewards' movement itself to the Red International of Labour Unions.[3] Even when, in June 1922, the National Administrative

[1] R. Martin, *Communism and the British Trade Unions, 1924–1933* (1969), pp. 8–9; V. I. Lenin, *On Britain*, (Moscow, n.d.), pp. 526–7, 529; Kendall, *The Revolutionary Movement in Britain*, p. 231.

[2] Pribicevic, *The Shop Stewards' Movement and Workers' Control*, p. 107; Murphy, *New Horizons*, p. 152.

[3] *Solidarity*, October 1920; Kendall, *The Revolutionary Movement in Britain*, p. 262.

Council of the shop stewards' movement finally merged with the British Bureau of the Red International the *institutional* independence of the 'mass movement' from the Party remained a primary tenet of Communist Party organizational theory.[1] The mass organizations, whether the Minority Movement or the official trade unions, were to be subordinated to the Party only in so far as the individual members of the Party could win leading positions in the policy-making organs of these movements.

During the same period the shop stewards came to accept that the naive revolutionary optimism underlying earlier attempts to identify the growth of extra-factory unofficial organization (in fact an index of defeat) with the struggle for soviet power could provide no solution to their political problems. The triumph of the Council of Action – which apparently prevented further British intervention in Russia during August 1920 – had owed more to war-weariness and the non-class nature of the issue than to any mass revolutionary enthusiasm.[2] In November 1920 Dave Ramsay pointed out in *Solidarity* that the call for the establishment of soviets issued by the March 1920 conference had been profoundly mistaken: 'The soviets could only be strong and effective in as much as the situation was of such a character that the workers instinctively accepted them as the only form of organization suitable to meet the requirements of the times . . " There was, therefore, no object to be served in issuing calls for the formation of soviets at a time when the workers were not already 'spontaneously' throwing up organizations of the soviet type.[3] The struggle for soviet power was, for the time being, postponed. The full implications of this recognition for a party formed primarily in order to promote that struggle cannot be discussed here. But this study would be incomplete without some explanation of how it was that the ideological advances made possible for the revolutionary movement by the wartime struggles of the engineers were so very rapidly blurred or lost altogether, why the central lessons of the shop stewards' movement for revolutionaries were forgotten almost as soon as they were learned.

In November 1920 Jack Murphy, replying to Tanner, had

1 MacFarlane, *The British Communist Party*, pp. 110–11.

2 R. Miliband, *Parliamentary Socialism* (London, 1961), pp. 76–82; see also L. J. MacFarlane, ' "Hands off Russia" in 1920', *Past and Present*, no. 38, December 1967.

3 *Solidarity*, November 1920; see also Murphy, *Preparing for Power*, p. 189.

pointed out in *Solidarity*: 'It is folly to think of our movement as a political party, or think it can perform the same functions. It belongs to the category of extra-union organizations. It has its own important tasks to perform . . .' In the communist theory of socialist transition a sharp and categoric distinction was drawn between the Party, the trade union and 'the category of extra-union organizations', i.e. the factory committees, shop stewards' movements, Workers' Committees – the embryonic soviets.[1] In a situation of rising unemployment, however, and falling revolutionary expectations, 'the category of extra-union organizations' tended to become an empty theoretical box. The work that could still be done by the surviving rump of the Workers' Committees was increasingly difficult to distinguish from the work that could in any case be done by the industrial fractions of the party itself. It was because of this objective weakness that the fundamental theoretical contribution of the shop stewards' movement to the revolutionary movement was obscured and forgotten.

As their position in the workshops weakened and the balance of power in the unions shifted from shop floor to head office the shop stewards naturally turned increasingly to face directly the problem of reconstructing trade unionism, to the work within the branches. The national conference in January 1920 adopted a resolution emphasizing the movements' desire to 'revolutionize the aim of trade unionism and to remould its structure', and calling for 'active propaganda inside the trade unions and . . . fuller participation in the internal work of those organizations'.[2] J. R. Campbell made the first serious attempt to work out the tactics of such a fight, arguing the need for a 'co-ordinated rebel movement' within the branches, and by the beginning of the next year a Socialist Industrial Unionist group had been established to work within the AEU branches in Scotland.[3] Similar efforts were being made in England.[4] The second post-war conference of the movement, held at Sheffield in March 1921, recognized that 'the time has arrived when the rebel elements in the unions must be consciously and scientifically organized to work within their unions for a definitely formulated policy',

[1] Cf. J. Degras, *The Communist International 1919–43, Documents*, vol. I (Oxford, 1956), pp. 145–9.
[2] *Solidarity*, June 1920.
[3] *The Worker*, 12 June 1920, 1 January, 26 February 1921.
[4] *Solidarity*, 25 March 1921.

and the new constitution provided for the establishment of branch groups of Workers' Committee members conducting systematic propaganda, and attempting to capture all elective offices within the unions.[1]

At first the shop stewards' leaders denied that this turn to the branches represented any fundamental change in their policy.[2] In wartime the movement had not been positively hostile to working within the official structures of trade unionism, and as unemployment enhanced the importance of the branch as against the workshop it was reasonable to concentrate more energies within the unions, while maintaining independent rank-and-file organization where possible. The second Congress of the Third International in July 1920 firmly rejected IWW dual unionism and inisted on the necessity of working within the trade unions. But it also fully endorsed the need for autonomous rank-and-file organisation capable of leading 'the spontaneous direct action of the proletariat' independently of reactionary trade union officials.[3]

Within nine months, however, the shop stewards were forced to accept the implacable logic of unemployment and victimization and to suppress the central principle of their movement. The move into the unions, which at the conference of January 1920 had represented only a change of emphasis, was now consolidated into a fundamental change of principle. Neither in Murphy's preparatory document for the conference, nor in Campbell's report of it, nor most significantly, in the very lengthy restatement of the policy of the Workers' Committees, *Consolidation and Control*, published in *The Worker* during the summer of 1921, was any reference made to the need for independent rank-and-file action.[4] The policy statement expressed complete confidence in the revolutionary potential of the trade unions, unaccompanied by the usual qualification that if a revolutionary opportunity were

---

1 *The Worker*, 21 May, 16, 25 June, 27 August 1921.

2 *Ibid.*, 14 February 1920.

3 Degras, *The Communist International*, vol. I, pp. 148–9, 145; see also Lenin, *Selected Works*, vol. III, pp. 400–2.

4 *The Worker*, 19 March, 21 May 1921. But J. R. Campbell, in the course of a polemic with the SLP early in 1922, did briefly acknowledge the change of emphasis and the reason for it: 'We talked about building Workers' Committees to create a feeling of solidarity, and to act as an alternative to the official unions if the officials sabotaged the mass movement. That was a possibility in periods of good trade. It may be a possibility again. We have nothing to apologise for on this head.' *The Worker*, 4 February 1922.

to occur before the unions had been reconstructed as revolutionary instruments, the rank and file would act independently of them. Where previously the imminence of such a crisis had been an argument for concentrating on the construction of a rank-and-file organization independent of the union bureaucracy, now the same presumed imminence was used to justify the exclusive emphasis on capturing the unions. The old problems of maintaining the revolutionary integrity of trade unionism while it operated within a relatively stable capitalist society, the problems which the theory and practice of independent rank-and-and-file organization had relegated to a position of secondary importance, now came back into the centre of the stage. *Consolidation and Control* contained an elaborate scheme for ensuring constitutional rank-and-file control over the trade union bureaucracy, while ignoring altogether the possibilities of extra-constitutional guarantees of trade union democracy which had been systematically developed by the wartime movement.[1] The conference of March 1921 had delivered the final blow to the movement, not by the explicit repudiation of its wartime practice, but by the silent supression of its central idea: 'We will support the officials just so long as they rightly represent the workers, but will act independently immediately they misrepresent them.' By 1922 the shop stewards' leaders had replaced the Workers' Committees by Trades Councils as the basis from which Soviets, Councils of Action would spring.[2] How far this was from the earlier position is clear. In 1917 Murphy had drawn a sharp line between the potentialities of the Trades Councils and those of the Workers' Committees:

'It will be similar in form to a trades council with this essential difference – the trades council is only indirectly related to the workshops, whereas the Workers Committee is directly related. The former has no power, the latter has the driving power of the directly connected workers in the workshops.'[3]

In 1920 he had reinforced this distinction, in a polemic against the inadequacies of the BSP as a revolutionary party:

The Trades Councils are not the nuclei of the Soviets. Their

---

[1] *The Worker*, 13 August, 28 August, 3 September 1921, 18 February 1922.
[2] J. T. Murphy, *Stop the Retreat. An Appeal to Trade Unionists*,
[3] *The Workers' Committee*, p. 12.

ineptitude in all industrial disputes provides ample proof of this. They possess no executive power over the unions, and action comes either through delegates from the workshops, etc., or the local district committees of the unions, which bodies improvise strike committees composed of Stewards and the district committees, etc. leaving the Trades Councils in the background or playing a reactionary part. It will be in such manner that Soviets will be formed, and not through the Trades Councils, as suggested.[1]

Yet mass unemployment, and the elimination of the militants from the workshops was bound to force the revolutionary movement back on to the Trades Councils for its 'nuclear cells of the future proletarian state'. It was on the basis of the Trades Councils, and of co-operation between the local District Committees of the unions, that the Communist Party's hopes (in so far as it had any) of a revolutionary dénouement to the general strike rested.[2] The Minority Movement remained, like the Amalgamation Committee movement before it, primarily an organization for propaganda in the branches, rather than an organization for action in the workshops. This is not a measure of any avoidable failure of the Communist Party in the 1920s: rather it is a measure of the degree to which the skilled engineers in the First War came nearer to 'throwing up Soviets' than the miners and their supporters in 1926.

---

[1] *The Socialist*, 6 May 1920.
[2] This would appear to be the conclusion to be drawn from A. Mason's study of the general strike in the Communist Party's 'model' region: *The General Strike in the North East* (Hull University Press, 1970).

Chapter 13

Conclusions

It is no accident that it was the practice of the shop stewards' movement which made the major contribution to the development of the theory of soviet power in Britain. Their identification of the Workers' Committees with the Russian soviets – as 'nuclei of working class political power' – certainly represented a most optimistic interpretation of the potentialities of the Committees; but it cannot be written off merely as an arbitrary imposition of quite alien categories on a movement whose own potential was intrinsically and unalterably non-revolutionary.[1] The contemporary international communist movement saw, in the independent rank-and-file movements that sprang up in most European countries during or after the war, evidence of the profundity of the revolutionary crisis:

> 'We say that the present period is revolutionary precisely because we can see that the working class, in all countries, is tending to generate from within itself, with the utmost vital energy (if with the mistakes, gropings and encumberances natural to an oppressed class which has no historical precedent, and must do everything for the first time), proletarian institutions of a new type: representative in basis and industrial in arena. We say the present period is revolutionary because the working class tends with all its energy and all its will-power to found its own State.'[2]

Britain shared in the international revolutionary crisis whose

---

[1] Cf. G. D. H. Cole, *Workshop Organisation* (Oxford, 1923), pp. 96–7.
[2] A. Gramsci, *Soviets in Italy*, Institute for Workers Control, Pamphlet Series, no. 11 (n.d.), p. 7.

centrepiece was the Russian Revolution, though in Britain, of course, the revolutionary movement existed in a subordinate relationship to the reformist institutions and ideology of the labour movement. Nevertheless, within the Workers' Committees, there were in addition to the seeds of defeat, genuine possibilities of a mass revolutionary politics, possibilities that made their impact not directly in the material arena of class struggle, but indirectly on the development of the revolutionary movement, in the elaboration of the theory of the struggle for soviet power after the war.

The influence of the shop stewards' movement has been analysed in eight different centres – Glasgow, Sheffield, Manchester, Woolwich, Barrow, Tyne, Coventry and Birmingham.

Two related phenomena have been under examination: the emergence of representative workshop organization recognized for bargaining purposes by management, and the construction out of this of independent rank-and-file organization at a local level on the model of the CWC, i.e. a local Workers' Committee capable of taking action independently of local and national trade union officials because of its hold over the membership at workshop level. The second clearly cannot be established without the first. Thus in Barrow, where the exceptionally close relationship between the District Committees and the Vickers management made it unnecessary for the latter to grant recognition to the shop stewards, the Workers' Committee remained a merely propagandist group.[1]

The growth of workshop organization clearly owed much to the pressures of full employment and dilution on the traditional wages structure. But the emergence of an earnings-rates gap and the growing importance of the workshop in wage determination did not necessarily lead on to the establishment of local independent rank-and-file organization. The Workers' Committees were not merely a product of the advance of wage determination in the workshops. The wages issue alone was insufficient to generate independent rank-and-file organization beyond the four walls of the factory. In fact, due to its inherently fragmentary character, 'wage drift' was in some respects less conducive to the establishment of Workers' Committees than the tensions which had

---

1 In Woolwich, on the other hand, the shop stewards' committee played the role of a District Committee in negotiations, and, being outside Procedure, was permitted to do so by the Executive. Consequently there was little reason for conflict between the Arsenal shop stewards and the Executive.

arisen out of local wage movements prior to their supercession by national bargaining procedures in February 1917. Before that date unofficial strike committees arising out of local wage movements in Glasgow, Sheffield and Manchester had provided a jumping off point for the establishment of the Workers' Committees.

In contrast, the most dramatic period of 'wage drift' in Manchester, during the autumn of 1917, coincided with the destruction of the Workers' Committee by the local trade union officials. Moreover, the pressures that the growth of workshop organization placed on the traditional sectionalism of engineering trade unionism and on the inadequacy of the collective bargaining procedures in the industry were as likely to spark off, as in Coventry and Birmingham, a process of adaptation and reform in the local official structure of trade unionism, as they were to throw up an effective Workers' Committee. The success of such a reformist exercise did not rest upon the goodwill or vigour of the local District Committee members or the full-time officials alone: the Sheffield District Committee was just as anxious to adapt itself to the needs of workshop organization as was its counterpart in Coventry. Yet the result, in Sheffield, was a Workers' Committee led by many of the same people as sat on the District Committee.

The critical difference between Glasgow, Sheffield and Manchester, on the one hand, and Coventry and Birmingham on the other, was the difference between the relatively archaic technology of the northern engineering centres, and the extremely modern technology of the motor car/aircraft complex in the Midlands. In the northern centres, when war broke out, the complex of trade union structures, work practices and attitudes that underpinned the traditional labour aristocracy still remained essentially intact. Craft unionism, though under pressure was still in the ascendent: the less skilled workers were still relatively badly organized and their organizations were not capable of asserting equal status with the craftsmen in the councils of the local labour movement. Wartime dilution was, therefore, explosive in its impact. It appeared to challenge and render indefensible the entire world outlook of the craftsmen. On the Clyde the Workers' Committee developed in 1915–16 in direct response to the dilution struggle. In Sheffield it was the associated menace of conscription that sparked off the leap into independent rank-and-file organization. In Manchester, where dilution on munitions work was relatively unimportant, it was the emergency over dilution on commercial work which gave the Joint Engineering Shop Stewards' Committee its one brief period of power.

The most conclusive evidence that the Workers' Committees rested upon the abrupt disintegration of craft controls derives from Coventry where the Workers' Committee was strangled at birth and the local officials proved most capable of containing rank-and-file militancy. Wartime dilution in Coventry was not experienced as a catastrophe because dilutees, the semi-skilled workers, were already well established and well organized in the motor car and allied factories before the war broke out. The integrity of the craft tradition had already been thoroughly breeched. During the war the less skilled workers showed greater militancy in grasping the new opportunities opened up for them than the skilled showed in defence of their privileges, and the dominant single union in the Coventry engineering factories, both numerically and at crucial points of policy formation, was not the ASE or the Toolmakers, but the Workers' Union. Because the craft aristocracy no longer existed in Coventry (and Birmingham) as it existed in the northern towns the explosive insecurity created by dilution in Glasgow, Sheffield or Manchester was absent, and the militants who laboured to build an independent rank-and-file movement laboured in vain.

It is clear, then, that it was the sudden impact of dilution on craft aspirations in the areas where those aspirations had been relatively well preserved up to the outbreak of the war that threw up the Workers' Committees as mass organizations. It has been suggested earlier that the craft tradition contained aspects of tenacious resistance to capitalist rationality, to the reduction of craft labour power to commodity status. When the craftsmen felt themselves pressed beyond endurance these aspirations, traditionally expressed in the defence of craft controls and of local autonomy, were forced to seek new modes of expression. The catalyst of war, the intolerable demands it placed on the attitudes and practices of skilled engineers, promoted an interaction between the doctrines of revolutionary syndicalism, Industrial Unionism and the craft tradition of local autonomy. In this interaction the Workers' Committees were born. The experience of the Workers' Committees, of independent rank-and-file organization, made possible a transcendence of the limitations of syndicalist theory that was to be crucially important to the post-war development of the revolutionary movement in Britain. No struggle for soviet power was actually launched in Britain. The Workers' Committees only came to be defined in terms of such a struggle after they had been defeated as a mass force. But when the revolutionary movement in 1919–20 rallied around the standard of soviet power it was expressing not merely the desire to imitate the Russians, but equally the perception that the Workers' Committees had embodied (and might again embody) genuine possibilities of the transcendence, by mass organizations of the working class, of the limitations of trade unionism.

Gramsci and the early Comintern saw expressed in the Workers' Committees and their equivalents elsewhere, not the instrumental consciousness of 'wage earners, the slaves of capital' (specific to trade unionism), but the aspiration to 'direct responsibility for production . . . the psychology of the producer, the creator of history'.[1] From the outset the shop stewards' movement was committed to the revolutionary goal of workers' control of production. In a typical formulation the object of the movement was described as 'obtaining an ever increasing share in the control of the workshops' which would culminate in the 'abolition of wages slavery' and the 'complete control of industry by the workers'.[2] Underpinning this demand was that 'psychology of the producer' long nurtured within the tradition of craft control: but nurtured in a narrowly individualistic and restrictive context.

Craft control rested on the defence of personal freedom in work, on a regressive aspiration to the status of the old millwright hired to do a job and to do it from start to finish without interference from the management. Craft control was a negative, defensive response to managerial encroachments on customary rights and contained none of the positive aspiration to industrial sovereignty expressed in the socialist demand for workers' control. 'The desire to be let alone, to be free from the irksomeness of control by others, is not identical with the desire to co-operate actively in the work of controlling.'[3] The craftsman as such aspired to personal freedom, to freedom from managerial interference; the revolutionary engineer went beyond this to the claim to participate in the exercise of a collective workers' control over the whole economic system.

With this distinction in mind it has been argued that the demand for workers' control arose solely out of the ideological inheritance

[1] Gramsci, *Soviets in Italy*, pp. 11, 13.
[2] *The Socialist*, January 1917; *Solidarity*, February 1917.
[3] C. Goodrich, *The Frontier of Control* (New York, 1920), p. 34.

of those revolutionaries to whom the craftsman turned for leadership when the traditional props of their economic security were apparently knocked away by wartime dilution. After all, the formal acceptance of a remote revolutionary goal was a small price to pay for the leadership of revolutionary socialists who were needed for the much more immediate practical reason that only these leaders had the audacity required to challenge established trade union practices to the degree that seemed to be necessary. The revolutionary goal of workers' control is thus seen as being artificially tacked on to rank-and-file aspirations of a quite different order. It does, however, seem unlikely that so clear a distinction can be drawn between the consciousness of the leaders and that of the rank and file. The 'militant craftsman' and the 'revolutionary engineer' certainly describe categorically different states of consciousness; but both states may well have co-existed, and interacted, in the same head. 'Our policy', wrote Gallacher and Paton in 1917, 'is that of invaders of our native province of industry, now in the hands of an arrogant and tyrannical usurper, and what we win in our advance we control exclusively and independently.'[1] It is impossible to distinguish in this between the revolutionary engineer's hostility to capitalist parasitism on industry, on the one hand, and the militant craftsman's resistance to the 'arrogant and tyrannical' encroachments of managerial prerogative. The two states of consciousness are fused in a unified rhetoric, each reinforcing the other. Within the wartime shop stewards' movement an interaction was taking place between syndicalist doctrines of workers' control and the non-instrumental aspects of the tradition of craft control. The development of the movements' attitudes to workers' control, and of its political consciousness as a whole, can only be understood in the light of this process.

At the outset the movement's attitude to workers' control was extraordinarily confused. The Clyde Workers' Committee's demand for the nationalization of all industries and workers' participation in management was not only wildly unrealistic: it was also a very odd demand to emanate from a movement composed of craftsmen and led by members of the Socialist Labour Party. The demand for nationalization flew in the face of SLP doctrine, which saw nationalization as a device for reinforcing the tyranny of private capital with the power of the state. Moreover, as the Dilution Commissioners soon discovered, it was the

[1] W. Gallacher and J. Paton, *Towards Industrial Democracy* (?1917).

recognition of workshop organization and negotiation in the workshop that the rank and file were primarily demanding as the condition of dilution – this was what workers' control meant to most workers – not wild schemes of general nationalization.

Following the débacle on the Clyde workers' control was not again raised as an immediate demand in the movement.[1] It became an 'ultimate goal', and when it was discussed in the movement, as for example, by Gallacher and Paton in *Towards Industrial Democracy*, the strategy for achieving it was discussed essentially in syndicalist terms. The shop stewards spoke of the development of 'a powerful and comprehensive industrial organisation based on the workshop which would, in the process of its development, assume an ever increasing share in the control of industry, until in the end the capitalist system was abolished'.[2] The shop stewards were for the time being blind to the fact that their own practice of independent rank-and-file organization was causing a fundamental disruption of the projected organizations basis – the revolutionary industrial union – on which this syndicalist strategy of transition to socialism rested. This contradiction in the thinking of the movement could survive only because the leaders did not believe themselves to be operating in a revolutionary situation. Because workers' control was an ultimate goal rather than an immediate demand it was not urgently necessary for the wartime movement to clarify its position. The discussion of transition to socialism thus remained locked in the syndicalist categories that the movement's own practice was helping to undermine. Only after the war was this confusion resolved, when the demand for workers' control was subsumed into the theory of the struggle for soviet power, and the notion of a strategy of encroaching control co-ordinated by a massive and tightly organized revolutionary industrial union was finally abandoned.

The war precipitated a combined offensive of management and the state against the traditional values of the engineering craftsmen which threw the positive aspects of the craft tradition into high relief. Where the craftsman retained his pride in his skill and the conviction that his work should afford him spiritual as well as economic satisfactions, then no amount of consultation

[1] For a partial exception to this see Gallacher's attempt to revive the workers' control demand on the Clyde in the spring of 1917, pp. 248–49 above.
[2] Cf. B. Pribicevic, *The Shop Stewards' Movement and Workers' Control* (Oxford, 1959), pp. 129–30, 149.

and negotiation, no purely financial reward for his sacrifices, could prevent the head-on collision between the two value systems, between craftsmanship and capitalist rationality. At all times this conflict had existed, and no doubt there were large numbers of engineers even on the Clyde and in Sheffield who had long since received nothing but money and misery from the exercise of their labour power. But in wartime the struggle was generalized. In order to meet the demands of war, capital and the state were driven not only to undermine once and for all the possibilities of exclusive craft unionism for most of the skilled workers in the industry, but at the same time to attack a vital part of that minimum spiritual reward that the craftsmen customarily expected from their work. Challenged in this way the subversive potential that had always been locked within the craft tradition was suddenly released, and released into fruitful interaction with the syndicalist doctrines inherited by the leadership. The political creativity of this central pillar of the old labour aristocracy flared brilliantly in the final years of its power. Its contribution made possible fundamental innovations in the ideology of the British revolutionary movement.

The fact that it was only the theory of the struggle for soviet power, and not the struggle itself, that arose out of the experience of the Workers' Committees is to be explained partly by the abrupt and unavoidable collapse of the economic power of the shop stewards' movement when the war finished. More fundamentally, however, it is to be explained by the ultimate failure of the craft tradition to yield up its revolutionary ore without the clinging dross of exclusiveness. Whether it would have done so had the general political context of January 1918, the degree of war weariness and readiness for action among other sections of the working class, been more advanced is a matter for speculation. In the event, faced with the prospect of making a decisive challenge to the Government, the craftsmen's élan shrivelled into a conservative militancy, the defence of vested interest. But, however subordinate the revolutionary possibilities, they had been there, and had been seen by the revolutionary movement to be there.

Appendix

ASE *Membership by Locality, 1914–19*

Area (as on map on p. 340)	ASE membership, June 1919	% total ASE membership in Glasgow	Growth 1914–19 (1914 = 100)
I East End	2,069	10·4	358
II Scotstoun	863	4·3	266
III Springburn	2,368	11·9	197
IV Dalmuir	497	2·5	176
V Cathcart	564	2·8	159
VI Central	7,072	35·5	153
[VII Clydebank and Renfrew	2,521	12·6	146
VIII Govanhill	2,526	12·8	132
Miscellaneous	1,451	7·3	128
Total	19,931	100·1	163

Branch membership figures were published monthly in the ASE *Monthly Journal and Report* during 1914–17 and 1919. The growth rates of individual branches do not vary widely within the areas designated on the map.

ASE *membership in different sections of the Glasgow engineering industry.*

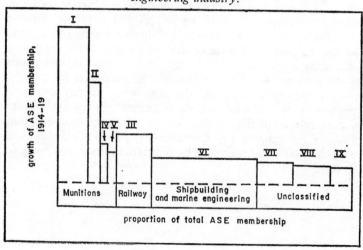

Key to factories shown on map

1. Beardmore, Dalmuir	munitions, shipbuilding and marine engineering
2. Singer	munition—largely semi-skilled
3. John Brown	shipbuilding and marine engineering
4. Yarrow	shipbuilding and marine engineering
5. Albion	munitions and vehicles for the army
6. Meechan	munitions and general
7. Barclay, Curle	shipbuilding and marine engineering
8. North British Diesel	marine engineering
9. Coventry Ordnance Works	munitions
10. Barr & Stroud	munitions and scientific instruments
11. Rowan	marine engineering
12. Burmeister & Weir	marine engineering
13. Napier	general
14. N.B. Railway, Cowlairs	railway engineering
15. N.B. Loco., Hyde Park	railway engineering
16. N.B. Loco., Atlas	railway engineering
17. Caledonian Railway, St Rollox	railway engineering
18. Mavor and Coulson	mining machinery
19. Beardmore, Parkhead	munitions and foundry
20. Arrol	bridge and crane building
21. Alley and Mc'Lellan	general
22. N.B. Loco., Queens Park	railway engineering
23. Weir	munitions and marine engineering
24. Dunsmuir & Jackson	marine engineering
25. Harney	munitions and general
26. Howden	marine engineering
27. Ross & Duncan	marine engineering
28. Harland & Wolff	marine engineering and shipbuilding
29. Fairfield	marine engineering and shipbuilding
30. Stephens	marine engineering and shipbuilding
31. Babcock & Wilcox	boilermaking

The major sources for this were: *Kelly's Directory of the Engineering Trades* (1917); and Glasgow Chamber of Commerce, *Handbook* (1919).

The address of the branch secretary, published in the *Gazetteer of Trade Union Branches* (Fabian Research Department, 1918), was used to establish the location of the branch. Branch organization was based upon residence, but it is not unlikely that some unavoidable error is involved in locating the branches on this criterion. However, in all cases where the name of the branch clearly indicated its location, the address of the branch secretary was bound to tally.

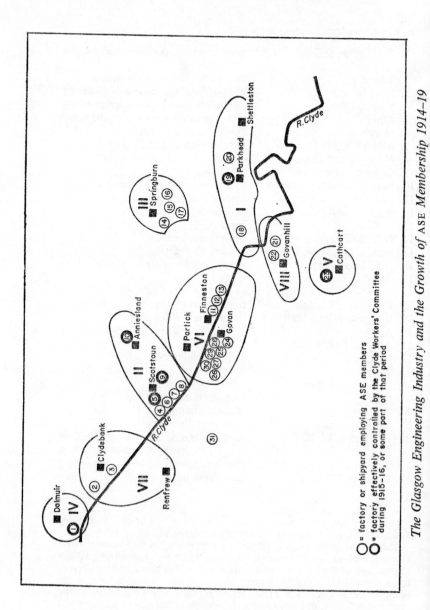

■ = factory or shipyard employing ASE members

○ = factory effectively controlled by the Clyde Workers' Committee
during 1915–16, or some part of that period

The Glasgow Engineering Industry and the Growth of ASE *Membership 1914–19*

Bibliographical note

Only the major primary sources on which this study is based are listed here. Other primary material, and secondary sources are indicated in the footnotes.

1 Government records

Records of the Ministry of Munitions in the Public Record Office:

Mun. 1, vols. 1–14, Daily Reports of the Munitions Council, August 1917–October 1918. Vols. 4–14 also contain daily reports of existing and imminent strikes provided by the Labour Department of the Ministry. In order to distinguish Munitions Council Reports from strike reports the abbreviation MC has been added after the volume number in footnotes referring to the former.

Mun. 2, vols. 27–8, Secret Weekly Reports of the Labour Department of the Ministry of Munitions, September 1915–December 1917. Reports for 1918 are bound in with the reports of other departments in *Mun.* 2, vols. 14–17.

Mun. 5. These are the records from which the official history was written. The title of the actual document referred to, together with the box number, has been given in the footnotes. There are about 400 boxes altogether.

The Beveridge Collection on Munitions in the British Library of Economic and Political Science. These papers were collected by Beveridge when he worked at the Ministry between 1915 and 1916. It also contains some Board of Trade papers from the period 1914–15. There are eight volumes. The page number and title of each document has been given in the footnotes.

History of the Ministry of Munitions, 12 vols. (1920–4). Each volume is composed of several booklets paginated independently.

Cabinet Papers in the Public Record Office:

Cab. 23, War Cabinet Minutes, 1917–18.
Cab. 24, GT Papers, 1917–18.

2 Trade union and labour records

Amalgamated Society of Engineers:

Annual Reports, 1914–18.
Quarterly Reports, 1914–18.
Monthly Journal and Report, 1914–18.
Executive Minutes, 1914–17. (The volumes for 1918–19 have been mislaid.)
Coatbridge *Branch Minutes*, 1911–18, in Coatbridge Public Library.
Sheffield No. 12 *Branch Minutes*, 1914–18. (See *Moore Collection* below.)

Trades Councils

Glasgow Trades Council, *Annual Reports*, 1914–18.
  Minutes, 1914–18.
Sheffield Trades and Labour Council, *Annual Reports*, 1914–18.
  Minutes of Delegate Meetings, 1914–18.
  Minutes of Executive Meetings, 1914–18.

Highton Collection, Department of Economics, University of Glasgow.

Moore Collection, in possession of Bill Moore, Leeds.

3 Labour and socialist press

The Call, 1916–21.
Daily Herald, 1913–14, 1919–21.
Firth Worker (Sheffield), 1917–18.
Forward (Glasgow), 1914–18.
The Guildsman (Glasgow), 1916–18.
The Herald, 1914–19.
Justice, 1914–16.
Labour Leader, 1914–18.
Sheffield Guardian, 1915- 16.
Sheffield Worker, 1919–20.
The Socialist (Glasgow), 1910–22.
Solidarity, 1917–21.
Trade Unionist, 1915–16.
Vanguard (Glasgow), 1915.
Workers' Dreadnought, 1916–21.
Woolwich Pioneer, 1914–18.
The Worker (Glasgow), 1916, 1918–22.

4 Local Press

Birmingham Gazette.
Daily Record and Mail (Glasgow).

Glasgow Herald.
Manchester Guardian.
Midland Daily Telegraph.
North West Daily Mail.
Sheffield Daily Telegraph.
Sheffield Independent.

Index